IN FOR LIFE

IN FOR LIFE

Confessions of a Three-Strikes Prisoner

DAMIEN LARTIGUE

WITH ERIC W. SENN

RIVER
LANE
PRESS

ANOKA, MINNESOTA 2017

In for Life: Confessions of a Three-Strikes Prisoner

© 2017 River Lane Press

All rights reserved. Except for brief quotations in critical publications and reviews, no part of this book may be reproduced in any manner without prior permission from the publisher.

River Lane Press
RiverHouse LLC
802 River Lane
Anoka, MN 55303

Cover: Susanna Mennicke

ISBN: 978-1-940447-29-2
Printed in the United States of America

Table of Contents

FOREWORD, *John B. Cobb, Jr.*,   *i*
PREFACE, *Eric W. Senn*,   *v*
Prologue

PART ONE

ONE:	*Beginnings*	5
TWO:	*A Child's Hell*	10
THREE:	*Yelling, Shots Fired, Family Illness*	15
FOUR:	*Friend or Foe*	20
FIVE:	*The Turning of a Page*	26
SIX:	*Strive, Achieve, Excel*	32
SEVEN:	*Integration*	37
EIGHT:	*Promotion*	44
NINE:	*A New Science*	50
TEN:	*Unexpected Qualities*	55
ELEVEN:	*Hell Restored*	61
TWELVE:	*A Strange New World*	67
THIRTEEN:	*The Road to Recovery*	72
FOURTEEN:	*Group Therapy*	80
FIFTEEN:	*Detours to Adulthood*	87
SIXTEEN:	*Making House Calls*	97
SEVENTEEN:	*Turning Wheels*	105
EIGHTEEN:	*Night Life*	110
NINETEEN:	*Striking Home*	119
TWENTY:	*Rescue and Search*	126
TWENTY-ONE:	*Tackling Monsters*	134
TWENTY-TWO:	*Graveyards for the Living*	138
TWENTY-THREE:	*Oops, I Did It Again*	150
TWENTY-FOUR:	*Do Time, Don't Let Time Do You*	156
TWENTY-FIVE:	*Independence*	161
TWENTY-SIX:	*Linguistics and Logistics*	170
TWENTY-SEVEN:	*Future Destinations*	181
TWENTY-EIGHT:	*Growing Support*	191

PART TWO

TWENTY-NINE:	*Seeking Answers*	199
THIRTY:	*Newfound Freedoms*	209
THIRTY-ONE:	*Baneful Relationships*	220
THIRTY-TWO:	*Higher Education*	230
THIRTY-THREE:	*Screwing the Pooch*	241
THIRTY-FOUR:	*On the Road Again*	252
THIRTY-FIVE:	*Becoming More Centered*	264
THIRTY-SIX:	*Death and Rebirth*	273
THIRTY-SEVEN:	*Miss Vicki*	280
THIRTY-EIGHT:	*Fundamental Analysis*	289
THIRTY-NINE:	*Two Loves Develop*	300
FORTY:	*Increased Development*	309
FORTY-ONE:	*A Day in the Life*	316
FORTY-TWO:	*Learning a New Process*	324

PART THREE

FORTY-THREE:	*A Good Ol' Boy and a Country Girl*	333
FORTY-FOUR:	*Please Stand Up*	342
FORTY-FIVE:	*A New Family Is Born*	349
FORTY-SIX:	*Arrivals*	357
FORTY-SEVEN:	*Finding Ohio*	366
FORTY-EIGHT:	*Unexpected U-Turns*	373
FORTY-NINE:	*Ever Increasing Excrement*	381
FIFTY:	*A Reintroduction to Hell*	390
FIFTY-ONE:	*Man in a Bottle*	399
FIFTY-TWO:	*Illogical Inconsistencies*	407
FIFTY-THREE:	*Regressing Reputations*	418
FIFTY-FOUR:	*Returning to What Works*	426
FIFTY-FIVE:	*Only Halfway There*	435
FIFTY-SIX:	*The Fight of the Decades*	443
FIFTY-SEVEN:	*Celebrating My Recovery*	454

Acknowledgements	465
Suggested Reading	466
About the Authors	469

FOREWORD

John B. Cobb, Jr.

This book is written by a victim of California's Three Strikes law. His third "offense," which was largely a misunderstanding, demanded a sentence of twenty-five years to life. He is certainly no danger to society. The state goes to great expense to confine him. This is called "justice."

He has worked on the book with a friend who is also in prison. Their joint style makes for good reading. The spelling and grammar are not perfect, but the occasional mistakes of this kind rarely invite misunderstanding. We are offering it "as is." We think the imperfections may bring us closer to the real people we are getting to know.

The chief author is not only a prisoner but also a lay theologian. He thought his way into something like process theology before he encountered other representatives of the movement. He wants to explain process theology in understandable ways, and he offers and reports on more and less successful efforts to do that. But his story as a whole teaches as much theology as do the explicit presentations.

The book is almost an autobiography—a remarkably honest and open one about a life that most of us middle-class folks can hardly imagine. It is about a life spent in and out of prison. The author makes no effort to exaggerate the evils of prison life or to conceal them. He does not claim to have special scholarly knowledge about the prison system.

He just tells us his story. I encourage you to read a little. I believe that if you do, you will read more. In one sense a hundred incidents stand on their own, with their immediate individual interest. But each also leads into the next. Again and again the reader's hopes, like that of the author, are raised and then dashed.

There are parts of the story that I can barely stand to read. That is not because the author is manipulating the reader's emotions. It is just that what happened was so brutally unfair. The straightforward, unembellished account draws the reader in. One feels each new blow — some are physical, more are psychological. It seems too much, much too much, but the reality is that life goes on. There is recovery and then again new loss.

It is all too easy to understand his attempted suicide and occasional thought of trying again. His evaluation of that as wrong calls forth our reflection. He interprets suicidal thoughts as a lack of faith that God has work for him.

I said that this book is "almost" an autobiography. It is not quite. Proper names are changed, and in a few instances other readily identifying features are modified. If you read, you will understand the need for a bit of concealment. I can assure you that the purpose is not to change the picture of prison life or of the author.

Of course, the author tells the story from his own perspective. That is the nature of an autobiography. But the resulting distortion for the sake of self-justification is minimal. He does not conceal his sins and failures. His worst crimes, such as his abuse of the friendship of the man who helped him most, are not the ones for which he is imprisoned. He acknowledges guilt and makes no effort to excuse himself.

But he also shows how his story can be, and has been, distorted by others to convict him of crimes of which he was not guilty. From this perspective, the "justice system" does not look very just. His experience in being arrested and convicted and then in being released and left to his own devices with nothing but a bad record are almost worse than his life in prison itself. One feels the urge to cry out a demand to reform the system that is obviously constructed so as to fail.

I recommend the book as an interesting, sometimes gripping, read. But it is more than that. The California prison system is in the news for several reasons—none of them good. Its overcrowding is a scandal already condemned by the Supreme Court but still hardly relieved. Efforts to prepare prisoners for life outside have been virtually abandoned. The whole system is set up to make recidivism normal.

Some of us have read about the experiment with a group of Stanford students, having some play guards and others prisoners. The intention was for a two-week experiment. But within one week the treatment of the prisoners by the guards had become so vicious that the experiment had to be ended.

We are learning from that and other experiments that giving power to one group over another brings out the worst in the former group and perhaps in the latter as well. We do not need to regard prison guards as unusually vicious people to expect that they will often abuse prisoners. We do not need to regard prisoners as unusually vicious people to expect that the strong often abuse the weak. But these generalizations take on a different quality when you read the story of a man who has spent many years in many prisons and experienced the worst as well as the relatively benign.

If you read this book you will never again think of our justice system or our prison system in the same way. You may already have your facts and your statistics straight. But these facts and statistics "on the ground" are real people with their individuality and special needs, and with hopes often dashed by shortsighted budget cuts that actually add to costs over a few years. I am glad that I am supporting the "Justice not Jails" program of Progressive Christians Uniting. But I can hardly rest comfortable with that gesture, when I think of millions of people whose lives are being destroyed by "jails not justice."

From the beginning of the book we are introduced to a boy with Aspergers, an absent mother, and an abusive father. That the boy ended up with a criminal record does not surprise us. What is surprising is the extent to which he transcended his condition and his situation. He knows that Aspergers has denied him the ability to read the emotional response of others. He tries to learn from experience what he does not sense directly. He was and is a thoughtful and committed Christian, one who, like the rest of us, remains a sinner.

He has sometimes felt that, being in prison, there is little that he can contribute. But one senses that he has contributed, and is contributing, quite a lot to a good many people. This book may prove to be his greatest contribution of all.

PREFACE

Eric W. Senn

Recently, during the post-production of this book, Damien asked if I thought our manuscript needed an Introduction or Preface. Mind you, we already had spent nearly a year trying to put this story together, and suddenly my friend wanted me to do even *more* typing! I already was exhausted and wanted to move onward with my next project. So, naturally, I tried to weasel out of doing any additional work by saying, "Naw, it's fine the way that it is." Also I didn't want to put anything at the beginning of the book which might rob its readers of any later discoveries or of enjoyment of the plot.

Well, as you can see (by the mere fact that you are reading these words), I failed at getting out of performing extra typing. However, these few "behind the scenes" pages into how this book came into existence shouldn't reduce the overall, and extremely positive, impact this story very well might have on your own life!

In late 2012, a man I barely knew approached me at a Celebrate Recovery meeting, and my first impression of this person was entirely wrong. I had believed him to be embarrassingly awkward, perhaps suffering from mental retardation, as well as having really poor taste in clothes. Looking back now, at least I got the "clothing" part right, but this man was anything but unskillful.

This stranger, who called himself Damien, was one of the small-group facilitators, although not of the small group in which I participated, and, although I'd missed hearing it, had given one of the most unimaginably distressing public testimonies ever heard. Damien had learned that I'd made some success at getting my stories published; so he told me that he'd written something about his life and needed help getting it ready to be submitted to literary agents.

I had not a clue what I was getting myself into when I said the fateful words, "Sure, I'll take a look at it." In fact, I may *never* utter these words *ever* again in my entire life! One of my future self-help books might have a chapter dedicated to teaching readers to never ever repeat that phrase, or they may suffer the same consequences that as did, months of frustration, confusion, and hair-pulling!

Normally, I'm a rather sarcastic person—if you couldn't tell this about me already—yet what Damien handed me that day was horrendously inconsistent, and I am trying to be a polite as I can. Even though he referred to those 310 pages as a "manuscript," I found it difficult to even consider it a "rough draft." There were just too many incomplete sentences, grammatical errors, and conversations between unnamed parties for any reader to follow along smoothly. Also, some chapters were entirely redundant concerning topics.

Nevertheless, I swallowed quite a few Tylenol to get through the document and dreaded answering Damien when he asked, "So, what do you think?" How do you tell an enthusiastic young author that what he's thinking of mailing off to agents and publishers isn't even close to being considered as a presentable final draft?

I'm not saying that I do not make mistakes, nor that every manuscript has to be absolutely perfect before being sent in for consideration, but Damien had *four* distinctively different characters all name Steve! You just can't do that to your readers.

Looking past all of the mistakes in spelling, grammar, continuity, names, ages, page numbers, etc., the message I found in those pages was quite profound. This book, originally entitled "The Roads of Life," *needed* to be written; its story, told.

The importance of what the main character goes through—his

less-than-perfect childhood and his battle against a learning disability that, before the 1980s, did not yet have a name—*shows* that anyone can achieve a lasting relationship with others and with God. That someone like myself, a person without the author's neurodevelopmental disorder, should not be having *any* difficulty in communicating, and building a stronger bond, with God.

Although this book discusses theology, the study of the nature of God and the relationship to the Divine One, it does not endorse nor promote any specific denomination or religion over any other. We have tried our best to respect non-Christian faiths while editing this story, removing anything which could be considered offensive. Still, much of this incredible tale depends upon discussing the very nature of God the Creator and of human evolution. Damien's development revolves heavily on absorbing and acquiring a better vocabulary and way of expressing his beliefs to others.

One of the most important duties of every Christian is in spreading the good news of salvation to those in need. Although sufferers of Asperger's syndrome face a daily struggle of introversion and disassociation, a struggle that hinders them from starting new friendships or even initiating conversations with strangers. Damien, as the reader will soon discover, trouble himself greatly with not being able to get his point(s) across when he wanted, or needed, to do so. In any case, He *never* doubted the one solid relationship which he could count on; the only stable parent Damien had throughout his life was his Heavenly Father.

I am hopeful that each reader of this book will agree with me that this story goes beyond just the biography of one person's troubled childhood and lack of support during adolescence. What happened to this young boy was, indeed, a nightmare; the ongoing obstacles were at times subjective, at other times voluntary. However, the misjudgments during Damien's growth came more from a lack of knowledge and parental guidance that from deliberate ignorance or disobedience, as many believed.

Damien also has offered, within these heavily edited pages, positive suggestions towards prison sentencing reform, replacing years of confinement with prerequisites towards release. Currently most state prisons only incarcerate criminals, and that makes them older, <u>not</u> safer. Instead of sending bad guys to play handball or basketball for five or more years, our legislature should replace the word 'years' with reformative programs, such as completing *five or more* emendatory classes in order to be paroled.

"Time doesn't make people more civil, only their bones more brittle."

Regrettably, I also experience the lifestyle and conditions of state imprisonment for several months, after being unable to exonerate myself from a false accusation. The state's Department of Corrections merely is a department of 'collections.' From what I saw, inmates only matured physically, not mentally. There was almost zero behavioral modifications nor was there any encouragement—outside of general education classes and of religion—offered to prisoners, No earnest rewards for good behavior, for being disciplinary free, or for showing the desire to better were inspiring prisoners to do so.

Sure, as Damien did, some of the luckier inmates made productive use of their prison time, whether starting... up a Bible study or obtaining work assignments within a kitchen—learning how to undercook pancakes and burn spaghetti. Very few other forms of rehabilitation went on within those walls and electrified fences. This situation upset both Damien and myself quite a bit, both as taxpayers and as human beings. Changes desperately need to be made; there are just too many good people in prison, people who simply need reassurance and civil training.

I agree with several of Damien's principles as found within this book; I would not have spent months rewriting the manuscript with him if I didn't. Originally, I told Damien that I'd only help him with its editing and that I didn't want my name associated with <u>his</u> book. Now, however, I am extremely proud to say that we wrote this phenomenal memoir together. I know in my heart that Damien's story will change lives, will change perspectives of the world around us. These few pages can assist anyone journeying along their own personal roads home!

I can only hope that our voices, our words printed herein, may help each and every reader to find their true home, wherever that might be.

PROLOGUE

Coleman, a small town in the middle of the state of Michigan, is where she was born, lived, and educated. Miss Vicki was born a farmer's daughter. However, she wasn't born to be a farmer; she earned a bachelor's degree in Education from Central Michigan University. Miss Vicki was a well-loved young lady in her community, the church, and the world in general. So, how did Damien ever have the pleasure of meeting Miss Vicki? As far as Damien is concerned, and in his own words, "That was a miracle, if ever there was one." However, I see that I have forgotten to tell you about my friend Damien. Let's start with him…

PART ONE

First Missteps

"To be human requires the study of structure. To be animal merely requires its enjoyment." ~Alfred North Whitehead

CHAPTER ONE

Beginnings

Damien was born in the mountains of Northern Washington, not far from the Olympic range, and was given a name that he no longer wears, Damien Shelden. He lived in these mountains throughout his youth. It should be noted that those years deeply affected him. Damien became a part of the mountains, and they became a part of his being. He was born a blond-haired, blue-eyed country boy, and he'll die one.

In the month of November 1960, a number of events were occurring at the same time. Not that Damien can recall such things from his early youth, like the fact that his biological father skipped out on his mother and him before Damien was even eighteen months old, or that his mom had that marriage annulled, or, for that matter, the fact that his mom met and quickly married Mr. Arthur H. Collins, mostly out of convenience and lust. All of these events occurred before Damien was two and one-half years of age. Yet, the events of that November were paramount.

Also, the nation had just elected a Democratic senator from Massachusetts as its latest president, the first Roman Catholic ever elected to that office. Tensions were building between the U.S. and Cuba, while Americans everywhere held protests to support and to oppose civil rights. Alfred Hitchcock's newest film, "Psycho," was busting box-office records. Then came the births of Damien's half-brother, Martin, and half-sister, Michelle...too soon, too many.

Damien recalls, barely, that they went to his step-grandparents' farm, just north and a little west of Olympia, for Thanksgiving Day. It was during that holiday that the twins, Martin and Michelle, were born.

As Damien recalls, *I didn't know what was going on. We were all having a great day, at least 'til my mom 'broke water.' I was told that Mom was ill and that she needed to see a doctor at the hospital.*

My step-grandparents, who I hardly knew, did a good job in keeping me occupied at their place 'til the phone rang. I remember being woken up. I still have no idea when or how I ever fell asleep, but sleep I did. When I awoke I cried so loudly because I was afraid for my Mom. My step-grandmother tried to calm me down, using soft baby-talk words which only frustrated me even more. I just wanted the same information that they were getting.

Finally, we got a second phone call and, although it was the middle of the night, we jumped into their car. Even now, in my 50's, I still cannot find sufficient words to express my joy at seeing my mother, in the maternity ward, healthy and ready to come home with my new brother and sister.

Following that holiday weekend in 1960, on what's now more commonly marketed as "Cyber Monday," it was time again to get things together and head out on the road again. This time, the newly-formed family of five headed for Damien's maternal Grandfather's house in Culver City, California. This would be for a longer stay because, according to what others told Damien, *Mom was not well. For some reason I was never told, she still needed to recover.* The medical term "hysterectomy" wasn't used too often back then.

Arriving at his Grandpa's house, they were warmly greeted by the man and Damien's mother's younger half-sister, Sharon, also known as Cha-cha. Walking into the pink-walled house, Damien was surprised because the house looked so small from the outside; yet, once inside, it felt plenty big enough to comfortably hold all of them with room to spare. In actuality, it was only a two-bedroom house which, to that three-year-old boy, seemed four times larger than their own farmhouse in the mountains.

Another actuality, Damien's mother wasn't born in the United States. The truth was that she'd been born in France, and that Damien's Grandmother divorced his natural Grandfather back when his mom was all of five years old. During the German occupancy of France in World War II, Damien's mother's mother fled from France, arriving by cargo ship in New York, where they lived with his great-aunt Daniel. Damien's Grandmother quickly remarried--much as his own mother had, out of financial need—and gave birth to two more daughters, then passed away two days before Damien was born on December 6, 1957. Meanwhile, the man who Damien would know all of his early life as "Grandpa" was yet another step-grandparent, further clouding Damien's true genealogy and understanding of relationships.

Aunt Cha-cha helped out in every way that she could, both as a makeshift nurse and diaper changer; although she didn't have, nor would have, any children of her own. Damien was likewise put to work as Cha-cha's "assistant," in charge of handing her the bottle of baby powder, towels, clothing, and bedding. The first few days were not symmetrical and haywire, while nearly everyone ignoring their own personal needs for those of the bedridden or soiled.

Damien, still a diaper wearer at night, felt just fine with being ignored during the excitement and disarray, except of course when he was hungry. Damien was a slim, borderline scrawny, boy for his age. At times, being able to "blend in with the woodwork" suited him; at other times, he required making a ruckus or "spectacle" of himself to get any assistance: Throwing tantrums instead of "using his words."

As things settled down in the household, Grandpa sat down with Mr. Collins and Damien. "So, Art, what plans do you have for little Damien? Are you planning to take him with you or to let him stay here?" the seasoned carpenter asked.

Explaining the situation, Arthur asked, "Could you folks keep an eye on the <u>four</u> of them? I'll need some time to get our place ready for <u>three</u> children. As you all know, we weren't expecting the third. And Damien, with his problems..."

"Oui. We've noticed," Grandpa interrupted. He fully recognized that Damien was having a real problem, for his age, communicating. For most of the time, the toddler would simply "shut off" altogether, ignoring the others around him. This was something that neither Arthur nor his bed-stricken wife were at all prepared for, and it was just one of the many beginnings.

Instead of feeling "put upon" by the extended stay, Damien's grandfather and aunt really wanted to help out during this transitional period of difficulty in his mother's life. The entire Collins family felt enormous appreciation for all the things that Aunt Cha-cha was able to do to make life as easy as possible, especially after Mr. Collins headed back to Washington. Alas, there were times that neither Cha-cha nor Grandpa were home, and that made things real difficult for young Damien and his mom, Christine.

Though she was "still ill," Damien's mom managed the round-the-clock breastfeeding of the twins and the changing of their diapers, but that was all she could muster. The three-year-old filled in the rest of the responsibilities, the ones he could conduct without adult supervision, while leaving the rest to pile up for Cha-cha or Grandpa to take care of later.

When Cha-cha wasn't home, Grandpa took care of my meals and needs, but I could tell that this was rather different for him since Grandpa had raised only daughters and had problems talking in English with a boy who spoke no language.

In comparison, taking care of the two newborns was easy, whereas taking care of Damien was like "swimming uphill." What did Grandpa mean by swimming uphill? Damien clarified for me. *In general he meant that he felt as if I was unable to communicate with anyone. Not that I wanted to, but that I couldn't. That we didn't speak the same language. For the most part, the one person I was able to communicate with was my Aunt Cha-cha. Simply put, she touched my soul in a way that not even my mom could. She spoke French, English, and spirit.*

Finally came the evening when Damien's step-dad came back to pick up his wife and kids and return to the mountains and the Olympic peninsula. Arthur had purchased new nursery furniture and moved it all onto their tiny alfalfa farm, then his family along with it. Christine rearranged everything, including Damien's room. Soon after their return, Damien's mother sat down with her oldest child and rather simply asked, "Damien? How do you feel about changing you last name from Shelden to Collings?"

You mean like yours?

"Mine and your brother's and sister's. We'd all have the same last name."

Damien clearly liked the idea, without any clear understanding of the significance of last names, nor what it truly meant to be adopted. The desire to fit-in and be liked by others was his only importance. So, following the paperwork and the need to wear a tie without going to church, Damien was adopted by his step-father and started a new life as a Collins.

Although neither Arthur's wife nor children knew it at the time, their visit to sunny California initiated a desire within Arthur to attend night school and work towards a more rewarding future for the five of them. However, it would become a future which was anything but rewarding.

CHAPTER TWO

A Child's Hell

Damien's life rushed passed him like water cascading down a mountain face. He was far from the easiest child to deal with and to raise. Damien spent quite a cumulative amount of time in his bedroom, both voluntarily and not. When he was all of a few years of age, not that he was trying to be difficult, Damien just didn't have the skills to build regular relationships. Well, that's pretty much true and still is today; although, he's slightly better today, thanks to much improved communication skills learned later in life.

When Damien turned five years young, his mother enrolled him in public school, that menagerie known as kindergarten. He had immediate and substantial troubles at school. Not only did Damien have difficulty having regular relationships with his teachers, but he had the same hindrance with students his own age. The kids at school couldn't understand him; most felt sorry for him or just plain didn't like him.

At first, I was strangely glad to go to school; for one thing, it got me out of the house. Boy, was I ever wrong! Neither the kids my age nor the teachers were willing to communicate, or be patient, with me. I felt as if I was constantly having to yell at them. I probably was.

It wasn't that Damien "wouldn't listen" to his teachers. No, he could not process the information like his classmates could. Damien operated at a much slower pace. His instructors labelled him as having a "learning disability," while his fellow students cruelly recognized it as "retardation" and called him as such.

As his mom grew more comfortable with letting Damien walk himself to and from the bus stop, without getting lost or into trouble, she'd immediately let him do so. After all, all that he had to do was to walk himself to the blacktop and wait. It wasn't a long wait for the school bus to pick him up, take him to that "horrible" school, and, at the end of the day, return him go the same piece of dirt and gravel near their driveway. How strenuous could that possibly be? Not surprisingly, on several occasions, Damien didn't make it to the place he'd come to perceive as "worse than hell."

The fact that Damien was unable to develop sustainable or "healthy" relationships, especially with other kids, made going to school a punishment more menacing than falling into a pit of snakes, having smoldering iron spikes stabbed into your eyes, or any other childhood fantasy. The other students at his elementary school, and later at his middle school, teased him mercilessly, oftentimes violently; bullying Damien seemingly without end!

Then came Steve.

Steve was a slightly older, African-American boy of thirteen who was homeschooled, which was rare in the 1960's and unique in their small town. One sunny afternoon at the township meeting hall, Steve met Damien and took a shine to the quirky boy; that is to say, Steve liked Damien and his idiosyncrasies. In hindsight, Steve would greatly influence Damien's like.

Soon after I had mastered by way to school and back home on my own. I'd met boy who was a bit older than I was, and he took it on his own to walk with me to and from school, and that made me well pleased.

At first, Damien Collins, or D.C. as Steve would call him, was nervous "as all get out" about being along with this new, and only, friend. Indeed, there was that happened between them that Damien was scared of. It was merely a matter of newness; Damien has never had a "friend" before.

Steven was not what mom was expecting in friends, as he was nearly fourteen years old and half-black. That made her nervous to say the least, but she allowed it. For the time being, she ignored what my dad would say about my first friend. Arthur didn't care about Steve's age. However, Steve's being partly African-American meant that, as far as dad was concerned, Steve was a n—.

This heated disagreement between husband and wife regarding race strained Damien's new friendship, not only because of his father's refusal to allow Steve near their house, but because Damien didn't understand racism. He valued having someone to finally talk to much more than his step-dad's approval.

One afternoon, while Arthur was out operating the combine, Steve and Damien's mother for permission to get her son involved in the local 4-H chapter (a youth organization sponsored by the Department of Agriculture that offered instruction in farming and economics). She was both surprised and grateful that there finally was a boy that showed any interest in her, especially one wanting to involve her introverted some in something a outgoing as the 4-H Club.

Damien was in need of someone he could talk to, whenever he would talk. Although with Steve, it was different compared to other kids. It wasn't as if Damien didn't use words much; rather, he often used far more than was needed. Truthfully, Damien spoke in a disconnected way. Not only was the listener confused, so was Damien!

Not everyone had patience with Damien. Steve did, and this came from the friendship Steve had given to Damien. If he fell off the track, Steve had him repeat what he was saying from the point at which Steve has gotten lost. As patient as Steve was, even he would become frustrated with having to be the ultimate listener. Damien talked, or rambled, and Steve listened, for the most part.

When Steve took on the challenge of being Damien's only friend and getting the younger boy involved in 4-H, he didn't know how much of a challenge that was. Boy, was Steve in for a real mess! Steve, himself, was rather proud of his involvement in 4-H. He was learning how to work leather and in grooming. Steve was looking forward to taking over his ma's farm when she retired or passed.

During their first week together, Steve wanted to teach Damien leather work. Steve hoped that this would be something that "D.C." could do and be happier with being able to make his own things. Maybe something for his mom. What actually happened surprised Steve far more than he could have imagined.

Things got off on the wrong foot.

When Damien would get frustrated, he would sit on the floor and commence in rocking himself back and forth, and nobody was able to breakthrough except for a limited few people—his mom (although this often took more time than she could tolerate), a school nurse, and Steve.

On that first day, Steve left Damien in good hands. Miss Linda was one of the many volunteer parents who taught leather craft. In fact, it was Linda who was getting ready to teach Steve and the others how to make their own saddles when "it" started: Damien sat himself down against a wall and started rocking.

This was something new to Miss Linda, and she really didn't know how to deal with it. Damien was as quiet as the wall he was leaning against. Without any warning, the situation escalated as the kids began teasing poor Damien and making fun of him. Linda scolded the kids which quickly shut them up, yet the rocking didn't stop, nor did the scolding encourage Damien to start talking.

Miss Linda got the attention of Steve by saying "I love your huge heart and desire to help young Damien, but I don't think that this is a good idea to bring him here, to be part of 4-H. He's still rocking over there."

Approaching Damien, Steve asked, "How are you D.C.?

Hearing Steve's voice, or perhaps just knowing that his friend was there, Damien regained his sense of safety and, with that, he was able to stop his rocking. Willfully, Damien turned his attention in Steve's direction, although it took nearly a minute until Damien could manage a single word to affirm Steve's question or making any actual eye contact.

Hey Steve, D.C.'s good.

"Yeah, you're good. What happened over there?" Steve asked while indicating the workbench where Damien last stood.

Stuttering nervously, Damien began to rock some more, but only briefly, while he replied, *D.C. m-m-made th-them mad at h-him.* And again Damien broke eye contact with Steve and sat quietly with his back to the wall.

Well, that was the normal for Damien, and Steve realized that day that things would work out after this 'episode.' That he provided Damien with not only friendship, but something incredibly more important: confidence.

CHAPTER THREE

Yelling, Shots Fired, Family Illness

Stepping slightly backwards in time, returning the calendar to December 1963, a few curious incidents occurred a few weeks after Damien has just turned six years old, on December 6.

Damien remembers it being a school night and that he was helping to clear the dinner plates and remains from the kitchen table when his mother, Christine, started yelling at Arthur Collins. Damien missed what triggered their frenzied argument, especially since Christine was yelling half in French, half in English, as she usually did when absolutely furious.

For what seemed like hours to that six year old, although the time was likely much shorter, Christine continued to yell at Damien's step-dad, so loudly that a neighbor from the farm beyond the trees decided to check on the Collins family.

Mr. Henry Levant was a middle-aged hired ranch-hand who lived in an auxiliary bunkhouse with two other live-in ranch-hands on the cattle ranch next door. He often came over to chitchat with Arthur and/or to borrow cigarettes or a beer. Henry and Arthur weren't necessarily buddies, rather they were acquaintances due to career choices and their close proximity.

"Evening Art, Chris, how are you folks doing?"

"Hey Henry," Arthur replied first, "Sorry for disturbing you tonight. We're okay."

"Yes, Henry. We're doing just fine," Christine sarcastically answered. It was clear that she both didn't want Henry to see them scuffling or their debate to be interrupted. After all, she probably believed she was winning.

"Well then," Mr. Levant raised an unopened liquor bottle he'd brought along. "Anyone want a nightcap?"

"Vermouth?" Damien's mom replied, feeling the need for something to ease the tension. "Sounds good to me."

Prior to the first drink being poured, Christine sent her oldest son to bed, then checked on the two toddlers. Through a cracked-open door, she commonly would see that little two-year-old Martin was wide awake, lying on his back in his crib, while quietly playing with his own fingers mere inches above his face. Meanwhile, as expected, Michelle was down for the night. Christine knew well to "let sleeping dogs lie" and not to scold Martin nor otherwise intervene. Instead, she carefully closed that door in an effort to not get the distracted boy's attention, otherwise she'd be in for an hour of pampering.

As Damien recently told me: *It wasn't long before the sleep, which I was enjoying, was disrupted by yet <u>another</u> yelling match, this time with new dominating voices. One of these was that of Mr. Levant, and the other was that of a nine-millimeter!*

At some point during this second incoherent argument of the evening, the topic had changed to something very different and dangerous. Arthur and Henry must've traded more than just drunken, angry words with one another, maybe a punch or shove or some of both, which Damien didn't see. Then Arthur brought out his ultimate voice, his handgun.

Damien arrived in the doorway of the kitchen completely out of breath and out of comprehension. His mom was both weeping at the table and permanently scared of Arthur for not knowing if or when her husband might fire another shot. Not that he would ever again fire it at anyone, just the thought that he might pull the trigger again with the children still in the house frightened her to no end, and she screamed as such.

The bullet had apparently just missed hitting Mr. Levant's left arm. Although he was caressing it with his right hand as if he'd been wounded in battle, there wasn't any blood.

To be truthful, I have no idea what it was that had woke me from my dream, but I was, nonetheless, scared. Later, when I was twelve, I learned a little more of what happened that night and grew more frightened of my step-dad's temper.

Henry, who was sitting when Damien first saw him, quietly got up from the kitchen table and left through the backdoor of their house, which was commonly used three times more often than the front door, without another word to Damien's parents.

Arthur, still intoxicated and holding the firearm, went back to the drawer where the gun was kept and put it away as if returning an unneeded tool, spatula, or some other cooking utensil. He then staggered into a chair beside his wife who, as mentioned, was understandably weeping and furious at the same time.

"W-what if h-h-he calls the sh-sheriff?" she finally choked out between sobs.

In the background of their small farmhouse, Martin was crying his heart out, although this was rarely anything new or unexpected. Damien himself kept thinking that he heard a police siren or that the next pair of headlights coming by on the main road, visible from the front window, was a possible patrol car. He privately wished that the cops would come and drag his drunk of a step-father to jail, to prison, forever. It would be a blessing.

Yet, despite these fears and prayers that Henry might have reported this incident to the police when he got home, or later in the week, they were never fulfilled. No phone calls were ever made.

Coincidently, Damien rarely saw Henry again, and never upon their own property. Since Damien was only six when this happened, he couldn't have fathomed how much of a turning point this shooting would become in his step-father's behavior. The firing of that gun was like the starting pistol of an entirely different type of marathon.

Ever since this unnerving event, Damien began to notice a clear and distinctive split in the household.

On one side of the family, if one could call it such, one had physical abuse in the form of regular spankings by Dad; who, instead of the customary bare hand, used a redwood bread cutting board, nicknamed 'the paddle.' Even if there was no real wrongdoing to merit such a beating, they practically turned into his favorite hobby. When that cutting board eventually broke, he improvised with a wooden baseball bat or whatever else was handy.

On the other side was the emotional abuse, for those who were doted on by Mom, which, for the most part, never included me.

Despite having all of the trouble in building a relationship with his family—let alone the rest of the world—Damien really did want to please his parents. Yet, no matter how much he would try to be the child that they could be proud of, he was still the target of their wrath; mainly because he was the eldest, and they viewed his troublemaking and emotional outbursts or "shutdowns" as trying to get attention for himself. Likewise, because he was the oldest child, Damien was inconceivably held accountable or "influentially responsible" for the negative actions of his siblings. For any trouble that either of the three would cause, the punishment always included Damien as well, in order to "teach him" the misguided lesson that he was to be a role model for the twins.

When little Martin was born, the doctors were concerned—as is common with multiple births—that his mental development might be impaired. Often what happens with twins and triplets, especially when there's an even greater number of siblings, that one or more of the fetuses don't receive enough oxygen or other nutrients. Not that the stronger sibling was necessarily "greedy," but from either tangled umbilical cord(s), insufficient placental or amniotic fluid to support the multitude, or other unknown contingencies during the 1950s and 60s.

As Martin aged, it became apparent that he suffered from mild retardation or deficiency. This greatly troubled Damien's parents, who believed that Martin's condition would parallel Damien's own sociological disorder. They were starting to believe that their family was cursed.

My parents thought that Martin would suffer the exact same set of developmental problems that I had. This was something they never accepted. Did my family have a curse? Well, in a way, we <u>were</u> cursed, but for entirely different reasons.

We live in reference to past experiences and not to future events; however inevitable. -H. G. Wells

CHAPTER FOUR

Friend or Foe

Damien believed that his unique companionship with Steve was completely sufficient for him—what more could a person need or want than one solid friend? Yet, on the other hand, Steve wasn't satisfied with having only one buddy for the rest of his life. While he found Damien's quirkiness amusing at times, irritating at others, as a maturing teenager within the throes of puberty, there were adult topics which Steve couldn't or didn't feel comfortable discussing with a nine-year-old.

Then came Nathan.

Unlike Steve, who was still being home-schooled, Nathan was a twelve-year-old, light-skinned African-American boy who went to Damien's public school; however, until this moment neither ever had noticed the other in the hallways.

Steve invited me to hang out with him and a new friend, Nathan, after school the next day. I'd accepted the offer to hang out with the two of them.

The next morning, on our way to my school, Nathan caught up to us and agreed to meet at the park, after final period. I didn't know that they wanted to play to do, but Steve was always friendly with me. I felt safe with him, and I was.

When Damien first met Nathan, due to the similarities in both older boys' skin tone and facial features, he'd believed the two teenagers to be related. Not brothers, but perhaps cousins. "Mixed" or interracial relationships were still socially taboo in the 1950's and mid-60's; the marches for civil rights, protesting segregated business and public restrooms, the famous speeches by Rev. Dr. Martin Luther King, Jr. and Malcolm X, all were part of the everyday news. Yet both of these boys were "halves."

The three boys entered the mostly vacant park, and, although Damien's first impulse was to rush towards the swing set to reserve a pair of them, the more mature teens headed directly to the park's public restroom.

I remember saying that I didn't "have to go," but Steve urged me inside the boy's room saying that there's something he wanted to show me. Before I knew it, and much to my surprise, Steve reached out his hand and touched my penis. Nathan joined him, making me feel very uncomfortable and causing me to freeze in my tracks. I still called it "my wiener" back then, while the older boys called it my dick This uncomfortable feeling started to fade away and was replaced with a hint of pleasure; however, I still had a thrust to run away.

The teenagers revealed themselves to young Damien; the fact that they had already sprouted pubic hair and were rather longer than himself bewildered Damien. Naturally, they were a couple of inches taller in height due to their ages; thus their prominence in length shouldn't have been unexpected. Only the entire situation, as a whole, held the nine-year-old in wonder and aghast.

It was all very strange to me, but it didn't hurt when they touched mine or impelled me to grasp theirs. Without warning of any sort, Steve looked at me saying, "We've been here too long and I need to get you home. And I mean right now." So we pulled our pants back up over our knees and I, for one, washed my hands at the sink—my mom's rule about doing so after touching my wiener must've been buzzing in my head.

That day of basic touching, as it would turn out, was merely a trial run to judge the nine-year-old's reaction by Steve and Nathan. Their true and hidden agenda of orally copulating and sodomizing this young, strawberry-blond boy as often as they could get away with it, would start the next week.

From the very moment I returned home that day, I felt as if I was in a living hell. It started with Mom yelling at me—half in French, half in English—for being so very late from school. At first, I thought she'd somehow found out about the sexual touching...all moms have spies everywhere! I had started to explain that I was at Centella Park with Steve, yet that wasn't what she was mad about.

Damien's mother had started hollering, mainly in French, "What happened this morning? Where is Nicki?

Wh-what do ya mean? Isn't s-she here? Damien stuttered out.

"You let her out this morning!"

Mom, I don't...Dad told me...I thought... and with that Damien broke down and started crying hysterically.

His mother, Mrs. Christine Collins, was still furious yet knew immediately that her own mood would only further escalate Damien into an intensity of sobbing and uncontrollable outbursts, then he'd reach a point of complete incapacitation that would last for hours.

"Damien, Damien," she began to soothe, "I'm sorry about that Damien. I'm sorry. I do remember hearing your dad tell you to let her out."

The boy was still weeping on the floor, curled up in the tightest fetal position he could muster. He wouldn't talk any longer, perhaps stammer a little but couldn't communicate with whole words, yet his mother persisted.

"Where have you been all afternoon?"

P-p-p was all that Damien could emit.

"Playing with that colored boy? Well, that's shit! You should have come straight home first. Don't I always let you go play with Steve after you finish your homework?"

Damien managed to quietly nod, although his attention was focused at his kneecaps.

"You're grounded...forever! And that's the least of your worries 'til your Dad gets home. Now get your work boots on. We'll be looking for Nicki all night if we have to!"

Since Damien's half-sister, Michelle, was already tucked in for the night—she'd been the "the perfect, most angelic baby" and, since Day

One, she rarely cried or woke up in the middle of the night—Christine needed only to carry the wide-awake and crabby Martin around with them during their search for Nicki the dog. It didn't take long after trekking through all of their alfalfa and hay fields, for Damien's mom to find her dead dog along the side of the main road. Deamien's earlier feeling of aghast instantly returned at the sight of the carcass.

I was horrified about our dog and about my own mortality, once Dad got home. I wanted to run away and be with Steve. Sure, he made me feel nervous when he touched my dick, but that didn't matter as much as getting spanked like I was going to get when Dad got home. It was better than not feeling at all. After all, with Steve, I was safe... and without Steve, I had to go to my own private place where I rocked 'til I was at peace.

When Arthur got home, Damien still got a beating despite his own innocence of 'obeying orders.' Although his step-father did ask Damien to let the dog our to urinate or whatever, it was still the boy's responsibility either to walk Nicki properly or to let her back inside <u>prior</u> to going to school. Damien "should have known better," about coming straight home from school, and, as his step-dad insinuated repeatedly, Nicki might've still. been alive if Damien had.

"You're spending too much time with that n— boy! You're turning into one! A disrespectful, good-for-nuthin!" he'd exclaimed in between each belting upon Damien's bare buttocks.

That night, the nine-year-old tossed and turned in his sleep, both from the pain to his rear end and from the nightmares of dead dogs and hairy wieners.

The following day, Damien was escorted to the end of their long gravel driveway by his step-father. There would be "no walking to school with that colored boy today," and Arthur took it upon himself to be sure Damien got onto the bus. Since the school bus driver had grown used to not stopping to pick up little Damien over the previous few weeks, the quick-moving bus skidded to a stop <u>after</u> passing the father and son.

Later, after school ended, Steve met with Damien along their usual route, anxious to find out where Damien had been that morning and/or if the youngster had blabbed to his parents about what had happened at the park. Damien immediately went into detail: his letting Nicki outside before school, coming home late, his mom screaming at him, their search through the fields, and the discovery of the dead animal, plus everything his step-dad said while Damien was being spanked with the belt.

Steve was relieved that Damien never said anything about their sexual touching, as well as being ambitious to perform some more of the same, if not more that very day.

"Well, Nathan is waiting for us at the—"

I'm grounded!

"What? For how long?"

Mom said, 'Grounded forever.'

"Forever? C'mon, it ain't gonna be forever. My mom'll say I'm grounded for a month, then jus' forget about it after a cup'lah days. Bet your mom'll too."

Maybe.

"I'll walk ya as far as the creek,, but I ain't gonna keep Nate waitin.' You doin' alright otherwise?"

Yeah. Go ahead an' go, I'll be alright. And with Damien's permission, Steve eagerly ran off between two trees and was gone.

The following Wednesday, since both Steve and Nathan oftentimes had soccer practice after school, the three met again at that same filthy public restroom. Almost immediately after checking for vacancy in the three toilet stalls, Damien was introduced to sodomy. The older boys relieved days of pent-up sexual frustration in the single afternoon! Damien, who was still too young to understand most things, was also introduced that day to orgasm.

A few days after Damien's virginity was <u>manhandled</u> from him, quite literally, upon that smelly and disgusting tile floor, Steve and Nathan had a "falling out" and no longer were friends. Damien and Steve continued to meet before and after school throughout the remaining year. They didn't always meet for sex, didn't always have a private place to be together, but the inclination and pent-up frustration was always there.

Damien was consistently doing poorly in school, as reflected in his appalling grades and letters from his teachers; however, the relationship with Steve became his largest distraction. Damien's obsession. His only source of safety and stability. The cost of being persistently molested seemed reasonable to the alternative.

Then came the next devastating change in the life of Damien Collins. After his tenth birthday, his step-father came in from bailing hay and made an important announcement to the family: he'd been offered a job in Los Angeles, CA! Earlier that summer, Mr. Collins had earned a degree in Computer Engineering at the community college. This new job was going to be his way out of being a farmer for the rest of his life.

This was going to be a change that would greatly benefit the family as a whole, or so his dad hoped it would.

CHAPTER FIVE

The Turning of a Page

It was the fall of 1969, and Damien was all of twelve, going on his teenage year. To say that the last three had been frenzied would be an understatement! Shortly after the Collins family moved from Washington to California, the family stopped being one. To date, Damien is unsure what caused this latest dismantlement and dissolution, but his parents separated.

It was decided between husband and wife that the twins were too young to be estranged from their mother, whereas she couldn't possibly support all three children on her own. Damien became the consolation prize for their failed marriage.

This was a new page in my life, yet it proved to be tattered and worn by the events and emotional wear of the previous experiences of my youth, especially the abuse and lack of understanding, to say the least. I was indeed grateful that no one yet knew about my sexual involvement with other boys and my use of it as a coping mechanism in dealing with my broken family.

At age eleven, I lived, if that's what you call it, with Dad in a small apartment in West Los Angeles.

Prior to coming to California, Damien had self-taught to protect himself the best he could from the mess on the farm, but L.A. was a different story altogether. Everything happened at a faster pace than in the mountains; everything that is except for him.

I spent the majority of my time in my bedroom, very much along . . . which was how I felt anyway. You see, the apartment complex where I lived did not have any kids my age. No, not one! And there was the lack of communication skills which hindered me throughout my life. Without any youngsters younger than teenagers in the neighborhood, I didn't have anyone to play with or make a relationship. And, due mostly to my dad, had a huge distrust of grownups.

There weren't kids that understood him and his problems, no replacements for Steve nor the courage and safety that Steve had provided. Damien's classmates at this public school mainly kept avoiding him as much as they could or teased him viciously.

Again, it wasn't that he couldn't learn. If anything, Damien possessed a rather grand intellect, limited only by his provincial upbringing. He was getting decent enough grades in his schoolwork and on tests. He was just slower than most, and, worst of all, Damien didn't have anyone to talk or work things out with.

At this point in my life, according to the social norm, I was supposed to be either at school, studying, or out playing with other kids my age. Since I was lacking the former, I chose sexing other teen boys. It might've been the wrong way to go about making friends, but it took the place of loneliness and regular beatings from an abusive drunk.

Damien met after school either at a secluded place beneath a freeway on-ramp or a complete stranger's living room, offering oral sex to students he knew and to some he didn't know at all. Sodomy wasn't offered as often as it was forcefully taken of him. However, Damien was beginning to accept this way of life as normal. After all, what else could he do? He needed companionship, and others needed sexual release. Wasn't this what friendship was all about?

Thanksgiving Day at the Collins apartment was basically the same as any other day. Dad did cook the two of us a dinner of sorts, yet it was neither good nor bad. I believe I upset him once or twice when I'd mentioned how much I missed my mom during dinner. We didn't even do anything to celebrate Martin and Michelle's birthday! That was usual, but very sad.

The fact is, we did nothing like a family. We didn't even celebrate each other's birthdays. Dad and I did do some celebrating on the Christmas in 1968; we got each other a few gifts and opened them on Christmas Eve. Then went to Grandpa's house in Culver City for some real good dinner with Mom, Martin, and Michelle. I was real happy then, although my dad was obviously uncomfortable being there.

It was during this holiday that the separated couple discussed making their divorce final. Damien's dad, technically his step-father, told his mother that he was concerned with the development of their eldest son. Public school wasn't working out for Damien. Arthur believed that what Damien needed was a school with more structure. He found Mt. Lowe Military Academy in East L.A. and wanted Christine to register Damien there. This school had success with 'problem children' in the past, and there laid hope for Damien's education and growth.

As sure as I am sitting here telling you my life's story, something was about to happen that was strange indeed. And it did. On New Year's Day, that morning both my dad and mom took me out to IHOP for breakfast. That alone was a strange gift, the two of them together, and in public.

Damien was starting to believe that the two of them had rekindled their relationship and marriage, the ultimate dream of most children of divorced parents; however, this was not to be the case. They weren't getting back together, instead they had something important to discuss.

Much to my surprise, when we arrived at the restaurant, I was greeted by Grandpa, my great-aunt Daniel, and also the twins, plus a stranger. Without delay, Mom stood up saying, "Damien, I want to introduce you to your uncle Mike."

Damien was obviously confused. He knew that his mom had only two sisters, and if "uncle" meant his step-dad's brother, Damien probably would've heard about him earlier in his life. No, Damien was quite positive he didn't have any uncles.

Standing and offering me his hand, this bronze-haired man said, "Hello Damien. How are you?" With the feeling of uncertainty, I said I was okay and ended up sitting down in a booth directly next to this man I never thought I would ever want to sit next to. I just felt too uncomfortable sitting anywhere else. Well, except for, maybe, my grandpa, since Aunt

Cha-cha wasn't there.

The extent of Damien's conversation with "Uncle" Mike was done over breakfast and consisted mostly about the recent Christmas and school. A total of about five questions: Did you have a nice Christmas? How are you doing in school? All of which Damien simply answered *Fine* or *Okay* to.

I was relieved that we had come to an end of his uncomfortable questions. After all, I was eleven years old and he was never involved in my life, until suddenly, now here was this uncle interested in me.

This was the only time that Uncle Mike had made an appearance in my life, on that odd New Year's Day. After that, Uncle Mike disappeared all these years. AS what I thought was a strange coincidence, I also never saw my Aunt Cha-cha anymore.

It wouldn't be for several year until Damien found out he'd been sitting next to his Aunt Cha-cha's husband that entire breakfast.

The special breakfast, on that holiday to celebrate a fresh start at life, was one of Damien's favorites; however, not as much as what occurred after. Before long, Grandpa took Damien to his car, joined by his great-aunt Daniel, who likewise made almost as much sense as did "Uncle" Mike, plus his mom and the twins, all together in their car. From the parking lot, they were on their way to Disneyland! Now that was a surprise if ever there was one.

I don't remember all of the rides that we went on, but I can tell you that we had a ball! It was the very first time that I had the company of my great-aunt, and, for that matter, I was treated to a day of fun and excitement, anything close like that one. Part of me wanted to have Uncle Mike with us, so that I could've got to know him a little more. Why did he appear in my life and just then disappear?

When the day ended, I was returned to Dad in the same condition which I was borrowed in, with the exception that I was a whole lot more tired.

When Damien's mother and grandfather left their apartment, his step-dad said, "Damien, you know, I forgot to give you something for Christmas. Why don't you look under the tree and pull out that last present?"

I had a good time with my family, or at least the Disneyland portion of it, and I went to bed thinking that there was going to be an improvement in my relationship with Dad. I had thought that all was going to be just fine from then on, after all, Dad and I were talking more than ever.

Boy, was I every wrong!

Talking between Damien and his father quickly returned to the previous level of mostly noncommittal and nearly nonexistent. The joy of the holidays evaporated like a ice cube in the Mojave Desert.

Well, from my point of view, just about everything went south that January. One humongous problem was about to happen, not intentionally, but I thought it would be okay for me to invite a friend from school home. The "friend" was, of course, only interested in my body, and to make things worse, he was <u>not white</u>.

As you already know, that made things more than wrong with my dad. I guess that I never understood racism. How could any of my friends be only okay, only as a white boy, in my house? His being black just didn't mean a thing to me.

It is not that I was a Catholic boy, or colorblind, or ignorant to different races, but the fact is, I just could not see that there really was some sort of hidden differences between people based on the color of their skin. A peach-colored person was okay by Dad, but a brown-colored was hated.

It was the first day of the second semester, and Damien had invited a black boy from school to his house. Damien didn't know the boy very well, and honestly couldn't recall for me his name, only that it had started with a 'J', possibly Jamal.

I had him in my room, and not to have sex, I mean that I wasn't thinking about sex at the moment. My friend was glad to be invited to my house. He just wanted to get to know me a little, since he just moved to L.A. and lived really close by. Less than two side-streets away from our complex.

I must've thrown out my dad's clearly racist statements to me when we lived in Washington and there was just Steve. I was rather a social moron because these rules never made any sense to me whatsoever.

When dad came home and found me along with this black boy, no wondering what was going on, purely one thought came to him because my friend was black. Wow! Boy did things go wrong. Dad really went berserk! And yet, even with the beating of my life that I knew I was going to soon get, nothing had hurt my feelings more than to hear Dad call my friend a "n—" and me a "n— lover."

After heaving, practically flinging, my friend out the front door, Dad then told me to get the bat. Just the thought of the bat got me sick to my stomach and made me tear up something fierce! I cried all the way to the closet. I received the beating of all beatings, and he didn't quit until he audibly broke bones. He then all but kicked me out of his home—an eleven-year-old homeless orphan. Thankfully he didn't; although maybe not thankfully.

When the spanking, if you can accurately call it that, was over, Damien retired to his tossed and dismantled bedroom. The emotional and physical hatred and pain would not subside nor dull. Damien mostly howled and wallowed, thrashing at his pillows and bedding, hammering at anything soft, screeching into his palms from the agony! This continued unceasingly for nearly an hour until, of all tutelary saints, his step-father came to soothe and console him. Damien, naturally would've preferred to have seen Satan walk in.

I felt so angry at Dad for what he had done, that I just didn't know what to do with it. Despite my inability to always put into words what I was feeling or why I was feeling it, I knew that what Dad did was wrong.

Then Dad came to my room to do something that I saw as weird coming from me; he <u>apologized</u> in his own way and explained why he used the bat on me and why he was so angry. He attempted to explain why black people made him so mad and why he called them what he called them. The more he talked, the more he made me pissed at him, not less. No, the only becoming less was my ability to trust him again.

To the date of this writing, I still cannot make sense of his nonsense. The following weeks were so bad that both of us worked at not having to deal with the other, even at not being in the same room.

Gratefully, this didn't last long before Damien was finally enrolled and would soon be sent off to Mt. Lowe Academy. It would be while he attended Mt. Lowe that Damien would hopefully learn more about responsibility and how to be part of a team; granted, due to his "spankings," he held a resentment towards joining any baseball teams.

Science may have found a cure for most evils; but it has found no remedy for the worst of them all—the apathy of human beings. -Helen Keller

CHAPTER SIX

Strive, Achieve, Excel

Some two weeks into January, Arthur slipped into Damien's room while the boy was getting dressed for school. He announced that Damien needed to come with him to his office at the Trident Corporation, a DOD contractor working on defense projects. His stepdad explained that he'd called Damien's school and excused him for the day.

I'd never seen where my dad had worked before, Back in our more friendlier months of living together, he used to say only that he worked on "top secret government stuff," and images from <u>James Bond</u> movies would popup in my head. Not that I believed that my dad was an international spy or assassin, but, maybe, he was one of the engineers that invented lasers that fit inside wrist watches or cars that can turn into helicopters!

After clearing visiting checking-in procedures, they spent only a little time there; and most of it within a drab office with no windows. Arthur has absolutely no intention of giving his step-son a tour of the facilities. Instead, after Arthur attended a morning staff meeting in an adjacent conference room, they headed back out to the parking lot again.

We stopped at a McDonald's and ate breakfast, since it was still too early for burgers, then headed on our way to the city of Altadena. I didn't know where we were going, but it turned out to be good for both of us.

Mt. Lowe Military Academy had a vast campus of separate buildings and exercise grounds. This was something quite unique to the mountain boy. While being a student of a Los Angeles public school, Damien grew used to the large classroom sizes and crowded conditions—much like Mt. Lowe's—but the public school's buildings were interconnected by long hallways; Mt. Lowe was more like an ivy college. Understandably, Damien felt not only his usual "lost in a crowd" feeling, but flat-out lost—period—during his first few days of figuring out where any thing was.

Arriving at Mt. Lowe, Dad said, "C'mon, Damien," and they would prove to be the last words I would have to hear from him for the next three months...which suited me just fine. I was happy that I wasn't going home every night to face yet another beating for not living up to Dad's standards. At this boarding school, I'd be able to relax and to do my work at my level. Or so I thought!

After being processed by an Admissions clerk, Damien was introduced to Sergeant Rob Barker. It was while handshaking this much larger boy when Arthur disappeared from sight and from Damien's life for quite a while. Sgt. Barker took Damien to one of the barracks where another introduction was made: Damien's squad leader, Corporal Dane Jackson.

Jackson was likewise a student, yet in his tenth year at the Academy. He was seventeen, around six feet tall, and a dark-complexion African-American. In his freshly-ironed uniform, this burly soldier looked ready to wrestle even the huskiest of "commies" to the ground. All it would take, would be to parachute just one Cpl. Jackson into the heart of the then-Soviet Union, to put an end to communism worldwide.

"Nice to meet you, Cadet Collins."

"M-m-my name is Damien," the twelve-year-old corrected.

"Yes, it is. But for now, you'll be addressed by your rank and last name," the corporal explained, then instructed Damien to salute the sergeant when the senior officer turned to leave. His salute was understandably sloppy and crooked; he'd never saluted anyone before.

Sergeant Barker left me in the capable hands of Cpl. Jackson, who first took me to the warehouse to collect my "issue" of uniforms and other school items. Next, he instructed me in how to "stow" my belongings and to make a proper bunk. He put off teaching me other things in order to give me time to wash up and get into my uniform.

"Okay, Cadet. You need to shower and get dressed, in uniform, and make your bunk, and you need to make sure your footlocker is in order. Got all that?"

Yes, Mr. Jackson.

"Sir! You say, yes sir. And you say it proudly."

Yes sir! Damien practically shouted.

"Okay. Get ready then."

Um—sir? Where is everybody else? Damien asked while indicating an open palm to the twenty-plus prepared yet vacant beds.

"In classes, of course. I know it's strange starting at a new school when the semester already started, but you'll get the hand of it."

Damien showered and dressed as quickly and properly as he could. He had never been at a school which required a school uniform before, and almost immediately missed the feeling of denim and cotton briefs— he disliked wearing boxers.

The barracks were all wooden with a corrugated sheet-metal roof— no luxuries such as fiberglass insulation or air conditioning—but they were all immaculately clean and neat. Within his own "G" Barracks, Damien even took notice of how clean and shiny the five-person shower, the three toilets, and the large bathtub-shaped urinal were. He also had a bit of concern about how open and communal everything was: no doors, no dividers, no privacy.

Before long, the fellow cadets had finished and returned from classes. Damien was almost completely ignored; only a few finger-pointing and whispers about there being a "new kid" were made, yet everyone was too busy with their own needs to greet him.

They weren't even back inside the barracks for ten seconds before Cpl. Jackson blew his whistle and started yelling out commands. He repeated over-and-over the word "inspection" and that we were to get ready for one.

The twenty or so cadets quickly stowed their books, combed their hair, and straightened their collars; Damien performed the last two of these since he didn't yet carry around any books. Then they all lined up for a "chow time inspection" to be performed by Sgt. Barker himself.

The sergeant came slowly down the line and stopped to check on my progress, He was basically pleased with what he saw and because he was able to bounce a quarter off my bunk, he believed that I was a "quick learner." I was happy to do things right and even got to keep the quarter, which back in 1969 was plenty for a candy bar. On his way out, Sgt. Barker said, "Nice work, Cadet. The shoes need some work, but one can't expect absolute perfection on your first inspection. Good work, Corporal Jackson. Sound off."

"Sir, yes, sir," Cpl. Jackson automatically replied, then ordered the squad, "G Barracks, sound off!"

All together, all the boys (except for one) in the room bellowed on que, "Strive, achieve, excel!"

"I can't hear you!" Cpl. Jackson encouraged.

"STRIVE, ACHIEVE, EXCEL"

"Fall out for chow!" the corporal ordered—another military term which Damien was unfamiliar with, so he just mimicked the actions of others around him.

In two separate single-file lines, they marched around their dormitory and in near-perfect formation of two-abreast, the entire distance to the Dining Hall. I n walking yardage, their just happened to be the furthest from the "mess hall," as they called it; thus their squad was consistently the very first to go there and, as happened more often than not, the very longest to stand and wait until the kitchen staff were fully prepared to unlock and open their doors.

This was perhaps the first time I'd eaten dinner before 4:30 p.m.! My first meal was far better than I had hoped for, or than Dad could've cooked. I had thought that I would be missing out on my favorite foods, like anything barbecued; but to my surprise, we had two of the juiciest, grilled hamburgers, mashed potatoes, buttered corn—but not on the cob—and a ton of pudding. All of it tasted real good.

We weren't allowed to talk while we ate. If you wanted someone to pass the salt or pepper, you knocked twice on the table and gave American sign language letters for "s" or "p." They didn't give us much time to eat before we were returning our metals trays and marching back to the barracks.

Along the way, I introduced myself to another new boy who started here at the semester. He was about my age and both cranberry hair and freckles. He offered his right hand and said, "I'm Jensen." But, he only got one more sentence out before we both got yelled at for "talking in line."

When we got back to "G" Barracks, he turned out to sleep across the main isle and down one bunk from mine. He explained to me that names were important.

"For now, you'll be called by your last name. When we're on our own time, you'll get called by your first name. Mine is Jason, what's yours?"

Damien.

"Cool. Damien Collins?" he double-checked.

Yeah, well, sort of.

"What do you mean by 'sort-of'?"

Well, I hate my last name. It's the name of my step-dad, and I can't stand him. I don't even remember the last name I was born with, but anything would be better than Collins.

"Don't worry. I don't think anybody here likes their last name," he grimaced, then added, "Or their fathers very much."

So, what do we do for fun here?

"There's a bunch of stuff. We have sports, like softball, basketball, and last week, flagball, which is touch football. There's archery and swimming, come the summer, and board games when it rains. Probably soccer, too, but later in the year."

Damien could see right away that this place wasn't going to be easy for him; that nearly all the sports and other events revolved around teamwork or partnerships, except maybe for the one during the summer (archery and swimming); although those possibly would involve relay races or some other teammate(s). His problem in communicating with others and building regular relationships with people was about to be put to a daily challenge.

CHAPTER SEVEN

Integration

One afternoon, while his squad was assigned at working to clean-up the upper exercise field, Damien took a rare chance to see how receptive a fellow student would be of this newest of teenaged cadets. Approaching his senior officer, the older boy name Corporal Jackson, to engage him in light-hearted conversation, Damien greeted him saying, *Good afternoon, Corporal. How are you?*

"I'm well, thank you, Cadet, and you?"

Fine, sir, thank you. I...um well, have –

"Out with it, Cadet! I don't bite."

Sorry, sir...I have a, um, personal question, if you don't mind.

"Sure, what do you want?"

I guess, well, I was just wondering why you're the only Black boy in, at this school, here. Why do you think this is true?

Pausing for a moment, the corporal considered the question, as well as the child's motive, if any, by bringing the topic up. This half-Irish youngster hadn't meant any racist insult by asking this. In the deepest recesses of his soul, this young African-American corporal was fully aware of the life and mission of the late Rev. Dr. Martin Luther King, Jr. and the fight for civil rights which weren't yet even a full decade beyond them; the famous doctor had only been assassinated two years prior to this moment.

"You're right, Cadet, I am, and it's just not right. For that matter, most blacks still can't get the right jobs to afford tuition here, or at any private schools. You follow?"

Yes, sir.

"My people have a much harder time getting into colleges, so they could get the degrees needed for better paying jobs. Things are changing now, especially after this was is over. You remember Malcolm X?"

Damien simply nodded, not sure if this was the topic to open up with.

"He was the civil-rights leader they gunned down five year ago. He was big on seeing more opportunities for Blacks. More colleges accepting our people." Then Corporal Jackson noticed an expression on Damien's face and turned sternly towards the young cadet. "Why you askin'?"

I, uh, just noticed and, um, thought it was weird.

"Weird, how? That I'm the only black kid at this school? That maybe Blacks don't belong at this academy?"

Oh no! How does that matter? Damien adamantly responded, then almost immediately regretted doing so and explained. *"I'm glad you're here. Just because by step-dad hates people because of the color of their skin, doesn't mean that I should. There is but one God and he made all people from Adam and Eve. How can I dislike or hate anyone because of the color of their skin? That just don't, doesn't make sense to me.*

"It doesn't make <u>sense</u> to you? Cpl. Jackson repeated, somewhat bewildered.

No, I would hate it if I was hated by you, by anybody, just because I was born with a certain color to my skin. I'm already not liked much for <u>enough</u> other reasons, know what I mean?

"You're alright by me, Cadet. In fact, I like you. I like the way you think."

Thanks! Sir.

"Sure, now let's get this done," he ordered while handing Damien an extra rake.

With that said, they returned to their work. They continued with their unit's clean-up assignment when another cadet, named Blake or something like that—called to Cpl. Jackson, asking the officer to take a look at a rock he found and was holding. Damien gave his own opinion that it was a fossil of a leaf that fell from a tree a long time ago, back before anyone had invented rakes like the one he held.

Jackson stepped forward, "Let's see what you have here, Private."

Putting the rock in the corporal's hand, Blake asked, "What do you think, sir?"

"I think Collins might be right. Looks like a fossil. Let's take it to Mr. Guler in the morning." After giving it back, he announced to the two dozen sweaty faces, "Looks like we're about done here. Line it up."

Several repeated cheers of "Line it up" echoed across the field, as the corporal gathered his squad behind where he stood, then marched them back orderly to their barracks and finally dismissed them.

On the following day, Cpl. Jackson was still obviously pleased with the earlier conversation with Damien. He seemed glad to hear that this young kid from Los Angeles, of all places, wasn't prejudice in the slightest. He rather liked Damien Collins. True, Damien wasn't the same as the others he'd come across at this school, including several of the older instructors; yet that's what he like most about Damien: a diamond in the rough. That and the fact that Damien had a "kind heart." The corporal saw that this kid was more than intelligent; he just didn't know how much more Damien was.

Likewise, Damien was impressed with Cpl. Jackson. He was a thoughtful boy minutes away from being full-fledged. A true asset to the U.S. Army, if that's where he was headed. Damien admired the corporal and wondered how to become his friend, if that was possible. How could Damien even approach him about being friends?

Then another fear hit Damien: *Hell, I don't even remember his first name.*

This became Damien's conundrum: He's finally met a person who is intelligent and approachable, and yet he's had this lifelong difficulty in engaging others in conversation. Without the right amount of courage, the chances of developing any kind of friendship at all are zero. Also, knowing the right time to take such a risk is similarly nonexistent.

However, that night, Damien decided to risk making a fool of himself and try to engage the corporal in small talk.

It was approximately 6 p.m. (a.k.a. 1800 hours), when Damien went over to Cpl. Jackson's bunk and politely asked: *You got a minute, sir?*

"Sure, and if we're not in formation or I'm not addressing you officially, it's Dane or just 'Dee'. Okay?"

Seeing an opportunity, he introduced himself, *I'm Damien, Dee. You can call me 'D.C.' if you wish.*

"Thanks. So, what were you wanting, Damien."

Well, the truth is, I liked your questions yesterday, because, well, the answers told you a little more about me. I, um, I sorta hoped that we can resume that conversation, from time to time.

With a smile, the corporal summarized, "So, you wanna talk?"

Well…yes, briefly anyway, if you want to.

Damien's nervousness made Jackson snicker a little. He wasn't sure if the young cadet was just naturally shy, or, maybe, feeling subdued by their differences in military rank: him, a corporal, and Damian, a lowly cadet. In either case, Jackson didn't want to scare the younger kid away too quickly.

"So, where are you from, Damien?"

The mountains of northwestern Washington, originally, and you?

"Hrrm." Cpl. Jackson mumbles out, surprised by Damien's answer of Washington. He'd read that this kid lived in L.A., not far from his own parents' house. "I was born in Long Beach, but we moved to the city a few years back. So, tell me about yourself. Not the full details, but some."

As I said, I'm a mountain boy from Washington. My real dad left us when I was all of eighteen months young. He was an Irish drunk, or so my Aunt Cha-cha says. Mom got her marriage annulled and soon after, married again to another Irish drunk. I'm half-French on my mom's side. I got a half-brother, Martin, and a half-sister, named…

"You! I want to hear about you," Cpl. Jackson emphasized.

Um, okay. Well, I'm not the same as other kids, as you know. I can't make friends as other boys do. I had one friend in the whole world. Steve was there for me from the start,, helped me in my schoolwork, and got me involved in 4-H, although not with others kids.

"Wait. What's 4-H, and why 'not with other kids'?"

4-H is a youth club designed to get kids involved in farming and related stuff, while making the many activities of farming and farm life as rewarding as possible. I had fun making stuff out of leather and such.

"Alright, so whaddaya mean about not being involved with other kids?"

Because, when I get the feeling I'm lost, upset because things are happening around me all too fast, I lost it! I lock-up and out. Either I stand absolutely still as a statue or I have to find a quiet place to sit and rock. Rocking away the feeling of being lost for words or expression—a way to relate to others, because I don't understand the immediate situation. I—it, you see, I disrupted the 4-H projects and at school, I'd lock-up and interrupt the whole class.

"Okay, I get it. You hardly do that anymore, that rocking thing. I, well, I mean I saw you on your very first day…"

Oh, you saw that? Damien had been left alone to put on his uniform for the very first time, and halfway through doing so had a quick two-minute episode of intense nervousness which resulted in this sitting on the unmade bunk bed, curled up like a ball. He had thought he was entirely alone, yet apparently he hadn't been.

"It's nothing to be ashamed of," Cpl. Jackson reassured him. "You were in a strange, new place, feeling all alone; it's totally understandable. The good thing is, you haven't done any rocking since. What's changed?"

Because I got some really good advice once, from my friend Steve. He told me that I can do it all I need to on my free time. If I just waited for a quiet and private time. Sometimes, I take real long, hot showers…

"Yeah, good luck getting one of those here."

Yeah, b-but the point is, I didn't know I could relieve stress in small amounts by doing things that relax me. I also thought I had to get rid of all of it at once, or I'd explode.

"Alright, I see." Cpl. Jackson sat up a little straighter, taking a glance out a nearby window. "When you feel the need, you might also go to the rifle or archery range. You'd be pleased to know that I go to the range to relieve stress. It's always helped me."

Thanks, Dane. I just need a little nudge in the right direction in a nice way, and I'll adjust accordingly.

"Sure. I didn't see a problem, but I saw a need that needed shifting a little. You give a little and we give a little... you know, teamwork and all that. You're going to find that this place revolves around integrating with others and building unity with your fellow students."

I'm, uh, that's going to be hard for me.

"You'll be fine. Trust me, trust in yourself. So, tell me a little more about your mountain life."

Oh, well, we lived on a 185-acre alfalfa farm, you know, hay. We had neighbors that raised a ton of cattle. We raised a few too. When I was five, my mom enrolled me into kindergarten. School, for me, was hell! Partly because it takes me longer to process information than for others. Why? I don't know. My parents and my teachers thought I was just a troublemaker on purpose. The teachers really didn't want me in their classrooms because of my 'episodes.' I was about eight-and-a-half when I found fresh air in the form of a friend, Steve. I'm just a weird kid.

"Listen, Damien. You're intelligent and I've never seen or heard you do or say anything crazy or off-the-wall. You <u>are</u> an odd ball, I'll give you that, but this place is full of 'em! But look... I like you. So, we'll talk more often. Mainly after dinner, whenever. I'm thinking that we can be friends, when I'm not bossing you around. You don't have to be what you're not. Be <u>you</u> and you'll be just fine. Okay?"

Yeah, And thanks, Dee. Damien happily said. He walked to his bunk with a bit of a spring to his step that had never been there before. Perhaps Cpl. Jackson was right, perhaps Damien did fit in just fine here.

For the rest of the evening, Damien reflected on his life and what Steve had told him when he last had time to be alone with his one and only friend; Steve had told "D.C." to always be proud of where he came from; that he was, and always will be, a mountain boy. Truth was, regardless of the farm life and the spankings and the bullies, Damien <u>was</u> proud of where he came from. He could see how the mountains became a significant part of who he was, both in strength and grandeur.

He'd already overcome so much!

Steve also told him that he wasn't mentally ill, he just wasn't blessed with the same social gifts as others were, but he was gifted with other gifts.

"This" Steve said to Damien, "is what you need to figure out; which ones do you have."

As time ticked on by Damien, he kept alert to see if he could detect any area in his life that he was gifted in, but so far he just didn't see it.

Reflecting a little longer, he recalled how his parents paid hardly any attention to who he was and what his unique gift to life could be. His step-dad believed only that whatever Damien's problem was, it could be cured with stern discipline. Often a good whipping with that cutting board, belt, or bat. His mom blindly accepted the doctor's early diagnosis of early childhood schizophrenia, believing that someday medical science would find a cure-all pill; given that this was the late-1960s, and these were the days before psychiatrists just shove Prozac and/or Ritalin down children's throats to cover-up the symptoms of their disorders rather than solve them, a cure-all seemed unlikely.

Damien was on a separate, completely natural and un-pharmaceutical path to recovery, which all started with opening himself without restriction to others around himself. To uniting, and becoming more than just himself, to becoming a part of a harmonious whole!

CHAPTER EIGHT

Promotion

It was the third night at Mt. Lowe that Damien was kept awake, unable to sleep, because he was reflecting on the makeup of the Academy. Behind the Dining Hall was where the massive kitchen was. He remembered from his new student orientation that everyone, at some point in their school year, worked the kitchen in either serving food or as a part of its clean-up crew; something he wasn't particularly looking forward to.

Outside the kitchen was the basketball courts, handball, and even a tetherball pole. Up the hill from there was where soccer and football, or flag football as James called it, was played, as well as where their drills were done.

Marching was a daily requirement for all students. Mt. Lowe participated in many local events, including the Christmas Day parades and frequently marched in the Rose Bowl parade in Pasadena. So, they drilled everyday, rain or shine, in relentless, and absurd, pursuit for incorrigible synchronization. Mind you, we're talking about teenagers here.

Due to Damien's poor sleeping at night, he tried to squeeze in an afternoon nap whenever he could. Most students didn't return to the barracks in between classes nor during lunch hour, only a few did.

Damien took advantage of this time to get some much needed rest.

Waking up from a sound nap, I'd been dreaming about my two long-lost friends, Steve and Nathan. I found myself feeling a little embarrassed by the unplanned growth in my pants. It was pretty obvious.

This was a bad habit to have, but I didn't know how to kill it. I actually wanted a few cadets to take notice of it in hopes that they would seek out the relief I was willing to provide, as long as it was in complete secrecy. I didn't want to risk the good things I had going.

I was having fun at being a good cadet. And why not? I was out of trouble, didn't have to deal with any more beatings, and nobody knew of my past. As a "new kid," I received the usual new-kid insults and practical jokes; yet these weren't personal attacks against me, at least not yet.

I was twelve years of age and in the sixth grade when I started by first semester at the academy. I worked hard to attain passing grades. Boy, I'm telling you the truth when I say that I did do my best; and still, I was upset with the poor grades I earned at my class work. I had disciplinary problems, but if what I wanted was to go up in rank, I needed to work harder at my class work, especially in English.

Walking into the barracks on a nice February afternoon, Damien literally ran into James Jensen, exclaiming, *Whoa Jensen! Let's watch where we're walking.* This was once a favorite phrase of Damien's mother.

"Sure, Damien. And at ease, soldier."

Yeah, thank you James. I'm actually glad we ran into each other.

Really, why? What's up?

Are you any good at English?

"Well, I'm speaking it, aren't I?" James laughed out loud, but his chuckling quickly subsided at the seriousness expressed on Damien's face. "So, what grade are you in?"

I was put in seventh, but I . . . , Damien lowered his voice to hide his discomfort. *I think that I didn't do good enough in English to start there.*

"You? Poorly in English? No way!" James teased, followed by pointing out that Damien should've said, "do <u>well</u> enough."

Okay, James. You're kiddin' with me. We both know that my English really stinks. Didn't help that my mom was half-French and, although I'm ten times worse at French, I'm so bad at English. Horrible, actually. But I so much want to improve. I want to earn stripes.

"Well, don't let that bother you. We all have areas that we need help in. I can't fire a rifle for nothing! Maybe you should talk to Corporal Jackson about switched to Captain Kendal's class. He's great."

I hope so, James, 'cause I really need help there. By the way, I had my first shooting range yesterday, and I shoot pretty good. The one thing that really helped me was to breathe real deep and slow. Don't hold it in.

"I'll try that. Thanks."

Damien and James went about their own business, as Damien wanted along time in the shower. He got the time he wanted, and for once the water was warm, but it much too quickly became pretty far from alone time. He was soon grouped together with three other fully naked boys and their exposed-yet-limp penises. Damien's own phallus was inadvertently hardening.

A lightly older student to his left noticed that Damien had stopped bathing himself, standing motionless and awkwardly, and upon discovery blurted out, "Holster that weapon, soldier!"

It was meant as a joke, of course, yet Damien took it the wrong way, rushing out of the shower naked and concealing his erection as best he could with both bare hands, almost forgetting his towel on his way out of the restroom area. The other students weren't sure what was happening; all that they saw was a mostly naked twelve-year-old hurrying from the showers, holding a towel only over his privates, leaving his entire backside exposed, and leaving a trail of wet footprints and other drops all the way to his assigned bunk.

This spectacle along was embarrassing enough, fueling plenty of material for some of the more brash and cruel teenagers to create hours worth of insults; however this wasn't the end of it. For, this being the first real time since his admission into Mt. Lowe, Damien sat on the cold floor beside his bunk bed and started quietly rocking.

For the most part for the rest of that semester, Damien got along okay with the rest of the students. He was particularly good at both the archery and rifle ranges. These became his places of solitude whenever his emotions and memories built up.

Another thing he was getting better at was his ability to

communicate. The area he was consistently having trouble with was his ability to understand what people were wanting from him, mainly due to his maturing skills and having trouble dealing with being scolded. He would still 'shutdown and shutout' when dealing with stressful situations, although these episodes were becoming fewer and further between, thanks in part to the staff at Mt. Lowe.

Damien really enjoyed both science and world history (social studies). On the other side of the coin, he had a strong dislike for both math and English. His lifelong dislike for English was more out of the fact that he'd never fully understood the rules of punctuation and proper grammar. In many ways, even today, he still hasn't.

Naturally, it was difficult to learn anything in public school while persistently being picked on and ridiculed; and now, at this military academy, the heckling from fellow cadets was limited to outside of the classrooms, mostly within the barracks, out of earshot of officers. In other words, for the first time in his adolescence, Damien could finally pay attention to the instructor(s) without teasing and other nefarious distractions. At least, to some degree.

The semester went by smoothly . . . so much so that I was able to earn a promotion to Private First Class (P.F.C.). I was doing much better at the academy than I had done in all of my previous public schools combined.

I already had a few friends, and even became a "best friend." I was learning how to communicate verbally plus tolerating contact with more than a couple of people. This made life a lot easier to develop relationships with other boys, and for the first time I had hope for girls.

One of my good friends was Samuel. He tutored me in math and English. I did the same for him in science. I also discovered some private stuff about Sam during the Easter holiday. Not only had he been beaten on several occasions by his own abusive father, but he admitted to being bisexual too. This was the first time I had ever heard of this term: bisexual. And although I did like both boys and girls—even though I hadn't thus far slept with any females—I wasn't willing to put such a label on myself yet.

My relationship with Sam was indeed warm-spirited, even leaning toward brotherhood. Sam was there for me—that is to say that he was my right arm—my strength during times of learning about boundaries and the whose who at this school. He knew the in's and out's of a lot of things.

It was on a warm, sunny Saturday when both Damien and Samuel had passes to go to town and maybe see a movie. Sam, naturally, invited his best friend, Damien, to join him and his other friend in Altadena, where they could go "watch a flick." Together, they had bought tickets to see the western <u>True Grit</u> (the original with John Wayne) since they were teenagers, yet snuck in to watch the horror classic <u>The Exorcist</u>.

The day was a mess, but better than being back at school. I can remember Sam saying he enjoyed spending time with me, regardless of the fact that he was missing a football game. Sam tried to make a day of it for us. Before sunset, Sam took me to his favorite spot for girl, and in some cases boy, watching. This was nice to know; although on this first Saturday "out on the town," we just sat and talked a bit while watching the sum go down.

Little did we pay attention that it was the girls who were watching us. That night was when I believed that I finally understood real love. It wasn't just lust, as it had been with Steve and the others. Sure, I was indeed hungry for either "girl-gina" or "man-gina," and didn't care which—I thank my raging hormones for that—I just needed it to be private. To not get caught. And so did Sam.

Thankfully, it wasn't long until we found that seclusion and engaged in mutual sex. The experiences I'd had before paled in comparison, for this kind of lovemaking wasn't just rapid screwing, nor was it coitus with only one partner's enjoyment in mind. Sam cared about my level of pleasure as much as his own, and this was something new to me. Much more advanced.

Damien really liked his teachers at Mt. Lowe; his favorites were Captain Kendal and Mr. Guler. The latter taught science, while Capt. Kendal (U.S. Army, retired) was the dreaded English teacher. Not that he, himself, was dreaded—only the subject he taught.

For the previous reasons I've pointed out, Damien didn't do well because he was so far behind everyone else in his English class. Both Cpl. Jackson and the administration became aware of this and, in mid-February, had switched Damien back to fifth grade English and into the hands of this retired Army captain. Yet, thanks to Capt. Kendal, Damien was able to pass his first semester ever!

One of the things that Capt. Kendal did that helped to demonstrate the power of language was by reading from popular fantasy novels by J.R.R. Tolkien (best known for The Hobbit and The Lord of the Rings trilogy) and other authors which really moved the youngsters. The captain also read from one of Damien's newfound favorites: A Midsummer's Night Eve.

Now, how is it that Damien, a mountain boy with such an unusual social impairment and low level of literacy, could enjoy the formidable vernacular of Sir William Shakespeare? True, even for the most educated of twelve-year-olds, the laborious language of any 16th-century playwright is a major deterrent, and none more so than Shakespeare himself, and yet his works would become something that stayed with Damien all of his life. It was this love for both Shakespeare and Tolkien that would shape his next dozen years.

CHAPTER NINE

A New Science

Around this time, Damien truly believe that he couldn't ever become a published author nor a writer of anything. This thought saddened him for a long while, but even this would pass. What he loved most about writing was the power it had to create whole worlds, vivid characters, and various species of life . . . for that matter entire galaxies! Writing took the reader on adventures or placed him or her into the middle of a marriage squabble where only they knew who the true adulterer was. It likewise became clear to Damien that territorial and civil wars have both begun and ended by the force of writing. But, of course, this is only the beginning.

Each and every weekday, Damien was now eager to go to classes. To hear Captain Kendal teach and read what was once his least favorite subject. Not that Damien actually understood grammar graphs, neither had his punctuation improved much, but he <u>did</u> enjoy the creative skill of authors who did understand these pragmatics and rules.

There was also the aforementioned science class that he favored. The teacher, a civilian named Mr. Guler, spent an unusual amount of time debunking the Biblical story of Noah's Ark and the Flood. He gave Damien reason to doubt those who told him that the flood actually encompassed the entire planet rather than the known world. Mr. Guler demonstrated to the class that no matter how much water you pour into a container, it will level out.

So, putting the flood story to the test, he asked the students to imagine that the entire world was flooded. The United States, its Rocky Mountains, Asia and it Himalayas, all of Africa and Europe and their mountains. The students all realized quickly that there would have to be a while lot of water in order for Mount Everest and the entire Karakoram Range (a.k.a. K2) to be completely under water.

Damien had the only question after this discovery, *Where did all the water of the flood go?*

Mr. Guler told him and the rest of the class, "That's a rather good question," and praised Damien for "using his brains." Damien had never received a compliment like this before and did not know how to respond properly. Instead, Damien remained silent while the other students went on verbally to throw out illogical suggestions like "It evaporated" and "It all froze into the polar ice caps," the latter which Mr. Guler immediately shot down as an inadequate amount of water if melted completely. Regarding evaporation, "if it all evaporated, it would persist in the atmosphere long enough to keep the world in complete cloud cover and an ice age that would last thousands of years!"

This debate wasn't enough to shake Damien's own belief in the credibility of the Old Testament and in Jesus the Christ. No! It only taught him that the older scriptures weren't necessarily one-hundred percent accurate. The events written in that first book called Genesis were told and retold around campfires decades before papyrus and ink were invented! It's human nature that you can only tell the same bedtime story so many times until you start to embellish it a little. Right!

Damien also came to realize that the original authors of those first few chapters didn't have to be completely accurate to teach people about God. It was the principles and morals about the flood, the tower of Babel, and what happened in Eden that's important, not whether or not people really lived to be four-hundred or six-hundred years old, which Damien likewise had trouble believing.

It wasn't that I thought the Bible was wrong. The stories were told several times every year of each person's life, it was one of their only sources of entertainment back then. Generation after generation, these were verbally passed down, until somebody finally figured out a way to write them down. As well as coming up with a calendar. Until all of these happened, the ages of these people is biologically impossible.

Think about how shriveled up people <u>today</u> look at a hundred-years old, and then think of how wrinkled they'd be at two-hundred or three-hundred. No, I believe as inaccurate as they were at keeping track of birthdays, the plots told around those early campfires might have been embellished a little, but then again, <u>so what</u>! Something amazing <u>did</u> happen, and that's all that really matters.

If anything, Mr. Guler's arguments against the possibility or probability of Noah's Flood made Damien and some of the others study the Bible even more intensely, which might've had been Guler's plan all along. Damien never understood before what made him believe in God, or a god, but believe he did.

As kids, we didn't go to church often, only the few times that Mom took us. I didn't understand why Jesus had to die for all of our sins—wasn't there any other way that didn't involve him dying—but I was glad that God loves us and that we are forgiven for everything we've screwed up.

What Damien didn't yet understand was why his mother took him to a Catholic church and why at this version of religion people pray to several 'saints,' including the blessed Virgin Mother. He spent hours flipping through pages, and the scriptures made it very clear to him that praying to idols or anyone <u>other</u> than God wasn't correct. Indeed, in dozens of chapters, idol worship is against what God had taught his people, yet Catholics continue to kiss rosary beads, hand crucifixes everywhere, and hail the woman who gave birth to Jesus rather than the man Himself.

Church and the process of worship was extremely confusing to me. If Jesus had died by hanging instead of being crucified, would my mom really hand a noose in our living room? This thought really did trouble me for a while. That, plus there's multiple translations of the same Bible, and dozens of denominations, yet it's all the same salvation and the same God?!? Doesn't matter if you're Muslim, Protestant, Jewish, Mormon, Baptist, Agnostic, and so on-and-on, as long as you're doing what your pastor tells you, you're

A-Okay with God? Regardless of whatever the Bible says? This theory deeply troubled me, not only because I worried about picking the correct religion to follow, but because I've been misled so many times already in my short lifetime.

As you've previously read, Damien truly had relationship problems, except for his relationship with God and Christ Jesus. He was slowly getting better, yet it was clear that he was always going to have this difficulty. It was equally clear that his awkwardness didn't have to be an obstacle in his road towards developing meaningful relationships—after all, his friendship with Steve proved this much—if he'd only be more patient and take his time at this task.

More than anything at this moment, Damien's difficulty in building and understanding healthy friendships—the "science of friendships"— with his felow students distressed him the most. At the age of twelve, having a relationship with someone you <u>can</u> see seems more important than one with the unseen Creator of floods, improbable or otherwise.

It wasn't until late-April that Damien had received any news from home. He truthfully wasn't ever expecting to hear his name called when the mail was passed out, believing that his family, particularly his step-father, had completely forgotten about him, with the exception of when tuition bills from the academy arrived there.

Nothing that Dad had done really surprised me until Easter came, bringing with it both my dad and mild disappointment. Dad had written to me for the first time since I was in the academy; actually, it was the first letter I got from him <u>ever</u>! He wrote mostly to inform me that he was not going to pick me up for the summer vacation. Why should he?

First, I didn't have a family; they all made this fact perfectly clear. I hadn't heard from my own mother since the breakfast with Uncle Mike and the day at Disneyland, an entire lifetime ago. Second, I preferred the time I spent at the academy more than I even could enjoy any amount of time with Dad. It was sad, of course, that he didn't want me around, or I, him. Who doesn't want a family to have fun, celebrate birthdays and other holidays with?

I was also happy to have Sam to spend the summer months with. He was more than a good school friend and one I could, and did, delight in sexually. The only love I needed, or so I believed. Love was its own funny kind of science; it didn't conform to any logical rules or theories. And before the summer was over, my relationship—sexual and otherwise—with Samuel ended.

In the midst of the ambiguity of the human condition, God's grace still abounds. Grace is not a supernatural intrusion on human experience, although it may be experienced as radically transformative of our lives and relationships.
~Bruce G. Epperly

CHAPTER TEN

Unexpected Qualities

Damien was a fast learner, especially when events and challenges had to do with demonstrating that he would make a good leader. He was earning recognition for his decision-making and overall troubleshooting skills. As summer school came to a close, so would the days that Damien would remain a Private First Class.

Major Robinson, a retired officer of the U.S. Army, was the school's vice-principal. The final weekend of the summer vacation, the major decided that it was time for the annual inventory. This was acceptable to all involved because it was long overdue to do another order for cleaning supplies, new laundry stock, and regular food supplies.

Damien and a few other summer-school cadets had just cleaned the basement of the kitchen from the flood damage that washed a whole lot of mud down the hillside during early August. This wasn't what Damien would normally call 'vacation-time work,' but since he was available when the early rainstorm came, he was called on to volunteer and help out.

Even though the school rarely used the old storage in that basement, it just made sense to clean up the mess; after all, it wasn't a difficult chore, just an untidy one. Because there was a lot of equipment down there that hadn't been used for nearly a decade, Major Robinson left instructions with

Cpl. Jackson to inform Sgt. Barker to report to him when he returned from his summer vacation.

That Sunday afternoon, as soon as the sergeant was approached by young Damien and his friend, Cpl. Jackson, Barker extended a hand and asked, "How was your summer, Corporal?"

"Fine, it was real fine, Sarge. How about yours?"

"Swell, until my sister—you remember me telling you about her?"

"Sure, good looking, goes to Berkeley?" Cpl. Jackson recalled.

"yeah, that's here. Anyway it seems as if she has a new boyfriend. I hope this one will last longer that the last one did, but I smell something foul . . . I just hope not."

"Well, guess what?" Jackson said. "Guess who want to help you get Sandy off your mind?"

"Can't guess. Who wants me?" The sergeant asked.

"The major"

"Let me guess . . . Major Robinson had a problem during the summer?"

"All that he said was to tell you to report to him ASAP."

"Will he at least give me enough time to switch out of my civvies before spilling my blood?" Then, after they both laughed, Sgt. Barker turned to greet Damien, "Good to see you, Private Collins."

The fact that he'd remembered my name on sight after a ten-week vacation was a high enough compliment.

Cpl. Jackson turned his attention to Damien, then ordered, "Let's get this one done, so we can kick back for the rest of the night."

Both men were filthy and wearing only gardener coveralls over their skivvies. They continued back into that basement and took inventory of all the remaining food which, according to Damien, there wasn't supposed to be any since they'd stopped using the old storeroom years ago.

This turned out to be a bit of a headache, but a worthwhile one. As it turned out, we didn't take very long at all with the inventory, that is, until I'd discovered something that looked strange to me and wasn't supposed to be there.

Damien had found several cans which looked all wrong to him. First, they were food items, and most importantly, the cans were 'bulging' on the top, as if internal pressure was deforming these cans from the inside-out.

This looked all wrong, so I brought two of them to Cpl. Jackson, who sent them to Sgt. Barker, who gave them back to Jackson, so that he could show and report the cans to Major Robinson.

While Cpl. Jackson was doing that, Sgt. Barker joined me in the basement and asked if there were others.

Turning his attention to the sergeant, Damien answered, *Yes, sir. There're around twenty or so.*

"Okay, Private. Please bring them upstairs while I get the cook."

Spending about five minutes in locating the total of twenty-six other cans of food with the 'spooky bulges' on their lids, Damien also found another thirteen cans without bulges yet without labels.

When Sgt. Barker returned with the Head Chef to the top of the basement stairs, the Chef asked how many other cans were down there. Damien had already started hauling the water-damaged cardboard boxes up those stairs, and simply pointed to the opened cases. Then, although out of breath, he told them, *There's other cans without bulges or labels, but they look too rusted to be moved. I also found sacks of dried beans or something.*

Putting down one of the cans, the Head Chef said, "Okay, Private, show me what else you found/"

We spent a couple of minutes going over the sacks and decided to make a note of what was found and following that up on the inventory sheet. He then instructed the sergeant and me to discard the entire lot. Then Sgt. Barker asked something like, "Excuse me, Chef, but what's wrong with them?"

Picking up one of the cans of Beef Stew, the cook asked, "Do you see this bulge? Well, it's a sign of food poisoning. Air has gotten in and the contents are fermenting." Then he motioned to the sacks and other boxes. "As well as the rest; I don't take things for granted. I'd rather throw out the dry food, just in case. So, we'll get rid of it all."

"I guess that you'll want to use the animal-proof trash?" The academy attracted quite a lot of raccoons and other vermin.

"Good thinking, Sergeant. Look, I have to return to the kitchen to get on with tonight's dinner, or some of you boys will be something hungry. Here's the key to the lock. Please see to it yourselves. And thank you boys! You're both deserving of a commendation for having attention to detail."

"No need to thank me, it's all Private Collins this time." Then with a wink, he added, "or should I be calling you Sergeant Collins."

While Damien turned a little bashful at whichever rank was mentioned, he still privately wished that they'd leave off his last name.

The weekend had come like a summer breeze, here one moment and gone the next. Being that it was nearly time for 'chow' on that final night before the new semester officially began, Damien decided that he was going to shower and do it smartly. He spent a good fifteen minutes on giving his boots a spit-shine. He felt "dressed to the nines."

I had just gotten in ship shape for inspection, before I knew that there'd be no inspection this time before chow. Instead, everything was done banquet-style: A buffet! Only twice a year was dinner served like this, and the food truly was pretty darn good. We were served thick slices of roast beef, mashed potatoes, peach cobbler, and grilled Indian corn. Fantastic.

Although that dinner was great, it didn't satisfy me . . . food rarely did. Sex had likewise lost its importance in my life. It was no linger the nutritional value I craved. Instead, I was always seeking food for my soul. At the academy I'd found a far better and more appropriate kind of soul food. I found that school, and my fellow students, as well as the military code of honor, too easily outweighed sex in its value of significance.

Much to Damien's ascetic pleasure, he was getting a lot of positive attention from his fellow students, particularly Sgt. Barker. This was the soulful substance that he really was needing. That night, when the banquet dinner was over, Damien returned to his barracks only find Sgt. Barker awaiting him. He was standing near Damien's bunk bed, holding a freshly ironed short by its hanger.

"That shirt looks dirty," he said simply enough. "Try this one on." The newer shirt featured a two-chevron patch on each arm. Damien froze in his tracks, afraid to even touch the garment.

Sgt. Barker, in his own way, informed me that he was putting me up for promotion to corporal. This pleased me no end. Then he took the shirt from me and said he'd let me know when it was official.

Come Monday morning, the first day of school, after routine exercises and drills, we went to our classes. I dreaded the fact that I was again assigned in taking difficult courses that year, at least English and algebra had always been difficult for me. This had my nerves on fire; however, I had nowhere to go but up.

A couple of weeks later, Damien was called to see Major Robinson. He had forgotten about that evening with Sgt. Barker and the new shirt, and had no way of knowing what the major wanted to see him for. Damien knew that he was disciplinary-free, which was why most were called to report to his office. It was the October of Damien's thirteenth year, and he received from Major Robinson the greatest gift of his life: Acknowledgment!

He had seen me grow a lot since my enrollment in the academy. He was well pleased with my behavior, my willingness to grow, to mature beyond my comfort zone. My "hidden qualities," he verily called them for extra recognition, and, as a sign of his pleasure, he had promoted me to the rank of sergeant! Beyond what Sgt. Barker has put me up for.

I wish I could describe the feelings of that moment, or for that matter, any time after that! This promotion showed me that I had worth, I had value beyond what my dad believed. I'd gone from being a P.F.C. to wearing <u>three</u> chevrons, in a single day. This new school year was indeed going to be a good one.

The major had me report to "B" Barracks as their new platoon leader. I felt a little uncomfortable with the assignment because I really didn't know what I was supposed to do. That is, until I'd met Lieutenant Adams, who knew about my promotion and assignment in advance—before I did—and was glad for it.

As it turned out, Lt. Adams taught Damien all that he needed to know, regarding how to manage his new assignment. Since Damien had completely skipped the usual months, or year(s), at the rank of corporal, Lt. Adams was quite understanding of Damien's nervousness.

His schooling of me about leadership was refreshing . . . and for that matter, a huge help in my development. I felt almost immediately empowered without letting my new authority either overwhelm or consume me.

Then there was a personal setback. I learned something the hard way. For one, women are truly attracted to authority and a man in uniform. And two, I discovered that I liked girls as a much better way to enjoy sex again. In fact, whenever I entered a room, I was the most attractive thirteen-year-old around, albeit because of the stripes on my arm.

CHAPTER ELEVEN
Hell Restored

*I*t was during the first week in the fall of 1971, I was finally about to discover something about my manhood, something that I should've learned from a father and not from the other immature teen boys from my school. I was about to discover the natural beauty of girls and the fact that I would want to know more and more than I could ever be taught, except by rote, by extensive personal experience.

As an officer, Damien was doing well enough and given off-grounds passes to visit Altadena, and the luxuries in town, more often than as a private. This was one of the benefits of advanced leadership which he'd not previously considered nor was aware of.

Not to be confusing—because I've found more than enough of life to be confusing as it is—but I did still find boys to be attractive. When done right, they were safer than girls . . . at least they won't tell, rarely get emotionally attached, and cannot get pregnant. Yes, yet girls are more pleasurable, more tender in their loving, and much more playful—if you enjoy foreplay—than are boys. What am I to do with this problem?

But then, there was a girl that I'd thought was by far the single, most attractive and desirable; her name was Yvette. She truly was all that to me and more! My social skills, especially those having to do with 'going out' or dating were nonexistent. As I've said, I never had any guidance from Dad *and so very little contact with any girls, with the exception of those who came over to our apartment with their moms. I felt awkward as all get out!*

When Yvette approached me, I went from feeling as happy as a kitten in a basket full of yarn, to s sea lion in the middle of a highway, in a flash. I don't know how in the world I ended up saying just the right amount of correct things to end up in bed with her; it was purely the very last of my good luck and fortune for the remainder of that year.

Damien's troubles began to hit him in waves, and hit him hard. A month after his new position as squad leader went by smooth enough, it happened. He began having restless nights, and when he did sleep, he dreamt nightmares: dreams about being back on the farm where he grew up. He was eight again, just as skinny as he is now, only a foot shorter.

His dream revolved around his three very different relationships. The first was the neglect and oversight of his mother and her lack of love for him after Martin and Michelle were born. His dad, well there isn't need to restate the obviousness of the abusive nature of that relationship. The twins themselves were much too young when Damien had last lived with them to have built any sibling togetherness. No, they didn't count as a relationship.

Then there was the very special friendship that he felt between Steve and himself. What had started off as innocent and supportive, turned lewd and molesting after both Steve's hormones and Nathan entered into the equation. Steve's arrival in Damien's young and tender years, those impressionable days when he badly needed someone, anyone, to just talk to. Everything was fine until sex became involved, and even then, Damien thought things were okay.

It was at this point of his dream, this recurring nightmare, that Damien would awaken. This pattern of sleep continued for several weeks, depriving him of obtaining adequate sleep, leaving him fatigued in the mornings, which was hurting his leadership and decision-making skills, hurting his chances at earning higher rank. This was distressing him greatly.

Clearly, something had occurred in his past, an important event, which changed his life that his memory had repressed and was now regurgitating with a vengeance. Damien was unsure of what it was but knew that if he did not face this buried fear he'd never be able to sleep more fully than he was.

The following night Damien intentionally overdosed on cold/flu syrup—not trying to harm or kill himself—so he wouldn't wake up halfway through his dream, if he dreamt it. Thankfully, he did; the nightmare started on the day he'd met Steve.

It was a rainy morning, and I was on my way to the blacktop where I caught the bus, and I met thirteen-year-old Steve, the boy who sexually molested me, yet not by being violent or bribing me. No! Not Steve. He was hanging around the township building when he saw me standing at the corner waiting for the school bus. I felt beside myself that morning, and Steve reached out to this youngster.

I remember that he'd called out, "Hey D.C., how are you doing'? But there was nothing, absolutely dead silence from the autistic eight-year old. I'm not even sure when he'd learned my name, but he knew mine before I'd told him or heard of his.

Steven and his family of three brothers, two sisters, his mom, and no father, lived about two miles away from the Collins' farm. What was he doing that rainy morning two miles from home? Does this mean that our "chance" meeting wasn't that chance at all? Maybe Steve had been planning it all along like a modern-day stalker? He certainly earned my trust right away, yet I still do <u>not</u> believe that he was thinking about raping me that early in our relationship.

Granted, when Steve introduced me to sex, it was never meant to be harmful to my development, but meant to or not, it did do some harm. Not that I found gay sex horrible or that it's <u>being gay</u> is what was harmful to my development. No! It was the fact that I was all too young to have freely chosen to be a homosexual, which later in life I might've never chosen.

Steve hurt my ability to develop and "freely" choose to know about sex at all, gay or otherwise. It was just another stumbling block. My relationship with Steve wasn't all negative; as you've already read, he did give me good advice at times and tried to get me to break out of my "shell" by getting involved in 4-H and spending time around other kids. So, comparing "pros" and "cons" in what Steve did to me, the good somewhat ties with the bad.

Somewhat.

As the dream pressed onward, so did my growth and self-confidence. I rewitnessed several events involving my dad, nothing but "cons" there, and when my mom walked out on him. His drinking was the main reason why they'd split up; he was consuming more and more ever since they had moved to California and he started working at his stressful engineering job. Maybe the job itself wasn't as nerve-racking as the thought that he built weapons that killed people. He'd already almost killed someone, back when he'd shot at poor Henry Levant; so, maybe the thought that he built bombs or whatever that murdered on a more grand scale bothered Dad.

But, clearly, this recurring dream that was depriving me of adequate sleep, it wasn't trying to make excuses for the people in my past. No, something else had occurred in my life, some other reason for these images to keep popping up in mh head. A few night later, this dream faded, and with it, so did my fatigue and discomfort at being a squad leader. However, in hindsight, it had never occurred to me that the message of this dream, the true meaning towards why I kept having it, was prophetical—a warning of things to come!

Damien was about to have another life-changing problem which he never saw coming, despite those recurring dreams. It happened, of all times, during the single most joyful time of the year. His father, three days before the official start of the school's Christmas/Winter break, showed up at the academy's administration building. Without any warning, Damien was being dragged out of the academy! The one place where he not felt like he belonged but was also learning to be a gentleman! A true military officer and leader!

Even though I didn't have the skills that other boys had regarding how to behave around others, I truly desired the ability to engage in positive relationships, and the academy was providing me with those skills and the courage that went along with it. This was going to be another disaster! How can someone screw up a perfect situation like keeping a person like me in an ideal learning environment?!

Needless to emphasize, Damien was confused, frustrated, and above these: pissed! Within one hour, he tracked down as many of his companions and fellow officers as possible to say "goodbye." His old friend and former squad leader, Dane Jackson, who had become a sergeant at about the same time as Damien, was on the upper lawn performing drills.

Dee! Dee! Damien had shouted over the crowd. *Sergeant Jackson!*

"PARADE REST!" Jackson ordered his squad, then turned to Damien, "Well, if it ain't my old cadet, What's so impor –"

I . . . I've come to--to say goodbye, sir, the red-eyed boy stammered.

"Sir? We're the same rank Collins. And, what do you mean, "goodbye'?"

My son-of-a-bi . . . he stopped himself, then repostured, *My worthless step-Dad is pulling me out of sch-school! Damien exclaimed through obvious pain and welling tears.*

"What? Oh, Collins . . . shit, I'm so-so –sorry."

I can't be-be-believe this crap! I belong h-h-here at the acad . . . . He never got the final syllable out before Jackson pulled him into a tight, bear-crushing hug. Jackson did this mainly because he saw that Damien was losing it and needed his friend's support. Meanwhile, the members of the squad, especially those in the back who couldn't have heard a single spoken word, caught a rather rare glimpse of military officers expressing any kind of emotion. Of brotherhood.

The shock treatment continued, although completely uncalled for, as Damien not only returned to the "apartment of horrors" but also to the Los Angeles public school system. In the academy, there was strict structure. Damien understood how to be a student there. He had prestige and recognition, had boys and below him in rank.

What was I to do here in a public high school? What were the new social rules? I had no idea; I was the social moron, again. What I didn't know was how to be a teenaged boy—an officer, I knew, but not a high-school student. The rules regarding relationships and interaction were very different, as far as I could tell.

Another fact was that there were laws outside of the academy. The problem of not belonging to the society, was that the laws of society were not part of my daily life. I didn't know them, nor could I get a hold of them. I was just dropped, parachuted without a harness, into the life I thought I'd never have to live again!

It didn't take very long to rekindle one old habit at the apartment:

Arguments with his step-father. His dad still drank and did it well, and drank a great deal. The beatings had stopped, but only because Damien was now basically the same height and physical build as Arthur. No, punching and shoving had replaced spanks, or there was always an improvised blunt object or other weapon.

My misery had returned full circle. I was back with my abusive dad, in over my head with grief, disrespected, and bullied by students, and rejected by society as an outcast. My world was full of intolerance, hate, and flames that were scorching my soul!

Take sides. Neutrality helps the oppressor, never the victim. Silence encourages the tormentor, never the tormented. -Elie Wiesel

CHAPTER TWELVE

A Strange New World

I was now a student at Inglewood High School. I had lost all interest in sex with boys, as my obsession with girls grew, particularly in girls of color. I'm not saying that I specifically went after girls of different races on purpose, out of spite of my dad's racist bigotry, I just found them more exotic. As it turned out, I had two things going for me; these were booze and the fact that I could provide girls their fill of my company. Not that I was a "real catch," but that I was dedicated, had what they wanted, and I was willing to learn and provide their other vices, such as LSD (a.k.a. acid) or marijuana.

Keep in mind that it was the early 1970's. I had missed the "summer of love" while I'd attended the academy, and all of these hippy outfits and lifestyles were new to me. There was also the growing presence of <u>disco</u> which, as a side effect, increased the demand for even more illicit and experimental narcotics. Who was I to "just say no"? I was too busy trying to get laid.

In the news, Richard Nixon was still president; America was still fighting in some godforsaken war which nobody cared about—they only cared about stopping it, and some guy named Charles Manson and three of his cult members had just been found guilty of murdering seven people, including an actress whom Damien didn't know anything about.

Inglewood High became my entire world, very little of anything else.

And of that school, there was a beautiful girl named Lisa. Lisa was in my French class and sat in the next row over, one seat back. This seating arrangement was to my advantage, as was the fact that I was born half-French and had plenty of vented exposure to the language, albeit only when Mom was very frustrated, which was quite often. Grandpa was also French, yet I hadn't seen him in years.

Anyway, one afternoon, while in our French class, I "accidently," in other words, deliberately, dropped my pencil behind me. Leaning over to pick it up, I glanced over in her direction, and I was entertained by the full beauty of her sex staring directly at me. This, naturally, brought me great joy and hardness. Just the knowledge along that she favored no panties while wearing thigh-high skirts would keep me erect for the remainder of class, but this wasn't the end of it.

Returning upright in his chair, Damien heard Lisa express her frustration when saying, "Hey, Sleaz-oid. Bring a camera next time."

To which Damien smart-alecky remarked, *When you dress like that, half the class is wishing they'd brought a camera.*

Boy, was she ever pissed! Not only did this fourteen-year-old boy see her sex, she was a year younger by the way, but as things turned out, she became the laughing stock for once. Also, as things turned out, she later that week was willing too provide much more than a private view up her skirt; she was willing to have sex if I was willing to bring the booze. She actually said, "If you'll get me drunk, Sleaz-oid, I'll treat you to a fuckin' you'll never forget." Who was I to turn down such an offer?

Sure, Damien played things coolly, *Come by my apartment after school.*

"Cool, just give me the address, and I'll be there."

Without hesitation, Damien wrote down his address on East Plymouth.

"Yep, cool!"

Boy, did I ever have a good day. I was learning French and that day I learned how to <u>give</u> French. To my surprise, at about four that afternoon, Lisa showed up and brought a girlfriend with her; "Nancy" was also looking forward to getting drunk and laid, perhaps even more than Lisa was. Both girls, by the way, were partly or wholly, African. I'm sure you can *guess where this is headed, yet that afternoon was exceptional and worth any consequence!*

At around six that evening Damien's step-father came home to find this unpleasantness: Two mostly-naked, under-aged, and clearly very drunk girls "of color" sprawled out in his living room, while his adopted son appeared comatose or merely exhausted upon Arthur's own disheveled mattress! He had two real problems: The first, getting rid of the teenaged girls without the authorities getting involved; the second, the fear that his son may very well have gotten one or both of them pregnant.

Dad just didn't know how to deal with this mess, so he resorted to his standby punishment: the bat. He smashed a few things to both sober up and encourage the drunk thirteen-year-olds to get dressed faster, then turned his attention on me. He'd swung into me twice, both times into my side, before I managed to grasp hold of it and pull it from his hands. I was becoming equally strong as him, and this bothered him more than anything.

I admit that I was wrong in drinking his alcohol and having sex on his larger bed, yet I stood my ground when started using the "N" word. He was the one who needed to grow up! I stood there holding the bat by its thick end, saying so. Saying that the world was changing, it was new, and he needed to change with it. Dad's only response to this was a stern warning that his alcohol was <u>his</u> and must never again disappear.

Regarding the two girls, Nancy, who was darker than Lisa, because of our afternoon, <u>did</u> get pregnant and gave birth to a daughter whom I've never met. Sure, there's the possibility that the baby wasn't mine, after all Nancy was what you'd call "loose" and insatiable . . . it was the 70's. But I believe the daughter was mine.

As it turned out, Lisa's mother, understandably pissed to find her little girl sloshed, <u>did</u> call the police, providing them with his written-down address found in her pockets. Damien was charged with having sex with a minor and contributing to the delinquency of a minor; however, since they were both around the same age of fourteen, the charges were misdemeanors.

I went to Juvenile Hall for my acts. I really didn't understand why I could be the only one charged for sex acts, if both—or, in my case, all three involved—had sex willingly. Deliberately. My providing them with alcohol didn't help my defense. Nonetheless, I was locked up with a bunch of boys, most of them much older than I was.

In five short weeks, I'd gone from a sergeant at a military academy, to just another high-school student, to a juvenile inmate. Three separate worlds, isolated, in and of themselves. What was I to do? I didn't know how to act in this third new world. I'd barely gotten used to being around girls, and here I was again, segregated from them and living in a dormitory of only teenaged boys again—only these were different; these were undisciplined boys. Street thugs, thieves, and bullies. Not all of them were brutes, but the majority were.

I knew in my heart that I was not supposed to have sex with boys, but how else was I to overcome my hurts and painful memories? Just the fact that I once believed having sex with boys gave me courage now repulsed me. Yes, I felt attracted to them, some of them, but I now knew from my days at the academy that allowing boys to molest me was weakness, not strength. But, in that horrible jail for kids, I felt just so weak and along.

On the third or fourth morning in custody, Damien went to Juvenile Court for his arraignment and appointment of counsel hearing. An attorney assigned from the Public Defender's Office met him in the courtroom, as did his step-dad.

My dad was there and seemed somewhat please with the result, on account of the fact that he no longer had to deal with me at all. I had somehow solved all of his financial and parenting burdens just by wanting to get laid by Lisa and Nancy. But, while in custody, I was only making matters worse for myself, while handling the stress the only way I understood.

Damien was being charged with not only having sex with two under-aged and intoxicated girls, while himself being a drunk teen, but on the more serious charges of contributing to the delinquency of two minors—after all, he had provided them the alcohol—plus persuading a twelve-year-old in acts of fellatio while incarcerated. Damien had been caught by the guards in not only touching the younger child in a sexual manner but talking about performing oral sex. Any type of sexual contact between inmates is prohibited.

Again, I was fortunate that I was all of fifteen years young and dumb. I had violated the law by my attempts in engaging a "friend" in sex. I didn't understand why that was illegal, why it was wrong to even talk about having gay sex. Dumb and stupid as I was, I was most fortunate to have the probation office that I had.

The only thing that I remember at that very first, of many, court hearings was being assigned to Mrs. "Diane," as we called her. My probation office actually cared about my well-being and was the one who would start me down the path of healing.

A few weeks after my arraignment, a psychiatrist at Juvenile Hall diagnosed me with "latent or early childhood schizophrenia" and prescribed me the drug Stellazine. My probation office wrote a report for the court stating that I should be going to an adolescent psychiatric program at Metropolitan State Hospital in Norwalk. The judge agreed with both reports, and, with the hammering of his gavel, I went from inmate to patient.

For the first time, I was put into a program designed to help kids like me, not just merely be removed from the society from which they came, such as the case of the California Youth Authority which did and continues to do. My recovery would start right away . . . at still one more new world I had to experience.

CHAPTER THIRTEEN

The Road to Recovery

Damien was admitted to Metropolitan State Hospital on 5 August 1973, after spending some six months at the Older Boys Reception Center (or O.B.R.C.), prior to the court committing him to the Wuchium Program for Troubled Youths.

I was picked up from "Juvie" and taken to a place of healing—known by the kids at Juvenile Hall as just "Metro" or "the nut house." It was, as far as I could see, a place where caring souls worked and needs were met. I felt truly blessed!

The Admitting Psychiatrist, if that was his official title, was the absolutely brilliant doctor, Dr. Samuel Reily. He, above and beyond most doctors, truly cared for his patients. Within minutes of my arrival at Metro, I had my first conversation with this doctor. Here I was, a freshly admitted patient at a psychiatric hospital as ward of the court, and I felt closer to being treated as a human being than ever before.

"Good afternoon, Damien. You don't mind being addressed by your first name, do you?

Being in a new place always shut Damien down, except for this occasion. This time was important to him because Damien wanted a pair of things to happen: First, he wanted more than anything to remain out of Juvenile Hall; secondly, he wanted to be healed, if that was "doable."

Shifting in his sear, Damien answered, *No, please call me Damien. Thank you, Doctor.*

"Good. And I am a doctor, but my name isn't 'Doctor.' I am Samuel or Sam. Okay?"

This was different. I was asked by an adult to call him or her by their first name. It did take me a few tries before I called him Sam and not "Doctor Reily." I was unlearning the habits from my years at military academy. Also, the fact that he shared the same name as my former lover didn't help, although I should point out that I never felt attracted to my doctor.

Responding to Dr. Reily's request,, Damien said, *Thank you, Doc— uh, Sam.*

"Alright . . . . you know what brings you here to a hospital instead of to C.Y.A.?"

My pro-probation officer h-has hope that this place, will help me become a better me? Damien said, unsure if his answer is the correct one.

"Okay. Well, what we do here, if you choose, is help with the rough edges, so that you can be you. A healthy <u>you</u>. How's that sound to you?"

His question really floored me! I didn't want to always get in trouble, and I wanted to know what I was doing that was wrong and hurting me.

Trembling, Damien answered, *Good, S-Sam. It sounds good . . . to me.*

"Okay. Well, I was reading your chart and I see that your parents are divorced and that you are the eldest of three . . . " After flipping a few pages, unable to find the form he was looking for, he added, "We don't have a Family History for you."

I don't have a family history because I never had a family.

"Really? . . . well, are you not alive?"

Yes I have two parents. One left the 'family' before I was two years old. My 'mom' has never acted like a real mom. She left me with my fake 'dad.' But, I still don't have a family. You want to call my 'mom'? Please do and you'll see what I mean.

"Yes, I do see what you mean by 'no family,' neither of them notified the police of their home phone numbers in case of emergency." Clearing his throat, he offered, "Let's go on with you alone, for the time being.

So, you were born where?"

I was born in the state of Washington, in the town of Clearwater.

"When did you move here to L.A.?"

Umm . . . I think that it w-was in 1967, or eight. Beginning to stutter worse, Damien resumed saying, *"Th-that was . . . wasn't the first time th-that I was here. The first time w-was when M-Martin and Michelle w-were b-born.*

"Your brother and sister?"

Yeah. But half. They're twins.

"Half? Oh, I see," recognizing that the boy meant half-siblings. Thankfully, Dr. Reily had years of experience interpreting what children with speech impediments really meant. "So, your brother and sister were born in L.A.?"

Finishing what the doctor was asking, Damien shut down, not deliberately but 'usefully.' He began rocking, trying to protect himself from Dr. Reily's probing questions about his family. Damien had been struggling because all of this was new to him.

It made me feel like I was in a pressure cooker.

"Damien?" Sensing that the boy was already feeling 'under the gun,' if you will, Dr. Reily moved from questions to simply talking with him, "How are you doing, Damien?"

The boy stopped moving, but could no longer look Samuel in the eyes, *I'm . . . . I'm okay. Same. Really, I am.*

"Okay . . . that's good. But tell me, why are we here having this conversation."

Again, rocking, Damien expressed himself by raising his voice, *I! Do . . . I don't know! What did I do wrong?*

"You went to Juvenile Hall. You were seen touching another boy, sexually. Not only is it illegal, the court decided to get you help for your 'illness' and keep you off the streets until you're cured of your choices."

In the 1960-s and 70's, homosexuality was largely viewed as both a disease and/or a personal choice: That a person's attraction to members of the same gender wasn't innate or developed naturally, but voluntary and optional. Research grants were even issued towards finding a cure for being gay. Yet, young Damien truly didn't understand how preference of sexual participation was considered illegal. Even worse, sodomy was one of the most hated sins according to the Bible (Leviticus 20:13). His curiosity grew to the point that he was feeling insecure and needed answers.

I just wasn't tolerant at that age . . . I needed answers immediately—like now! Feeling a strong sense of urgency, I asked the doctor what was so wrong with two boys, of similar age, who chose to have some sex or share some sex.

"It is against the law," he simply said. As of October 2013, there remained to be an active penal code in California that has any act of sodomy—even between consenting adults—considered as a state felony. "Right or not, we obey laws . . . because our state representatives, our legislature, made it illegal to have any sex before the participants are of the legal age of consent."

Okay . . . I was wrong because the law says it's wrong. But, then, wasn't the other boy also wrong? Why am I the only one in trouble?

"I'm sure he also got in trouble, of one sort or another. For now, let's focus on your own recovery."

The conversation dwindled significantly as Dr. Reily pulled out his pen and began writing hastily. He called an end to their discussion until their next session, privately, together. Yet, there would be plenty of talking until then.

Dr. Reily immediately took me off of my Stellazine and started counseling with me weekly as a complete, uninhibited person. Furthermore, Dr. Reily started me in regular group sessions. My experiences at the Wuchium Program were honestly very liberating, more so than at the academy, Juvenile Hall, or anywhere/anytime else.

By the time Damien went to dinner on that first night, he was familiar to his new surroundings and fellow patients, both male and female. He was surprised at the fact that everything was done in a co-ed living style. This was a real change compared to Juvie Hall and Mt. Lowe; the girls' rooms were upstairs.

The Wuchium Program was very different than he had experienced in his past, at least as far as he could tell. The first obvious fact was that the patients weren't locked-up 24/7, nor confined to a strict regiment, but had substantial freedom during the day and after classes. Based on good behavior, patients could earn extra privileges, which included increased hours of indoor "dayroom" (common room) time, outdoor "yard" recreation, or even journey off grounds.

In "Juvie," positive behavior was rarely, if ever, acknowledged or rewarded, just the opposite. There was quite a bit of favoritism between guards and certain inmates . . . funny thing was, it was usually the guys that got into the largest amount of trouble who received the largest amount of favoritism and got the best inmate jobs.

At first, there at Metro, I only had some recreation room time after school time. I spent mostly this time to myself, which commonly turned into shutdown-and-out time. There already was a problem for me to solve before I responded by shutting out people of authority, and with all these kids that were nearly adults, I felt constantly on the defense, although needlessly.

It was around my third day in the program when I was approached by a fifteen-year-old boy named Alex, who would become an important friend. A strictly-platonic friend. And by Platonic, I mean he studied the philosophy of Plato and <u>other</u> philosophers, "Insofar as they assert ideal forms as an absolute and eternal reality." Alex was <u>himself</u> a self-proclaimed philosopher; albeit, it's because of his overzealous desire to spread his "words of wisdom" to teachers and grocery-store clerks and hundreds of complete strangers at what his parents persistently labelled as "inappropriate times," which caused Alex to become committed at Metro.

I rather enjoyed Alex's company and his "words of wisdom," although I can't really remember any of it. Most dealt with reaching a level of pure reflection and spiritual reality that a person could transcend to another plane of existence. It sounded too much like science fiction to me, but Alex swore that Plato knew all of this was possible four-hundred years before Jesus was born, and was himself transcended into the heavens.

"There is a spiritual reality beyond anything we can possibly imagine," Alex told Damien. "Yet, it's right here with us. Surrounds us, every single second of everyday."

"Y-you mean, like ghosts?

"No. no. Ghosts are supernatural, and I doubt that they're real.

But, angels! Now, angels are real. God refers to them in the Bible, so they must exist. Angels are around us, surround us, every day. We can't see them, unless they reveal themselves to us, but we can join them."

Join them? You mean when we die?

"No, Damien we can transcend to their level of existence. That's what's Plato tawkin' about in his books, reachin' a level of purity so pure, those angels will view you as one of their own."

Um, I'm not sure that's how it works. Damien stood from where they were sitting and said to his new friend, *Let's do something fun.*

"Alright," following the younger boy towards the dayroom. "So, Damien, Whatcha in for?"

Wha? Damien suddenly became uncomfortable. He'd heard Alex's question clear enough. In fact, he had been asked this question dozens of time while in Juvenile Hall. *What do you mean?*

"Why are you in Metro?"

I, um, Damien had no intention of admitting he'd been convicted of coercing a boy to have sex with him. He didn't want any of the other boys in the program to know that they had a homosexual living amongst them. Yet, at the same time, he didn't want to start their friendship on a lie. *I went to Juvie and they said I had early childhood schizophrenia.*

"Schizo?! You ain't even close."

When I get feeling lost, upset because things are happening too fast around me, I turn off. Lock-up and out. I either end up standing like a statue or sitting down and rocking away my bad feelings.

"Alright, I admit that's weird, but you ain't schizo. You should ask for a second opinion. You've seen the real nut cases and 'jay cats' around this place. Those are the <u>real</u> schizos."

What is a 'jay cat?' Damien asked.

"Uh, it's an old military term, I think. Short for "J" category. Kinda like what the police use . . . five-one-five-oh. Fifty-one fifty. Off your freckin' rocker! But you ain't crazy like most of the guys in here."

I never felt crazy. I just don't understand a lot about friends, how to make them, to keep them. There's a lot about society I just don't understand completely enough. My family has given up on me, thought I was a troublemaker on purpose. I got spanked lots of times, sometimes without knowing what I did wrong . . . if I *did* do something wrong.

"Well, you jus' sound confused to me. An' trust me, bein' confused is a whole lotta better than bein' wacko."

Damien wasn't sure if he liked being called either one! He didn't think of himself as 'confused' as much as he believed people just didn't explain the more important things in life to him. Again, it wasn't because he wasn't listening or lacked intelligence . . . actually he was brilliant in certain topics, would collect large amounts of facts or statistics about his favorite ones, and talk incessantly about them, on a regular basis.

No, the only lessons he'd received in earnest from his mother and stepfather either involved racism or some other principle that contradicted his deepest convictions. Together, his parents only taught him about replacement . . . and how easy he could be.

Turns out that Alex wasn't the only person thinking about 'second opinions' about Damien's diagnosis.

After our second private session together, Dr. Reily changed my diagnosis from childhood schizophrenia for that of autism or, rather, a mild form of autism marked by impairments in social interaction and repetitive behavior. I was what he called "high functioning" for someone with autism, which actually kind of puzzled him at first, fascinated him at second. As a rather young pediatrician, I was one of Samuel's very first autistic patients.

I had some "deep seeded" habits, as he called them. My speech was, at most times, either disjointed or overly formal . . . or both! Another significant part of my problem, as Dr. Reily further uncovered, was the fact that my defense mechanism had turned into an addiction. I was using sex like a drug user. Even if I didn't need to protect my hurt soul.

Damien's addiction was indeed "bad." Coupled with his behavioral deficits, sex became an all-absorbing interest that dominated both his thoughts and conversations. An autistic sex-addict! While living with his step-dad, Damien invited boys over either to his place or a place of privacy of the boys' choice, so that Damien could provide them with pleasure. On one side was the quick sexual release; on the other—to

Damien's benefit—was the getting rid of pent-up pain and insecurity. For him, sex was stronger than any drug.

Then came the first day of Damien's counseling sessions, a day which Damien wouldn't soon forget.

CHAPTER FOURTEEN

Group Therapy

Monday, the 13th of August 1973, came and Damien was called over the loudspeaker to the Nurse's Office, where a nice Polish lady named Nurse Bowen instructed Damien to "kick back for a little bit" in a waiting area occupied by two other boys. He wasn't at all sure why he'd been called out of school, but seeing how today was a geometry test he was rather pleased to be missing it.

One activity that was carried on were a number of therapy sessions of which there ere various group meetings. Not everyone participated in all of these sessions, except for the weekly community group one which was on Wednesdays and mandatory for everyone. Likewise mandatory were the weekly "psych sessions" with one's counselor, plus periodical visits with Dr. Samuel Reily (who, after our first two weekly sessions, split our private meetings to every other week and, eventually, to only once per month).

It was just under ten minutes of waiting when Damien was first introduced to Nurse Jessie Robertson, one of the psychiatric nurses, albeit the only male nurse Damien had seen on staff, worked with, plus the most formidable!

Walking out from the Nurse's Station came a young, six-foot-seven tall black man who was immediately intimidating. He reminded me a lot of Corporal Jackson back at Mt. Lowe Academy. He towered over us three boys and didn't look, at least to me, at all happy to see us, far from it; I thought I'd been caught doing something bad, and this huge male nurse was there to deliver my punishment! Thankfully, my first impression was false, completely wrong.

The six-and-a-half-foot black man asked the three boys sitting there, "Which of you is Damien Collins?"

Raising a nervous hand, the timid fifteen-year-old—and much shorter—replied, *"I-I am, s-sir."*

"Alright . . . let's talk for a couple of minutes, privately, in my office," and with that, Nurse Robertson lead the way down a short hallway. "Have a seat, Mr. Collins. Doctor Reily has asked me to include you in one of my groups," he directly began, in a no nonsense manner, while taking a seat of his own behind a cluttered desk.

"Every Monday, Wednesday, and occasionally on Fridays, I facilitate a small group specifically setup to deal with child abuse . . . " lowering his deep voice, despite the closed office door, he added, "sexual abuse in any form and against any person. I have come to understand that child—excuse me—sexual child abuse occurs far more often than it's reported. The 60's opened a broad range of depravity which, regrettably, exposed particularly young children to intense adult and age-inappropriate behavior. Too much, too early. You follow?"

Damien simply nodded.

"I would like you to become involved in our private little group, And I mean exactly that, 'private.' Whatever is said and shared in our group, remains in our group. You'll be able to trust us, if not right away, to keep everything you tell us to ourselves. Sound okay?"

Nurse Robertson, or just "Jessie," worked with both teenaged victims <u>and</u> offenders within the same group. He believed that the problem lied in the hands of both victim and violator, and treating them together helped in humanizing each one's role. That is to say, that both needed ongoing counseling to not only deal with a host of motivators and problems such as being molested or raped, as well as hearing the aftermath of what a victim goes through. Each session had its own level of shared turmoil and/or heartache from the patients brave enough to confide.

Walking into the meeting room that first time, I couldn't believe that there were so many other boys who were raped and/or molested by their own fathers. I didn't know much about female sex or sexuality in general, except for the fact that all it takes to get a girl pregnant is intercourse at the right time or if you fail to take precautions. I, at that time, didn't know that there was any such thing as good or bad sex.

It was at Metro that I would learn about the missing facts about sex and "healthy" relationships. I was glad, indeed to know about Jessie Robertson and this group he ran in Wuchium. I liked the fact that Jessie's group focused not just on sexual abuse, although it mostly did. He'd also toss in some bits of philosophy and questions that challenged our understanding of behavior.

It didn't happen as fast as I would have like it to, but I did come to learn through group that not only was I abused physically, but also sexually. I'd never considered that my early sexual exposure with Steve and Nathan was actual "abuse," and not just "foolin' around." I never thought of myself as being molested by them nor by anyone else. I'd simply accepted it as providing others physical pleasure while I, myself, received emotional slack . . . never as being a victim before. It was because of this belief that I initially thought I didn't belong in this group.

At first, attending meetings was difficult on me, mainly because I was new to doing so. To have eight other kids sitting around talking about sex, three of them girls—as freely and open as if discussing a TV show they'd all watched, was very different. Not exactly uncomfortable, but very unique, and something I so desperately needed without knowing that I did need it.

Sitting down at one end of the chain of chairs, Jessie opened that Monday's session by introducing Damien and another person: "Good afternoon, folks. I see that we have a coup'lah of new people, including a new girl. So, maybe, we'll start with you, Damien. I don't believe in ladies first," he remarked with a kind smile and chuckle. "Please tell us a little about yourself, Mr. Collins."

I'd started to feel my stomach churn and an instant pain it was generating. Here I was, a former military academy sergeant, a leader of young cadets, and I had "butterflies" in my gut. Then came a belch of hot gas and acid up my throat—boy, was that nasty and bad timing. There I was, a "newbie" and my insides were hurting an' all. I just knew that any moment I would shutdown and start rocking, that was what I was afraid of most.

"C'mon, Damien. You want complete healing . . . of that I'm certain. Please introduce yourself and that's all . . . I promise."

Damien cautiously responded, *"M-m-my n-name's Damien. An' m-my probation off*—he swallowed hard, *"my P.O. had me p-put here and I . . . I don't really know why. I mean, I know what m-my paperwork says, but I d-don't . . .why it's illegal. B-b-but, I'm thankful."*

"Thankful? To be here?!" wisecracked one of the boys to his left.

"And you, Linda," Jessie said, ignoring the sardonic teen. "Could you introduce yourself, please."

Standing the short blonde said simply enough, "Hey . . . I'm Linda . . . and I'm here because I use," then sat right down again.

Sitting up straighter in his chair, another young boy spoke up, "Hello, Damien and Linda. I'm James, and I'm here because I have a problem with cocaine and speed."

". . . and with waiting his turn," the smart aleck again aired openly.

"Thank you, Peter," Jessie gave the discourteous boy a quick—and apparently not uncommon—rebuke, then suggested, "James, what have you gotten from the--," he paused to calculate within his mind, "the four months of being in group?"

"I know that staying in the drug-for-hire world, I'll still be locked up . . . only next time, I'll be going to C.Y.A. or adult prison . . . or worse."

What's worse? Damien asked.

"Death . . . my death!" The young black boy answered frankly.

"So," Jessie continued, "tell the newbies what made you see the real danger with prostitution and deals for drugs?"

This conversation grew from James go three or four others sharing until the end of the hour. It didn't include all of the kids—most remained quiet, not wanting to draw attention to themselves or interrupt anyone else.

After the first twenty minutes, two more girls from upstairs made their very late way to the group and sat in the empty seats or just sat on the carpeted floor at the feet of a friend. The staff allowed the girls a chunk of leniency when it came to whatever they saw fit. Most of them were emotional wrecks with horrific testimonials.

"Hey, Damien . . . I'm Kevin and I live in Venice Beach—lived there—and the beach there is real cool. There's a huge supply of fun, sun, and hot chicks. I mean, if that's your thing, you'd love it." This last part of his statement was actually meant to probe Damien's reaction.

"Very good, Kevin," Nurse Robertson complimented, then faced both Damien and Linda. "You both just got here last weekend. Don't let any of our comments interrupt this work that you are doing."

Damien politely—although unnecessarily—raised his hand. *Can you help me understand <u>what</u> you mean when you say 'work'? I mean, what is it this group does? Do we just talk and listen to each other? Is that it?*

"There's more that goes on. <u>That</u> is part of your work. The healing. The rest will come to you in time."

Nurse Robertson knew from experience that the greatest amount of "work" comes from a patient's own self-awareness and when he/she relates to the hardships of others. As far as Damien was concerned, his first group meeting was pretty darn good, but he didn't understand how simply listening to other kids' traumatic experiences could change him, fix him.

After the first group meeting, I met and talked with Jessie. Well, I talked and Jessie listened, for a full three-quarters of an hour. At the end of our first "psych" session, I learned quite a bit more about myself and the psychiatric process. I had never really heard about depression nor autism before meeting Jessie. Boy, was he ever on the mark!

Autism was still a relatively new medical term in the early 1970's. Most "old-school physicians" continued to misdiagnose autistic children as being schizophrenic, which they subtly weren't. Likewise, kids were falsely considered 'manic-depressive' (the prelude to today's term of 'bipolar'), which they also weren't. Damien's level of autism and of depression were comparably minor to most cases, and he quite certainly wasn't manic . . . although he admits to using far more words than necessary when describing a situation.

Nurse Robertson also eased Damien's fears about homosexuality: That while being gay or lesbian might be a social taboo, "according to the American Psychiatric Association, homosexuality—in and of itself—is not a mental illness." This gave the boy an added sense of wellness, if not acceptance, about his attraction to both genders.

Jessie believed that I was not psychotic, not "schizo," but had a major—and majorly missed—depressive syndrome. Jessie would see about getting me put on an antidepressant, something like Prozac, by one of the doctors. He, being merely a nurse, couldn't prescribe it for me himself. It was the positive effect of his well-run group and our one-on-one sessions that brought healing to my soul, and to the other kids—usually nine or so—in our sexual abuse group . . . as well as the nearly one hundred boys and girls in Wuchium. It wasn't all easy to be sure. No, that's far from the truth of a well-run group.

For the first time in my life, I was feeling as if I could start lowering and releasing my defenses, and that I might enjoy the process of healing. I really felt as if I was safe. My problem was compounded by the fact that I couldn't easily trust adult persons. My "dad" would beat me for any reason at all. My "mom" was clearly crazy and, therefore, made me believe all adults as untrustworthy and not dependable.

Twice that I know of, Doctor Reily wanted to get my parents involved in my healing process. Failing in getting them involved beyond one scheduled family meeting which no one showed up for, told the all important story of my "family dynamics" . . . of which there was no family in order to have any dynamics! That, too, painted a living picture of my world of abandonment. In fact and indeed, I had been devalued as a human being and nullified as being a family member!

Things actually started to change without my being actively aware of them; such that I was able to reduce, even stop, thinking about having sex with other boys or girls . . . instead in working with the therapy. Seeing where it would take me. The therapy took time, but it took far less time than it would have had I not allowed myself to lower my hurtful defenses. I had done a lot come January 1974 . . . however there was more to do.

I was no longer craving sex at all. I was beginning to be able not to need acceptance to feel good about me and to feel for others. This was crucial to my development as a healthy person: It was important for me to be able to get to know who I was and get to like myself . . . the me without any addiction.

That was the end-all and be-all of Damien's twice-weekly group meetings and monthly visits with Dr. Reily. To learn self-value and self-worth without the need of social acceptance of any kind. Despite the obvious devaluing made clear by his parents, Dr. Reily and Nurse Robertson did a fantastic job of providing healing sessions in a safe, emotionally-stable environment. Together, both mental-health practitioners progressed through one-on-one meetings that—like the majority of sex-related reasons—the core issue remained of Damien's overwhelming lack of healthy relationship skills with anyone at large.

Then came yet another detrimental and unfortunate detour in Damien's road of life!

CHAPTER FIFTEEN

Detours to Adulthood

As one of his final acts as republican governor of California, Ronald Wilson Reagan (who'd eventually become President six years later) regrettably cut the funding to several state-financed youth resources, including the Wuchium program. Without the necessary money, the Metropolitan State Hospital had only a month to properly notify patients' guardians, relocate or fire staff, and shutdown the program.

I couldn't believe it! It was my last day at Mt. Lowe all over again! Having to leave Metro was a scary proposition for me. I was seventeen years young, forced into being an early adult despite having any clue on what was expected of a true grown-up. Although I still didn't know it at the time, I was also the father of a newly-born daughter elsewhere in this gigantic world. Then there was the fact that I still needed both psychiatric care and pharmaceuticals. The timing couldn't have been any worse!

I had no money, no insurance, no plans. To be rather frank, I was very scared because I had no means by which I could care for myself and live in society. I still didn't know what it meant to have an adequate income, how to shop for food, or manage any money. I was not mentally or emotionally ready to support myself.

During Damien's final week at Metro, Damien approached and asked Dr. Sam Reily if there was some way that he could stay . . .

another program, perhaps?

"It's not just Wuchium that's getting cut. All of the adolescent programs here at Metro are shutting down due to lack of funds from Governor Reagan. Besides, you're no longer a ward of the court, Damien. Without medical insurance you couldn't possibly afford to stay here."

B-but I . . . I've got nobody out there. Nowhere to go.

"Parents, yes. We've covered that. But, perhaps, you can reach out to someone else? An aunt or uncle?

My aunt Cha-cha married somebody named Mike. I don't even know their last name.

Damien, with Dr. Reily's help, decided to call his grandfather. Damien explained, at great length, the last five years of his young life; that he'd left the world in any real sense before he was allowed to grow up in it . . . had never been taught how to care for himself, get a job, or even buy groceries on his own. Also, he confessed to being a bisexual, in a world that actively frowned on such a lifestyle. He summarized his recent therapy at Metro and how it was a "good start," but that he knew he had a long way to go.

I was blessed by my Grandpa and his tough decision to allow me to live with him for a while. He came through, leaving me with merely getting my out-of-sorts self to Culver City . . .back to where it all started to fall apart.

The walls of his house were still pink, that much I remembered from my childhood. I was only three when I'd first met him and his house seemed foggy. Of course, when we moved to California, he was there, too . . . mostly to help unload the moving van. But after my dad separated from my mom, which seemed only a few weeks later, I'd lost contact with Grandpa, except for a Christmas or two.

Damien's grandfather was real kind and understanding about the boy's situation. He hadn't spent any meaningful time with his grandson since their day at Disneyland half a decade ago. Grandpa didn't at all mind with the lanky seventeen-year-old living with him for a while; however, the teen would not be a "freeloader" and was expected to contribute financially once settled. The French carpenter had been retired for years and living by making cabinets plus a life without having to support another person, family or not.

On top of all of my problems, was the issue of impulse control . . . which manifested itself not long after I moved in Grandpa's home. This impulse control revealed itself one day while I was out job hunting and went inside a sporting goods store. I applied for a job, then took a look around . . . almost automatically I located the Guns and Rifles section. To this day, I have no idea why their display of guns had made any sense to me, and I mean getting involved with them at all.

My guess is that guns stood for adulthood . . . and if I owned one, I would be an adult. Right? This was my goal, to become an adult! So, this display of handguns and rifles triggered my poor impulse control.

The Big 5 store featured a Remington pump-action .22 rifle which was cheap enough for the unemployed teenager to afford. The cash he had on hand wasn't meant to purchase any firearms, granted, the money had been given to Damien towards the purchase of items he actually needed. However, the attraction of the rifle was too overwhelming to pass up.

Now I was faced with a new problem, and that was getting the rifle into the house without my grandfather noticing it. That was a big one, but my lack of impulse control put myself into a case of stupidity, deluxe! And for no reason whatsoever! I knew my Grandpa would be strongly against the thought of me buying a rifle. Speaking of stupidity, I was the master of it . . . or was stupidity the master of me?

In Damien's reality, he felt abandoned by the state hospital. Normally, when a patient completed the Wuchium program's inpatient therapy, he or she received outpatient follow-up with a psychiatrist to maintain the patient's stability. Damien, as previously explained, would not be receiving any kind of follow-up. He was lacking competent survival skills and the ability to not only interact with society but to be a productive member of it.

"Damien? Is that you?" His grandfather questioned from another room.

Yeah, the boy's worst fear was coming true; his grandfather was not only awake but was approaching when Damien was only halfway to his bedroom. The bulky cardboard box which the rifle came in held in both his arms. *D-do, um, we have any cough drops?* he yelled out in a clear voice, then pretending to cough.

Amazingly enough, this worked. Grandpa froze in his tracks in the adjacent room, seconds away from having a clear view of his grandson and the long item the teen was holding. "Let me check." Grandpa turned on his heels and went towards the master bathroom.

Thanks! Damien quick-stepped to his bedroom, then frantically looked for an appropriate hiding place for the big box. No sooner did he find one and shove the weapon into position when the footsteps began to approach him again.

"Here's a couple," the old man presented the nearly empty plastic packaging, "Hope you're not gettin' sick . . . seein' how you'll be workin' now."

Working? Damien was puzzled.

"Yup. That fast-food place on Venice called. Carl's burgers."

Carl's Junior? Damien's enthusiasm instantly peaked. *They called?*

"You've got an interview tomorr'ah at ten. Where's your 'good' jeans, I'll iron them."

"I know how to iron . . . I was in the military, remember? Oh, this is good. Great, in fact. I can't believe I got a job." The teen was excited.

The interview only took minutes, it's not like they had much to read on my job application—I'd never worked anywhere before. Under arrest history, I put 'none' because, by the time they looked into it, I'd turn eighteen and my juvenile record would be sealed . . . or so I thought.

My boss, Mr. Jones, went from asking me a dozen questions to giving me a quick tour of behind-the-scenes: the kitchen area. Everyone started on the food preparation lines, putting the hamburger patty and all of its toppings onto the correct style of buns. They expected speed over precision, although looked frowningly on mistakes and wasted food. If I showed potential, I could be promoted to the French fries fryers or even cashier. I was uncontrollably excited! I would start my first day on that Friday.

I must've ran all of the way home, dripping of sweat and exhilaration. I couldn't wait to tell my Grandpa that I got the job! That I'd be making burgers and, most importantly, making twenty-cents above the national minimum wage! Two dollars and thirty cents per hour! I was ecstatic!

*Grandpa! I got it! I got the j—*Damien exclaimed as he entered the house, only to be interrupted by the sight of the object in the old man's hands.

"Tu veux, to tell me . . . about this!" His grandfather lifted the cardboard box containing the pump-action rifle to emphasize the item in question.

You searched my room?

It's my room. My house! I was putting your clothes away. Dieu et mon droit! When I found <u>this</u>! Who on God's green earth told you, you could buy a gun? And, and bring it into <u>my</u> house?!" The furniture builder shouted.

I-Ithought, well, I'm going to making some contribution f-for the rent . . . I, uh, just thought—

Rent?! Rent doesn't allow you to being a gun into my house! What's the matter with you?" he asked, hypothetically, then stopped Damien before the boy could provide an answer. "Are there any other weapons I should know about? In the attic, perhaps? Hidden in the garage? A lot of this was in French.

No, Grandpa, Damien said in a barely audible voice.

"Good. I want you out of my house by tomorrow."

You're kickin' me out? For buying a rifle?

"Buying the rifle, spending the night at your friend's house without giving me an adequate heads-up, that you—"

T-that was last week! Damien complained in a childish whine.

"Oh, I'm sorry . . . am I not supposed to remember what happened a week ago?" The old man rumbled loudly in French about 'not being senile enough,' then more clearly stated, "I forgive, I don't forget, just like God. But your constant disrespect for me and for my rules . . . <u>oui</u>, I'm kicking you out."

Damien was shocked. He'd only been living with his grandfather for about three months until finally landing this job at Carl's Jr., and now all of his enthusiasm had been deep-fried because of the impulsive decision to purchase that rifle. He hadn't being showing his grandpa the respect which he'd so richly deserved.

I felt sick to my stomach about my disrespectfulness of my grandpa, by causing him to wait up for me to come home the other night. He surely did not deserve this behavior and especially not from me, the one he'd opened his house to, due to my own urgent need. How self-centered that behavior was . . . that I was.

So much anger was generated by my lack of regard and courteousness, to cause him to ask me to move and find my own place to live. I was truly disgusted with myself . . . no, that's probably not true, since I was still only a teenager; I was more likely disgusted with Grandpa—with the innocent person in all of this.

Damien was exhausted after their argument and went to his bedroom to get some much needed sleep. Waking, he found himself wondering where on Earth he could live on such short notice and with his low income. He really was at a huge loss regarding where to move to.

I literally had no idea what I was going to do. I decided that I needed to get up and get something in my stomach before my search for a solution. Walking into the kitchen, I was greeted by Grandpa saying, "Bon matin, mon Damien," which was good to know that we were still on speaking terms. What wasn't so good was what else he had to say . . .

"You must have been really tired avant-hier, I mean with you sleeping all day when I told you to move out!" Avant-hier means day before yesterday.

Sitting down at the kitchen counter, the boy's mouth dropped, *Hold it. I slept all day yesterday?! The whole day?*

"You sure did. You must be hungry."

Damien didn't know what to say; he never slept over thirty hours before. He felt like flipping on the TV or finding a newspaper to prove it to himself that his grandfather was wrong or teasing him, yet somehow he knew the old man was correct: that somehow Damien had slept an entire day away.

"You want some breakfast this morning?" his grandfather asked again.

That, um, yeah, that would be real nice. Th-thank you.

"You go and wash up, and it'll be ready."

With that, Damien rushed to the guest bathroom and took a quick shower. He returned dressed in the kitchen just as his grandfather finished scrambling two eggs.

"Bonjour . . . and bon appetite. You want cheese on your oeufs brouilles?"

Grandpa, please, you know I'll never learn to . . . pas francais.

"Your eggs! You want Cheddar or, faute de mieux, that white cheese?"

The white kind. Por favor. Samien responded, defiantly saying 'please' but in Spanish, not French.

His grandfather sneered at the boy before grabbing a package of Kraft American cheese singles. Damien got himself a tall glass of orange juice from the fridge, then sat at the table moments prior to the older man handing him a plate of eggs, bacon, and French-style hash browns.

Thanks, Grandpa, this is fantastic.

"Je vous en prie," which means 'you are welcome.' Letting the conversation drop until Damien finished eating more than half the breakfast, his grandfather eventually asked, "Do you have anything to say to me?"

Damien paused, *About the eggs?*

"About what we talked about avant-hier?"

The boy put down his fork, knowing exactly what his grandfather was expecting. *I'm sorry. I apologized before for not calling you, telling you that I was spending the night with my friend.*

"And the gun?"

I-um, I just wanted to be, you know, own something 'adult.' I thought having it would make me feel more like an adult. Be an adult.

"I forgive you, but you still need to move out in a couple of days."

Do, uh, do you have any hints where I might find a place to live on, you know, minimum wage?

"Nope." Then his grandfather suggested, "Can you try your friend, the doctor?"

Doctor Samuel? I can't, I don't have his home number.

Fixing himself a couple of slices of buttered toast with cinnamon and sugar, he remembered something, "De bonne grace, I do! He gave it to me, when I picked you up at the hospital."

Do you know where it is?

"Ma foi! That was three months ago," his grandfather headed over towards an antique desk, pulling open one drawer after another. "I remember it being written on a yellow piece of paper . . . oh! Voila!

Cool, I'll call him right after breakfast. Thanks, Grandpa.

<u>Je vous en prie</u>, Damien. I am just surprised I kept it." Then, after taking another sip of his hot coffee, he asked, "<u>Excusez-moi</u> for sticking my nose in your business, but why do you avoid calling your mother? <u>Mon</u> Christine?"

Well, she stresses me out rather than helps. You know what I mean? She's never been much of a 'mom' to me . . . the twins, sure, but I'm just her, uh . . .

"<u>Ame damnee</u>" he muttered, then—after seeing the boy's shrug—translated, "It means 'lost soul.' Yeah, Christine has always been a bit to handle, and that's not what you are needing right now. Well, this Doctor Reily might be the right thing for you."

Maybe. I did learn some things, if that's what you mean.

"<u>Non</u>. What do you mean?"

Well, Damien cleared his throat, *of course there's the respect issue between you and I. But, I think that the greater issue for me to learn from all of this was that you gave me advice and that you did so freely. Any advice from family and friends should be listened to by the young. I am, if anything, still very young. I had no reason whatsoever to buy that rifle. I wasn't planning to go small game hunting or shoot for ducks, so why was I buying it? This made it clear that I was far more a kid in your eyes for the senseless of it. And, if nothing else, that's a reason for me to leave your home.*

"The senseless of it," Grandpa repeated this phrase with a subtle nod. Smiling, he then added, "Maybe buying that gun did make an adult of you. Not the having of it, but being able to see 'the senselessness' of a child." His grandfather left the room, only to return moments later with the rifle still sealed up in its box. "<u>Aux armes</u>!" which means 'to arms!'

What? The puzzled boy asked, looking for a translation.

"You bought it. Hopefully you've still got the receipt 'cause only one of you is staying. I'll drive."

Damien, being only a teenager, naturally didn't keep the receipt;

however the sporting goods store's manager informed Damien that even with the receipt, their store had a strict no returns policy on all firearms—this has since the 1970's changed at all Big 5 retailers. Even Damien's grandpa couldn't persuade the manager to provide them with any kind of refund or store credit.

"Back in my day, customer service took priority," he contended.

"True," said the similarly-aged Hispanic man, "However, back in <u>our</u> day, customers weren't robbing banks or liquor stores, then returning their rifles to where they bought them. I'm sorry, but we've had problems in the past and I can't—"

"But, look! The box is still sealed. Surely you can make an exception."

"Surely, I cannot."

Damien returned to his grandfather's car holding the accursed item in both arms. He felt sick to his stomach again, mostly because his impulsive buying of the weapon was once again causing frustration within his grandpa, and tension between the two of them. He deeply regretted purchasing the weapon now, and—although he did not know it ye—it would continue to develop into an even heavier ball-and-chain later on down this road.

I'm sorry, Grandpa, he admitted once they were both inside the old man's sedan.

"<u>Au contraire</u>, Damien, you should be embarrassed. Now we're stuck with that thing. I'll put it somewhere safe, hold onto it until you're truly a man. <u>A propos de bottes</u>, we have other things to take care of today. <u>En avant</u>! The lumber store awaits."

The rest of the day, Damien and his grandfather worked on a brand-new standing cabinet made of robust cherry with an inlaid mirror. It was going to take a bit of work. Damien felt pretty lucky because he was going to be a lot of service for his grandfather. The carpenter seemed more at peace with him.

That felt really nice, helping my grandpa. I would miss that part of my times with Grandpa. Nevertheless, I had a life before me and that brought me happiness. Part of the task that day was to drive the finished cabinet to his customer. It was tough work, and we bonded after all was said and done.

Now that was cool, Damien said while getting in the car at the end of their delivery.

"Cool? J'ai chaud, and sweaty all over," he exclaimed while wiping sweat from his forehead with the back of his hand, "I'm glad you enjoyed helping me, because I'm inviting you to join me tomorrow."

Cool! That would be fun. I don't start working at Carl's Jr. until Friday, and I'll need to buy a pair of black work pants . . .

"I take it that means 'yes'?"

Yes, I really want to join you tomorrow. Thank you.

"Je vous en prie. You'll need to be ready to go at seven; it'll be a long drive."

With that, they became quiet during the trip back to the house. His grandfather stored the unwanted rifle up in his attic, hidden away where Damien wouldn't easily find it. Once the boy turned eighteen or moved out, whichever would come first, Grandpa would return the weapon and assist his grandson with his eviction.

It were not best that we should all think alike; It is difference of opinion that makes horse races. ~Mark Twain

CHAPTER SIXTEEN

Making House Calls

When December 6th came, Damien came home from working at the hamburger place and went to his room to gather any dirty laundry to wash along with the filthy uniform he was wearing . . . only to be surprised by the fact that Grandpa had already washed and dried all of it, as well as placing them within an open suitcase. The luggage would count as his birthday present.

The day came that we'd talked about. I was no longer a minor and, as agreed, I'd no longer be a burden. I was feeling a mix of sadness and eagerness to start my new life with my former doctor, Samuel Reily, whom I'd called several times since the day Grandpa located his number. This was going to be different. I knew that I was going to have a better life than what it would have been if I had moved in with my mother or stayed with my grandfather, that is, if either two of these had been an actual option. Personally, I didn't want to be raised by either of them.

Doctor Reily invited me to not only stay in his guest bedroom, but had a job lined up for me; I would be working in his office as his Office Manager. He arrived at my grandpa's house just in time for a light dinner. I was very pleased to finally see him after all of our calls; we hadn't seen each other since the day I left Metro. With my bags packed and a warm smile upon my face, I was ready to move in with Sam, my true friend.

"Nice to see you, again, Samuel," Grandpa greeted him at the door. "Parlez-vous français?"

"Uh, no sorry. I studied only German and Latin in college."

"How have you been, Doctor?" the old man escorted the younger inside.

"I'm doing well, thank you. Smells wonderful in here," he complimented while stepping into the living room. Damien was visible in the adjacent dining room, setting the table. "Hello, Damien."

We're having tarragon chicken, Damien reported from the other room.

"It's pronounced, '<u>poulet a l'estragon</u>,'" Grandpa corrected the boy.

I don't care how it's pronounced.... I care how it tastes! The insolent teenager hollered back. Finally, after placing the last fork on the tablecloth, Damien rushed over to give Samuel a much deserved hug. *Hi, Doctor Sam!*

"Hello," he repeated after releasing the embrace. "It's good to see you, too. And, please, just call me Sam... I haven't been your 'doctor' for almost a year."

I simply couldn't wait for dinner to be over and until I was on my way to Huntington Beach. I even almost choked once on a piece of chicken I'd swallowed too quickly. Once done eating, I cleared the table, piling everything in the sink. For once I was excited that I wouldn't be the one to be washing the dishes after dinner.

"You got all of your things together?" Samuel asked the youngster. Doctor Reily wasn't that much older than Damien. He'd only recently turned thirty-one that previous summer.

Yeah, the eager boy rushed into the living room.

"Damien," his grandfather stood out of his chair, "aren't you forgetting something?" The old man showed a look of distain on his face.

I-uh, oh! Yeah, Damien said after recognizing his grandfather's expression, *I'll be right back.*

Damien started to go into his grandfather's bedroom to access the folding stairs which led to the attic, when Grandpa called out, "Damien, it's already out here."

Where? The boy said as he ran back into the main room.

"Right under the sofa," he replied , with an extended index finger.

Oh, the boy got down on his hands and knees, reaching underneath the upholstered couch. Seconds later he pulled out something wooden. *I found it.*

"Found what, Damien?" A slightly puzzled Samuel asked.

My rifle, the boy state, holding the weapon upside-down by its faux wood-grained stock.

"Uh, I see..." the concerned doctor stammered.

"Don't forget the bullets," Grandpa advised. "They're in my room, on top of the dresser." Damien wasn't in his room for more than a few seconds before he spotted them: two boxes of .22 caliber rounds. Damien had purchased them the same day as the rifle, yet—unlike the weapon itself—hadn't been allowed to open their boxes... nor had the desire to.

"<u>Excusez-moi</u>," Grandpa excused himself as we went into the kitchen, for no other reason than to give Samuel and Damien a little time to talk about this unexpected development: Damien bringing a weapon to the doctor's home.

"Damien," Sam stated calmly, "I don't really approve of having weapons in my house. But, of course, it is yours and I respect your privacy. Listen, you can keep it with you, in my home, if you'll give me your word that you will take lessons at a firing range and let me keep the bullets."

Um. Alright. To be honest, I really have no interest in shooting my rifle. I never really should've bought it.

"Interesting. So, why did you?"

I, um, well this was a few months ago. I was seventeen, and I wanted to own something that made me feel more adult.

Oh? So owning something that only adults normally buy made you feel older?

No, the only thing it made me feel, was sick to my stomach.

Hmm, we'll talk more about this later."

Samuel and Damien gathered the boy's belongings and loaded them into Samuel's one-year-old Pontiac Grand Prix—featuring a 450 big block—then returned inside for final hugs and an "Au revoir" from his grandfather.

We were off for Huntington Beach, my new home. I was certain that all would go well, that it would work out for the best. I just didn't know what or who was on the same road with me. I didn't know what obstacles and obstructions were awaiting me. As you can tell, by the number of pages remaining in this book, there's quite a few of <u>both</u> waiting to rear their ugly heads!

My first impression of Samuel's house was: He had money! Quite a lot, in fact. He also had something I didn't expect, a housemate named Nick Smith. Actually, as it turned out, Nick was a bit more than just a guest. I hadn't previously thought about Sam's sexuality; I was rather centered on my own; so, this discovery was a bit of a surprise. Keep in mind, though, that my being bisexual played no part in why Samuel want me to move in with him. I wasn't what you'd call "his type."

Both Nick and Sam were very generous and mature gay men. They knew how to treat visitors. Walking into their home, one quickly got the feeling of both being welcomed as well as "well to do." The first notable thing was Samuel's wonderful stereo system: Clearly these men loved their music! Then, was their beautiful leather davenport and love seats. On the opposite side of the living room was a gourmet kitchen and dining room, featuring a glass-topped table on an oval stand.

Nick and Sam were joint leaseholders of the impressive property.

Prior to that day, they'd discussed my staying with them and that neither expected that I would come up with an equal share of their excessive rent. Instead, they made it clear that I would earn my stay by both working for Dr. Reily and taking care of their house and yard. I was also to return to school and work on getting my diploma.

Samuel was still working as a rather well-paid state psychiatrist at Metro as well as establishing his own private practice within an office building; this would be the small office which Damien would help manage. Nick was a professional—equally well-paid—hair dresser/designer with a studio at Huntington Beach's Fashion Island. Neither of them were exactly "rich," yet they were rich for each other.

Problems seemed to follow me from the days before I first went to the hospital. I just seemed to find them or bring about trouble for myself and these two men who demonstrated such concern for me. I would never deliberately bring problems to either one of these men. Nonetheless, I was, indeed, bringing tension from my world into theirs, whether I wanted to or not.

At the time, I'd believed that the real source of the troubles was that monster of sexual inappropriateness showing its ugly head again. I was not doing anything that could be called sexual, but it clearly made a few young ladies uncomfortable to be around me. Sex was an excessive interest that just seemed so significant and <u>casual</u> to bring up in routine conversation.

It was this sort of socially inappropriate behavior that made people, in general, uncomfortable with me… and uncomfortable for Samuel and Nick; however, neither of my benefactors kicked me out of their house. All that they asked was that I fly under the radar, to "tone it down" a bit… or more. I think that what made things particularly uncomfortable was that there was not just one or two gay men living in a house together, in society, but now there were three. What would the neighbors think was going on next door? However, I wasn't lovers with either of them; instead, as it turned out, I was something more important…

Dr. Reily had an ulterior and career-minded motive for having the quirky young man move into his home. As mentioned previously, while Damien was first being diagnosed by the doctor, Samuel hadn't had many autistic patients, and none as non-stereotypical as Damien. In fact, Damien was such a nonconformist of conventional autism, the doctor was second guessing himself.

What's that you're reading, Sam? Damien asked him one afternoon.

"It's medical stuff. Just some case studies about children."

I didn't think you still had any children patients.

"Not currently," Samuel then eyed Damien, "but then again, do any of us truly grow up?"

Well, we most definitely grow older, I mean, I'm growing more and—

"I meant that… nevermind." Dr. Reily smiled while shaking his head. Damien rarely understood the doctor's sense of humor or irony.

What is that written in? It's not English, and I'm pretty sure it's not French.

"Oh, it's German. I think I've mentioned before that I speak German. Anyway, it's by an Austrian pediatrician names Hans Asperger.

Believe it or not, I'm reading this because of you."

Me? What did I do wrong this time?

"Ha!" Samuel laughed out loud. "No, no. I mean, I've been looking into whether I was right about you having autism. This doctor in Austria had been studying four children who, well, are a lot like you. Turns out, you're not along in the universe after all."

Damien scratched his head, a usual sign of growing frustration, then asked *What do you mean? How 'a lot' like me are these kids? I've never been to Aus-Australia. My mom was from France, not—*

"Calm done, Damien. I meant that I think *I'm* wrong. No, this Dr. Asperger—and he's in Austria, by the way, not Australia—he's been watching some children who he thought had high functioning autism, but lack the usual severity that autistic patients have. That's what I mean by 'like you,' just that these children have the same difficulty integrating with society."

So, I don't have autism.

"It's something very similar to autism. Dr. Asperger calls it 'autistic psychopathy' and I—"

Y-y-you mean, now I'm psycho? Like that Alfred Hitchcock movie? Damien was clearly becoming distressed by the conversation. His body still and arms rigid as he stood there in Samuel's study. The young man was sick and tired of being persistently re-diagnosed by medical officials, none of whom in his past seemed to agree with another.

"No, no. Psychopathy doesn't mean the same as 'psycho.' No, I believe that this syndrome that Dr. Asperger wrote about is the closest thing I have read." Samuel motioned towards the other books on his desk, "that characterizes your own social impairment and difficulties. I am now certain that this is what you have—what you're having trouble with."

So, you're saying that I don't have autism and I'm not psycho, but that I have some condition, s syndrome, that is both autism and psychopathy? I don't want to have any conditions or syndromes; I just want to be me.

"And, what I'm saying is, now that we know what kind of condition you have, the easier it will be to find proper treatment for it. You see, us doctors like to categories our patients to have a better understanding of what we're dealing with and how to research into what treatments and interventions worked best in the past. A proper diagnoses means now I can talk with other physicians and compare notes about what they've discovered. What works for them, you see."

I 'see' a little bit Damien admitted. Now instead of telling other doctors that I have something more specific than just saying I've got autism, I—

"It's the other way around," Sam corrected, "but go ahead."

Right. So, instead of saying I have autism, that I have autistic psychopathy, those other doctors can say that they found something that works even better than what we're doing now?

"Maybe. Unfortunately, this is all still pretty new. And," he said as he showed Damien the cover of the book he was holding, "written in German. If I made any phone calls right now asking my colleagues and old college buddies if they've ever heard of Dr. Asperger or 'autistic psychopathy' before, or had a patient with it, they'll most likely say 'what is that?'"

Maybe they would if it wasn't so hard to pronounce." Damien then quietly mouths the phrase 'autistic psychopathy' over and over again. *I think I liked it better when I was just 'high-functioning autism,' it's easier to say.*

"How about, between the two of us, we just call it Asperger's?" Dr. Reily suggested, not knowing for certain that this would precisely be what mental-health professionals would be calling it in the 1980's and still today.

Asp...burgers? Isn't an asp a kind of snake? Who would name theirs kids a snake burger? That sounds really disgusting to me. An asp burger.

Dr. Reily did make plenty of phone calls to fellow psychiatrists and physicians, several of whom he didn't know personally, to get a better understanding of Dr. Hans Asperger's observations. He routinely went over Damien's symptoms with these other professionals, describing the boy's peculiarities, lack of social and relationship skills, incoherence of conversation, speaking in a monotone pitch with poor modulation control of the volume of his voice—especially while indoors, such as a bookstore or movie theatre—and obsessive need to talk about his singular interest: sex.

This, of course, isn't completely true. Damien didn't always talk incessantly about sex… it's just that sex kept coming up. There were plenty of other times when the topic of choice would be music or Shakespeare, and the listener would be buffeted with outstretched minutes of that particular subject without end in sight. Not that the conversation would be boring or without merit, just that Damien would lose all concept of time and of timing while expelling his vast knowledge. Likewise, the topic of choice rarely coincided with Damien's surroundings, such as discussing French architecture during a group viewing of a major sporting event, such as the Oakland Raiders playing the Minnesota Vikings at Super Bowl Eleven. (The Raiders won, by the way.)

Not having the right job skills, people skills, and overall social training to be an effective member of society made Damien's situation all the worse. As agreed, he cared for the house of these two men, who allowed him to live in their world, would carve a path for Damien. With their help, he would become a welcomed member of their society, and if not welcomed, then as invisible as they were.

CHAPTER SEVENTEEN

Turning Wheels

Damien's life, up until this moment, had been a wild and twisting path not unlike a rollercoaster, however, clearly never as fun nor exhilarating as one. No, his ride had been constant detours down potholed streets! Such as obtaining a friend, only to be moved away from Steve; being enrolled and accepted at a military academy, only to be pulled out of it; finding his way into a state hospital with the perfect resources to help him, only to be evicted once the program's funding got cut. None of these digressions were under Damien's own personal control nor a result of something he'd instituted, yet all of them seemed to take him in completely opposite directions from where he needed to go.

I was grateful to be involved in the program at Metropolitan State Hospital; after all, I never would've met Dr. Reily and be living then in his house. However, I very much believed that such a program, even though its funding was cut, needed to have some sort of follow-up care that would have prepared each patient for either continued education or much needed jobs training. If the program hadn't been shut down when it had, I would've been able to graduate high school by taking an equivalency exam.

All record of my attendance in school stopped the moment I was put in Juvenile Hall; there was no official documentation stating otherwise. For all that the state of California knew, I was still only a sophomore, albeit I was now almost nineteen years old. Granted, although I was working for Dr. Reily and wouldn't be needing to go job hunting anytime soon, I promised both of them when I moved in that I would continue my education.

Damien, with Samuel's financial help, was enrolled in Huntington Beach Adult School. He immediately applied himself to his school work, oftentimes neglecting his chores around the house and in maintaining the yard. These were excused due to his long commute to/from school via public transportation; however, on non-school days, his unexcused negligence caused tension between Nick and himself.

Damien decided now, more than anything else, he needed to focus on getting his driver's license and a care of his own, which he couldn't afford alone.

Although he was living rent free off of Samuel and Nick, Damien was likewise living income free. Sam did pay Damien "under the table" an agreed upon allowance for helping out at the office; however, Damien would've been making more had he not quit his previous employer, Carl's Jr. In either case, he now needed initial funds to purchase a vehicle.

So, one evening, Damien went to Samuel, *Excuse me Dr.Reily?*

"Damien, please stop calling me doctor when we're at home. I start looking for my dad," he remarked with a smile. "Please call me Sam. You don't have to be so formal all of the time."

Being formal in one's speech is one of the "tells" of someone with Asperger's syndrome. Patient's frequently need to be reminded when it's considered appropriate or not… yet, in Damien's case, his years at military academy made the usage of titles and rank hard-wired in his behavior.

Sure thing, Sam. So, I—well, I have a predicament, and I wanted to tell you about my problem and see what, uh, what plan makes sense to you.

"Hmm, so what's the problem?"

Well, as you know, Nick and myself haven't been getting along, well… no, that's not true. We get along. I mean, uh, well we get along good or well enough. I mean, that he gets frustrated with me, about me forgetting to get all of my chores done before getting all of my school work done, which I hardly have any time to get done…

"Um, okay, but what's the problem?" The young doctor stands from his seat, removing a fresh bottle of very fruity red wine from a cabinet, then works with a corkscrew at removing both the wax seal and the cork. Sometimes, having a conversation with Damien requires a substantial amount of wine, for his web of thought is equivalent to that of the tool used to open wine bottles.

Well, traveling to school and back on the bus, which takes a lot of time, especially when the buses are running late... if I didn't have to go by public transportation, then I'd have plenty of more time to complete the chores, and Nick wouldn't be so upset with me forgetting to finish them.

"Alright, I'm following you," Sam said after taking a reasonable gulp. "You'd have more time to complete the chores if you didn't have to take the bus, is what you're saying?"

I would have a lot more time that way. Waiting for the bus—

"Okay. So how do you suggest we solve this problem?" the psychiatrist asked. "Maybe a helicopter? Your own personal submarine."

I—well, yes, a helicopter would do quite nicely. I could clear all of the leaves off the back lawn real easily. But, I was thinking more along the lines of a car.

"*Oh! A car, really?*" Samuel asked sarcastically. Oftentimes, Damien would not recognize the doctor's facial expressions and sarcasm—it's another Asperger's trait—nor would he catch the humor in the situation. Instead, sarcasm is often taken the completely wrong way by Damien, which leads to frustration.

Never mind, forget it! Damien exclaimed suddenly as he turned to leave. "*It was a stupid idea of—*

"Wait! Damien, no it wasn't a 'stupid idea' at all. Come here and tell me your plan. How do you think we should go about getting you a car?"

I just—well, I guess I would need more of an allowance, maybe some help each week, or a loan to buy a car right away.

"That's not a problem. I already know that Nick would agree."

There was hope for me after all. I felt so good about my future that I went right back to the kitchen and to work and made a really good roast that night. I spent hours nose-deep in the classified ads of the newspaper, looking at car I could never afford even with Samuel's and

Nick's help. Nineteen-year-olds never look at the used cars section first, it's always the Ferraris, Porsches, and Lamborghinis.

During the years that followed, I regularly felt like a fifth wheel in their home. Only occasionally did I feel warmth or as a friend by Nick. What did I do to cause him not to like me very much? Well, that happens to be fairly easy: Sam was very much in love with me. No, I don't mean in a sexual manner, I mean that I was a fascination in every sense of the word. A puzzle he couldn't quite finish, yet was unwilling to give up on. And, yes, there was endearment, too. Samuel doted on me in ways that made Nick, his true lover, quite jealous.

Damien went on to complete his G.E.D. at Huntington Beach Adult School, then proceeded onward to Golden West College, despite the fact tht he'd only earned a G.P.A. of 2.05. At this community college, he enrolled in mostly general education classes. The purpose of going to college was to earn any available degree that would serve him long after graduation; however, his goals weren't turning out as expected.

I just became willing to accept the idea that I might not be equipped for the mental-health field. This would prove to be a major stumbling block for me, because I was already determined that the right job for me was to earn degree in psychiatry-related fields. After all, Sam was an M.D. in child psychiatry, why shouldn't I? My greatest problem was: not only was I still a patient myself, but I'd developed dyslexia when it came to both talking and my writing: saying words in a reverse order than I'd planned to. This started to show up more often with my use of adjectives; by saying the noun it's supposed to modify first, then either the adjective or start my phrase all over.

That, plus, as someone with Asperger's syndrome, I wasn't what you'd call an empathic listener... I'd usually concentrate on my own thoughts while others were speaking. Not that I was trying to ignore them, just the opposite: I was struggling to hear them over my own processing of a response. I've been called self-centered and "not paying attention" when, in fact, I'm paying the highest possible attention to what the other person is saying even when it looks and sounds like I couldn't care less.

I failed to perform well enough in school to get accepted into either the psychiatric technician or nursing programs, which was a major letdown. It was time to reconsider my educational options. I wanted to earn a degree *in a field that would allow me to be of service of repairing souls, not just people like me but anyone! I thought that would be my way to repay Dr. Reily for all that he had done for my <u>own</u> soul.*

None of the academic choices were panning out as a promise in my future. I became very angry! Indeed, I was hurt. I really didn't know what to do, or how to accomplish my seemingly impossible goals. I wanted, more than anything, to give reasons for Sam and Nick to believe in me, to feel a sense of pride in my accomplishments. I failed horribly in this task, and that also hurt; I got even angrier because of it. I really had no idea of what I should've done differently nor what would lead me in the direction of some success. I was just spinning my wheels.

Damien had another goal which he was failing at—added to his aforementioned anger—which was at meeting women. He wanted to prove to himself that he wasn't gay or bisexual, that he could be a "normal" heterosexual man. Yet, at this too, he failed. He continued to find himself attracted to both genders, viewing other men just as alluring as women. Any relationships he started with a female left him desiring to be with another male, causing the friendship to fall apart.

You want to know what I did to change this set of failures? Wow! That's a really good question. There, again, I failed at that. The fact is that I was trying hard to "fix" the wrong things in my life. It really didn't matter to anyone that I was a bisexual man. What mattered was that I lived a life that respected others and the laws of society, starting with my local community of Huntington Beach, California. The problem which really needed "fixing" was that I didn't know this. That I had no understanding about how to live in a society, since I had never done so before. Not as a child, let alone as a fully grown adult.

The problems that I faced were created by my own "need" to work on skills that I ended up overworking. Like I'd said before, I was like a car stuck in some deep snow and just spinning my wheels without moving closer to the solution or destination. I worked at skills that I both didn't need and ended up overworking them; I ended up out of the snow, yet deeper in the malarkey!

CHAPTER EIGHTEEN

Night Life

1979 was not a good year for Damien on account that he would be given the boot from Sam and Nick's home, due to a combination of problems.

The previous summer, Sam was planning to attend a conference of the American Psychiatric Association, and he invited Damien to join him as a guest. Although the conference didn't interest the young man, for some reason Damien agreed to go—felt compelled to go. He wasn't going to attend college in any related areas, but was still rather interested in the field of study.

I had misread the obvious hints that Sam was attracted to me, even in love with me. Really? Why? Nick was fairly handsome and closer to Sam's own age. Nick was also trouble free. They were both mature men who had romantic feelings—strong feelings—for the other, and knew it. So why me? I still don't know for sure, however, I think that the reason might be that he liked the challenge of loving someone that has a need for the sort of healing which only love can heal. Well, there's the idea that Sam liked to serve God and he found that the best service came when he helps the one he loves.

So why not I?

Up until this moment in their living arrangement, their patient-doctor relationship, Damien's understanding of Samuel Reily was as a caregiver. They were strictly platonic, in a friendship of pure brotherhood.

Samuel had an interest in both Damien and Damien's disorders—had even written an article about this anonymous child with high-functioning autism, depression, and addiction to sex as a coping mechanism for parental abandonment.

On the day they boarded their flight to this conference, Damien asked Samuel what the doctor saw in him that wasn't obvious to the rest of the world.

"What I love about you, Damien, is what I see in your heart, in your soul. It's a good one."

During their second night in a hotel room together, Damien took Sam's romantic overtures to the next level, engaging in an ill-advised sexual experience. Samuel awoke the following morning stating that what they'd done was a mistake. Damien didn't take this rejection well, and the tension which followed continued to build even after they'd returned home to Nick.

Then, not long afterwards, a day came when Nick's late mother's wedding ring—apparently she'd been divorced several years prior to passing away—went missing. Nick was in a panic, searching their home from attic to basement looking for the missing ring. Almost immediately, Nick began accusing Damien for its theft. Sam did all that he could to help calm Nick down, as well as to defend Damien against any such blame. This only triggered a long-awaited arugment:

"Sure, I knew you'd take _his_ side!" Nick accused.

"What's that supposed to mean?" Samuel approached his lover.

"You're always so quick to defend you little boy-toy!"

"You're wrong, "Dr. Reily insisted. "Damien wouldn't—"

"Wouldn't what," Nick interrupted, "wouldn't steal my mother's ring or wouldn't be your boy-toy. Pick one, 'cause it sure as hell ain't both!"

"He didn't take the ring," Sam insisted. However, as all three of them noted, Samuel wasn't willing to say anything about the second accusation.

"I want him out of here," Nick said to Sam, then turned to reiterate directly at Damien as if the boy were deaf, "Out . . . of . . . here!"

"Don't talk to him like that!" Sam once again defended.'

"I'm sorry, I didn't mean to insult your free-loading, retarded, do-nothing kleptomaniac! Oh! Did I forget to include home wrecker? Guinea pig?"

Nick continued to furiously rant as he left the room, "I want him out!"

B-b-but, Damien finally spoke out, *I didn't take it! I'm not any of those other things he said—*

"Nick!" *Sam yelled while walking after the other man,* "Nick come back here..."

Nevertheless, Damien was moved out of their home that very night.

This was very scary, because I had no idea how to live as a citizen of the streets. Sam couldn't convince Nick that he was wrong about my having anything to do with the missing ring. There were previous times when small amounts of money or other items disappeared, and I was blamed... sometimes rightly so, other times not. But now, with my prior acts as evidence enough, I was homeless. Coincidently, Nick found the long-lost ring several months later within his closet.

On my last night in their house, I asked Sam for a little cash to tide me over for a little while. Sam was indeed kind. He gave me a couple hundred dollars and gave me a ride to West Los Angeles, as well as putting me up on a motel on Santa Monica Boulevard. Again, I owed him a debt of gratitude for all of the help he was generous enough to freely provide. If you wondering why he had to give me a ride, well, I guess I forgot to mention that I'd smashed the used car they'd help me purchase not long after purchasing it. I seemed to have ruined everything that Samuel or Nick provided me with.

In the days which followed, I was in temporary good shape. All I needed was to hunt smartly for a job that'll cover the weekly rent of a room and, of course, my food... although I could survive on very little. Sam had told me that he might be able to send me some cash to hold me over at the end of the month, that is, until I could get a job on my own.

One morning while I checked out my immediate surroundings, not two blocks from my motel I learned that not only do women prostitute themselves for money, but so did young men, and—sadly—as did very young kids. In fact, on my way to turning in a job application at a diner, a "john" as I later heard them called, asked me if I was working. "I sure hope to be soon," I replied, showing him the application. The man laughed really, really hard, and it took some hours until I finally figured out what was so funny.

Damien spent a couple of hours each days watching the streets and learning who was doing what... and how. Not knowing the streets was, at first, his handicap, but he grew out of it. The riddle was learning the terminology used between prostitutes and johns—or 'tricks' as some called them. The hookers, themselves, had a network of communication of their own, as well as rules which were meant to be followed, even if you didn't know them.

When the afternoon arrived, Damien continued onward to deliver yet another application at the famous "The Golden Cup" coffee shop on Hollywood and Vine. It was a bit on the dirty side back then, but the food was cool, especially for the money. Keep in mind, this was 1979 and the area hadn't yet turned into the tourist trap that it is today.

The more I considered it, prostitution wasn't that bad of an occupation. I recognized that I had one highly-experienced and marketable skill, which was bisexual sex. I knew how to please either gender; however, johns are almost never female unless married to someone interested in threesomes. How bad could that be? I would have sex and get paid for it, maybe even sharpen my existing skills.

The first lesson that I had to learn was the need to operate as far under the radar as was possible. This would be fairly easy for me, since I'd been doing precisely that from when I was ten-years-young. I bought a pair of denim jeans two sizes two small and a "tank top" muscle shirt, even though I had little physique to speak of. The—the no muscles part—would turn out to be an advantage because I looked even younger and vulnerable by being a scrawny blond.

Within minutes of me walking out of my motel room, all of the other prostitutes knew what I was up to. Even the undercover police in the area would know. It was colder than all get out that night, and here I was in a tank top and skin-tight jeans at a notorious street corner, Salem and Vine. It took only a few minutes until I was sitting nervously in a passenger seat of a complete stranger's car.

For the next several days, after lunch, Damien would venture out to what he'd soon nickname as "his office," that same street corner. His uniform was now the exact opposite of anything he would've been allowed to wear at Carl's Jr., and he hand-washed these clothes each night. Occasionally, he was forced to buy new muscle shirts as these were frequently torn and ripped by overanxious customers, if not lost completely.

There I was, an almost twenty-two-year-old, college-educated, somewhat handsome and gay white guy, and the nearest thing I had as a job, as an office, was the street corner of Salem and Vine, or—at times—other such streets. I sold my only recognizable talents, which for me was limited to oral and anal sex, meaning it wasn't "kinky" sex... however, if it would increase my income, I was willing to learn more about any sexual acts. Yet, I wasn't risky, in fact, some johns called me "picky" about what I willing to do and with whom.

Then came the realities of prostitution: What I'd once presumed as an "easy" line of work was anything but! First, there was the concern about the law ever catching on or doing an undercover cop sting as a john looking for prostitution. Second, although there wasn't yet the fear of AIDS and HIV—it existed but didn't even have an official virus name yet—there was the concern about catching any of the dozens of other STDs; plus, the fact that they were even more contagious when anal sex was involved. The most common were Chlamydia and Gonorrhea. Both would let you know when you had them by giving you a horrible burning sensation every time you urinated, sometimes a disgusting or bloody discharge would leave your body part. Very gross!

The third, and scariest of all, was death. Johns were known to be over-aggressive with their whores, beat them whenever it pleased them, or straight up murder a prostitute simply for fun or whatever personal reasons. Hookers died in Los Angeles at an alarming rate in the early 1980's, which it would soon be. No, I was trying to keep myself safe; however, you can't always judge a book by it cover, sometimes the most quiet and passive johns turned out to be the most violently explosive.

Despite the fact that most adult theatres and other clubs, such as "The Cave" or "Pussy Cat" were heterosexual in clientele, there were always plenty of men who—in dark corners of the place—would gladly receive oral sex from gals or guys. Nevertheless, there were people who gladly paid for services regardless of the gender or age of those providing the services.

Damien might not have had what you'd call "regular" job skills, but this bleak underworld lifestyle paid for his rent and other needs. Thankfully, unlike most hookers, Damien wasn't addicted to any illicit street drugs. In the late 1970's, marijuana and cocaine were still the drugs of choice. Neither ecstasy nor crystal meth had been discovered yet, and likewise crack hadn't yet hit the market. No, less-addictive hallucinogens like LSD were still king.

Although I needed to make myself self-sustaining, able to afford all of my expenses, prostituting myself really got in the way of my going to college classes. Not to get into the details, but I felt exhausted all of the time. It also didn't help that I wasn't taking my antidepressants anymore—couldn't afford them without insurance—and was falling deeper into an underground and hidden society of the homeless...the world of street urchins.

Street urchins, or homeless and/or runaway kids, often find themselves living in the alleys and under freeway onramps, forced into the lifestyle of the underworld—if one can call it living. These children are society's responsibility and mankind's future! They deserve secure, safe, and healthy housing, not to be forgotten and ignored. Sure, there are a few children who survive the streets and grow up to become healthy members of their community, but more often than not, the majority of California's lost children—and pretty much every other state's—remain hopelessly lost!

I was a witness to the creative ways these urchins cared for themselves and, occasionally, for each other. Living on the streets of "Lost Angels"—as we recognized the entire L.A. County—caused me to rethink my perception of homelessness, especially my fellow urchins. These little ones are our hopes for the future, yet they were living like raccoons and badgers...and respected by adults as such: vermin. Sponging off of city and state resources which could be spent on personally more viable things like pothole repairs. Yes, I witnessed and felt the effects of what these lessons taught our homeless: that you're less important than the street you're living on, less important than the pavement.

Moreover, the conditions of living on the streets are unnatural and hurtful as a whole. This meant that by my being homeless—although I still had a weekly-rented roof over my head, so not completely homeless—was damaging to my living soul. This wasn't what I was born for, this wasn't what any of these homeless kids were born for. God's purpose for my life most definitely never included prostitution and giving up on my goals.

God's purpose for all of these homeless kids these street urchins, and even the grown-up ones living underneath freeways or in gutters, was never meant to be like <u>this</u>!

I had been told by my original and first friend Steve—or maybe it was my Aunt Cha-cha—that we all have gifts. A hidden gift which we were born with, and what a shame it would be to go through life without ever realizing it! Without putting that gift or gifts to use. I knew for that my gift to the world wasn't as its punching bag or gay sex-toy... that I still had a much more important talent to offer! I just needed to discover it.

Again time was passing Damien "like a warm, summer breeze." The 1980's had arrived, and although he was still prostituting himself for rent money, things were changing that he hadn't known about.

Without any prior warning, Samuel decided to pay me a visit at the motel one morning. I had been at the window, cooking my breakfast on a portable, electric grill, when I saw a canary-yellow Corvette sports car pass right by, reverse, then pull into the parking space in front of my motel room's door. The drive looked familiar, although the bright-colored car did not—Sam had been last driving a fairly new Pontiac Grand Prix when I'd moved out.

I rushed to the door and poked my head out, yelling his name. The driver seemed unexpected to see me, and after getting out I saw it was Dr. Reily sure enough. It actually took him a few seconds to recognize who I was, even though I don't believe I changed that much, other than my hair length and tired-looking eyes.

"Get over here, kid!" Sam suddenly called out and the two of them tightly embraced and lovingly. "This is a surprise!"

Surprise? Damien pulled away, not believing that the doctor was at the motel to see him.

Don't get me wrong, Damien. I <u>was</u> looking for you, but didn't expect you to still be living <u>here</u>."

B-but you were the one who put me here.

"Yeah, but that was months ago.... I never thought you'd stay put. Not forever anyway," the doctor smiled warmly, then followed his former housekeeper inside the messiest, disarrayed motel room he'd even seen. "Hmm, no maid service?"

Not for us 'weeklies.' We get clean sheet and towels twice a week. Damien cleared off a chair and offered Samuel a seat, although the doctor—wearing a rather nice suit—preferred to stand. *"How are you doing, Sam?"*

"Not bad, thank you. And you?" he needlessly asked. Looking around the distressed room, the piles of unwashed laundry, and—more importantly—the unshaven whiskers on Damien's neck, answered the doctor's own question.

I've got to tell you, Sam, that I've seen better times. These past few months have opened my eyes.

Dr. Reily, always the psychiatrist, asked Damien to explain himself.

Well, where to start? I wasn't in college for very long, what was it? Some six months ago I moved out?

"Something like that. You mean you gave up your classes after moving?"

Had to. I couldn't find a real job, I applied everywhere. I couldn't afford to keep going <u>and</u> pay my rent.

"I see," Samuel was quietly taking inventory of the motel room. There were empty food containers, a plastic bag full of aluminum cans, and other items which looked salvaged from a dumpster. "You've been recycling for cash?"

Oh, what? No, those are Tony's, Damien half-explained.

"Who's Tony?"

Him and Carl stay here some nights when it's real cold and they have no luck at the office. Just don't tell the manager, we're not supposed to have guests spend the night over. I don't want to get evicted again, Damien instantly regretted this last part, since the last person to evict him was standing there in front of him. *I've been trying to help out the other homeless kids around here.*

"I see," the doctor automatically commented out of habit.

I don't think you do 'see.' The first thing that one notices is the filth that one has to live in. That is trumped only by the cold nights of winter. Neither Tony nor Carl had anything to cover up with, and I learned in a hurry that many, if not most, of the people on the streets have nothing to keep warm with, except the trash. There is thrown out newspaper and other items that help to keep out some of the cold.

Then there's another need, no food. Of course, the trash will provide some 'food'—if it can be called that—and that's not the worse part. No, It was seeing all the young kids that I've seen... who also live—if you want to call it living—on the streets. Most of the young, including young adults like me, end up selling their wares. For the most part it's either drugs or their sexual experiences, but they need to survive somehow.

"Yeah," the doctor finally got a word in, "it is horrible out there. So, what can you do to get yourself off these streets?"

I've been doing it. I'm one of the lucky ones; I have a room, a bed, and—best of all—a door I can lock when I'm sleeping. It's not the best or cleanest of places, but I'm still better than most.

Dr. Reily shook his head, "That's not what I meant. Ever since I first met you at Metro, you had such great potential and even came up with some good expectations and ambitions towards what you wanted to do: to heal hurt souls. But, Damien, us care-givers need to heal ourselves before we heal others."

What are you saying? Damien asked. He was hoping more than anything that Sam would give him another chance to live together with him. Although he really did feel so very badly for the kids on the street, at the same time he knew that moving in with Sam would put an end to his prostitution and personal homelessness.

"I'm saying... well, let's go have lunch," he motions towards his car parked just outside the window. "How does I.H.O.P. sound?"

CHAPTER NINETEEN

Striking Home

*T*he last time I ate at an International House of Pancakes was back when I was thirteen and hoping to be going to an amusement park full of exciting and wild rides... now I was eating at one again and hoping to get off of rollercoasters! Get out of this amusement park of homelessness and prostitution. Off of my self-created Ferris wheel of life. Yet, walking into that restaurant, I still had no idea if Samuel was to be my hero... or if I was to be his.

For the next half hour, Sam and Damien talked about both of their predicaments. Samuel earnestly wanted to know how Damien was fairing as both homeless and a male hooker—although he never once used the term 'hooker' nor anything else derogatory. Damien, at length, told Sam that although he really did not like the homeless aspect of his life, being a male prostitute was—in an odd way—sort of cool, so long as the john was clean and could afford the cash for the services. This admission disturbed Samuel, however—knowing Damien's background with sex as a defense mechanism—he couldn't have not expected the younger man to find a certain level of fascination with getting paid for something he used to do for free.

Samuel, on the other hand, talked about Nick and his lover's arrogant attitudes of late. The two of them had been growing more insolent in their arguments since Damien moved out—although he wasn't to blame for any of this—and had fallen in-and-out of love on several occasions. After their latest opposition over financial expenses—namely the brand-new Corvette—Sam and Nick broke up. They were still living under the same roof, but not for much longer.

He informed me that he'd broken up with Nick and that he was wondering whether or not he should invite me back in. To be his new housemate or not. He wouldn't be able to afford the lease alone, so I would need to contribute. And, of course, I would have to give up prostituting all together, even my regular men who I thought were young and very cute.

After his lease was up, there'd be the need to find something smaller that we'd could more feasibly afford on just one paycheck, because he really wanted me back in college. As we sat there, he was planning it all out in his head and everything seemed so perfectly logical. Unfortunately, Sam forgot one important thing and that was that I was part of his mathematical equation. Me, the most unsolvable of variables in any math problem.

With all said and ate, Sam paid for their lunch and from there walked a little ways uphill, leaving the sports car behind in the parking lot. Samuel stopped right in front of a nice looking apartment complex with underground parking and completely enclosed fencing. When Sam buzzed the manager's office and no one answered, he decided to take a look with Damien anyway. This was a little confusing to Damien since Sam had just minutes ago invited him to move back into the Huntington Beach house.

Sam pulled out an apartment key and invited me to come in and see it together. I replied, "So, that's why we're here? To look at apartments?" I had little understanding of how he suddenly had a key to the lobby. We took the elevator to the third floor, then Sam told me an apartment number and handed me the key, saying, "Here you go Damien. Let's see if it's right for us." Sam was full of surprises that morning.

As things would have it, Dr. Reily not only had the key to this apartment, but the place wasn't an empty one. Sam already had moved himself in. There were recognizable pieces of furniture and photographs everywhere. In fact, it was apparent that the doctor had been living there alone for one or two nights. Suddenly, everything made sense to Damien: The selection of the I.H.O.P. restaurant a block away, the sudden desire to walk to this specific apartment complex, and the ruse of going apartment hunting; it was all preplanned.

How did . . . wait? This is your stuff? Your apartment?

"No, our apartment. There's a bunch of your stuff that you left at the Huntington—"

Th-th-thank you! Damien said, stumbling over his own words. He didn't and couldn't express his gratitude any better than this. He was so incredibly happy. *"Wh-what, um, what do we-we have to do, to finish moving in?*

"Relax, Damien. I already moved everything that would fit in yesterday, and paid a couple of guys to unpack the kitchen. We still, of course, will need to check you out of the motel and get your stuff there."

I don't care to see any of that stuff ever again," Damien admitted of his belongings at the motel. This apartment represented a clean, blank slate for his life. A new start. Why bring anything from his past into this future?

This was indeed a huge, a new page in both of their lives.

Um, Damien felt very tired and wanted to pinch himself to be sure he wasn't dreaming all of this. He'd dreamt events like *this* before, where Sam would rescue him from that dismal motel room. This thought suddenly triggered a concern, *B-but what about Tony and Carl?*

"Who? Oh! Your friends staying with you at the motel?"

If I'm not there, they'll be back on the street.

"Damien, I'm not a miracle worker. I'm sorry, but..."

No, I don't mean that they'd live with us. Or that you'd hafta get them an apartment, too. But I have a few dollars, maybe we can give them two weeks rent? I'll even give them my electric grill; I know Carl would like that.

"Your heart never ceases to amaze me, Damien."

The summer of 1981 was, as far as Damien could recall, actually a good one; except, as it concerned their apartment, was the fact that he didn't always obey Sam's wishes. On the positive side, Damien didn't get the two of them evicted; on the chaos side was that Damien invited over a lot of visitors. Not that the number of guests meant that much, but that the other residents of the complex felt unsafe due to the fact that these were young men, all male prostitutes Damien had befriended, and residents had run-ins with 'their kind" in the past.\

Another problem was that when Samuel first moved in, the question of whether or not he'd be able to locate Damien was still up in the air. For all the doctor knew at that time, Damien had moved on with his life and maybe even was in a stable relationship with someone else. Because of this conjecture, only Sam's name was initially placed on the apartment's lease. Once it was discovered that Damien would in fact be moving in, the manager had her qualms about adding an unemployed youngster who wasn't related to the doctor on the lease. And now, with a fistful of complaints, the manager's misgivings were justified.

"I'm really sorry, Doctor Reily," she reported while standing at their open door, "but I've received several grievances about your roommate's behavior."

"He is more than just a roommate. I thought I made the relationship quite clear when we added him to my lease."

"True, but what was also made clear when we added him, was that all new tenants are subjected to a probation period. Things are clearly not working out. I have too many other tenants to be concerned about. Either he'll have to move out, or you'll both be—"

"Fine! Then we'll <u>both</u> move out." Samuel countered.

The following weekend, Damien did all that he could do in getting them packed and ready to move into their new place on Gower Street in Hollywood. Unpacking was for them more tedious than packing was. The house was an even smaller place than the apartment was—which was half the size of Samuel's previous Huntington Beach address—and also only one-bedroom. Yet, they somehow made all of the furniture fit inside this latest of rentals.

I was twenty-three in the summer of 1981, and because of me we moved to our first house together. I was living in Hollywood; however, had no intentions nor qualifications of becoming a movie star. What I did have was some meat on my bones which I never really had before—Sam called them "love handles" and frequently used them as such—as well, my having a man who not only cared so deeply for me but foolishly trusted me in ways that he probably never should have.

For example, that summer I used Sam's 1974 Porsche 914 to take care of a little shopping chore. A quick little car for a quick little errand. And, sure enough, I had an accident causing the expensive sport car's hood to buckle. Oh hell! I did it now. Between the Porsche and the Corvette, the former was one of Samuel's favorite toys of all time.

Understandably, he had the right to be pissed, but he surprisingly forgave me. Unlike me—and this could be another one of those Asperger's traits—Sam didn't have that much attachment to objects, only to people. He was more concerned with my welfare and well-being than the cost of repairing his favorite car. He was just built that way.

Samuel and Damien lived at the Gower address for roughly a year. During their last two months, Samuel's younger sister, Barbara-Anne, offered to help with some house-hunting, as Sam was much too busy helping patients. She looked for a house that Sam could afford to buy—no more leasing—and one that suited his style and desires. It took a little time, but it was well worth the wait. Barbara-Anne really came through for her big brother; the place she located was back in Huntington Beach not far from the one he'd shared with Nick.

Before long we moved into Sam's new house. Technically, it was "ours" but he was paying for everything. Once again, I was living how my Grandpa considered me as: a free-loader. Actually, he wasn't the only one, there was my step-dad and also Nick who all believed me to be self-indulging others' hospitality. And, unfortunately, I couldn't really prove any of them wrong. Not then, and not now.

On the day after moving in, Samuel sat down in a recliner beside Damien and asked, "You know, Damien, how would you like a real job?"

Damien hadn't worked anywhere since quitting from Carl's Jr. almost six years ago—unless you'd like to consider helping Samuel out at his office or waiting at street corners as <u>working</u>—and almost forgot what a paycheck looked like.

Why do you ask? Sure! I'd love a real job.

"Well, in a little bit I'm going to need a new assistant."

Damien became confused. *What does an assistant do that's, well, different from what Barbara-Anne does?* Samuel's sister took over the role of office manager after Damien moved out and had since been vital to its operation.

"Nothing, she's returning to school and it would be useful to have you take care of some of her errands. How's that sound?

Cool, Sam. I'm looking forward to doing something other than housework and textbooks all day. You won't mind me working on some of my school work in the office?

"As long as you think you can concentrate on both at the same time. You sometimes forgot to answer the phone when it was ringing last time you were working for me."

It wasn't that I forgot, Damien insisted, *"it's I thought it was your private line that was ringing, and when I realized it wasn't, they'd already hung up or you answered it yourself.*

"Well, now that you're older and more experienced, we'll see if you can handle it."

Damien rather liked working for Sam. Ever since being admitted to Metro, Damien had become interested in psychiatry, both as a subject and as a career. His goals of becoming a mental-health specialist fell apart years back when his development of dyslexia and grades were below acceptable levels. However, just his working around patients in an office setting vicariously gave him the belief he needed that through assisting the doctor, he was likewise assisting the patients.

I really wanted to earn a degree in these areas, because I wanted to help people in the same way Sam did for me. I also wanted to be responsible for the things that I did. Life as an adult was a little scary and confusing at times. When I'd first left Metro, I was better than I was when I'd entered there, that's for certain. However, I was still unprepared to live on my own, as both my motel room and chosen profession proved. I wanted to learn how to do it correctly if/when there would be a next time.

Don't get me wrong. I didn't see the two of us, Samuel and I splitting up anytime soon. However, I'd been kicked out and evicted from so many homes and other living arrangements since the age of ten, that I felt the need to prepare myself for the next lightning strike!

For Damien, it was rather stressful moving into Sam's new house in

Huntington Beach; however, it was all worth the strain on his nerves. Both of them were very glad that the house was fully ready to be moved into. This was particularly good because neither of them wanted another delay. Their lives were to start completely over again in many ways than just having a new place.

With all of the additional space available after moving in everything from the Gower house, Sam had a perfect place to setup a one-hundred-gallon salt-water fish tank. The collection of colorful coral and exotic, tropical sea life made them both very happy.

You should have seen him on the morning after we moved in: he was so pleased to no end! For the first time, he was able to make changes to things like the carpeting and light fixtures, all without first contacting the landlord. That fact along made his house truly his. This was also <u>my</u> house, at least as he was concerned, which I was grateful for but—in all honesty—I never looked past who <u>really</u> owned it.

CHAPTER TWENTY

Rescue and Search

About four months had passed since their return to Huntington Beach, when Damien came across a young man freshly out of high school and in trouble. His name was Robert Jackson, or "Bob" as he preferred to be called, and he was equally unprepared to live on his own as Damien was. Bob still lived with his parents down the street from Damien, and almost instantly Damien was feeling the young man's need simply by seeing him out in front of their house.

I call it dysfunctional magnetism: that someone raised in a dysfunctional childhood and family can identify and even attract somebody else from a dysfunctional family. I didn't actually know of his troubles until we talked, then witnessed him in a yelling match with his dad. I guess that it was the sincerity in my voice that he heard, that opened the door which invited him to briefly share his troubles with me.

Bob was living with his parents for the time being; however, at any moment he knew his days there were numbered. His father was much like Damien's own step-father: both abusive and husband. So, instead, Bob was actively looking for a job which would pay for a studio apartment's rent and other household expenses.

After their first brief encounter, Bob later accepted Damien's offer to join him for lunch at Damien's and Sam's house. Over lunch, both young men described their situations to each other; albeit, Damien's story took immensely longer to tell in comparison. Not long afterwards, Dr. Reily returned home from work at Metro. Damien described Bob's disintegrating family plight and simply asked Sam:

What do you think I could do to help?

Actually, Sam didn't know. "I think that it is possible that I could talk to him personally… and then you'll have a better idea of what can be done, if anything."

What do you mean by 'if anything'? Damien asked.

"Damien, not everyone wants to be helped. Not everyone's problem has to become your problem to fix. Challenges are a part of life, they are meant to make us stronger. If you solve Bob's problem for him, then who'll become the stronger? Bob or you?"

Okay, I get it. But can you please talk to him?

"Let me think about it," Samuel responded, which—for him—usually resulted in a 'yes'."

Sure, Damien nodded, *I don't think that it's an emergency, but I… well, never mind. I wouldn't be bringing it up if my gut didn't tell me that it could be urgent.*

"Always listen to your gut, Damien. That's where you soul resides. And it's through your soul that God is trying to get your attention."

With that, Samuel took the rest of the night to think about what Damien had suggested of young Bob's troubles. The next morning, the doctor had told Damien to invite bob over to the house for dinner the next time Damien saw the boy. It wasn't until a couple of days later, but invite Bob he did.

I was glad that I had the opportunity to be of some potential help potentially—to young Bob. I thought I had a lot of advice that would benefit him; not that he was to become homeless, but I knew that he felt <u>hopeless</u>. I'd read somewhere, some book, that George Bernard Shaw once said:

"He who had never hoped can never despair."

I took this to mean that I could ease his despair and return hope to his life. I could provide him all of the assistance that never came for me during my own troubles.

Driving down to the house, on his way back from picking up

groceries for their dinner together with Bob, Damien was indeed glad to see the boy walking down the street towards the house. Passing Bob, Damien yelled out and waved his hand, almost losing control of Sam's very yellow Corvette. While unloading the trunk of groceries, Bob arrived to their driveway asking if he could be of any help with the bags.

Being our guest, I didn't think it was good manners to accept his offer to help carry things. I told him that it was a nice gesture, but I could manage. I believe I only dropped one of the many bags before reaching the front door, but I might've miscounted.

"God," Bob exclaimed while following Damien inside the foyer, "your house is real big next to my dad's." Bob, of course, meant this as a compliment; however Damien has always had trouble accepting compliments—the few he'd ever received thus far.

That might be true, but we don't live on Skylark. Those houses are two-bedrooms and much larger in comparison. Better view, too.

"If you say so," Bob stated while continuing to look over the expansive front room and dining room. "So, what kind of work do you do, to afford all of this?"

Actually I go to Golden West College. I want to go on and become a physician's technician, or at least, earn some sort of degree in whatever program that'll allow me to get a job in the medical field. You know, a doctor's office? When I'm not in school, I help out Doctor Samuel—err, I mean, Sam—around his office.

"Yeah, that's cool . . . ."

Just as Bob's last word faded away, Sam came into the living room and introduced himself. The conversation shifted from there to the kitchen, since Damien was still holding those grocery bags. For dinner, Damien whipped together a fresh tomato and basil soup, a cheese-stuffed chicken breast similar to chicken cordon bleu yet without the ham, grilled cheese toast, cottage cheese, and a fruity dessert. Damien was well please to see that Bob was every bit the eater, because Damien would've hated to have fixed a meal Bob wouldn't like as their first.

After dinner, Damien excused himself to clear the table and give Sam all of the privacy he needed with his new patient. Damien respected the confidentiality that came with helping people, between doctor and client. Only when the dishes were finished and the conversation in the next room died down, did he venture back into the dining room.

"It's okay, Damien, C'mon in," Sam reassured. "Your friend, Bob, here is in much better shape than the two of us put together were at his age."

Really? Damien was surprised by this. *Better shape than you were at his age he asked Samuel directly.*

"You'd be surprised about my college years," Sam simply smiled. Then, after clearing his throat, added, "How do you feel about Bob moving in with us for a few weeks?"

Once again, Damien was shocked. *Really? You're gonna let him move in?*

"Until he gets his feet under him financially, yes." He turned to Bob, "Give or take a few weeks."

I can tell you now, in hindsight, that it wasn't only for "a few" nor was it only "weeks." Bob ended up living with us for nearly five years! But, naturally, none of us foresaw this length . . . nor did any of us predict the amount of problems that this would cause. Excuse me, that I've caused to Sam by getting him and our house involved in the first place.

The biggest problem was that Bob was a straight guy living in the house of two gay men. More precisely, Bob was a vivacious and promiscuous heterosexual, whereas Samuel preferred the sanctuary of his home—a place completely absent of females... until now. It's not that he resented women for being women, just that he'd prefer to never hear one within the throes of lovemaking or orgasm! The grunting and moaning of a female nearing climax was revolting to him. Nauseating!

On more than three occasions, he'd addressed Bob about his personal abhorrence of hearing a woman having sex through the walls of his own house. Bob was prohibited, forbidden, under penalty of eviction, if he ever brought another "hook-up" home with him. Unfortunately, the combinations of lust, youth, intoxication, and forgetfulness in the form of time would result in yet another pretty coed crawling in and out of Bob's bedroom window.

Unfortunately, for events yet described to you, Damien would miss a handful of these confrontations between the disgusted Dr. Reily and his lustful house guest.

Time once again slipped by Damien and he was about to celebrate his next birthday, his twenty-fourth. He wanted to do something extra special to celebrate his surviving a quarter of a century. For all intents-and-purposes, he felt like it was simply amazing that he'd survived long enough to become a teenager—let alone an adult—considering the number of times he was "spanked" by his drunken step-father.

I admit now that I got some bad advice from Bob. I once asked him how he'd go about celebrating his next "big" birthday, which would be his twenty-first. He stated he'd party hard and get higher than a kite. Up until that time in my life, I had smoked weed (marijuana) plenty of times and even "dropped" acid (LSD) more than twice. Neither drug was addictive to me; I could go several months without desiring another "hit" or trip to La-la land.

It was the fourth of December and based on Bob's advice I went to pay a notorious neighbor down the street a visit. It was really strange for me to do this, considering the fact that the only time prior to this visit that I had ever visited "Mark" was when he'd moved into the neighborhood last spring. On that day, I simply visited him and his wife in their driveway and welcomed them to the block by helping to carry two or three boxes off of the moving van. I didn't have any rapport with him at all!

Seeing Damien walking up to his porch Mark—who was in the garage—greeted, "Hi. Lookin' for someone?"

You're Mark, right? Damien changed directions, heading towards the grease-and-oil smeared stranger within the wide-open two-car garage.

"Not if you're the law, I'm not." After a quick snicker he nodded. "Yeah, I'm Mark."

I'm Damien. I live just over there, he said, pointing out their house with a forefinger.

"Ah, yeah! You helped us unload the truck when we moved in." Mark quickly cleaned his right hand on a rag dirtier than his hand was, then offering it for shaking. "How are you doing, Damien?"

Not bad, thank you. And you?

"Good. I'm just closing up here," he motioned to the exposed engine of his Chevy pickup and the discarded motor oil cans. You want a beer?"

"*Yeah, actually, I'd love one. Thank you.*"

A few minutes later, Mark finished his oil-change project, slammed the hood shut on his truck, and invited Damien to follow him inside, which he both gladly and foolishly did. Mark was a professional mechanic and occasionally brought some work home with him, he explained. But this was only one of his occupations; the other was the distribution of narcotics. Both were quite lucrative, although the latter of these made higher profits.

He pulled out a bar stool and offered it to me. We sat across from each other at a glass-topped kitchen counter. After several minutes of polite conversation, mostly small talk about where and what I did in school, Mark took the discussion to a whole other level. Pulling open a drawer, he asked me if I'd ever done cocaine.

Coke? Damien double-checked his hearing. *No. Why do you ask?*

Guzzling the last of his beer, he raised a small brown bottle, "Wanna?"

Yeah, I guess so. What kinda high is it? What's it do?

Uncorking the little vial, he explained, "Trust me, Damien. This shit's the bomb! It'll make you so high that you'll... touch the stars."

Damien was about to say something like: I don't want to go that high, I'm afraid of heights; but Mark continued to explain, "You see, this kind of cocaine you don't snort. I changed it by getting rid of the impurities making it smokable. Although there's some loss of weight, it's far better than the gram I started off with. I'm guessing you've smoked weed?"

Damien simply nodded, watching as Mark pulled a glass pipe of a sort that he'd never seen before out of that drawer. It was made totally of glass and there were two stems and an apple-sized bowl which held water. This was where the heated gas was cooled before inhaled, for a more comfortable smoke. It was a rather pretty pipe and Damien did get used to it, quickly.

Putting the pipe down, he exclaimed, *Damn it, Mark! You were right, it's a blast. It's the shit!*

"Want another hit?" Mark needlessly asked.

You know I do!

"Cool. Then we'll wait until my wife calls."

That's cool, Mark. Damien accepted the filled pipe and lighter, *Thanks.*

The rest of that day was mostly a blur…

There was one real problem with the drug, and that was the fact that getting high the first time was the best and all that… however, trying to get as high as that first time was a constant search. Chasing that high was expensive to say the least: both in money and emotions.

My expectations that afternoon was that we'd smoke another bowlful and I'd go about my business at home, just as I would if we'd been doing weed instead. Boy, I never could've been more wrong. Clearly, it was Mark's expectation that I would spend more time with him and his wife, who turned out to be rather addicted to this stuff. This, of course, was good and bad for Mark the drug-dealer; he could keep her well loaded directly from his supplier, but it cut into his profits. That's wy he needed new customers, like me.

After that second hit, I didn't worry much about going home to make dinner. Coincidentally, I had already prepared both dinner and dessert; they would merely need to be heated. Instead, I fell head over heels for this drug—which is a phrase, in itself, which doesn't make much sense since my head in normally above my heels on any given day. Very little of this day made any sense, now that I think of it.

When Mark's wife got home, she didn't only look forward to getting loaded but in getting screwed. We engaged in a drug-enhanced <u>menage-a-trois</u> of wild exhibition in which I'm not at liberty to discuss—this isn't that type of book. After finishing the last of the "freebase"—as it's called—I dragged myself home at around nine and, if coming home late with the scent and "walk of shame" all over wasn't bad enough, I was still higher than the Empire State Building.

After locking the front door behind me, I retired to the back room where Sam and Bob were watching a little TV. It was only at that moment, seeing the familiar prime-time show being shown, that I'd realized that it was late … and, worse of all, that I hadn't called to say I'd be late.

The first thing that Sam asked when Damien entered the room was, "Where've you been all night?"

I was across the street, with Mark and Dianne, having dinner.

"Mark? Mark who?" he asked while standing up, stepping closer.

Our... um, our neighbors.

"So, were you going to tell me? Or—," Sam's facial expression suddenly changed, "or should I take a guess?"

Wha—what are you talking about?

"I can smell the sweat and perfume from here. You're obviously high on something, either coke or phencyclidine. Which one?" The latter drug mentioned also goes by the street name of angel's dust. It was used primarily by veterinarians as an animal anesthetic until college kids figured out that they could get high on it... that is, if it didn't outright kill them.

How, um, did you know?

"I'm a doctor, remember? Also, I am your friend."

Oh, Damien sighed, then finally answered, *"Mark called it freebasing cocaine. He'd washed the coke in ether and we smoked it.*

"Uh huh. And how often has <u>this</u> been going on?"

I... I'd just met Mark, today.

"And his wife?" Sam asked, to which Damien only silently nodded. Sam rarely got upset or mad with Damien and, even with this confession, the doctor never once raised his voice.

We talked, Sam and I, for a while about drugs and my history with them. I promised Samuel that I wasn't an addict—saying that one phrase that nearly every drug addict says at some point in their life: "That I have it under control." That I could quit at any time.

Before retiring for the night, Sam turned to Damien and warned, "You better not get hooked. Promise?"

I promise. I won't get addicted, I'll quit first before that'll happen.

With that said, Damien went to the kitchen to make sure that everything was put away. Instead, he found a messy sink, stove, and plates of food which had been left out. He spent a little time cleaning up and even had a piece of cheesecake he'd made the day before, prior to going to be in his separate bedroom. Damien was still much too "high" to find any sleep, and ended up watching hours of late-night television, unceasingly flipping through channels in search of shows that weren't as dismal as he felt.

CHAPTER TWENTY-ONE

Tackling Monsters

Regardless of Damien's promise to Sam, he grew more addicted to cocaine thn he possibly could have imagined or controlled. He likewise found himself in debt "up to my eyes" with Mark, and borrowed money to get his debts paid. The drug was also impairing his abilities at managing Sam's medical practice. He was more distracted than ever before at the office, which was ruining both business and his friendship with Sam.

I figured out that the first thing that I needed to do was to flat out quit cocaine and then pay off all of my debts. Easier said than done. I couldn't stop cold turkey (nor any other type of poultry). Getting off the drug was a monster, but I forced myself not to buy more than I had money for... as well as covering all of my bills and personal needs before going to see my dealer. That, too, might sound too easy... and I'm not suggesting that this was easy. Nothing that I ever did was!

No, I usually found a way to accomplish what I needed to accomplish by mere accident or out of desperation. This time, when I discovered that my financially-allowed amount of cocaine was less than a gram, I realized that simply running myself out of money on purpose before seeing Mark would prevent me from smoking cocaine. So, naturally, I took up buying cigarettes... exchanging one deadly habit for another! Smoking cigarettes was a lot cheaper and it was a legal way for one to kill themselves, albeit more slowly.

One problem with doing any kind of drug, is that when someone does drugs they tend to hang around other people who both do and have access to another drug. During my efforts to quit cocaine, I not only added smoking cigarettes to my list of addictions, but I started using pot (marijuana) again. True, it was "only" pot, something which I believed myself as not needing any help in order to quit; in other words, of my three addictions—not counting sex—smoking weed seemed the least harmful.

Damien was indeed becoming a stern addict: cocaine, marijuana, and nicotine. If not for his hatred of his step-father's own nasty habit, Damien would probably be adding alcohol to this growing list. The earlier promise he made to Samuel over cocaine only further damaged his self-esteem as yet his addiction was taking over his ability to sort out what was reality and which was imaginary.

Thanks to using both weed and cocaine at the same time, my inability to clearly tell what my mind was making-up, the real from the unreal. The year of 1982 was a disaster, and it was only about half over, except for me. No, I was done. Freedom was about to vanish altogether, and I couldn't have cared less. Only my imaginary, fantasy world seemed to matter; however, even that, too, contained monsters.

One summer afternoon, Damien went into Samuel's bedroom—while the doctor was at work—loaded several rounds into his Remington pump-action .22 rifle, opened the back door of their house, took aim at the back fence, and fired! He unloaded three shots into the planks of fencing.

Why? I simply "saw" a person climbing over the fence and was in fear for my life. The fact is, there was no person on the fence... I was in no real danger. The cocaine I had used that morning had magnified my sense of being watched and that there <u>were</u> people out to cause me harm. This paranoia had built up and became so bad that I felt impulse to grab my rifle and defend myself, using the bullets I swore to Samuel that I'd never ever touch without his permission.

Unfortunately, this firing of the rifle wasn't a victimless crime. Although Damien was only aiming at a vacant fence, one of the shots which penetrated the wood found second target on its own. Beyond the backyard of their home was a manmade storm gully approximately thirty-feet across. Beyond this culvert were the backsides of several small businesses: a liquor store, a dry cleaners, and—most importantly to our story—a gas station. An entirely innocent man, who was busily filling up his car and minding his own business was shot by Damien.

This innocent man, for no reason at all, had become my victim. I'd thought, at the time, I fired my rifle at nothing but empty space... at some villain working for county agency out to get me. And, behold, I did end up hitting someone near the base of his neck, above the joint of the collarbone. Mere millimeters from killing him, but enough to put him in critical condition for days.

Although I was not high at the moment, I was suffering from the paranoia that was magnified by its abuse. I'd gone back inside, none the wiser, totally oblivious that my actions had actively caused a man twenty yards away to be fighting for his life, bleeding all over the rear fender of his car, collapsing to the dirty ground, yelling for help! No, I didn't know I'd caused any of this. In fact, I was still holding the "smoking gun"—as it were—when the police kicked open our front door and arrested me for the crime of assault with a deadly weapon. I am very glad—and lucky—that I didn't cause any greater harm to this poor man who had done me no harm whatsoever. I could use the excuse that it wasn't my fault, that it was the drugs—the monster inside of me—yet I was the one who had pulled the trigger.

It was while entering Orange County Main Jail that Damien learned that race and racism really meant something, particularly in the world of incarceration. During his experiences in Juvenile Hall, race wasn't as important an issue as age was. However, as you've previously read, racism was a concept which Damien thoroughly hated and wouldn't accept.

Once I was arraigned, I was cuffed and put inside another holding cell and waiting transfer to the county jail's "overflow" annex. The county jail was so over-crowded that I was celled in a designated "black man's cell." I quickly learned that regardless of the fact that most of my best friends in life were black, and that I hated any source of "hatred of people because of race alone," that I wouldn't be accepted by either whites or blacks.

While I was being housed in the old county jail, I was "classified" according to a number of characteristics. As it turned out, I was determined by staff as both "soft" and gay, and I'd be housed accordingly. To this day, I still don't know how they came by this conclusion—most likely from looking at my juvenile record, since I was never questioned by them about my sexuality—however, I am ever grateful to've been placed in protective custody. I know that if I'd been, instead, housed in general population that day, I most likely wouldn't be alive today.

The end of Damien's freedom came at the moment when the jury read its verdict: He'd been found guilty of assault with a deadly weapon, although acquitted of the more serious charge of attempted murder, which the overambitious deputy district attorney tacked on at this arraignment—hence the need for the costly jury trial. Indeed, Damien freely admits that we was reckless when he fired his rifle at his fence; however, the intent to hurt anyone at all just couldn't logically be proven in a courtroom. For this reason, the fact that Damien hadn't actually been aiming at anyone with his rifle, the sentencing judge would impose a rather lenient sentence: the statute minimum of three years in state prison.

Man, was I lucky or what? I mean I deserved and could've received up to nine years. If the jury had found me guilty of attempted murder—which my court-appointed public defender never believed as a reality—I would have spent the rest of my life in prison. Instead, this sentence of only three years for nearly killing an innocent man is astonishingly short, especially when compared to California's current liberalism of dishing out "to life" sentences as if they were pieces of Halloween candy.

Who are the real monsters to society? The ones committing crimes or the lawmakers who—after years of campaign promises of "being tougher on crime"—have locked up nearly a tenth of the state's population? If I had committed the same crime I'd committed in 1982, in the year 2012, I would've become a financial burden on state taxpayers for the remainder of my life as well as never being able to experience the further events of this book.

While there is a lower class, I am in it; while there is a criminal element, I am of it; while there is a soul in prison, I am not free. -Eugene Victor Debs

CHAPTER TWENTY-TWO

Graveyards for the Living

You ask why I named this chapter the way I did? As you might have noticed, all of my previous chapters fit into a particular theme. This "grave" chapter and the image its name creates is really quite accurate to my own personal experiences and view of the California state prison system, as it was in the 1980's, 90's and currently. Prisoners in these institutions are neither dead nor living, they are simply breathing!

While taxpayers are unwilling paying for those inmates who failed to complete high school—many of whom aren't even citizens of this nation—and helping them towards earning their diplomas; the rest of these prisoners who already graduated in one way or another, waste their time (and those tax dollars). They spent hours drawing artwork, playing sports or other forms of recreation, without any true rehabilitation or job skills provided; doomed to reoffend upon their release.

The lucky ones blindly become involved in Christianity or another religious service purely to have additional time out of their cells or dorms, then "accidentally" discover a life larger than just themselves and their incarceration... at no credit to the prison system itself.

About six weeks after Damien's conviction and sentencing, he was transferred to the California Institution for Men in China, California, which was one of the state's oldest prisons—originally opened in

1941—and served as a short-term "reception center" to process and classify incoming inmates.

The first day of being processed into the prison system was a pain in the ass; indeed, a real day in hell. Arriving at C.I.M., we were instructed what to do in a step-by-step process; which included fully-naked strip searches and other demoralizing procedures, not least of all: to shower as a group and be dusted for lice or other related insects. Hours of bare-nakedness later, we were given a set of stretched-out and/or threadbare clothes and a bed roll of sheets, a blanket, and our first supply of hygiene items.

Reception was tedious and boring. Inmates are under constant lockdown, only out of their cells for showers and hot meals. There were no telephones or recreation at our reception center... you weren't entitled to anything but hours of sleeping or regret. Any despair you hadn't already gotten over while in county lockup, you could freely enjoy at reception—staring at those paint-peeling cinderblock walls.

Once I was there for about six weeks and had gone through the process of being fully admitted and classified into the prison system, I was transferred to my parent or "full-fledged" prison, which in my case was Tracy D.V.I.

Deuel Vocational Institution in Tracy, California had originally opened in 1953 as a prisoner training facility. As its name implies, these vocational programs were both numerous and beneficial towards preparing an inmate for a job in sheet-metal welding, automotive repair, masonry, plumbing, and even in aeronautics—they had a broken-down DC-10 aircraft parked near the visitor's entrance; albeit, without its wings attached.

Unfortunately, state budget cuts to the then-Department of Corrections, took a huge hit to the salaries of vocational instructors. The original intent of the Deuel Vocational Institution was swept under the state treasurer's rug! Classes were cut in half, then eventually cut completely; the hiring of new instructors cancelled; unneeded textbooks and other supplies tossed into local landfills... along with any prisoner's hopes at job training.

Prison officials began stating that having inmates work in their prisons' kitchens and laundries were vocational enough. The manufacturing of automobile license plates—which, to date, was only available at one of the thirty-plus prisons—and other state department items, such as CalTrans reflective vests, eyeglasses for both prisoners and the poor, chocolate milk for public schools, and various other food and clothing items needed throughout the prisons themselves. Non-violent prisoners could also earn the privilege of training to become firefighters... putting their lives on-the-line for mere pennies a day.

My arrival at Tracy D.V.I. was a little similar to my arrivals at both C.I.M. and even Mt. Lowe academy. We were stripped searched—which didn't happen at Mt. Lowe—then were issued our initials clothes, bedroll, and "fish kit" of personal supplies. We went through yet another orientation process where after interviews with various staff members—it was determined where each inmate best fit in the institution.

Before I was sent off to "F" Wing to being my orientation, I was escorted to be seen by the Receiving and Release sergeant... who promptly advised me to "keep my mouth shut about being gay" and to "stay out of other people's business." Oh, what I wouldn't do to be able to go back in time just to undo my stupidity of my first night in that prison. Why did I not comply with that good piece of advice?

Sure, of course, if I had a time machine, I could've prevented both my shooting of that innocent man in his neck, my addiction to freebase, maybe even my being pulled out of Mt. Lowe in the first place! But, for now, let's focus on this most recent of situations. Simply put, I must have utterly misunderstood the sergeant when he advised me to stay out of other people's business. I should've kept to myself, but no... not <u>this</u> high-functioning autistic man.

Damien unloaded his armful of bedding and other items into his cell, then felt compelled to introduce himself to a group of men playing a card game. He just felt it would be rude not to say hello; while, at the same time, seemed to ignore the common sense that he was now living in a "rude" world of convicts.

From the table rose a young man, who—for no given reason—walked over to the new inmate disturbing their game, and just popped Damien in his mouth, putting him "on his ass." An observant prison guard immediately blew on his referee-style whistle and all the inmates were ordered to lie prone on their stomachs. After determining who was involved in the 'fight.' Both Damien and the assailant were simply ordered to their separate cells for the remainder of the night.

How stupid can I be? Thank God I learned this lesson quickly in my years in prison; however, I was about to learn another lesson about grudges. On my way back to my cell after evening chow the very next day I was approached by a young white guy who passed me a "kite"—what we nicknamed a short note—telling me that the same guy that popped me in the mouth wanted to meet with me during evening dayroom. The kite was signed with the name "Danny."

Regardless of my not knowing anyone there at D.V.I., I agreed to follow the deliverer of this note to Danny's cell. Arriving at his open cell, he invited me inside. What kind of idiot was I anyhow? Was I just trying to be brave or did I really not think I was walking into a trap? I don't know, but I wasn't going to allow him to pop me in the mouth again… at least, not as easily as the night before.

Walking into Danny's cell, Damien immediately saw two other youngsters standing against the box window to the rear, which was wide open making the cell quite cool. Each cell at D.V.I. was about nine-feet long, roughly six-feet wide, and eight-feet high. It goes without saying that these cells were small, especially when you throw in the factor of having two inmates share that same tight space. Roommates or "cellies" learn quickly to both compromise and accommodate each other's need to move around or use their shared stainless-steel toilet/sink unit.

Looking at the one called Danny, Damien said right away, *"Look. I'm sorry about last night. I should've stayed out of your business."*

Danny smiled and replied, "That's okay. I shouldn't have been that rough with you on your first night off of orientation. Where're you from?"

I must've have lost my head altogether. *I'm from Huntington Beach.*

"Where's that?" the boy standing behind Danny asked.

Orange County, kinda near Fullerton.

"Oh, al'ight," that nameless boy replied. He looked to be around nineteen. Actually, all three of them seemed younger than Damien, two boys—including Danny—voluntarily shave their heads bald, while the talkative other kept his dirty-blond hair cropped.

"That's cool. Have a seat,' Danny offered to Damien a spot on the metal bunk—its saggy mattress rolled up tightly into a log at the head of the bed. Blanket neatly folded and lying on top.

Damien became the only one sitting, a rather intimidating situation to say the least, until eventually Danny sat down beside him. "So, Damien, want some weed?"

Damien was uncertain, of course, whether or not to accept such an offer from someone who'd only twenty-four hours ago punched him in the face, but the temptation of smoking some marijuana was irresistible.

You know it! I haven't had any in months.

'"Cool." Danny nodded to the previous boy who had spoken, then decided to make some introductions. "This is my cellie, Jim. Next to him is my dog, Bob." The terms 'dog' and 'big dog' are relative to the word acquaintance. A level of familiarity just below that of <u>true</u> friendship… which is beyond rare within a prison.

The twenty-year-old identified as Jim was the tallest of the four of them, and wore unkempt Levi's jeans that were so oily and dirty that they could quite possibly stand up on their own. In fact, with the exception of their tradition to roll up their mattresses each morning—a habit ingrained by active gang members in the general population—the cell was rather disorganized and dusty. Their floor hadn't been swept with a broom or towel in weeks, hard-water stains all over the sink, and algae was growing in a ring around the toilet bowl's water level. They were filthy men living in a filthy space.

It seemed to me as if both Danny and Jim were "well-schooled" in the politics of prison life. Not only did they have the behaviors of someone whose lived their entire teenaged years incarcerated, but Jim had no "canvas" remaining—that is to say unmarked skin. No, there wasn't much blank skin anywhere along his arms nor on his chest and back. Danny had even <u>more</u> ink work, including tattoos of skulls and fire up and down each leg, and probably more underneath his two-layers of boxer shorts; which, with the exception of a simple gold-chain necklace, was all the clothing he was wearing.

I have to admit that I was scared. I didn't know how to deal with this situation, and—naturally—I didn't want to say or do anything to piss these three men off. Men? Why do I keep calling them 'men'? They were still twelve-years-old on the inside. Their maturity stopped the moment they first entered California Youth Authority, the same juvenile prison system which I would've been sent to if my probation officer hadn't recommended my placement at Metro. To think that I nearly missed becoming just like one of these "lost souls" on that day I was committed to a state hospital; and yet look at where I was sitting now!

Danny asked Jim to hand him a joint from their hiding spot within the metal framework of their bunk beds. Receiving the joint, Danny lit it up and passed it over to Damien, for which he was grateful.

Picking up the conversation from where he left off, continuing on his hidden agenda, Danny said, "So, tell us a little about yourself, Damien."

What do you want to know? Damien asked cautiously.

Why don't you tell us how you ended up in our little, uh, hole in the ground?"

Taking another drag off of the joint before passing it on to Bob, Damien explained what he did to end up in prison, exaggerating the part about him shooting "some dude who climbed over my fence," for some other reason than pure paranoia. He thought it was very important to make it look like he was justified in this shooting., but little did Damien know that it was just as unwise to lie about your case.

"Were you ever in juvie?" Danny asked, and Damien went on for about ten minutes about how he'd gotten two girls drunk and screwed them both. Neither of the three other inmates believed a word of this. Instead, Danny got confrontational, "Are you gay?"

What was I to tell them? If I lied they probably would've known it. The fact that I was taking longer than a second to think over my answer was admission enough. So, since I'd already lied enough for one day I told them the truth—going against the R&R sergeant's second piece of advice.

Yeah, well, I'm bisexual.

"What's bi-" Jim was about to ask until Danny interrupted.

"You like both boys and girls?" Danny asked and Damien nodded. "Well, that doesn't make you a bad guy. We just need to know if you have a man yet. Do you?"

The joint was suddenly urged back into Damien's hand. Taking another drag to comfort him—and his answers—even further, Damien passed the joint back to Jim before answering, *No, do I need one?*

Unbeknownst to Damien, by the words 'have a man' Danny was actually asking Damien if he had a <u>pimp</u>: Someone to procure his prostitution deals and to provide Damien any protection he would need.

"Well, yeah. That's how things go smoothly around here. See what I mean?"

"You got it?" Jim suddenly added.

I, uh—how do I choose a man? Damien asked. Again, unknowingly to Damien, the asking of this question illuminated dollar signs within Danny's own eyes. Everything was going as according to plan.

"I suggest you do it carefully. You really don't want a man that'll take advantage of you as soon as you choose him."

No, I guess not. Damien decided then that he should take up Danny's unspoken offer to be his pimp, to be his own private prostitute. Danny, of course, accepted under one condition:

He wanted me to take care of him and his cellie's sexual needs, starting immediately. I had no choice but to agree. With that said, Danny told me that Jim needed a blow job, while he got some backs. Jim, the unkempt boy smelt like he hadn't bathed in weeks, with or without those disgusting jeans on. So, I went ahead and take of both of their sexual needs. Somehow I knew I'd be paying for those drags off of that joint, one way or another—nothing in prison came without a cost.

Danny took full advantage of Damien's submissive nature, regardless of his own personal warning to Damien about not picking a man that would take any such advantage. No, Damien was put to good use right away and fairly often for the next few weeks.

Without any warning one day in October, there was a stabbing on the yard. A big, black inmate almost lost his life. Damien and his fellow prisoners were locked down for about two weeks. The prison guards caught the stabber and, after interviewing each individual inmate, determined that the issue was resolved; that there wasn't any retaliation pending. The prison soon returned to normal program... and Damien returned to his normal homosexual duties.

As for me, well, all that I had to do was to keep my own nose out of trouble—which amounted to keeping my mouth shut—and Danny would take care of the rest. I always had my canteen food items, plenty to eat and smoke; plus, thanks to Dr. Reily, I had mail and quarterly packages sent from home. I would always share some of my packages and store, whether I wanted to or not, with Jim as I was expected to, yet I never suffered from any lack of needs.

Nonetheless, I still felt a very strong sense of being alive in a graveyard where people didn't really exist; except, if lucky, to one's family or a few outside friends. Otherwise, we were dead to the world beyond these fences. One's whole world existed in the space provided by the prison: a nine-by-six room stacked with bunks, a pair of footlockers, a metal shelf used as a table, the aforementioned toilet/sink combo, and a pair of dudes. That was our entire world or graveyard, if you will.

The prison staff was made up almost entirely of custody officers who couldn't care less about the welfare of the inmates under his or her charge. The nurses should some empathy, but only because they were being paid to. The "free staff"—as we called them—which were noncommissioned state employees who handled support services such as laundry, food management, and the canteen's stock, did care for the inmates to some degree. However, all of these staff members and their concern for inmates was quickly fading away with each new generation of employees who desired only higher paychecks, sleeping on the job, or a total lack of actual utilization or duty—instead, to get paid for newspaper reading or crossword-puzzle solving.

Damien's cellie was a motorcycle rider from way back: Mark the biker, not be confused with Mark the dealer, both dressed as a hardcore motorcyclist, a Harley man, and carried himself as one. At first, upon their earliest discussions as new cellies, Mark wasn't sure if he'd get along with Damien. Although Mark stated that he wasn't gay and never had any kind of sex with another man, this later turned out not to be true. One of the initiation steps of a biking gang he used to belong to included an undescribed homosexual act. By their second month together—and come the middle of the night—his previous denial in oral sex by another man proved false... and he grew increasingly interested.

There were two creatures that would pop-out late in the night. One was Mark's lust and the other were actual insects: the water bugs. Now, these water bugs were basically really big beetles of the genus family Belostomatidae, some big enough to carry one's boots away on the backs, or so the myth goes. And, they were bigger than Mark liked! I took care of his needs anyway both the dick sucking and bug squashing.

An example of what Damien called "a glimmer of hope" was about to happen in late December of 1982, just in time for the holiday season yet would become extinguished before most families would take down their Christmas lights.

There was a new state law that affected the amount of time an inmate would serve in prison. It was called the Work Incentive and Training Program, or W.I.T.P.—although nicknamed W.I.P. by the inmates—and most prisoners would qualify for it, but not all. Under the old system the two-thirds credit law, inmates needed to complete sixty-six percent of their sentence prior to be released on parole, as long as they remained disciplinary free. This newer program offered "half-time" or a full month of good behavior credit for each month an inmate was either working or going to school.

Just about as fast as we heard about this new law and how it was going to work, things got messy! First of all, there were riots between the inmates that had jobs and the ones who couldn't get any. Students started intentionally failing tests in order to remain in education or their vocational classes. Then, as if things weren't muddy enough, Mother Nature released her own fury in the form of seemingly endless sheets of rain! As if nothing could get any worse, the basements of the old prison flooded with all of the electrical equipment, such as the transformers, ineptly shorting out.

The problems were so bad that the warden of Tracy D.V.I. decided to send a portion of his inmates to several different prisons. I was transferred to California Men's Colony in San Luis Obispo. However, on account of the simple fact that the torrential downpours had caused flooding to several major arteries to that college town, they drive our busload to the world-infamous San Quentin state prison for a several-day layover.

As life had things, we were getting rained on all the day long! When we arrived at San Quentin, we were instructed to disembark and line up outside a building until told otherwise. We stood their shivering in the pouring rain wearing these paper-thin jumpsuits—with nothing but our skivvies on underneath—and flip-flops on our feet; handcuffed behind our back, so we couldn't even rub our arms to circulate body warmth. Finally, the misery came to an end as we were ordered to enter the century-old and foreboding rotunda—which gave me the impression straight from an old vampire movie! After all, the prison was built back when Abraham Lincoln was still only a congressman.

More precisely, California State Prison—San Quentin, opened in October of 1852. It's located along the coastline of the now-San Rafael Bay, a branch or cove located right around the corner from the famous Golden Gate Bridge (built eighty-five year later). It placement, directly at the waterline, was crucial due to its then remoteness and access primarily by boat, much like its slightly more famous <u>cousin</u> prison, Alcatraz... which was a federal prison—not state—and constructed decades after San Quentin.

Another half hour passed before I was assigned my new—well, new to me anyway—cell. Even though I only spent a few days there, I still remember the cell and its number quite well: 5E-143. That translates to the 143rd cell on the fifth tier of East Block. Back then, only the first two or three tiers of East Block were considered "Condemned Row"—those lucky few awaiting state execution—however, nowadays, all six-hundred-and-fifty cells within that maximum-security block are designated for this cause.

The cells were oddly cool in one way, painful in another. The only way that it could be considered "cool" was the fact that it was truly a place of American history and that from the height of my cell and its direction, I had a pleasant view of San Rafael Bay. Actually, it was also this fact—being able to watch the ferries and other boats sailing all day—that made my situation far more painful than the lower tires which had no windows at all.

Another "painful" feature: Would you believe that these cells were actually smaller than at Tracy D.V.I.? Well, it's true. In fact, people back in the 1850's must have been a whole lot shorter (and thinner) back then. If, for example, one sits on their bed with their back flush to one wall and extends their legs, he or she could touch the other wall. In fact, I could place the palm of each of my hands completely flat up against each wall, with my elbows still bent! With my head at the head of the bunk, my heels dangled off and out through the bars of the cell; if you slept the other direction, with the top of your head pressed up against the bars, your heels could almost touch the edge of the toilet bowl.

From a pal's personal experience in 2007, San Quentin's South Block was being utilized as an aforementioned reception center for new commitments. However, these exact same measurements of cell size and space were now used to house two inmates instead of one! The number-crunching geniuses at what is now called California's Department of Corrections and Rehabilitations (or CDCR) thought that adding a second bed in a cell barely big enough for a single person seemed perfectly reasonable... well, financially reasonable—if not entirely inhumane.

The meals there were alright, probably the best prison food I'd experienced throughout my incarceration; although, because we were only layovers, we were fed in our cells. Our 'yard time' was likewise limited both in time and to a fenced-in area that was used for those who were in disciplinary lockup—or, more affectionately known as "the hole." Other than this outside recreational time, us layover inmates didn't have access to anything else, especially canteen or telephones, with the only exception of a shower once every three days.

Approximately two "very long and boring" weeks passed until Damien and a handful of others were escorted back to the R&R building. They were once again strip searched—which Damien considered as totally unnecessary due to their constant confinement, *What did they really expect to find up our rectums which wasn't there two weeks ago?!*—and switched into one-piece jumpsuits. They were then loaded onto a bus to transfer them either to the prison in Soledad, south of Salinas, or further onward to C.M.C. in San Luis Obispo—located just north of Santa Barbara, and home of Cal Poly State University.

I grew excited as the bus approached "San Luis," and I saw familiar road signs for Highland Avenue and the intersection with Highway 101 beyond that... which we would never get to. As we turned off of Highway 1, my fellow passengers frantically looked all around; yet, from their bus seats and the speed at which we were travelling, everything felt uncommon and distant.

My experience of life in state prisons, whether in Chino, Tracy, or San Quentin, was covered—or cloaked—with the scent of spilt blood, gunfire, and overall violence. Not only was the air at these places foul, murderous, but also the grounds—such as they were—occasionally peppered with spent rifle-shell casings of various calibers. It is a fact that such places have their own nicknames given to them by inmates and staff alike, such as Blood Alley and Death's Corner. There were particularly ghastly references in San Quentin to the area where the old gallows once stood before electricity was considered a more guaranteed method of execution... as well as more gruesomely thrilling to watch publicly.

I was overjoyed when I found out that, unlike previously named prisons, California Men's Colony was nothing like them. This fact was made crystal clear to me the very moment we disembarked. From the transportation officers on down to the ones in charge of actual custody, I was in for a pleasant-and-welcome surprise: None of them carried billy clubs, there weren't any tale-bearing bullet holes in the walls, nor ominous crimson stains along the pavement. It was an incarcerated version of paradise.

Upon entering the reception building, Damien and five fellow newcomers were immediately advised by the active sergeant there that, "If anyone wants to get sent out of this place, the quickest way is to pick a single fight. Violence of any sort isn't tolerated here!? In fact, C.M.C. was constructed very differently than any other institution in the state; it was considered a "program" or privileged yard where positive behavior wasn't only the norm but rewarded.

For example, there were four prison yards made up of two housing units, each held a maximum of three hundred men, each man with their own single-cell; although, as with San Quentin, there wasn't enough in each cell for all of its occupant's personal property... they were quite small. However, with the amount of recreation time offered, inmates were rarely inside their cells! This was the next obvious uniqueness, as well as each inmate actually having a key to lock and unlock their own cell's door! Completely unheard of at any other prison throughout the state, perhaps even the entire nation.

Keys? Damien remember asking another newcomer standing next to him. *We can come and go whenever we please?!*

"Well, to out cells, anyway," the other white youngster smiled, "I don't think they'll work for the main gates."

Yeah, only Saint Peter has the keys to those," Damien whimsically replied.

CHAPTER TWENTY-THREE

Oops, I Did It Again

Damien wasn't housed at C.M.C. more than ten days before he was assigned to work in the facility's Dining Hall—or "Culinary" as it was improperly referenced by custody staff. Due to this job assignment, Damien was also moved to yet another new cell, as inmates at C.M.C. were housed according to their work or educational placement. On that very same day, one other pleasant thing happened; Damien received his personal property which he hadn't seen since leaving D.V.I. in Tracy.

I was able to reread all of the old letters Sam had written to me while I was in Tracy. There weren't many, but you see, he never wrote anyone else more than me, and there weren't many at that. He constantly talked about his caring about me, and that I could return as his housemate upon my release. Two letters talked about coming to visit me while I was at Tracy, which he did once. From Huntington Beach to Tracy would take eight or nine hours of driving, each way... that's a lot of hours to be away from his medical practice, and just to visit little ol' me. But, now, I was about half-an-hour away!

I really did care about him and I was beginning to care about my own welfare again. I was also caring more about other significant others. For the very first time since my incarcerations started—since my arrest, actually—I felt more relaxed... when I slept, I'd feel sleep flow down my body like a warm river, gently washing over me, causing me to drift off to a different place entirely. Well, at least, until the announcement to stand up for count time. In actuality, I was so busy and active, I didn't sleep for more than a couple of hours, but when I did, it was healing to my soul.

It was getting closer and closer for Sam and I to start talking about and making parole plans. For that I was happy; I was "short timing it," as we called those running low of their sentence. Not wanting to do anything that would jeopardize my approaching release date, I wouldn't actually have any hope if it wasn't for Sam and for the friends I made at C.M.C. Yes, I did say the unheard of word "friend" didn't I? Inmates aren't supposed to make friends in prison, as outlined in Danny's relationship with his "dog" Bob. But a friend is exactly what Charlie would become... and in record time, too.

Charlie "Oops" Osborne was a young African American man whom Damien had seen at Tracy D.V.I.; they'd both been in the same auto-repairs class, yet due to their differences in race, didn't socialize. Neither did they notice each other during their equally-brief time at San Quentin or on their lengthy bus ride. These combined experiences were, by far, the only things they had in common at all, yet proved to be enough to initiate a familiarity.

Race was a real issue in prison, as I've mentioned before; except for there at C.M.C. No, on the year we were both getting used to, it was considered not just "soft" but "super soft" when it came to politics. Nearly every inmate there had at one time or another been involved in a street or prison gang, "snitched" to officers about something criminal, had a highly offensive case or criminal charge—including those jury trials that caught any serious media attention—or were homosexuals. In fact, there were several homosexuals there out in the open about their sexuality preference.

Charlie "Oops" and I rarely said more than a couple of words to each other at D.V.I., and the ones we did were primarily in our mechanics class to-or-from the tools cage. No, it wasn't until C.M.C. that we began having brief conversations, one of which included us sharing the fact that we were both gay and even attracted to each other. However, naturally, we kept this information a secret from anyone else, plus never acted on our impulses until we knew each other better.

Damien never thought, after leaving D.V.I. that he'd see anyone from there ever again... at least, nobody that he'd recognize or that knew him. With Danny the pimp completely out of his life and no one at C.M.C. knowing who or what he was—bisexual—he'd have a clean slate. Yet, he became so very pleased to see his old classmate coming out of Building Six.

Hey there, Charlie Oops! He blurted out in passing.

Stopping dead in his tracks, Charlie about-faced and responded, "Wait, what? Is that you, Damien?"

You remember my name? They had only been in class for roughly a month before the torrential rainstorms started.

"Yeah, the instructor kept yelling: 'Damien, don't touch that,' and 'Damien, put that down.'"

I don't remember him—oh," Damien noticed Charlie's demeanor, *you're fuckin' with me.*

"Yeah, I wish," Charlie replied, both stating his humorous side and hidden sexual desire with the same phrase. "So, how long you been here?"

About two weeks. You?

"Huh, I got here almost two weeks ago, too."

Wait, Damien suddenly realized, *where'd you go from Tracy?*

"I went to Quentin, how about you?"

No way. I was in Quentin. I can't believe we were in the same joint all that time; how did we miss each other?

"Well, it's easy to miss something you're never looking for," Charlie theorized, then asked, "What building are you in?"

Afterwards, Charlie needed to continue on his way, yet promised to catch up with Damien and resume their conversation the following day... and that's exactly what he did.

The next day, walking from the quarter-mile track together, Charlie "Oops" and Damien talked about all matters of things, from favorite movies and music, to how lazy prison guards were; that is everything except the "being gay" issue.

Seeing that Charlie had been avoiding that particular topic, Damien turned to him asking, *So, are you going to open up about being gay here?*

Or, are you still in the closet?

"Oh, I'm not in the closet," he replied. "Have you noticed yet how, you know, gay-friendly it seems to be around here?"

It is a blessing, Damien agreed. *"I, for one, don't want to hide behind cell doors any longer, but I don't want to catch any extra time, too.*

"Well, I'd like to get to know you better," Charlie admitted, which is a popular euphemism for wanting to get sexually active.

Damien acknowledged that the two of them faced two difficult challenges. The first is that prison mirrors the society from which it came, in that both interracial relationships and homosexuality were seriously frowned upon, and yet they desired to launch forth; the second, any sexual activity between inmates is not only forbidden but criminally prosecutable. Were either of them willing to risk losing good-behavior time credits towards early release just for a "roll in the hay"?

Nonetheless, we did the impossible. We risked the prejudice of an openly gay black guy hanging around a questionably queer white guy. Being of two different races meant that we'd publically be rejected by anyone racist, especially someone of our own race. However, since this was a "super soft" yard, only a handful of inmates at C.M.C. still held onto such hatred.

Then came the assumptions: The fact that Charlie was knowingly gay and I was hanging out with him, it would be assumed that I was getting sex from him <u>before</u> either of us even started doing so. Certainly, neither of us could do as our bodies desired with all of this attention bearing down on us. Still, due to how drop-dead handsome Charlie "Oops" physically was, jealously was building amongst the homosexual community to the point where I needed to keep my distance from the other gays in order to keep my teeth in my mouth and my skin on my face!

No, these threats to my body and life caused me to do whatever I could to get around this hatred in my world. I liked Charlie, but not enough to fully engage him in some much desired hot sex—desired equally by both parties, mind you—regardless of how cute he was... and, as I've said, I found him to be gorgeous!

Damien admitted to me during the compiling of this book, that it's difficult to understand how he could freely offer himself up to inmates such as Danny the pimp, Jim the sloth, or Mark the biker; none of whom he was at all attracted to—Jim was the exact opposite of gorgeous!—and yet Damien seemed paranoid to become sexually involved with this man he did find amazingly sexy and handsome?!

Damien felt inclined to ignore his urges towards Charlie simply because he didn't want to fully alienate himself from his race. The three perverts named above, were all white guys... and having sex with them wasn't looked down upon as much as would having gay sex with another race member. Yet, as I already mentioned, regardless if Charlie and Damien had been actively engaging in sex or not isn't important, since they were already perceived to be doing just that.

It was a quiet evening on "C" Quad. I was grateful for the gentle and warm breeze sweeping across the hills just outside of the prison causing the tall grass—to their own rhythm—to dance for God's enjoyment and my own. Very few others outside that night seemed to take any notice.

Truly, I was blessed... inside prison, yet fortunate. So very fortunate. My transfer to C.M.C. was an act of Mother Nature, my friendship with "Oops" an act of grace. I sat there, that night, quietly next to Charlie and nothing would make me happier without the removal of clothing. Sure, to find a bed where we could make endless love with each other would be the icing on an already delicious cake, but I was enjoying the slice which life had served me so far.

Yet, of course, I have to ruin a good thing. I would not be me if I didn't push for something more. You could call it greed, maybe selfishness, but I don't think I was either of these... I just didn't want what we had to become stale or boring for either of us. So, I sought Charlie out on the matter, making the centerpiece of our conversation.

Hey Oops? Damien started, jabbing his friend with a forefinger to catch his attention. *Can I ask you something serious?*

"Depends on what you mean by 'serious'." He didn't want to wreck the current mood of their night out together.

Where do you see our relationship going? He asked straight-forward.

"Where do *you* want it to end up, Damien?"

Well, I want to wake up to find you in my bed.

"Oh, that's good. Because that's something that I'd love, too."

How could we do that? Damien asked, believing that with the prison's count times and security sweeps, he was suggesting the improbable.

Charlie put down the glass bottle of root beer he'd been nursing, then responded, "I'm thinking on that. Be patient, Damien."

Cool, he nodded.

Putting his warm arm around Damien's shoulder, Oops said, "This place is amazingly cool for being a prison. We'd never get to see the hills all dressed with tall grass at Tracy."

Yeah. Damien tilted his head towards his best friend, *Charlie, how about if we just sit and take in the moment, and the season, and all this blessed quiet.*

With that said, they sat and quietly enjoyed the peace and comfort of each other's company. Before long, Damien found a new pleasure in feeling his friend resting his beautiful head on Damien's shoulder, as he ever tranquilly fell asleep.

CHAPTER TWENTY-FOUR

Do Time, Don't Let Time Do You

How do I mean? This is an old prison saying which still rings true today, and even for those who aren't incarcerated. It's completely factual that many people have significant problems living life, and end up letting life do them. This is true of those involved in loveless marriages, working thankless jobs, or sacrificing their own dreams and happiness to raise unappreciative children. They let time steal life from them, instead of living life to the fullest!

Indeed, even in prison, having leftover a quantity of "zest for life" remaining for the next day that follows is good. We must stop the destructive ways we "live" our lives, because so many of us aren't living to our true potentials. We are simply existing through life, "making a living," with no zeal or zest for life. This is bad not only for ourselves as individuals, but it is hurtful to our communities! To our future.

In the world, people don't know how to live life. This is especially true for those in prison; but, honestly, it's everywhere. We have all forgotten that when we live life with—and for—each other, we live life fully. Our *families become less safe because we are no longer living for them. All that does is to ensure that our neighbor has a better chance of "catching our cold," adopting our misery. Our communities are fading away into the future of street gangs... for, of all the evil and crime a gang commits, at least they understand how to live life with and for each other.*

Damien thought about his desires where it concerned becoming physical—sexual—with Oops, but what he didn't yet know was that by living his life in a state of self-centeredness, he didn't think about how his actions affect the society which he was living in.

I was more than blessed with a unique tenderness that whispered, "I love you," from Charlie. Our many early morning laps around the yard were, at times, concluded by Oops resting his head on my lap, or mine on his. I had begun to learn about and believe in the soul thief, that evil deceiver named Satan, and how he tempts your character, tests for weaknesses.

My soul needed restoration—it still does—and Charlie "Oops" provided me with exactly what I loved about him: He provided his whole self, blanketed in love. The truth is that I was falling deeply in love with Charlie and not lust. We hadn't even kissed yet, hadn't seen each other naked... no, our love for each other wasn't physical at all, regardless of how much we both wanted to take it to that level. I was glad that I still doing time, because, despite being in prison, I wasn't about to let time do me!

"What's the point of surviving, if we never truly live?" Charlie asked Damien, and he wasn't just talking about 'surviving prison' neither.

About a week after Damien started his inmate job in Dining Hall "C", he requested being switched to a different shift, so that he and Charlie could work the same early-mornings shift, the same hours and regular days off (or RDO's). They were pleased to no end; this made it possible for Charlie and Damien to have more private time together after they cleaned up and were released to the yard.

When the time was right, Charlie had a most pleasant and desirable surprise: He announced that we were going to make love, finally. I was amazed when, after a particularly long shift one morning, he told me, "Damien... both of us deserve this chance with each other." Needless to say, I wasn't expecting it to be <u>that</u> very day, but was hopeful.

You're right, Damien replied, *I don't just deserve to make love to you, I* *want to do it. My God, Charlie, you make me so very happy. I never wanted anyone the way I <u>want</u> you.*

Drinking from his coffee mug, he replied, "We could be neighbors. This way we could have access to each other, simply slip into each other's cell in between counts."

Damien was pleased; Charlie seemed to have spent some time considering this plan. *That would be great, Charlie. Let's do it, no matter what the cost. I'll pay my current neighbor to move. But for now, we need to act like nothing is going on. We don't need to air our laundry out on the tier, you know?*

"That would be great, Damien. When can you talk to your neighbor?"

Tonight, maybe. I'll get at him, but it has to be private.

After the serving of breakfast was done and the last person had left the chow hall, the cleaning would begin. Damien's job was to assist in sweeping and mopping the floors, then helping out wherever else he was needed. Charlie's main tasks were the dumping of leftovers—more about this in a sec—and the cleaning of the serving line, which was one long hot-water table with "bays" for each pan of food to sit in and be kept warm by the steam. Draining all the water and then scrubbing it all down, inside and out, actually didn't take all that long, it was just a real pain.

You wouldn't believe the amount of wasted food we dumped out each meal. Scrambled eggs, oatmeal, sausages... here were so many pans at the end of each shift that just went to waste. I asked once or twice why we didn't send all of this unused food to a local homeless shelter—thinking about all those cold nights wishing I had something more to eat and my street-urchin friends—but I was told "because of health reasons" or "security reasons" they couldn't give the food away, only throw it away. My argument was simply: The homeless already eat our of dumpsters, you think they'll care about reasons from leftover, previously handled prison food?

Back to me and Charlie; we would often finish our cleaning before the rest of the crew. This was good because that meant we sometimes had private time before our shift was done. On some days, especially when the dumpsters out on the back dock needed to be picked up, the waiting to leave work was long, but only meant more time for us to talk, or explore other opportunities.

Much of the time the correctional officers and the free-staff cook who supervised the inmate cooks, didn't mind leaving us alone in the kitchen briefly while they handled the unloading of the supply trucks or garbage pickups. We were both cautious at first, then realized that this was the perfect time to have some limited pleasure. On one such morning, the bakery truck arrived late and, from experience, we knew it took fifteen minutes to unload.

Getting up from the dining room table, Charlie looked at Damien, "Are you ready?"

Damien looked around the large chow hall, there were eight other workers sporadically seated in groups of two among the fifty tables. *You know I am, but... how are w-we going to do this?*

"Oh boy," Charlie chuckled, "look who is impatient!"

I'm, uh... I'm not impatient, Charlie Oops!

Ignoring this remark, Charlie asked, "What do we want right now?"

Keeping his voice down, Damien replied, *I really want to make love to you.*

"And that's what I want. C'mon," he urged Damien to follow.

What? Where? Damien blindly chased after Charlie, not sure where in the kitchen they possibly have any privacy. Both of the guards were right there at the back doors.

"It's not the cleanest," Charlie warned, then motioned with his hand, "How about the broom closet?"

Ain't it locked?

"Nah, look at the door handle. It's not latched all of the way."

Taking Damien's hand, Charlie walked hungrily into the smelly closet, closing the door behind them. Moving in closer, they Frenchkissed without any further delay, stripping each other's pants and boxers down to their ankles. In case of needing a quick getaway, they left their shirts and shoes on. For more than ten minutes, they made steamy hot love in that awfully confined space.

I never experienced anything like our lovemaking before in my life. Maybe it was the panic of getting caught, the claustrophobic conditions, and our lack of time, but we were beastly! Hot and fast! Neither of us required much to reach climax, we'd both been suffering from weeks of anticipation and anxiety!

Once we were done, we rushed to put on our clothes, tucking in shirts, running fingers through our hair, and tidying up the brooms and other stuff we'd knocked over. Then, I believe Charlie started it, we began kissing heavily again. Suddenly, from beyond the door, we heard the jingling of keychains and voices, and knew that both cops were on their way through the kitchen. It would look strange if we both came out of the closet as the same time, so I grabbed a broom I didn't intend to use and slipped out unseen, Charlie wasn't so lucky.

"What the—" the officer exclaimed after realizing the closet wasn't locked all of the way. "Who's in there?" he asked while pulling the door open.

"I am, sir. Just finished," Charlie reported from inside. He'd been pretending to organize the bottles of disinfectant.

Wait, Damien suddenly came around from the corner he was hiding behind, walking towards the officer, *here's one more,* holding out the broom.

"About time," Charlie played out in an upset manner, "Okay, sir. Now I'm all done." Both inmates stepped out of the guard's way while he firmly closed the door, then pulled on its handle to confirm it shut. "Good. Let's get out of here. Tell the others t grab their shit."

Damien and Charlie headed back out to the main dining room and unnecessarily hollered to the other inmate workers, "They're coming! Time to go!"

All ten or eleven kitchen workers gathered around the table nearest the door leading out to the yard, gathering their prisoner identification cards tossed onto the table by one officer, while the other found the correct key on his massive keyring to unlock the chow hall door.

"Here you guys go. Stay out of trouble."

Walking out onto the prison year, Damien replied,, "Yes, sir. Have a good one." Everyone seemed completely oblivious to what he'd just moments ago experienced in the closet. Well, except maybe for the amount of happiness he seemed to be radiating.

"You feeling okay, Collins? The officer asked from behind him.

Oh year! I'm loving life! Damien yelled over his shoulder.

> The thoughts of a prisoner—they're not free either. They keep returning to the same things.
> ~Alexander Solzhenitsyn

CHAPTER TWENTY-FIVE

Independence

During the last week of June 1983, Damien had become more involved with the inmate population than ever before. Representatives of the prison's Inmate Advisory Council—sometimes referred to as the Men's Advisory Council (M.A.C.), which was just a group of elected inmates who presented any grievances which inmates had to the facility's captain or associate warden, as well as their primary task of advising the population to changes to daily operations or upcoming events.

One such M.A.C. representative approached Damien about any problems or suggestions he might have. Both Charlie and Damien were of the opinion that inmates should have a way to "partake in the nation's birth" on the looming holiday, the Fourth of July.

Although Charlie and I had specific dates which we were going home, both of us had Earliest Possible Release Dates (EPRD's) set in September— his way ten days before mine—a few at C.M.C. had no such date to be paroled. So, although on July 4th we celebrate our independence from England, some cringed of the fact that they may never know personal freedom ever again.

As things turned out, the staff already worked a plan so that both the officers and inmates could have a ball... by way of playing softball, that is. Inmates against guards! The correctional officers actually played ball, literally, and as the visiting team (since they technically were only visiting the prison each day; it's the inmates who lived there). Tensions were high during the first inning, nobody knew what to expect, especially if an officer had been beaned by a wild pitch; but by the third inning, nearly everyone overlooked the fact that this game was being played within the confines of a state prison!

No, due to the amount of excitement, it was merely the blue team versus the green uniforms. It was simply phenomenal: The guards stopped being guards, and the inmates weren't inmates; they were just human beings and ballplayers. That is, of course, until the end of the ninth inning.

How can I tell you how special this was for Charlie and I? Then, we found out that after the game—the inmates won, coincidentally—there was also going to be a gigantic barbecue on the quad. The captain allowed the inmates to half a 55-gallon steel drum using some metal cutting tools slicing the barrel from top down, into crescent-shaped basins to burn charcoal in. Some rebar or other rods were welded across the top for the actual grills. The food, itself, was paid for and brought in by the facility lieutenant herself, and cooked entirely by the inmates: hot dogs, burgers, even potato salad.

To be honest, if I hadn't been there myself, I really didn't think that such an event was possible within a prison. The staff really pulled through and made it all happen. That the level of respect and support us inmates had with these officers back then... I'm not saying that there still isn't the same level currently in prison; however, I'd be rather surprised. The 1980's were a very different time; prison employees didn't only care about the size of their paychecks as much as they do today. No, the camaraderie of that July 4th was incredible, although—and unfortunately—brief.

For the first time in years, Damien agreed to join someone in going to church. He never would have done this "bit of insanity," except that the person who invited Damien was none other than Charlie "Oops" Osborne, his lover. One reason that Charlie invited Damien was because he was interested in seeing how Damien would react to and/or accredit the inmate preaching. Damien decided that it would be good for him to see how he'd agree with this inmate's sermons or not. The last time Damien had touched a Bible was to prove Mr. Gueler wrong about

Noah's flood (at Mt. Lowe).

So, Charlie and Damien went to the Chapel on the very next Sunday after the invitation. On their way to the building, Charlie asked, "So, are you ready to meet him?"

'Him' who? The chaplain?

"No, Tex Watson."

I don't know who that is, Damien confessed.

"You don't know who Charles 'Tex' Watson is? Charlie asked and Damien shrugged his shoulders. "He was the principal murderer of the Manson crew."

The what? Who were the—

"Seriously?! You don't know bout Charlie Manson and his crew? They killed, like, a dozen people." Actually, it was seven; one of whom was an actress named Sharon Tate, whom Manson was rumored to be obsessed with. The murders occurred in 1969, back when Damien was around eleven. Manson, Watson, and two female cult members were convicted of first-degree murders in January 1971, twelve years previously to Damien meeting Watson.

"C'mon, Damien," Charlie said as they approached the chapel's door, "Let's go and meet a celebrity."

Charles "Tex" Watson, or just "Tex" as he preferred, had the look of an assistant chaplain or pastor, not of some wild serial killer as the media had once portrayed. He was a solid-built six-foot white man or middle-age. Plus, as Damien discovered, he was also well-versed in Christianity and both Testaments. Several months prior to Damien's arrival at C.M.C., Tex Watson convinced the prison's chaplain that he'd fully repented, both full of regret and remorse, for his past behavior and gruesome murdering of the helpless. His resilience was outstanding, Tex truly took on the look of someone who'd spent half their lifetime in a rectory, as a spirited member of the clergy.

Charlie and I went into the sanctuary and waited for the service to start. Almost immediately, Tex identified that I was new there—how out of fifty other guys did he single me out as never being there before, I've no idea—and invited me on a quick tour of the chapel. He described the many different services and programs they had, as well as their tiny library. He even handed me a book which featured him in its chapters.

Tex then asked us to stay after the service, and he would be glad to answer any questions we might have. We took out seats in our handcrafted pew—each bench was built decades ago by inmates—and watched as Tex lead several other men to the altar. Quickly, everyone else took their seats and the service was underway. I have to admit that it was kinda cool. The prison's chaplain, a man from the local Lutheran church, delivered an engrossing sermon and related his message to a personal experience which we all enjoyed.

It wasn't long before I found myself listening to Tex give his testimony and explain how the church program made a drastic difference in his life. I got the impression that he was well-educated and not at all shy about who he used to be when he'd both hung out and committed crimes with Manson. There was once even a two-million-dollar hit out on him by members of the Folgers family for killing their young daughter!

Time was running out between when the next service that morning would begin, yet Tex wanted to continue their conversation, so he invited Damien to return during the week. Damien, however, wanted to resume talking instead of going back to the yard, and that's what they ended up doing. They stayed for the second service and an encore of the chaplain's same sermon, just so they could continue where they'd left off.

I was so blessed with Charlie's patience. He waited through that second service, a complete repeat of message and testimony, just for Tex and I to bring an end to our earlier conversation. Later, I knew that we had spent a lot more time talking about Tex than the time spent with him. Charlie was truly a good friend—and lover—and when I warned him that I sometimes get fixated on a single subject, because of my Asperger's; he was understanding, as well.

Tex and I did meet again and resumed where we'd left off that Sunday. I have to admit that I'd become interested in Tex Watson because he was an example of someone who God is willing to forgive and "save" by the blood of Jesus Christ. A murdered who had completely turned his life not only around, but turned over... over to God. Before we went our separate ways <u>that</u> day—we'd met again that Sunday, as agreed—Tex asked his favorite question. He asked me if I was "born again" or not.

Born again? No, I can't say that I have been.

"Do you believe in God? In Christ Jesus?"

Those are good questions, Tex. Let's grab a seat on the bleachers, Damien suggested, and they did. *Yeah, I do. But I can't say for sure that I am comfortable dealing with it.*

"Oh? What do you mean?" Tex represented his earnest curiosity with both facial expressions and hand gestures, encouraging Damien to elaborate. Little did Tex know how much Damien enjoyed elaborating on any topic!

Well, yes, I absolutely believe in God, though my belief is very different than what the chaplain teaches. I've heard priests preach about a god that's all powerful, and, for me, that simply doesn't make any sense. For me, God is everywhere and at the same time, everything is in God.

"I'm not sure why that wouldn't make any sense. Is God all-powerful to you or not?

Well, Damien scratched his head, then asked, *do you have the power to ask that question?*

"The power to ask—well, yeah. I have the 'free will' to ask the question, like you had the power or will to answer it or not."

Exactly. If I have the power to answer the question or not, then God does not have control. He doesn't have the power to cause me to answer it or not. I have my own power, my own choice, not to be a robot. I have the power and will to be human, and as you fully know, I am obviously a human because God's robot wouldn't be either homosexual or in prison.

"You're trying to say that we either have our own power to act the way we choose or we don't. Correct? That if you have some control over your life, then God isn't completely in control? Am I right?

Exactly. How can God be all powerful, if we have enough power to screw up and sin against Him. He has lost control of us.

"Tell me something," Tex asked politely, "did you ever believe that God was all powerful? If you did, when did you throw that belief away?"

No, I can't really say I did... until I was six, I had no belief in anyone I couldn't see, and by then I believed that if God existed, He would not have wanted my life to be going the way that it was. Nobody possibly could have wanted my childhood to be the way that it was. But, although I honestly believe in God, I also believe we have power to not do what God wants us to.

"Of course, we have free will."

But that's just it. God doesn't have the power, the control is yours. If God did, then that would make you a robot. As for your question about what I believe… about an all-powerful god and when I got rid of that belief, well, how can someone have all of this power and, yet, not be in control? I got rid of that belief while I was at Mt. Lowe Military Academy. We read about all the wars in the world, all of the people who lost their lives, and all the evils caused by dudes like Adolf Hitler and Joseph Stalin. If God is an all-powerful god, then how could he allow so many people to suffer? Was the Holocaust of the Jews and Stalin's genocide of millions all under God's control and power? I have wondered how can all the wild flowers on that hill bloom, unless an all-powerful God has to cause each one to open individually. They, too, must have some free will to open or not. None of what I was taught in school made sense.

"So," Tex finally got a word in, "you don't understand it… and that makes it not real?"

Tell me, do you believe in free will? Countered Damien.

"Absolutely! This is why I am so dead certain about the teachings about our all-powerful, all-knowing Heavenly Father. In one teaching, we have God as having all the power, yet in other teachings, that we have independence to choose, as do most animals. However, having free will doesn't take power away from God. See what I'm saying?"

"I, uh," Damien couldn't get his words and sentences the way he desired, and he felt frustrated. He knew what he wanted to say at that moment, the point he wanted to get across, but he just couldn't compose it. *You're saying that God doesn't control everything and every event. Right?*

"That's almost it. I believe that our Heavenly Father, God Almighty, does have a plan for our lives. He might not control your every choice or reaction to every single situation, yet in the grand scheme of things," Tex then looked up at the beautiful sky to emphasize his next phrase. "I believe that our loving Lord steers us in the right direction to achieve what He expected us to."

Wait, Damien admitted. *You lost me there. So, you think that God has our lives all figured out: beginning, middle, and end. But we still have the power to change all of that. Yet, we still end up reaching 'the end' that God planned for us all along? How is that possible? If we have the power to change up what God wants us to do, how can there be a 'plan' for our lives? That... there's no way that can be right. The way my life has been going, there's no way that my life is part of some great plan.*

"It might not feel like your life has a greater purpose, but—"

No, Damien interrupted. I'm not saying that. I know my life has a purpose, but I can't see how God could have planned any of my childhood. I was beaten, molested, constantly bullied in school, became a prostitute, an addict, and I even shot a guy. How could God be behind all of that? That He wanted me, before I was even born, to become a prostitute, get addicted to freebase, and end up in here?! I can't buy that.

"I am not saying that I understand why God allows certain things to happen in our lives. Everything has all the power that it can have over their own daily choices; there simply is no <u>being</u> without power. But, the word 'power' can be understood as both the ability to affect and the ability to be affected. Don't get me wrong, the ability to be affected isn't a defect nor a weakness. God affects our lives by the choices of the other around us."

At around this point of their conversation, Damien's friend Charlie sat down next to both of them; however, he didn't want to disturb either of them.

"I believe," Tex continued, "that when our own independence, our choices take us too far off the path God wants us to take, he involves others around us to affect the outcome of our choices. Take, for example, your shooting of that 'innocent' man. Who is to say that he was innocent? Who is to say that if he'd finished filling up hos gas tank and drove away from that gas station, as usual, he would have done something irreversible. That we would have ended up so completely off of God's plan for his life, there would've been no going back."

So, Damien stammered, *if, uh, I hadn't shot him in the neck, he would have done... what? Something so terrible th-that God would've had to ch-change His plans?*

"No, I don't think so. Who is to say that it would've been 'something terrible'? But, the point is, through your actions, you affected where that man's life was headed. It most likely wasn't headed in the direction God would've liked, otherwise He would have diverted that bullet or stopped you from pulling the trigger."

Yeah, but by me pulling the trigger, I ended up in here. In prison. How could've that been part of God's plan for my life?

"Well, for one, it gave you the chance to meet me?" Tex smiled. "I'm not saying that meeting me is worth a trip to prison, but the path you were heading down before meeting me, before coming to prison, probably would have headed your life towards an ending which God never intended."

"And me," Charlie spoke up. "You never would've met me."

To tell you the truth, Damien replied, *I don't just accept that what happens to me is just people making mistakes, because I make a lot of them. I just know that I cannot be the only one. To make mistakes, I mean. How can God know that my mistakes are heading me down the wrong path.*

"Stretching his legs, Tex asked, "Why can't God know about the future?"

Because, I believe, nothing exists there. We are so concerned with the things that may or may not occur, when, in fact, we owe it to ourselves and our community to focus our attention on what is! On our families! Okay, yes, we need to keep in mind how our current actions would likely affect our families, our homes, including our universal home...the Earth, in the potential future, but need our—our focus...it needs to be in the present.

"Where on earth did you get these ideas?" Tex asked.

To tell you the truth...I learned a lot by asking the questions and I don't accept what I'm told is the truth. I know none of us can really know God and what He has planned for us. And what He does, why He does it.

"True," Tex agreed. "Right now, I'm giving you the best guesses that I can. But, I promise you one thing though."

What's that?" Damien asked.

"If you continue to get educated and learn all that you can about God and our relationship with the world, you'll know as much as you'll need to about Him and yourself. You'll feel His love for you."

I will! Damien grew excited. *I'm really interested in believing and experiencing Him. I also plan to be able to help people develop healthy relationships with Him.*

With that said, Tex admitted that he was exhausted, and it was time to quit. However, after Tex shook both of their hands and walked away, Charlie struck up a related topic.

"I have a question that I don't really expect an answer," Charlie began. "Why do we call God, 'He'?"

What do you mean? Damien asked.

"I mean just that. You and Tex always talk about God in male terms. 'He does this, He does that.' Why do we address God like a man?"

I don't know. What are we supposed to call Him?

There! You just did it again," Charlie chuckled out.

I'm not sure, Charlie Oops. But, now that you've pointed it out… Damien paused to drink some water out of a drinking fountain and to compile his thoughts on the subject. *It's not really fair to girls or women, is it? Look at it this way. Eve, the first ever woman, was made from the rib of Adam, and Adam was made in the likeness of God. Since Adam was first, I guess we just assume God is male.*

"Yeah, but nobody else was around in the garden of Eden. Whose to say that God created Adam first? Maybe whoever came up with that whole story was just a male bigot."

I think you mean male chauvinistic, Damien corrected. *Then they headed back together towards their neighboring cells to change out of their state-issued clothing and into summer wear.*

I had a very strong belief in God and Christ. I believed in the salvation for those who asked Christ into their lives and souls, to be their Lord and Savior. I have always had a real difficult problem believing that God was male or female—it made more sense that God was both: Creator of life, author of wars, monarch of all. I wasn't certain that those concepts mattered much in the Kingdom of God. He or She is our leader, full of love, mercy, and power over everything of this world. We are God's independent children, some of us more disobedient than others… some needing pushes in the right direction.

My notion would be that anything that possesses any sort of power to affect another, or to be affected by another, if only for a single moment, however trifling the cause and however slight the effect, has real existence; and I hold that the definition of being is simply power.
~Plato, "The Sophist"

CHAPTER TWENTY-SIX

Linguistics and Logistics

At this point in my life, I still have more questions than answers... and most certainly, no real clear-cut ones of either. Another thing that I was certain about was I believed that the Holy Bible could be called sacred, but it wasn't 'holy,' in the sense that God neither wrote nor dictated it. I was of the belief that man wrote down their experiences with God, and that nothing could be more sacred than that! But, I simply couldn't overlook the "typos" in it.

The following Sunday morning, Charlie Oops and Damien were on their way to have another discussion about God and God's nature. Damien was both happy yet a little disappointed by the fact that he still didn't have a language that would allow him to adequately talk about the nature of God.

Both Charlie and Tex definitely had an advantage over me, in that they had a complete language by which they could talk about God. I was struggling a lot more than I've expressed to you so far in this book. No, my sentences weren't at all crisp as they appear on these pages. I was often fighting with my thoughts and my tongue at the same time and they rarely got along with each other.

Arriving at the chapel, Charlie extended his right hand in offering Tex a handshake: "Top of the morning to you, Tex."

"Back to you... both." Tex shook both of their hands, then—although in a hurry—asked, "How are you two doing?"

Fine, Tex, Damien replied. *"Do you think you might have some time later?"*

"Between services, maybe. That good for you?" He asked while adjusting books and furniture around the sanctuary.

Whatever works for you, Tex. I mean, I'm free all day, today.

That wasn't exactly true. Charlie and I had some plans that involved his bed and my naked body in it. Each and everyday, I saw how Oops loved me. It's true that I was uncomfortable about what would likely happen if we were found out by the officers. Nonetheless, we were content with each other regardless of the moments or reasons to have pause in our relationship.

We were also pretty sure that nobody outside of the gay community, the few inmates who knew Charlie was homosexual and that I likely was, didn't know. Especially not Tex, neither of us wanted him nor anyone else to find out. It was not guilt or shame that we wanted to avoid comments, but rather we wanted to avoid private hurts caused by the briefness of our loving friendship.

That morning's church service seemed to slip by Damien. Actually, time in general often had a sense of flying by him without a hint of putting on any brakes. That is, until Charlie tapped Damien on his right arm, bringing him back to the present moment.

Making eye contact, Charlies asked, "Hey boy, you okay?"

I, uh, Damien responded, snapping out of an unexpected daydream.

"Where did you go?" he whispered. The service was still going on, although the chaplain was still minutes from wrapping up his sermon.

Actually, Damien started to respond in his normal volume until Charlie gestured to lower it. *I was at my cell's door, looking at yours. Was I talking in my sleep?*

"Ah, no. I just was wondering is all."

Putting his right arm around Charlie, yet not actually on him, Damien sat up straighter in their pew. The lengthy service was coming to an end, and the other seated parishioners were anxious to stretch their legs and/or leave the church. Although kissing in public, especially inside a chapel, would be complete craziness, Damien wanted nothing more than to embrace Charlie at that moment. Instead, he settled for a restrained and "masculinized" pat on the back.

About five minutes later and rather suddenly from the rear of the chapel, Tex arrived at their pew, reaching across to say good-byes to the inmates leaving the pew ahead of them. He turned to Damien and Charlie, finally, and asked, "Well boys, are you ready?"

As usual, Damien responded. *You know it.*

"Me, too," Charlie spoke out. "I have a few questions."

To be honest, I felt like I didn't deserve this man's time, but I so desperately needed it. Sure, it didn't have to come from him, from Tex Watson... and, no, I'm not being personal. This man, who had abused innocent souls, who now helped run the Sunday church services... and, I, I was no exception. Look at what I had done with a rifle, responding to a paranoia brought on by a drug rather than a convincing and manipulative cult leader like Manson. Who was I to pass any judgment?

Picking up the Bible, Damien asked, "Where do we start?"

"Why don't we let the Bible tell us?" Tex plucked the Bible out from Damien's hand and, starting from the back of the hardcover book, randomly flipped pages like an old-fashioned flip book, until the pages themselves seemed to clog up behind his thumb, becoming difficult to flip. This is when he stopped, right at the third chapter to the gospel of John. "This seems like a good place to start. Here, what's the sixteenth verse say?"

Uh, it says, 'For God loved the world so much that He gave His only Son, so that everyone who believes in Him may not die but have eternal life. For God did not send his Son into the world to be its judge, but to be its savior.' Should I go on?

"No, hold on," Tex wanted to reflect on these quotes. "So, what's that mean to you? That God gave His son?"

That He sent Jesus to Earth, Damien answered.

"But it doesn't say "God sent His son,' but that He 'gave' Jesus."

What's the difference? Damien contended. Charlie wordlessly agreed that he didn't see any contrast between <u>sent</u> and <u>gave</u>.

"Alright." Tex explained, "Imagine you're a dad. It is just you and your son living in some crappy apartment and you 'send' your son to the grocery store to buy some milk. Okay? Now, compare that to being a dad, living in a house at the top of Mount Everest, and you send your only family member to a faraway place like Australia or Zimbabwe, knowing you're not going to hug him again for, like, thirty years! Imagine the heartache and loneliness of that poor father."

Oh. Damien could feel what that would be like. *But what about verse seventeen, where it does use the word 'send'? That God sent Jesus but not to be the world's judge?*

"Actually, it says He did not send Jesus to condemn the world, and so on, because it wouldn't sound correct to say that God did not give his Son. But, my point is that in one sentence it says God gave Jesus to us, and He did not do this because he wanted Jesus to pronounce judgment on us, but to offer us an escape route... a path of salvation."

"I've got a question," Charlie jumped in. "Why does the Bible say that Jesus is the only Son? I thought that we were all God's children. I'm His son, you're His son," then he pointed at Damien, "we are all His sons, aren't we?"

"We are, now!" Tex simplified. "But when Jesus was with Him, and I mean before Jesus became human and born of the virgin, it was only the two of them plus a couple of angels. Jesus, at that time, was God's only companion within His Kingdom."

"Wait, what about Moses and Elijah? Aren't they also in heaven?"

"Now you're going a little deeper than we can go on." Tex said, referring to the facts available in the Bible. "Sure, they are likely in God's Kingdom, but like all the rest of the prophets and servants of God, it's possible that only Jesus could enter the holiest of places like the throne room, much like the priests in the Old Testament handling the ark of the Lord. But, again, we're getting off topic."

Okay, so what topic are we talking about? Damien asked.

"The most important one... are you a Christian?"

Putting down the Bible he'd been holding, Damien replied honestly, *"I don't believe in all the same things that you do, Tex. Or you, Charlie. I believe that there is a God, there's God's only Son, begotten of a virgin—like it says in Luke—which I find interesting being that only a woman who was pure could give birth to someone as pure as the Christ.*

That, with my whole being, I really do believe! That Christ is my savior and Lord. My king of all kings.

I know I'm a sinner, Damien continued, *and that only by the blood of the Christ Jesus can my sins be forgiven. You can't buy that blood in any stores, it's already been spilt out for us. We only need to believe in the man it came from.*

"Very true," Tex agreed.

However, like I said the last time, I don't believe that God or any other spiritual; being knows the future, nor can he or she know all things about to happen, because even God doesn't have all the power. I believe that all beings have their own power to be what they are and that all humans have the power to do as they will. So, God can't have power that other beings have.

Shuffling through a stack of notes Tex had for the upcoming second service "Whoa! Let's take this apart first. It's a lot to consider. So, you accept our God is real and that He exists?"

Yeah, I do. Damien admitted. Charlie likewise nodded.

"You believe that although you have some control over your life, you don't have complete control of it, and neither does God?"

Well, unless I gave up all my power, He doesn't have control of it.

"But," Tex suggested with a smile," you could relinquish some of the control over your life, over to God, if you wanted to, Right?"

Well, yes... if I wanted to give up my power.

"And, you believe that Jesus is the only begotten Son of God, that he died on the cross for your sins?"

Yes, I really do believe in that. Damien adamantly agreed.

"Me, too, Tex!" Charlie equally admitted.

"So, what's there to discuss?" Tex grinned from ear to ear. "You both sound saved to me."

Damien was quiet for several seconds, looking at Charlie, then back at Tex. His thoughts were racing a hundred-miles-per-hour yet his lips were stuck in 'Park.' Finally, he found his inquisitive voice again.

You mean, that there isn't one or two points that are worthy to discuss... theologically?

Changing his gaze so that Charlie would be addressed, Tex said, "To tell you both the truth, there are probably hundreds of points which we could agree and disagree on, but that's not the important things."

"What is the important thing?" Charlie asked.

"The ultimate, consequential, all-important thing is that you recognize that Jesus is the Son of God and that he died for your sins. That we was raised from that death, and that you are now—for all time—washed clean before God. We can argue about anything else you'd like, but it'll be a waste of breath."

A 'waste of breath'? I don't think so. I'd like a good conversation about God, regardless if I'm already saved or not.

Shifting in his seat, Tex asked, "Do you believe that everything found in the Bible is one hundred percent what God wanted to be written down? That God told the writers to write, and they obeyed completely?"

Ha. That's a resounding, no! Damien responded.

Picking up another Bible left on the pew beside him, Tex asked, "What is it, then, if it's not the word of God? Have you ever read Second Timothy, verse 3:16... "All Scripture is inspired by God and is useful for teaching the truth, rebuking error, correcting faults, and giving instruction for right living." Tex recited from memory.

Damien opened the Bible he was holding and reread the biblical quote, pointing out, *this one's a little different. It says 'correcting and training in righteousness,' and goes on from there.*

"Yeah, that's an N.I.V. translation. I'm sure it's also different in original King James, but the message is still there. That everything in this bible or that bible," he said while pointing at yet another abandoned book on an adjacent pew, "was originally written under the inspiration of God."

But, why are there so many translations? I mean, this one's N.I.V., the one you're holding is Today's English Version, and that one over there, with the red cover, that's New King James. How can they all be correct? Or accurate?

Well, just because one Bible uses 'thy' instead of 'your', it's still the same story. The fact that language has evolved over the last one-hundred years alone should show you that a book written two-thousand years ago would have words in it that nobody uses anymore. Take the word 'gay'," Tex suggested and almost immediately Damien felt a bit fidgety. "Just 20 years ago, it had only one meaning, which was to be merry or exuberant. You know, full of happiness. Now, it's hardly ever used for that definition anymore… only something or someone homosexual."

So, if the Bible had the word 'gay' in it, a hundred years from now the reader wouldn't know that it meant 'merry'?

"Actually, I believe some versions do have the word 'gay' in it." Charlie pointed out.

"True. So, when the word loses its original meaning, future readers will be confused by what exactly the Bible is trying to say. Hence, they publish yet another new translation. There are several Hebrew and Greek words in the Bible right now which not even the world's best historians can find a translation for, such as <u>shiggaion</u> and <u>gittith</u>. Neither had been used in so very many hundreds of years, they lost all meaning. Yet, one unknown word doesn't destroy nor diminish the overall message."

"Um," Charlie began, "you said that 'All Scripture is… useful.' right?"

"That's what Second Timothy, chapter three says."

"So, then, why isn't all the scripture in the Bible?"

"I don't follow—" Tex started to say, then asked, "you mean the Apocrypha? And the Deuterocanonicals? The so-called Additional Books of the Bible?"

"Yeah. The books of the Maccabees, the gospels written by the other Apostles. Why aren't they in the Bible?"

"Well, it took a while for them to officially be declared as sacred and canonical. You got to remember that back in the First Century, ninety years or so after Jesus was born, ink and paper—or papyrus, actually—was really expensive back then. If you wanted a full and complete copy of <u>all</u> of the scriptures, you had to pay almost your entire life savings to hire scribes to spend eighteen hours a day, for five years, to copy by hand every single word ever written about God and the children of Israel. So, some cost-cutting must have been agreed upon."

So, they left out the books of the Maccabees to save themselves some money? Damien asked. He found this topic rather amusing.

"Well, we really don't know, for sure. But, no, it took almost fifteen-hundred years until these left-out stories were finally considered a part of Scripture. Unfortunately, most versions of the Bible still don't include them because, well, to be honest, I'm not sure why not."

Well, Damien was aghast, *that's not right. I mean, I believe, they are a story of a people's expressions, of their experiences with the world in relationship with God. And fills in the huge gap between Testaments.*

Tex was suddenly impressed. "You've read the Apocrypha? The books of the Maccabees?"

I read <u>everything</u> I can get my hands on. Those books are—their stories were—their best effort to record these experiences and communication with God, But not as if it was dictated by God. In fact, all of the Bible that they wrote, these experiences they'd written down and have survived this long, is in itself a miracle. If God didn't want something to be written down in the Bible, all He would need to do is snap His fingers and those writings would cease to exist. But, the fact that they still exist in the world tells me they must be of some importance!

"Hmm, the same could be said about certain people I know."

Personally, I believe that God does inspire writers today, and that these people may have the blessing of being writers of future scripture. The fact that nothing has been officially added to the Holy Bible in all this time is wrong to me. In the basement of the Vatican, there's rumored to be all kinds of unpublished letters by Peter, Paul, James, and others. There's also a contested gospel written my Mary Magdalene, whom the church continues to rebuke as an Apostle due to her gender. I don't think this is fair nor right.

At some point in the near future, hopefully sooner rather than later, Jesus David our Christ and Savior will be returning to planet Earth. It would be impossible to believe in today's society that if a female news reporter were the first one to "stick a microphone" up to Jesus, that her reporting of the facts would have any less actuality or truth to it than that of a male news reporter. Yet, we currently have trouble accepting any scripture written by a woman thousands of years ago as being accurate or sacred. Why is the Vatican locking these scrolls away from us?!

Later that same Sunday, Damien and Charlie took seats on the bleachers overlooking the prison's soccer field. It was an incredibly warm

August afternoon, but a pleasant "on shore" breeze was slowly picking up with each passing hour. Their conversation hadn't strayed much from the topics shared with Tex that morning—once Damien got stuck on a favorite subject, it took quite a bit of effort to change it!—and now they were discussing "questionable mistakes in scripture."

Yes, Charlie, Damien began while looking at his lover with wonder, *there are a bunch of suspect verses. Next time you get a chance, look at—I believe it's—Second Kings, chapter 16, verse 20. Then compare that to Second Chronicles, chapter 28, verse 27, and you'll see two perfect contradictions. The Second Kings verse says that King Ahaz died and "was buried in the royal tombs in David's City." But the Second Chronicles one specifically says that King Ahaz "was buried in Jerusalem, but <u>not</u> in the royal tombs." Yeah, this mistake is rather tiny, but wouldn't God the all-powerful, all-perfect want these errors not to exist?*

"So," Charlie responded, "one author wrote one things, and one wrote the exact opposite. All it proves is that these two author's didn't copy off of each other's notes."

Maybe, Damien contended, *"but Ezra, who they gave credit for writing Chronicles, probably read Second Kings <u>before</u> contradicting its author. At least, by the way it's worded, it sounds like Ezra was pointing out a mistake in that other writing.*

"Well, Damien, I don't know about that. I'm not a thinker like you are, and this is one hell of a subject...a very difficult subject."

But that's just it! Reading the Bible shouldn't be difficult. God wants us to read His Word, yet it's the most laborious book <u>to</u> read. The four Gospels overlap each other, talking about the same events during Jesus' ministry...and yet, even though these four people followed Jesus everywhere he went, some gospels completely overlook miracles He performed. Only some of the parables were written down here and there. The gospel of John has several events that don't appear in any of the other three at all. It makes you wonder why only one of the four authors thought that certain events were worth recording when the other three decided not to.

"Or, maybe they weren't there that day?" Charlie suggested.

I don't believe that either. These Apostles left their homes, their families to spend every possible moment with Jesus, everywhere He went. Why would only one gospel include the raising of Lazarus from the dead? Did the other three writers think this resurrection wasn't that big of a deal?

"That is interesting, but…"

But what? C'mon, Charlie, you can't believe that if God really wanted everything written down, then all four of the Gospels would coordinate with one another. God likes things to be perfect and pure, just like the gold used to build His temple. But there's just so many mistakes in His recorded word. Take the very first chapter of the Bible.

"You mean, the book of Genesis?"

If you look at the first chapter, on the fifth day God created animals, then on the sixth day created humans. Right?

"Okay," Charlie wasn't sure where this was headed.

Then look at chapter 2, verse 19. It says that after God created Adam, the first man, he <u>then</u> created animals. So, which is it? Did God create animals first, or create man first? These two chapters contradict each other, and they are the first two chapters of the whole thing! This is why so many people don't like to read the Bible cover-to-cover. Because of mistakes like this one, and because the books aren't written in chronological order.

"What do you mean by 'chronological order'?

Just that the Bible doesn't read like a book: beginning, middle, and end. Like I said, both Kings and Chronicles talk about the same events in a slightly different way. All of the minor prophets, their timelines are all over the place. Some write about the destruction of the temple, then you read one written before the temple was destroyed. Why did they publish these books in such a slip-flopping order? The Bible is hard enough to read with having to remember if the story your reading happened before the Jews were dragged off to Babylon or after.

"So, you think that the Bible should read like a paperback novel?"

Some of it does read like a novel, From Deuteronomy to Second Samuel, the story flows nice and smoothly. But then the nation splits in two, there's two separate kingdoms to keep track of, and then the Babylonians show up, you forget whose running things, and there's impossible-to-keep-straight names like Jehoahaz, Jehoiakim, Jehoiachin, wishing that everyone just went by Robert or Mike Junior. Of course, some last names here and there would've been nice instead of: 'Ezra, son of Seraiah, the son of Azariah, the son of Hilkiah,' the son of this guy, son of that guy, son of another Azariah, and so on.

"They do, don't they? I mean, they call Judas, Judas Iscariot. And, call Jesus, Jesus Christ."

Christ isn't Jesus' last name! Damien exclaimed, then realized that Charlie was only kidding. *Yeah, Charlie. I got you. But, seriously, Jesus was of the family of David. His full name should be, Christ Jesus David of the city of Nazareth. But we prefer to just call him Jesus the Christ, sometimes forgetting the 'the' in there.*

"I don't know," Charlie shrugged, "I just follow along with the people in the chapel. That's why I'm not one to ask questions, especially things in the Bible."

Well, me neither. I don't want to mess with people's minds or step on their faith. I believe that their living life as a Christian is far more important.

"Wow, I—" Charlie defended himself, "I didn't mean to suggest that, uh, that you're messing with people's minds. No! Not at all, and that comes from me. I just, you know, think that you're really smart and that you merely need a way to express yourself, your thoughts, and your opinions regarding God and the Bible."

With that said, their conversation faded away, leaving Damien and Charlie in the blessed quiet that they enjoyed so much enjoyed. Damien sat there with his forbidden lover, just watching the tall grass of the nearby hills dancing in the breeze, and the sound of the herd of wild turkeys just on the other side of the prison walls. It was while in this mood that Damien best was able to dwell on his thoughts of the Creator, leaving the mess of that prison behind.

CHAPTER TWENTY-SEVEN

Future Destinations

Following dinner, Charlie and Damien spent some free time in repose—relying on the stillness of the night for the refreshment of the mind—so that they could resolve some important issues. The biggest of these, was where they were going to live once released on parole and what they'd be hopefully doing for employment. It sounded to Damien as if Charlie had already solved these problems for himself, which made Damien fairly happy, yet—still—Damien was very uncertain about his own future... and that made him very nervous.

I was indeed scared, I was slipping. I had stopped thinking about this all-important problem: Life after prison. I had stopped making any plans for this blessed and upcoming event only a few weeks away and rushing ever towards me. Frankly, I was scared; and to make things worse, back then the prison system didn't have a program for those returning to the real world or out on parole. No, the days of halfway houses was gone, and the more current days of readjustment programs for ex-offenders hadn't yet been dreamt up... and, from what I heard, these programs have about as much substance as a dream!

Part of my problem was that, on most days, I would regularly lose track of time. In prison, it's awfully easy to become stuck in a routine that quickens days at a time. Another problem was, I had been getting myself so involved in my church groups and even putting together a Bible study group, the reality of going home soon seemed still months away instead of weeks. Charlie wanted to have a study group mainly because he was interested in hearing my notions about God and my beliefs and faith as a Christian. He knew that I was different than others in my beliefs…for that matter I was just as different in many other areas.

Anyway, Charlie was glad to recognize that my notions made more sense than most other people's ideas. He wanted to mature in his depth of insight and thought, but there was one thing blocking his progress: Neither him nor I knew anyone that had somewhat similar notions about God and Scripture. This is what triggered our desire to start our own Bible study group. Well, that, plus it was a huge distraction from our worries and fears about preparing for our parole.

Charlie and Damien formed a Bible study group made up of three Christians and an atheist, plus themselves. Most of these guys worked with Damien and Charlie in the kitchen, except for a young white boy named James who was a yard-crew worker. In fact, at their very first Saturday meeting, Damien was really—and pleasantly—surprised at the sincerity of interest building in and around their little study group.

Charlie opened their first meeting with a question to Damien, asking: "Damien, please tell us why you have such a hard time calling the Holy Bible, you know, something <u>holy</u>."

Okay, Damien started, *I have a problem with the notion of holiness, because I believe that if it were 'holy', then it would be completely without any errors or differences in opinion.*

Sitting to Damien's right, and one row of bleachers below him, was a young black man named Guy Davis. He asked, "Damien, what are you comfortable with?"

Well, Guy, I know them as sacred because of their subject, and because it is clear that the sons of Israel were truly inspired to convey their many experiences with God, in comparison with the outside world. For this reason, their stories are sacred. If there were no errors or differences in textual meaning, then—and only then—I would call them holy.

"Why's that?" James asked.

Well, several stories—I should call them recorded histories, but not all of them are historical—contradict each other. How could something have been dictated by God have mistakes? God disliked impure things. He wanted everything which represented Him to be without blemish. This is not the case with the Bible... God's written word.

Smiling, as if catching Damien in a contradiction of his own, Guy asked, "Sure, Damien. But if God didn't dictate them—didn't pick who would tell the great stories of God—then who would?"

Guy, I'm not a biblical historian. I have read my study Bible from cover to cover, including all of those footnotes and introductions. I'm not an expert, but I have found imperfections in the historic account. There's a lot of events told by the prophets that don't match up with the book of Daniel. Wrong dates, wrong names. There's a big inconsistency with the Creation story, in Genesis chapter one and two.

Damien then went on to describe the two verses: the Fifth Day versus Genesis 2:19, and how they refute each other. Charlie and James seemed interested with this retelling. Both had their Bibles with them and read Genesis 1:20–26, then 2:18–26, then 2:18–20 out loud. Everyone noticed the contradiction right away except Peter.

Peter was a young Mexican with a shaved-bald head and an ensemble of mono-colored tattoos of Spanish words and "low rider" artwork. He was here in the United States illegally—without documentation—and had a little trouble with the English language, other than from what he'd learned so far in prison. Immediately after Damien pointed out the quarrel found in Genesis, Peter raised his hand and said, "Damien! I thought you were a Christian... but you're not. You are just going to hell."

Waving his hand as if to wipe away what Peter had just said, Damien replied, *So, condemn me for not seeing the Bible the same way as you do.*

Peter responded, "Well, I no judge you... but how you going to call the Bible something less than holy? And accurate?

Taking off his gray beanie cap, Jeff interjected, "Tell us, Peter, what do you believe?"

"Well, Jeff, I don't call it holy or sacred... for a very different reason. I'm an atheist."

"A what?" Charlie asked Peter.

"I don't believe in God... at all."

Really? Damien was honestly surprised. *Then why'd you want to come to a Bible study?*

"I'm here 'cause I thought the conversation might be interesting. So far I'm right. It's interesting."

"I dunno if I like the idea," Charlie contended, "of having someone that doesn't believe in God, to be in our group."

No, hang on, Damien defended, *If anything, having a nonbeliever in our group allows us to view the Bible more, um, adversely.*

Charlie started to ask, "What does 'adversly' mean?", when Jeff interrupted with: "Damien, there's still your question of holiness. Why don't you believe that the Bible is holy?"

That's easy, Jeff. Because God clearly didn't write or dictate its Creation. He gave us the Ten Commandments—those He wrote down Himself—the rest of the Bible was written by man. This, he held up his copy of a N.I.V. study Bible for emphasis, *is supposed to be God's word. Yet, it's one of the hardest books that there is to read. See what I mean?*

"Guess that you have a point there," Jeff replied, "except for Paul's declaration about all Scripture." Referring to the aforementioned Second Letter to Timothy, starting at verse 3:14, instead of only at 3:16: "But as for you, continue in what you have learned and have become convinced of, because you know those from whom you learned it, and how from infancy you have known the holy Scriptures, which are able to make you wise for salvation through faith in Christ Jesus. All Scripture is God-breathed and is useful for teaching."

Yes, Jeff, and that's a good point. However, we didn't have the same 'teachers' that Timothy did. What we only have is this book, except for the fact that God didn't strip any of the writers of their ability to be opinionated or creative. That is also a power that God lacks, to error is to be human. He allowed us to write His Word, rather than write it Himself. See what I'm saying?

"So... tell me," Jeff responded, "can they—the books in the Bible—be seen <u>as</u> holy, since each one deals specifically with living a spiritual life?

Charlie interjected first, "This suddenly has turned to be a difficult subject. Ya know?"

I fully understand, Charlie, Damien replied. *Yet I think that it doesn't have to be. What we must be willing to do is to pray and think clearly about the various subjects. We'll need to be willing to set aside our current beliefs, so that way, we can examine our faith without any previous contaminations. Then, after we are done, we can believe as the Spirit of God leads us to.*

"If there *is* one," Peter added with a smirk. Damien only nodded quietly to this comment.

Stretching out his football playing legs, Jeff remarked, "Well, certainly we know where Damien stands with the Bible. The accuracy of it. Does anybody want to share their thoughts and feelings about the Scriptures? Doug?"

Doug, another huge football player type, was a white guy in his early thirties. He'd been "in the system" since childhood, mostly for several short commercial-burglary terms of three years or less. Unfortunately, his latest charge was "erroneously" bumped up to a more serious robbery conviction due to an employee showing up early for work while Doug was making what would've been a clean "getaway."

As a strong-and-silent kind of guy, Doug merely replied, "Nah, I'm good."

A passerby along the jogging track suddenly stopped at the bleachers, looking up at their little group. "This is a Bible study, right?"

"Sure is, Tim. Why do you ask?" Charlie asked of the newcomer. 'Tim', as Charlie identified, worked as one of the clerks in the sergeant's office.

He was likewise black, and about the same age as Charlie...although, according to Damien, not nearly as good looking.

"Well, because I decided 'bout a week ago to check out church and, you know, the faith. I just wanna learn more, so I can make up my mind, you know. That's okay?"

Waving him up to join them, Damien said that guys like Tim were the main reason for the group to exist. And that he and anyone else he knew were more than welcomed. Tim appreciated this comment more than anything.

Well, Tim, Damien turned serious again, *we've just started today, and we are studying about the nature of the Bible. Not so much about what's in it, as much as what it physically is. We seem to be at an impasse. I believe that its stories are sacred, but not holy. I maintain that for something to be called holy, it had to have been actually written or dictated by the Creator, by God, but it has too many errors and mistakes here and there to be something He would have created.*

Jeff, here, Damien introduced, *believes that anything written by God or that can help someone's spiritual life is holy. Peter,* again he pointed out the named person, *doesn't believe in God yet, so naturally doesn't think anything is holy—.*

"That's not true," Peter rebuked, "I know cheese has holes." This caused the few chuckles it intended to.

And, Damien continued straight-faced, *Charlie pretty much goes along with whatever I say.*

"Hey," Charlie lightly punched Damien on the arm, "that's what friends are for."

Drinking some more of the coffee that he'd brought along with him, Tim said, "Well, guys, I find all this very interesting… and I do agree with Damien. The Bible can't be holy if God didn't write or dictate all of it, as he thinks."

"My being an atheist is not what I base my judgment by," Peter spoke out, "I am stating what reasoning led me to accept or not."

"Although you jus' came to us for the fun of it, Peter," Jeff said. "I believe that you're right. Careful reasoning will lead a person to accept the truth that the Bible is sacred… if not completely holy."

Charlie then jumped in, "So, Tim. Do you accept Damien's belief about the nature of the Bible?"

"Well, I know I jus' got here, and I missed wha'ever you all were sayin' earlier… but, yeah, Charlie. You got me right."

Okay then, guys, how about if we move on to another topic for now? Damien suggested. *We can always return to this one if there comes a need. Is that cool with everyone?*

For the next and final twenty minutes before "yard recall," the five of them talked—Doug only listened—in peace about various beliefs they had before really getting into the Bible itself. They just "let the candle dwindle" until it was time for them to return to their cells.

Damien was very pleased with their first ever meeting and where their group was headed. Even though they were of mixed races, with mixed backgrounds and strengths, they wouldn't ever have any physical fights nor out of control arguments. That, in and of itself, showed that they could be good Christians.

Actually, I love studying and talking about God... and to God. I can't think of anything that I'd rather do. God doesn't just want us praising Him or His greatness, He wants to be our best friend. Someone that any of us can just chat with—even if you're doing most of the talking—that is what a personal relationship with God is all about. This coming from a guy who spent half his life unable to created healthy relationships with anyone... well, at least, with anyone I could see with my own eyes.

So, why couldn't people love to share with others how God has moved them in their own lives? All of the positive changes God has made in their own lives? Who wouldn't want to record, to write down for all to read, everything that affected them so many centuries ago? To teach the people many centuries in the future? Who wouldn't want to share such with the people of this planet, or any other, all that God did for their cultures and nations?

Shakespeare once wrote, "O! Call back yesterday, bid time return." It is from our past, our history, which we'll move forward. Now is the time to prepare for what will be... the "then" is there to guide us along. What was "then" might soon be, what will be... unless we change now.

Once again I was at a rare loss for words. There simply weren't any adequate enough to describe what I felt when I heard that I had a visitor waiting for me! No, not even the word 'surprised' would do. I just didn't know anyone other than Samuel who would come to my prison to visit me, and on that weekend, I already know that it would be impossible for Sam to do so... I believed he was in Chicago at the time.

So, that Sunday morning, on my way to the Visiting Room, the only person that I could imagine other than Sam was my Grandpa. And sure enough, it was him, only he wasn't alone. No, a woman was with him who I didn't recognize in the slightest... that is, until I heard her loving voice. It was a voice very much like that of an angel's; however, before you jump to any conclusions, no... it wasn't my mother, although the family resemblance is a sure thing.

His caring grandfather had brought along Damien's long-lost Aunt Sharon—who still went by the nickname of "Cha-cha," but now preferred Sharon. They had arranged to visit Damien not as a regular six-hour visit, but as an overnight "family" visit which lasted roughly forty hours and took place in our of the prison's conjugal visiting motel-style rooms. Visitors, back then, were allowed to bring food along with them, as well as photo albums and memorabilia from home. Damien had a fantastic and healing visit with them.

Caring was what I needed, and as I was growing up, caring was not coming from my mom. That was the hole which my Aunt Cha-cha had filled while I was only three, back when the twins were born. I had continued to see her off and on during my parents' divorce… she had been the only one I could relate to at that time. But now, years later, although I felt love from her, there was also an unexplained distance.

The truth is that I still don't know my family. Currently, at the age of fifty-five, I know as much as I did when I was five. That's the true shame of my life. What I did find out differently at that pleasurable visit, was that they loved me; although, they really didn't know what was wrong while I was young. I told them that I'd wished they had raised me instead of my parents, because I likely wouldn't have been in as much trouble. My Aunt Sharon cried when I said she would have been a better parent than my mom. I had no idea at that moment how often she had tried to become pregnant, nor that her divorce from my Uncle Mike had been in part due to her infertility. No, of course, this would be explained to me later, after it was too late to apologize.

While Damien had been growing up, he'd caught snippets of a conversation between his mother and aunt which made it clear that there were family problems in their childhood home also. The grandmother whom Damien never knew was both a French native living illegally in the United States and rather brash with her daughters. Much like Damien's own mother, his grandmother picked favorites of her children and lavished affectionately to the point of suffocation ontwo of them while practically ignoring the third.

Not that I'm trying to find excuses for my mother's actions, there just simply is no defense for how she'd abandoned me. However, history somehow managed to repeat itself and, like her own mother, she chose to ignore a child just as she, herself, had been ignored. I vowed at that moment that history would not repeat itself beyond my current generation. No, the Collins family curse would end with me and proceed no further.

At the end of Damien's visit with his Grandpa and Aunt Sharon, he returned to the yard and his cell nearly in time for "mandatory standing count" and chow release. Frankly, he couldn't possibly tell anyone what they had for dinner—probably some variety of chicken casserole would be the best bet—since his mind was still filled with the overwhelming joy of the visit. Both of these two family members—the only ones he considered himself as having, albeit, only Aunt Sharon was biologically related—cared about him and wanted Damien to be part of their lives, their future.

It was already decided that Damien would be moving back in with Samuel upon his release, but his Grandpa and Aunt Cha-cha very much wanted to see him on the holidays. What neither of them nor Dr. Reily knew was anything regarding Charlie "oops" Osborne, his current lover, and man of the hour.

I had completely forgot that our Bible group had changed our meeting time to directly after dinner. So, after chow, I returned to the yard where—who should I find?—but Charlie relaxing on the bleachers. "Our" bleachers, as we considered them. I noticed that something was bothering him.

Gently grabbing Charlie's shoulders, Damien asked, *Tell me, what's on your mind?*

"Nothing. Just I haven't seen you in almost two days. So, what our subject of the evening?"

<u>Subject</u>? Damien was dumbfounded! Not being able to remember what he had at all planned for the evening. *I—crap. Why must we work out the group's subject all the time? Let's just have them work it out.*

"Now that's cool," Charlie enthusiastically replied. "We'll let <u>them</u> pick the subject? That's why I'm glad that you're our leader."

Hold the horses, Damien countered, *we are co-leaders.*

"Yeah, I've been meaning to talk to you about that. You know I'll be leaving pretty soon. We should be finding a replacement."

Yeah, Damien suddenly turned depressed, *but not today. Right?*

Taking Damien's hand for a moment in a rare—and forbidden—public display of affection, Charlie replied, "Sure... you're right. Let's focus on right now. The future will take care of itself."

CHAPTER TWENTY-EIGHT

Growing Support

Damien and Charlie waited at the bleachers for the other expected four or five to arrive. Shortly, the overcast sky started to trickle down on them while the other group members, themselves, trickled in to join them. Luckily, the light sprinkling of rain stopped just as quickly as it began, although the same can't be said of the sprinkling of believers.

The first to arrive was Jeff, who once seated quickly asked, "So, what are we working on tonight?"

That remains to be seen, Damien answered.

"Wait, what? You haven't already picked a topic?"

Nope, this group belongs to you guys. Charlie and I only facilitate and learn along, like you guys do.

"Cool, 'cause I sorta want to talk about God tonight."

"We'll see," Charlie replied.

Soon the others showed up and were likewise eager to get started. Charlie made mention of Jeff's suggestion for that night's topic, to which, there weren't any objections. Even Peter the atheist was ready to tackle this subject. All attention was turned towards Jeff, since it was his topic choice.

Okay, Jeff. Tell us what your concern is regarding God?

"Well, it's like this. Is there any way that God can know all things from the beginning to the end of time?"

"You mean, that word…omnipresent?" Charlie asked.

"Yeah, but I think, in the Bible it says that God exists everywhere <u>and</u> at every time at once. Omni—past, present, and future. How can that be?"

Just as the group was getting started with Jeff's question, a fifth and completely new person popped in, asking if there was room for one more.

Sure, replied Damien, *this isn't, like an inn in Bethlehem.* This comment earned Damien a few peculiar looks from those unfamiliar with the second chapter of Luke; although a snicker from James, who was. *Really? Didn't any of you ever see the Charlie Brown Christmas special or read the Gospel of Luke?*

"Cartoons are for kids," a rather macho Peter spoke out.

"Isn't Luke after Matthew and Mark?" Charlie asked, then admitted, "I skipped Luke. It only repeats what the first two Gospels say, anyway. The same miracles and everything."

"Well, now I know what tomorrow night's topic should be," James said in a rather humorous way.

"Anyway," Charlie said while offering the new guy his hand to shake, "I'm Charlie. That's James, and Peter. That's Doug. And over here is my best friend and fearless leader, Damien."

"Well, I'm Kevin," the new guy introduced. He was a middle-aged white guy roughly Damien's height and lanky weight. "I was raised, you could say, as an agnostic. By that, I mean, I believe that something out there created the world and human beings, but I'm not quite ready to call our Creator a god, or the God."

"And why's that?" the atheist among them asked.

"I, uh, well…it's clear that human beings, our bodies, weren't an accident. That we were intelligently designed with 'backup' organs, and, um. An immunity system that heals and repairs us. Have you ever sat and thought about how complicated our eyes work? The fact that we have two kidneys when we really needed only one."

"Well, Kevin," Jeff responded, "I can assure you of one thing, whether or not you believe in God, or want to call our Creator, 'God', that this place is here and real. You're right that our bodies weren't some freak accident, and that we aren't alive by accident—"

"I'm not willing to go that far," Kevin said with a smile, "not yet."

It's nice meeting you, Kevin, Damien said. He was rather pleased with how their conversation was going. That so many other inmates were eager to be involved with their very theological discussions. During the span between their last meeting and this one, while Damien had been blessed with that unexpected family visit, he wasn't sure if their little group would last longer than a week; and yet, new members like Kevin were popping up out of nowhere to lend their support and views about the Bible.

I wanted people to love the Scriptures and God as much as I did. We discussed everyone's beliefs briefly, what each person thought about God... well, each person except for Doug, who hardly ever spoke. I was glad to explain my thoughts openly with anyone for the first time in my life! Jeff's sincere topic really got-the-ball-rolling—you could say—with our growing Bible study group. But, truthfully, after only half an hour I was tired, mentally exhausted, and I longed for the end of the day.

I went to my cell and prepared a snack for Charlie and I to enjoy. We looked forward to the two hours between inmate counts that we could spend alone together in his or my own adjacent cell. An evening alone with my best friend, my lover, if only for a few hours.

Although, as mentioned earlier, Damien thought that their following meeting's topic would be about the Gospel of Luke, as James suggested... it instead returned to another familiar subject of Damien's: Noah and his Ark.

Tim, who had missed their previous meeting, showed up for that night's group and asked, "Why are there two very different descriptions of the animals that Noah brought aboard the Ark?"

"Where's it say that?" James asked, opening his Bible to Genesis, chapter six.

"Towards the end of him building the boat, and chapter seven, verse three. Why do you think God changed His mind?"

Before anyone said anything else, everyone who had a copy of the Bible with them read the two chapters in question. Charlie was the first to ask, "What's a 'ritually clean animal'?"

"Oh," James was the first to answer, "That's the ones you can eat. It's in Leviticus, chapter eleven."

"B-but, if it's in Leviticus, then how would Noah know which animals were clean, and which weren't?" Suddenly there was a lot of page flipping, back and forth through Genesis, with a few guys jumping all the way ahead to Deuteronomy chapter fourteen, verses three and onward.

"It says right here," James pointed out, "'You may not eat camels, rabbit, or rock badgers. They must be considered unclean…' They got pigs, owls, vultures, and winged insects in here, too."

"Okay," Charlie contended, "but that was all in Moses' time. How did Noah know which animals were clean or not?"

"God must've told him," James theorized. "Maybe Noah memorized it instead of writing it down."

Damien raised his hand to get everyone's attention. *I think we're missing the point Tim was trying to make. Right, Tim? You wanted to know why God suddenly changed His mind and told Noah to collect seven pairs of one kind of animal but only one pair of another. When, just one chapter ago, he said only one pair of every kind of animal.*

"Hey, isn't that favoritism?" Charlie outburst.

"The whole Noah's Ark story," Peter added, "is favoritism. Only Noah's family members were selected to survive that flood, meanwhile millions would drown."

Excuse me, Damien tried to gain control, again. *But the topic is that there must have been more than one writer—one author—of the account of Genesis. In fact, most theological schools of the day had to compile the stories from verbal accounts shared during several different families and their lifetimes. Keep in mind, that they hadn't invented a written language until much, much later. They had paint, but not ink back then, and told stories around campfires using hieroglyphics and pictographs—.*

"You mean, graffiti?" Charlie simplified for the other uneducated members of their study group, "Cave pictures?"

"Well, yeah. *They could've used drawings on walls to help tell their stories, Until, finally, generations later paper—papyrus—was discovered and replaced them and chiseling into stone tablets. God gave the writers various experiences which inspired early man to write down. God intended them to be shared not only between the Israelites, but also all of the people opportunity to share and make these stories known by as many people of their world until their great-great ancestors could finally write them down. See?*

"Yeah, I sorta do," Jeff replied. "It's difficult, nowadays, to think that they didn't have pencils and ballpoint pens back then."

No, Damien replied, then suddenly recalled, *Ballpoints pens were invented only a hundred years ago. In 1888.*

"What? How do you know that?" James asked.

I own last year's The World Almanac. That, and I watch a lot of game shows.

"Huh," Tim suggested, "you should get on that one with Alex Trebek. Make yourself some money."

I don't think so, my mind doesn't actually process questions fast enough to be the first one to push my buzzer. But, again, we're getting off the subject.

"What was the subject, again?!" Peter smart-alecky remarked, poking obnoxious fun at the new group's apparent disorganization.

"Hey guys!" A sudden and rather authoritative voice boomed from the bottom of the bleachers. It was a correctional officer whom both Charlie and Damien respected, perhaps more than any of the others. "Sorry to break up your little powwow! It's emergency count! Take it back to your buildings!"

"Crap," said Kevin the new guy. "Jus' when things were getting' good."

'Good'? Damien repeated to himself, then a feeling of overwhelming joy seemed to flow through him from head to toe. Their small Bible study group was indeed working… it was being admired, which would also make it attractive to even more new members!

After the 'emergency count' was cleared, Damien and Charlie left their cells to go to the TV room, and watched a little "boob tube" until it was recall time. The correctional officers didn't normally look inside the cells between the dinner meal release and their 9 p.m. count time. Being that inmates all had keys to their own cells, Charlie would visit Damien several times… both after this count and in between other known inmate count times in the middle of the night. This was when they'd make passionate love to each other and be done before the first osunds of boots or jingling key rings could be heard coming down their tier.

Some nights, we would return from chow to one another's cell. Then, done with our sex, we would shower and return to the bleachers to wait for the group to show up. This was one of the only ways that we could concentrate on the Bible and our group without being distracted by each other's closeness on those benches. Once in a while, Charlie would bring out with him a blanket for us to enjoy while we sat on the grass at the foot of those bleachers.

At each Bible study group, once everyone was seated, I asked the group to share their concepts and emotions about God. It was very important that we were all "on the same page," if that was even possible. I never thought this could be probable, especially with Peter the atheist and Kevin the agnostic; however, both of them surprised me at times. They had various understandings about the very same God. We all did! But, more than anything, I also wanted them to see that we had different interpretations of what it meant to worship Him as our Heavenly Father.

PART TWO
Divine Detours

Although the result of Jesus' message, life, and death should have been to redefine divine power in terms of divine love, this did not happen. Power, in the sense of controlling domination, remained the essential definition of deity....

God seeks to persuade each occasion toward that possibility for its own existence which would be best for it; but God cannot control the finite occasion's self-actualization.... [S]ince God is not in complete control of the events of the world, the occurrence of genuine evil is not incompatible with God's beneficence toward all His creatures.
~ *John B. Cobb, Jr. and David Ray Griffin,* Process Theology: An Introductory Exposition

CHAPTER TWENTY-NINE

Seeking Answers

California Men's Colony is set on top of a hill located rather close to the beach in San Luis Obispo, almost directly across the Pacific Coast Highway. Summertime at C.M.C. were warm for sure, yet rarely unbearably hot, thanks to being so close to the Pacific. Occasionally, one would see temperatures rise above 95 degrees F, and when it does, Californians would have their battalions of air-conditioners going; however, C.M.C. only had ceiling fans.

We also had our mini-market, or "canteen" open whenever the yard was open at night, where one could buy sodas or ice cream...which made things so much more comfortable. The summer evenings were also nice because the Warden gave us permission to keep the night yard going until 10 p.m. Normally everything shuts down at 9 p.m. So, for a prison, C.M.C. and especially its staff, was a pretty good deal! Although, I don't recommend doing anything to end up there, it's not worth the ride; the price of admission! It's all bad!

Sunday morning came and Damien nearly missed Charlie on his way to breakfast, or so he thought. There hadn't been a single meal since they'd met that Damien and Charlie didn't sit and eat with each other, especially on their days off from the kitchen; but, even then, they usually ate their worker meals within eyesight. That morning, there Charlie was waiting for Damien at the landing of their housing unit's stairs.

The fact was so wonderful though, he and I did most everything together. Or, we took time out to admire the handiwork of God... at least, what of His work that was available to be experienced from our fenced-in yard.

To Damien's surprise, Charlie was also as eager to visit with Tex Watson and witness how Damien would express his various questions, as Damien was. The truth was that Charlie wasn't a Christian—he freely admitted to Damien that he did not believe in the Bible at all—but he clearly thought that Damien's understanding of God simply made more sense than that of Tex's... whom Charlie viewed as "the extreme theologian" as well as a Manson family murderer.

After breakfast, they headed back to their cells, washed up, then got ready for church. Damien wasn't trying to convert Charlie over to his own beliefs, however, Charlie did express interest in what others believe about God and Scripture. As you might have noticed, Damien wasn't at all shy about sharing his knowledge and opinions to any specific topic; although, he was known to often become stuck on one.

Walking in, we were greeted by Tex's assistant—yes, an inmate had another inmate assigned as their assistant—who asked us if we had ever been there before. Obviously he was new, since we'd been coming there for five or six Sundays in a row! We explained who we were and that Tex was expecting us, even though we were standing in an open auditorium, not a doctor's office, and Tex could clearly see and hear us from where we stood. I was glad to see that Tex was busy enough for the Chaplain to believe he needed an assistant, even if the whole thing was rather bizarre.

Damien and Charlie waited in the sanctuary and sat through Tex's lengthy sermon, which they'd both found interesting. Well, Damien rather liked it, for the most part anyhow. Only while giving his speech, one issue—Damien varied with—Tex did make the point that God had control of each and every occurrence on Earth... of the universe, for that matter.

The reason for my problem was that if God had control of every single moment, only to later blame us for tons of sins and mistakes just made no sense whatsoever. Yes, according to Exodus, God affected the Pharaoh of Egypt and hardened his heart against Moses' repeated requests to free the slaves; and then, God punished the Pharaoh with plagues, embarrassment, and killing his first born—as well as everyone else's first-born son. Does this make sense that if God was controlling pharaoh's feelings then Pharaoh justly deserved to receive such horrible punishments?

Tex's belief that God was behind every major decision in our lives also meant that these subjects—or victims—had no power over the occurrences of good or evil in their lives. This troubled me greatly. How could He take someone's "free will" away from them, only to cause that person to fail or to sin? No, I couldn't accept this... God couldn't have controlled when I became addicted to freebasing cocaine or selling my body for rent. Why would He want me to become or continue being a prostitute when doing so was against His own Law?

When Tex Watson was done with that morning's service—first of two—Tex made his way over to Charlie and Damien with a warm greeting, "Good morning, brothers. How are you doing?"

"We're doing well, thank you," Charlie replied on their behalf.

"I'm glad to see that you brought questions and your Scriptures," he said, referring to the study Bibles both were holding and the piece of scratch paper in Damien's hand.

Charlie turned and pointed at the notes Damien held, "Here they are. I hope you brought ammunition, and plenty of it. Damien did his homework."

Sitting down in a metal folding chair, Tex expressed that he wasn't at all worried. "Ask away! We only have fifteen minutes until the next service."

Alright, Damien lifted his chicken-scratched handwriting to eye level. *Well, Tex, here's our group's first question. In Genesis 6:19-22, it looks like God changed His mind about how many pairs of animals Noah should have taken onto the ark. My question is why did He change His mind?*

"Okay, Damien. <u>How</u> did God change His mind?"

Well, in chapter 6, we read that God directed Noah to take a pair of each and every kind of animal. But then, in chapter 7... Damien then started thumbing through the pages in his study Bible, but Tex not only wasn't holding a Bible, he didn't need one.

"Yes. Clearly chapter seven makes God's instructions clearer than in chapter six. There really isn't any mystery there. Next?"

Come on, Tex! You of all people, I expect better than that from you. The fact is that God gave two different sets of instructionsOvery-Brownor, well, the author does. There are differences in the numbers, and these can be accountable by the fact that one school of writers wrote chapter six, and another was, in fact, the author of chapter seven. There is the notion in chapter seven of clean versus unclean, as is discussed in the teachings of Mosaic law, which—as you know—didn't exist until many generations later. Noah would have no idea what a clean or unclean animal was.

"Well, I see what has you bothered, even confused, but I can assure you that the one and only number of animals was—likely—only one pair. You're right about different authors, I'm impressed. Yes, the story of the great flood was a composite narrative that came from two separate sources, with the Yahwist source having some later editorial additions which produced duplications and inconsistences to that of the Priestly source. Much of the chapters one through eleven required the interweaving of the two sources into the intricate patchwork we have today. But, I assure you, the importance of the overall message of the flood isn't diminished if Noah took seven pairs or only one.

"What's next?" Tex eagerly asked, as if what he'd just said was common knowledge which anyone should be able to recite from the top of their heads, as he had precisely done.

Wait! So, it's not important enough that one author—what you called Priestly—and the other, which I'm not even going to try to pronounce—

"Ya'vist. It's just the name they gave to the putative author of the earliest known writings of the Bible. Yahwist, or 'author of Yahweh,' a Hebrew name for God."

O-o-kay, Um, well, I think that the number of clean animals might've come from Levitical law, as it may have been seen to symbolize the number of days God took to create the earth and then rested after.

"Ah, I see someone's been reading their study Bible's footnotes. Yes, the number seven stands for both the day of creation in which He rested and as God's special number for perfection. The numbers six and seven are very symbolic throughout the Bible: Seven is pure, six is impure."

With that said, Damien flipped his Bible to Second Timothy 3:16, pointing out the famous chapter and verse to establish the inerrant nature of the Bible. However, as Tex then pointed out, "The Bible doesn't have a verse that assures the reader that there aren't any errors in the pages of the Bible."

But, Damien contested, *it's supposed to be God's Word. The perfect representation of God's mindset.*

"Whoever said that God had a perfect mindset? God is all-knowing, the source of all love, wisdom, and mercy. He is omnipotent. But, even God admits that He changes His mind. You've read the story of Jonah?"

"Yeah," Charlie spoke out. "the whale guy!"

Tex merely shook his head at this reference. "Yeah, the swallowed by a whale guy. Anyway, God wanted him to go to Nineveh, to tell that capital city of the great Assyrian empire, that God would destroy it. Jonah didn't want to go there because he was convinced that God wouldn't follow through and carry out His threat to destroy the city. Finally, after a series of dramatic events like being thrown overboard and, yes Charlie, being swallowed by a really big fish, he went to Nineveh, delivered God's message, and—poof!—nothing happens, just like Jonah originally feared."

"So, God lied to Jonah?" Charlie questioned.

"No, there wasn't any lying. Read the final chapter of Jonah. Actually, I invite you to read the whole thing, Charlie. It's only four chapters. But, yes, after the leaders of Nineveh repented upon hearing God's warning, God did change His mind... and He even gives Jonah a very good reason why He did."

Okay, Tex, why don't we move on to salvation?

"Yeah, I'd like that," Charlie agreed.

"Before I start," Tex said, "tell me, Charlie, what you know about salvation?"

"Uh, well, salvation means... to be saved. That we don't go to hell."

"How about you, Damien. What do you know about salvation?"

Well, salvation is a gift from God, which can in no ways be earned, and—like Charlie said—it is the only way out of going to hell for all of existence.

"Hmm," Tex shifted in his chair. "I noticed that both of you focused on the negative, not on the reward of salvation—"

Not going to hell, Damien interrupted, *is the best kind of reward.*

"On the opposite side of the coin, it's what happens when you <u>don't</u> go to hell. Both you and Charlie will be spending 'all of existence'—as you call it—in the glorious presence of our Lord and Heavenly Father. Instead of going to hell, you'll be spending a new life together with God and Jesus for all eternity."

"Yeah," Charlie nodded, "I've got you on that!"

Tex turned his attention back to Charlie, probably because he saw him as a little more undeveloped in his faith or knowledge. "So, you said that 'if we believe in God and do the right things,' then we'll receive salvation. Are you sure about that?" As an answer, Charlie merely shrugged. "How about you, Damien? Do you know how you can receive this gift?"

Well, I've always been told that it's 'ours for the asking.' By asking God to forgive us for everything we did wrong, and asking His only begotten Son…Jesus the Christ to be our savior.

"You have to ask Jesus to be your savior?" Tex scrutinized, "Or, do you simply need to believe that Jesus is your savior? That He died on the cross, then was resurrected?"

I always thought that 'asking' was a part of 'believing'…that you wouldn't be asking someone to do something if you didn't believe that they <u>could</u> do it.

"Okay, Damien, I can see that. So, what we must know is that there is no forgiveness without accepting the fact that we are, in all ways, guilty of sin. This is a crime against the very being of God and His Law, for which there is but one penalty: a prison sentence in an abyss for a thousand years, followed by being tormented day and night in a lake of fire and sulfur, forever! Or, so it says in the Revelation to John, Chapter 20."

"There is but one way out of this punishment, and that is salvation through the blood sacrifice of Christ Jesus. The earnest belief that He allowed Himself to be captured, flogged, and crucified as the ultimate sin sacrifice. That we have been washed clean by that blood He spilt for us. And, most importantly, that Death had no power over Him…

that after three days in a grave, Jesus conquered Death, returned to life to spend forty days with His dedicated Disciples, and now sits on a throne beside God."

"So," Charlie squinted in frustration, "that is all that's involved?"

"Isn't that what Scripture days?" Tex questioned him back.

"I get salvation, just by asking God for forgiveness and for me believing that Jesus died and came back to life? That's all I have to do?"

"If you'd like to do more," Tex smiled wide, "you could clean my cell. Maybe volunteer here at the chapel once in a while. God appreciates 'good deeds' and the love we express to one another, but it's not through our deeds or our 'fruits of labor' that we earn salvation. No, you are saved through your forgiveness and belief. Period."

Yeah, Charlie, Damien reinforced Tex's statement, *so long as you have done these from your heart, then you'll be my brother in Christ. You'll have salvation and be a true Christian.*

Unfortunately, especially in prison, many people 'pretend' or simply say that they are brothers and sisters in Christ, so that others will feel obligated to prove them with charity—even when they aren't in poverty—stricken or otherwise in need. Little do they understand that a Christian is equally as happy to help out a non-believer as a believer, perhaps even more so. Yet, in prison, the word 'Christian' does get thrown around a lot for all the wrong reasons.

After we had this brief conversation about Tex's favorite subject, we had to return to "C" Quad just before the next church service began. Charlie actually liked having our friendly debates about religion; however, he had an understanding about Christendom that troubled me from our very beginning. He thought that by calling himself a Christian, he would be opening a door for other inmates to take full advantage of him and his personal property. It was a misunderstood label he wasn't inclined to put on himself.

Although I was somewhat willing to change what I precisely believed about the Bible and of salvation—for that matter—the substitute would have to make far more sense than the belief I held. However, what Tex was offering was a really basic, or elementary belief in God and the Bible, along with a nature of the created Earth, which was far from enough for me. No, I wanted all the answers, True, when Tex gave his sermons, he was limited to the level at which his audience was at; and during our private discussions, Tex spoke at a level that wouldn't exclude Charlie. But, instead of Christianity 101, or Christianity 201, my Asperger's kept pushing me to desire Christianity 777.

Damien was spending as much quality time as he possibly could together with his best friend—and undercover lover—for the remainder of Charlie's stay at C.M.C. prison. The upcoming release date troubled both of them greatly, instead of providing either joy or the usual excitement of finally getting out.

The very best part of my days in prison was seeing Mr. Sleepy Eyes walk through his door. I was moved to smile when I saw my partner walking to the chow line ever so slowly, to his seat, practically crawling there. At the end of every meal or shift in the kitchen, we went to the bleachers and entertained each other with conversation or other distractions.

I read somewhere, that if one wants to get through boredom, all that one need do, is to become one's own entertainment. That might work in other parts of the world, but not in prison. It can be damaging to one's sanity! In prison, inmates will do exactly the same things every single day… or, expect to be able to. Each day in prison, they greet the same people in the same way, participate in the same sport, recreation, or other entertainment, day in and day out. The fact that even the grass-covered hills are the same year in and year out, sometimes more brown than usual, but pretty much the exact same.

So, one must make himself the "entertainment department manager" of his own soul, or get prepared to seek psychiatric help! The only other tool against boredom is to make changes to one's routine and do whatever new activity they can periodically, otherwise life becomes totally stagnant.

Charlie loved playing basketball, it was "his" sport, and his only true source of entertainment besides television and, of course, Damien. On the other hand, Damien didn't enjoy sports, although he'd stay and watch Charlie play. Instead, Damien found the grass on the hills as entertainment in its own right. At C.M.C. prison, they also offered shuffleboard, weightlifting equipment—although they removed all the weights in the 1990's—and a tennis court.

I liked the sport of tennis, but couldn't play. Both my eye-hand coordination and reflexes just weren't there, weren't quick enough. I enjoyed watching women's tennis on TV, since they were really showed off phenomenal abilities... as well as legs. Otherwise, I found prison quite boring without Charlie by my side, which he soon wouldn't be. Following his release, I would have about three weeks before going home myself. But, I considered myself to be so much more—and incredibly—fortunate than Charlie... I had a part-time job and Sam lined up; Charlie had nothing except his freedom.

Charlie "Oops" Osborne was returning to the same streets, same gang members, same old drugs and problems he'd left behind. The prison system didn't actually care what the inmate—or parolee—had to return to when his time was up, and this was a huge problem. Previously, prior to the 1960's, prisoners were given the benefits of a halfway house and, usually, a job at a grocery store or car wash already assigned to them upon their release. Currently, however, parolees are given two hundred dollars and a free plastic trash bag to carry their personal belongings to the local bus station. That's it!

Somewhere between eighty to eighty-five percent of parolees have nowhere to go once released, unless a family member is willing to offer them a couch to sleep on for a few nights. Nearly all of them are likely to reoffend or to violate their parole conditions, in major or minor ways, and wind up back in jails or prisons, simply because they can't get jobs and don't have a better living environment to be released from prison to. The State of California basically never developed a meaningful pre-release program; its prison system just cannot handle any enormous amount of prisoners and parolees... it still can't.

This was what Charlie was returning to: anticipated failure.

The day before Charlie's release, we were heading back to "our" bleachers for a final conversation between him and the Bible study group. But, as usual, this wasn't in the cards. There was an altercation, a small fight or riot—we rarely know the full details—on "A" Quad, and the prison was on 'emergency lockdown' until the problem was isolated... and all of the paperwork completed. After all, the world would cease to exist without mass amounts of paperwork!

At any rate, we were told to return directly to our cells, so that's what we did. Things only got worse when, following an unexpected inmate count, the officers threw the main security lever into deadlock, securing us inside our cells. Charlie and I wouldn't be having our last night of sex, as planned. No, in fact, the officers gave us not even a single moment to say our goodbyes to one another. I felt completely dejected! If I hadn't already been taking anti-depressants, I would've needed some. The system robbed us of any closure, not even a final kiss, to our relationship.

Damien was fully awake and standing at his cell's door when two officers arrived at Charlie's own door to escort him off of the yard, to the main Receiving and Release office, where he'd be processed out. Although it was before sunrise, and therefore disrespectful to make such noise, Damien knocked loudly on the inside of his cell and yelled through the cracks of the door. With the officers standing right there, he couldn't even get a clear view of his lover being chaperoned and ushered out of his cell and the building.

Not long after this upsetting event, Damien had the awkward moment of—for the first time in months—walking to breakfast without a companion, having nobody to converse with in between bites, and nothing to do afterwards. He headed over to "their" bleachers, only it wasn't "theirs" anymore, only "his"... although, technically, this wasn't accurate either. Damien's life had turned from a life he shared with someone else, into one of separation. Of isolation.

This feeling, I came to realize, was what God must have gone through when He sent His Son down here to us. Imagine spending everyday with someone, falling into a routine of that person always being there, only for that person, your constant sidekick, to be sent away somewhere unreachable. They aren't dead, nor did they die; but, they aren't beside you anymore. You still seem to go through a period of mourning, not knowing if you'll ever see them again. This was the only benefit God had, that He knew that He would see Jesus again after thirty-some years. Actually, for the rest of us, as long as we achieve salvation, we'll likewise know that we'll see our lost ones again.

CHAPTER THIRTY

Newfound Freedoms

Several lonesome weeks later—lonely with the exception of the moments spent in the chapel or running the Bible study group—Damien's life had come "figure eights." At first, he had been removed from society for getting two girls drunk and one of them pregnant; went to juvenile hall and then Metro; to be released back into society... that was his first circle. Then, he'd been removed from society again—this time justly—for injuring another human being; went to jail and then prisons (Chino, Tracy, San Quentin, then San Luis Obispo); to finally being released back into society... back in the center of things.

Finally, it was the day of my going home, which brought me much joy if not some sadness. I would miss the Bible study group Charlie and I had together started, even arguing with Peter the atheist had become my favorite pastime, and I'd miss it greatly. The previous evening, I'd returned to my cell from group, showered extra long, and rested my neck. Everything I owned was already in knotted-up trash bags near the door. I couldn't sleep a single wink, my nerves wouldn't allow me to.

I felt certain that I could do all three years of state parole without violating any of the conditions or laws—not even a traffic ticket. There was little fear of being returned to prison, little desire to do anything reckless or to contact my old drug dealer; to be honest, I had even forgotten his name at that moment. Instead, I experienced an intense happiness rush over me the instant the sound of the boots approached my door that morning.

Not only was it the end of Damien's imprisonment, but the last day of summer. A "summer of learning" he called it, and correctly so. It was while housed at C.M.C. that Damien had some of the very best conversations about God, religions, creation, and the nature of "sacred" Scriptures. Was he better for the experience? Damien had learned a lot while locked up; a lot of growth and maturing, all around. But the most important question which remained to be answered, to be realized, was: Is Damien rehabilitated? Did he grow enough?

Leaving the prison felt understandably strange to Damien. After nearly two full years of being surrounded by concertina wire or cinder-block walls, or wearing handcuffs whenever not fenced-in, things were nice but different. He walked out through the visiting room of the prison without being searched—which, too, was uncharacteristic—then was hailed by an officer in the overlooking control tower, "Collins?"

Yes, sir.

"What's your C.D.C. number?" The officer ordered, which meant his prisoner I.D. number. About thirty seconds after yelling this up to the guard, Damien saw the gate before him open with the same officer saying, "Good luck out there."

Thank you, sir. Have a good one. This joyous moment, completely out of temperament or personality of a hardened inmate, proved that Damien had somehow retained his humanity; normally, prisoners would never 'waste' their breath in giving a guard any kind of salutation.

Through the opened gate, Damien both saw and was warmly greeted by his only other friend in the world, Dr. Reily—albeit, in hindsight, with Charlie out of the picture, Sam was really all that Damien had. Sam embraced Damien much in the same way a father would hug a son returning from a war in another country, which wouldn't be far from the truth. Sam walked Damien towards a parked car, loading his two bags of property into the trunk.

"You're not hungry, by chance, are you?

Are you joking, Sam? Yes, I am starving. Especially for some real food.

"Good, how about Denny's?"

Yes, sir. That sounds good about now. Thank you.

"Sir?" Sam quoted, as he turned the key in the ignition.

Sorry, force of habit. It then dawned, at that moment, that he'd not be needing to call anybody 'sir' for a <u>very</u> long time. No more correctional officers, no more inmate count times, no more of quite a lot of things which came only with living behind bars.

It wasn't until Sam had driven down P.C.H. for a few minutes before it hit me that I really was free. It felt like how it must be to be born! Okay bad simile... but boy did it feel good. Sure, I still had responsibilities to the state, such as weekly reporting to a parole agent and having random tests, but I was <u>free</u>!

Oh, something else that took me a few miles of driving down the P.C.H. before realizing, and that was I wasn't sitting in a Corvette. No, in all the excitement of seeing Sam and being released from that awful prison, I had completely overlooked the fact that we inside a brand new Ford Escort two-door hatchback. Robin's-egg blue. In case you're confused, a canary-yellow Corvette sports car looks nothing like a robin's-egg blue Escort hatchback. And yet, in the thrill of everything going on it took me that long to realize the difference in style... and avian-inspired color.

Most people never experience freedom, that is, until it has been taken away from them. No, freedom doesn't matter in the slightest little bit in their daily lives and routines. And those trapped in a lifestyle of constantly needing a larger income never realize the freedoms which they actually have! The freedoms which they take for granted. No, to really experience freedom, you need to know someone who has been either kidnapped or imprisoned for any measurable amount of time, if not being such a person yourself.

Being "not locked up" is not the same as being free. There's a huge difference between freedom and not being locked up. It is part of being free, however, occasionally even an inmate can experience true freedom behind bars! Freedom is a state of mind that even jail cells and barbed-wire fences cannot take away, if one refuses to let it slip away from them. It's a spiritual experience. Even the Apostle Paul wrote several of his letters while in custody, admitting that he had freedom, even though he might not of had liberty.

At Denny's, Damien ordered a Grand Slam...a *real one*, he commented. On Sundays in the prison, inmates were served what was referred to as a "grand slam" breakfast which paled greatly in comparison. For one, there wasn't any crispy bacon: for another, the pancakes were either undercooked ovals-of-dough or overcooked—sometimes cooked on a previous day, then reheated—pieces of cardboard suitable for playing Frisbee or, perhaps, doing some skeet shooting.

I had forgotten just how food could be filling, as well as tasty. I also needed to apologize to Samuel for my lack of table manners and "speed eating;" we rarely had enough time to finish everything on our trays before being rushed out of the chow hall. Sam was actually appalled when, purely out of habit, I folded a pancake in half with my fingers and shoved a quarter of it into my mouth, completely ignoring my fork.

"Seriously, Damien, Are you five-years-old?"

No, I-I am sorry. I'm guessin' that there'll be a bit of bad habits I'll need to break out of.

"Hmm, how many is 'a bit'?" Sam sarcastically asked, then— remembering that Damien rarely recognized sarcasm—apologized before Damien started to name them all. "Sorry, that was uncalled for."

No, Sam. You're right. I realized at prison, a lot of things about myself that need changing, and...well, I know that I've developed some habits of my environment. The cussing and rudeness of my fellow inmates rubbed off on me, but can just as easily be rubbed-off, off of me.

"Well," Sam started to laugh at his own joke, "try not to rub any of it off onto the carpets." And, for the first time in many, many months, Damien actually laughed.

The whole experience had overwhelmed me such that, a mere few minutes after leaving the restaurant, I fell fast asleep. Keep in mind that it was only around nine in the-morning, and that we lived roughly two hours away from the prison. However, the last thing I remembered was thinking about just how beautiful the Pacific Coast Highway was.

I am not sure what awoke me, but waking up I found myself still in Sam's small car driving near Sunset Beach in southern L.A. County, just north of Huntington Beach, where—in case you forgot—our house is. Actually, I still considered it Sam's house, since he paid for everything, but

I was planning to change that, to contribute. I was happy to hear that Sam didn't suffer from any consequences from my actions while I was in prison. There was some damage caused to the front door when the police came to arrest me, but as incredible as it sounds, after filing a claim form, the city actually paid for a new one... keep in mind that it was the 1980's; I don't think you'd get as lucky nowadays.

I was indeed grateful for the ways that Sam was willing to take care of my needs. Okay, maybe grateful isn't the correct word: lucky and/or extremely fortunate fit also. We'd agreed during our last collect phone call from prison that I would go back to taking care of the house and yard until things settled down. I had every intention of getting back to work right away, besides that being a requirement of my parole conditions.

Arriving at Sam's house in Huntington Beach, Damien got out of the car and looked at a small planted box where Sam had planted a small cactus only a few weeks prior to Damien's arrest. The cactus was the kind which only bloomed once each year and with only one or more flowers at the same time. Damien had originally thought that the one Sam planted wouldn't grow as fast nor as large as the one beside it which Damien had planted; however, it was now peeking over the roof!

Have I been gone that long? Damien asked in reference to the enormous cactus.

"Prepare yourself," Sam warned, "but it's been a busy two years."

The living room looked pretty much the same, with the exception of a huge 56-inch rear-projection TV. While none of the furniture was different, some were arranged in a different way which made them seem different to Damien. *Is this a new love seat?*

"No, it's the one from the front room. Notice the wine stains," Sam indicated. "Yeah, we have Bob to thank for those."

Bob? Damien had forgotten all about him until that very moment, *He's still staying here?*

Sam merely nodded, yet the frown on his face told a story of frustration which he was unwilling to share at the moment. Not now, not when Damien just now returned home, safe and sound.

"How about some music?" Sam then suggested.

I was very much in need of a concert, and knew exactly what I was in the mood for. It was the album which, since over a year ago, I had been missing and listed on my list of "first things to do once I got out." Carefully, I'd leafed through Sam's impressive record collection—yes, record, as in big, flat, disks of vinyl—and took out Leonard Bernstein's performance of Gustav Mahler's second symphony. Turning on Sam's turntable, turning down the lights, and tuning out the world, I sat down in the center of that much-missed room to enjoy the satisfying piece of recorded music on Earth ... at least, that's what I believe.

Halfway through the playing of the album, Bob made his appearance. He was respectful enough not to disturb Damien during his enjoyment, simply stepped into the room and offered a silent handshake. After the concert ended, Bob and Damien sat to figure out how they should "split up" the responsibilities and chores around the house. In the entire time Damien was in custody, Bob hadn't retained a single, meaningful job. He found some odd jobs, here and there, to supplement whatever money he sponged off his family, Sam, and/or unemployment checks. Most of this income, however, went directly towards bar tabs and entertaining girlfriends.

As far as splitting up the chores, my only problem with that was Bob hadn't been handling the chores very well in my absence. There were four-foot high weeds in the backyard! His only requirements for living in Sam's house rent-free came with the promise of housework, and now he wanted me to take over half of those responsibilities—probably the only half Bob had been doing. This, in his own logic, would leave Bob with nothing to worry about, nothing to do.

It was agreed that Damien was the better chef, that the kitchen would become his ultimate domain and responsibility. To very little shock, Damien found the refrigerator and pantry practically empty of any food. Sam and Bob apparently ordered a lot of take-out food or only bought items needed to make that particular day's meals at a time. Even the spice rack contained only empty jars or rarely used ones like allspice and cardamom.

While looking in the barren cabinets, Sam entered the kitchen. Damien turned towards Sam and, although uncalled for, repeated the same insult that Dr. Reily gave him at Denny's, *Seriously, Sam. Are you five-years-old?*

The sting stung for a brief second, but eventually Sam found the humor in this, "Ouch! What's wrong?"

Pointing to the now closed pantry, Damien reported, *There's nothin' in there but empty peanut butter jars and raw garbanzo beans. How in the world did the two of you survive without me?*

Sam chuckled, then playfully defended himself, "I know how to make oatmeal. Bob's a master at grilled cheese sandwiches. We survived didn't we?"

Damien, still quite serious, replied, *What's the point of surviving if we never truly live? A good meal isn't a luxury... it's a lifestyle. Haven't you ever heard that you are what you eat? That saying isn't talkin' about the ingredients, it's talking about the overall quality of the dish.*

"So, if we eat 'junk' then we are junk? I can agree with that."

Actually, instead of 'junk' I was thinking more along the lines of 'depressingly sad,' 'bland,' or 'unappetizing.' Food that's appealing makes it's eater more appealing.

"Well, then for tonight's dinner, please cook me something—" he then winked, "extremely appealing. Irresistible, even."

Damien was comfortable with his being a bisexual—even proudly admits this now to others—however, he'd become uncomfortable with Sam's romantic interests in him. True, before going to prison, they'd shared a few sexual experiences together. But, Damien still saw him as only a friend and former therapist. Truthfully, the word 'former' shouldn't be in that sentence.

He was a most excellent therapist and best friend, but I just couldn't see Dr. Reily as a lover. Perhaps, I should have. He clearly loved me. I hadn't yet told him about my relationship with Charlie, my desire to locate him, or the fantasy of finding a woman to settle down with and raise a family. Yes, I actually wanted to have children, someday. But, was I really making a mistake? I just wasn't wanting a gay relationship with Sam... fun, yes; partnership, no.

What was I to do? I didn't know what to do with my emotions, my feelings, or how to express myself effectively without stomping all over the feelings of others. Heck! I rarely understood what it was that I felt, how was I supposed to predict how I'd affect others?! Knowing about social rules was something that—regardless of their importance—I really didn't know. I've blamed this earlier in the book on how I lived—rather, how I "existed"—with any of my parents, a childhood much like a ping-pong ball. Or, better yet, like someone forced to play a game of "musical chairs," never getting the same seat twice.

Throughout my life, up until that moment, I had learned several different collections or "sets" of social rules, which never mixed well together with my following environment. First, there was being an awkward kid in kindergarten in a rural town; Second, there was becoming a sex toy—nothing but a plaything—for two teenaged boys; Third, we moved from a farming town of a few thousand, to the crowded chaos called Los Angeles with its then 2.8 million; next, it was off to military boarding school and a completely new set of structure and lifestyle. I learned about teamwork and being valued.

Suddenly, I was back in public school—high school of all the worst places—where there wasn't any such thing as teamwork nor value. Shortly after starting there, I was introduced to incarceration at Juvenile Hall... another new set of structure, lifestyle, and even language! Then came the blessings of paradise in the form of Metropolitan State Hospital—a totally different world of smiles and support. Followed by a loving foreigner who had his own rules, customs, and culture... as well as language. Next came the world of illusions, of phantasms, of psychedelics, where normal rules simply didn't apply, only the next high did. This led to my trigger-happy suffering and readmission to the unique world of incarceration—only that the original rules I'd learned in Juvenile Hall no longer applied. No, there were new social laws in adult prison, even more language to learn, as well as a different structure.

Finally, we arrive at where I was—back at Huntington Beach. I was a huge failure, and I had before me an opportunity to learn and grow all over again. This time, I wanted to trust Sam's judgments, simply because he was a success in his own life. It was my plan to not only register for classes at Golden West College again, but to do much better than I did when I last went there. I really wanted to make something good of myself.

Returning from the grocery store, Damien called out to Bob, *Bob!*

I need a hand out here ... getting food out of the car.

Getting himself up, Bob replied, "No problem, Damien. What's going to be for dinner?"

Walking to the hallway, Damien replied, *Just about anything that pleases you. I think I bought-out the entire store! What do you feel like?*

"How about a beef stew, or one of the quee'shis you used to make. I don't know. You make it and I'll know I'll love it."

You mean, a quiche? Sure, I could whip up a quiche Lorraine, but with crumbled beef instead of bacon.

"Why not both? Beef and bacon?" Bob greedily suggested.

Guess we can try that later. First, I'll need your help cleaning this house up, so that it doesn't smell like an unclean locker room... or worse, a prison cell.

About fifteen minutes later, Damien had finished putting all of the refrigerated and frozen foods away, plus most of the cans and boxes onto shelves in the pantry. He hadn't seen nor heard from Bob since the young man brought the last of the grocery bags in from the garage. The hunt for him ended at his ajar bedroom door.

I went to Bob's room, where I found a very horny twenty-one-year-old man taking care of his sex drive. On a fourteen-inch TV screen on his dresser, played out a lesbian-porno tape. According to an earlier conversation I'd had with Samuel, apparently Bob had grown quite addicted to these videos, especially since Sam wouldn't allow Bob to bring living-breathing women home with him anymore.

C'mon, Bob. I really need your help with the house. Put that gherkin away.

"I...will...be...there..." he panted out, during his exertion.

Damien, walking away disgusted, wanted to gather all the laundry, vacuum, and finish some much needed general cleaning before he did any cooking. Nobody would want any dust in their food. Too much surprise, albeit five minutes later than expected, Damien did get some much need help from Bob, for which he was glad. It wasn't so much that Bob was lazy, but when he did help out with the chores, he'd work up a sweat.

After the housework, Damien washed up, ran the dishwasher, and listened to Pink Floyd's "The Dark Side of the Moon," while he prepared the aforementioned quiche plus a delicious chocolate soufflé, which turned out great, if he says so himself.

I love Pink Floyd; they were one of the greatest rock groups of all time. Sure, most of their music was targeted towards the marijuana-smoking or acid-dropping crowd yet, even totally sober, David Gilmour's guitar playing took any listener on a journey of the mind's eye. Samuel had about one-thousand, five-hundred records in his collection, which included some of the very best of rock and classical music. Both him and Nick had amassed the albums together, yet Samuel ended up with the majority then paycheck-after-paycheck filled in the gaps throughout the years.

After making dinner, I called Sam to see what time he was coming home. I would let the meal stand in the oven while I took care of any remaining indoor chores… the backyard would need to wait until the following day. I rested on the couch with a glass of wine, although I never was much of a connoisseur… mostly I drank Cabernet Sauvignon, the cheap stuff. I guess it's a good thing that the old saying I gave to Samuel wasn't "you are what you drink."

I didn't see it coming, but I was becoming addicted to yet another substance new to me… it was called "the shopping mall." Even if I didn't have any extra money to buy anything, I loved going there. One of the draws to that place was the other customers, the actual watching of them, I mean. People are interesting, especially when they don't know that they're being watched. "She is in a hurry." "That guy must be shopping for his wife." "Why would anybody pay <u>that</u> much for <u>that</u> shirt?" It was the best movie available.

However, and speaking of movies, the Westminster Mall had one of the original United Artists theatres in Southern California, before they started popping up everywhere. I went to the mall often to enjoy a film alone— yeah, it sounds rather depressing now that you've mentioned it—after Sam went about his business. It was there, at the movie theatre, that I started to become carelessly irresponsible. No, movie going was not itself irresponsible, but the fact that I began going several times a week is! I was beginning to go even though I still had chores and homework to get done.

Why was I going? Lord knows, I was not that interested in the movies I *saw. The answer was the I wanted to grow beyond my friendship with Sam. I believe that I just needed to meet more adults, especially single women, and develop my future from there. <u>Being wrong</u> must have been my hidden ability, my favorite prevalence, because of the fact that I kept returning to it. I also kept on damaging the one relationship that really meant anything to me, my relationship with Sam.*

Man was born free, and everywhere he is in chains.
~ Jean-Jacques Rousseau

Freedom and slavery are mental states.
~ Mahatma Gandhi

CHAPTER THIRTY-ONE

Baneful Relationships

*A*s you know, starting and maintaining friendships or romances were my greatest weakness, and I should have known that <u>myself</u> because of the fact that I continued to ruin them. To tell you the truth, I simply did the opposite of what was working. I was improving my inability to have a meaningful relationship... I was learning, but—as with most people with Asperger's—I was really impatient with progress.

I had no reason to think that if I kept going to the Westminster Mall, I would be able to develop a worthwhile friendship with someone. I just needed to meet more adults—especially women—and work from there. And, as actor Tom Cruise said in the movie "Top Gun," the place was "a target-rich environment." I saw a young black man by the name of Cameron—a manager of one of the many fast-food restaurants there—and I thought I could develop a friendship with this guy. <u>Wrong</u>! Get a clue, Damien. I went about my task altogether in the wrong way, and for all the wrong reasons.

As Damien explained it to me later, he had laid his eyes on a lovely and young lady named Kristy who also worked at the fast-food joint. His personally developed reason for wanting a baneful relationship with Cameron was under the misbelief that only through that friendship he'd then have a shot at Kristy.

I guess my ego was in the sewer. I had no idea that my actions were about to create a disaster for me, and all for the sake of my being able to be in a romantic relationship with a young lady. Yes, I now know what I really needed at that time was to earn an A.A. degree as Dr. Reily encouraged me. I had the mind to do just that if I was willing to be patient with the college classes I was taking. Problem was, I thought I could take 12 to 15 units of classes in the same semester, which I was not yet prepared for.

I foolishly decided to do what my sex drive told me to do, and not what God had prepared for me to do. I realize now, in hindsight, that God had laid the groundwork and path—through Sam—for me to get out of my all-male relationships and to compete my educational goals... however, at a far slower pace than my immature soul decided to work things out, but I wanted speed!

I really did and still do care about Sam a whole bunch. I just had an immature response to my situation which quickly outgrew me and became a lot more than what the Apostle Paul call "a thorn in my side." My personal problems were with engaging others into a romantic relationship... and no wonder, when one deals with reality.

Damien was nearly thirty-two years old, although he looked and mentally behaved at a much younger age. Likewise, the young men and women he was most attracted to were in their early twenties or late teens, which paralleled his own level of delayed maturity. By society standards, he wasn't supposed to be engaging eighteen-year-old ladies into a romantic interest; he should've focused on women around his own age... and, in his own opinion, might have gotten further success in doing so.

In the middle of all the social blundering that I—unknowingly—was in the middle of committing at the mall, I cultivated a friendship with Cameron Hearn rather quickly. I guess that if the truth was told, I would say that I had little—if any—self-esteem, yet I was oddly willing to do Cameron a favor that involved me carrying some things to his apartment. I really had no business going to his place. If I had cared for myself at all, I would have told him that I was too busy or had some other reason why I couldn't go to his apartment.

At around that time in my life, I was starting to have problems with school… the previously mentioned overload of classes was harming my health and self-image. I had begun to believe that I needed to pretend to be someone other than I was. In the day that Cameron asked me to go to his apartment, before doing so and after school, I had showered and put on a nice suit that Sam had bought for me to wear at his doctor's office. I wanted to look good and get lucky.

Kristy, the object of Damien's true affections and interest, lived with her boss, Cameron. She was very young, although Damien had no idea of just how young until later, and a runaway from home. Damien didn't know the full details of her reasons towards becoming 'voluntarily homeless,' yet after his own months of life as a street urchin, he knew that these reasons were better off not to be known. He had heard plenty of testimonies about abuse—physical, sexual, and emotional—both on the streets and at Metropolitan State Hospital to last him <u>two</u> lifetimes of nightmarish images and blessings.

Cameron and Kristy were uninvolved roommates, as well as coworkers, and strictly heterosexual or 'straight.' Their apartment was typical of college-aged students, more organized than clean, with a lot of garage-sale furniture and hand-me-downs. The once-white walls and ceiling were tinged from cigarette smoke, as well as from other substances which both of them smoked.

When Cameron asked me to go to his apartment to drop off some things, he had given me his copy of the key to their apartment. He also got on the phone and called his housemate Kristy to explain that he was sending me over to drop off some things from their work. Arriving at the place, I knocked on the door and anxiously waited before eventually using the key that Cameron supplied me. Kristy, however, opened the door from the inside before I finished turning the key.

Oh! Damien yelped in surprise to the door opening itself, *Um, hi. You're Kristy, right?* He asked, as if he didn't know already. As if he hadn't been thinking unflaggingly about her over the past few days.

"Yeah—how'd you g-get a key?" the bikini-wearing girl asked.

Didn't Cameron tell you why I'm here?

"No, I don't think so," she took two steps back from the door, "only that you were. That's cool. I didn't know you were a friend of his."

Damien picked up the items he'd left on the doorstep in order to knock, then took a step inside. *I'm kinda a new friend. Maybe friend isn't even the right word, yet. Not yet. But he did trust me with his key.*

"I've seen you at the shop," Kristy identified with him. "You've been coming there quite a bit lately. Cam will be here within the hour, you wanna wait?" The fact that she was practically naked provided his answer.

Cool, if you don't mind. Damien straightened out the winkles in his suit, then sat down on Cameron's couch. His nervousness with this situation made it nearly impossible to sit still. She was very alluring.

For the next forty-five minutes, the two of them engaged in nonchalant small talk about the apartment, the weather, and the community college classes which Damien was enrolled in. Kristy, who turned out to be all of seventeen-years-young, had no interest in returning to high school to earn her diploma, nor to go onto college. The more that they talked, the less interesting her future ambitions, goals, and overall personality seemed to Damien.

It wasn't long before Cameron—or "Cam"—returned home carrying two bags of groceries, which included a sixteen-bottle pack of Coors beer. After offering both Kristy and Damien a bottle, which they both accepted, Cameron walked into the rather quiet living room.

"Now that that's done," he said, referring to the groceries being put away. "So, Damien. You might not remember telling me this, but you had let it out that you used to smoke coke from time-to-time."

Did I? Yeah, I guess I told you that. Damien admitted, then sheepishly turned towards Kristy, *Before I went to prison, I was hooked on freebasing.*

"You were in prison?" This topic sparked a hidden interest within the young girl.

Yeah, it's nothing to be proud of, but I accidently shot a guy—somebody I didn't even know—and he almost died. I wouldn't be sitting here if he did.

"Wow!" Kristy was suddenly hanging on Damien's every word. This wasn't the kind of attention which Damien was interested in. He didn't want here to find him fascinating because of his crime or prison sentence, but for who he was. However, sitting there in that suit, any interest she had in him was more than simply welcomed.

"So," Cameron returned to the topic of drugs, "how much do you buy?"

Buy? Not I. Every once in a while, I come up with some, get it ready to smoke. You buy and I smoke. Follow?

Drinking from his beer bottle, Cameron asked, "You got some on you now?"

Well, friends, yes I do. You wanna buy some? spoken like a used-cars salesman, as he was similarly dressed.

Cameron look at his roommate, then back at the drug dealer, "We're wanting a sample first, Damien, Is that possible?"

I don't normally do samples... but this one time, I think I can. Okay? We can split up these two grams. Damien produced a small brown vial from his pocket. Damien had been fronted this small amount of drugs in order to sell and make a little bit of profit, not to dig himself further into debt with his supplier, Mark... yes, the same Mark the Dealer who originally got Damien addicted to freebase.

Kristy grew agitated while Cameron fetched his pipe; she had never been involved in a drug transaction before. "I don't understand why we have to pay <u>you</u>, if you're going to be smoking <u>with</u> us."

"I told you, Kristy, Damien is cool. He's not trying to profit off us, he just wants to recover his share of the costs."

Cameron and Damien got busy making up the two grams of freebase for all of their smoking pleasure. While they were busy fixing it up, there was a knock on the door. Unbeknownst to Damien, Cameron was expecting a friend to join them and share in the party, in an all-out smoke-a-thon. His name was Joseph Langly, and he was head of security for their apartment complex and lived a few doors down the hallway. At first, seeing the man in uniform, Damien thought Joseph was a police officer and nearly had a heart attack.

There I was, being stupid, about to smoke coke with people I didn't even know. Like I really needed to do drugs at all! I was still freshly out of prison, on state parole, and pretending to be an experienced dealer, complete with my cheap suit. The fact that my parole included random drug testing as one of its many conditions meant nothing to me at that very moment. No, my having a drug connection had earned me instant popularity with these people. After two years of "forced sobriety" provided by thick prison walls, I dove back into the deep end of the pool.

Joseph, as it turned out, was not only a security guard but also a composer of some of the best hip-hop music I'd ever heard. He was well-versed in music history, especially in what's more commonly called "urban music." He was really cool to talk with, plus—as an added bonus—he brought some weed to our improvised party. Later, we all three went in for food, supplying what little money we could, for the delivery of both Chinese take-out and pizza. There was lots of pizza.

Walking into the apartment, Joseph pulled off his expensive leather coat. "Whose hungry?" he needlessly asked. They had been smoking the weed he supplied for over an hour. Joseph thought it best to meet the delivery guy down in the apartment complex's lobby, since it was pretty obvious what was going on inside the apartment.

"Fantastic, Joseph. You want the final hit of freebase?" Cameron offered.

"A perfect end to the day," he gladly accepted.

So, Damien returned to an earlier conversation, *"Joseph? You both live and work here?"*

"Yeah, it's kinda cool, too. I get to live where I work, and the rent is free...well, sorta. It's part of my salary."

Still, you get paid to protect your own place, as well as others'.

"I see whatcha mean. Yeah, I do get paid to protect my own stuff. Th-that's pretty witty of you Damien. You're peachy keen."

I...I'm just stating the obvious, Damien contended, refusing Joseph's compliment in his usual fashion.

"Nah," Joseph shook his head, "it ain't that obvious. You've got good insights. Cleverness."

Well, I don't know about that, Damien self-criticized just as he raised the marijuana pipe to his lips.

There I was again: abusing my body with the very same poisons that I had used before going to prison. This regular and constant drug abuse of my soul was ruining my changes to grow from my mistakes. To evolve from the past. I couldn't believe that I was doing this to myself again, not after all those months of sober living—whether I wanted to be or not—inside prison. But I so much wanted to start a relationship with these people, especially one of romance with Kristy. Yet, the only baneful relationship I was kindling was with the smoke entering my lungs!

It was beyond time for me to quit this abuse! I was putting myself in the position to violate my parole and be sent back to prison. Two failed urine tests sent the usual parolee back, yet I was considered "high control" and would only need to fail just one "piss test" in order to be locked up again. However, as most drug users do, I didn't care at that moment about any consequences. I also, unfortunately, didn't care about my best friend's advice... heck! My only friend.

As you may have noticed, I commonly disregarded Sam's advice and for no reason at all. Sober or not, his words never sunk in. Not that I was evil, but I didn't know how to deal with my depression and insecure life. Also, I was unaware that by abusing myself with drugs, I was causing Sam harm... both financially and emotionally. How could he receive so much abuse, as I dished out, before he would just give up on me and quit?

Despite my wanting freedom, I started abusing that privilege day-after-day. For the current ways which I was a constant threat to society, as will about to be proven to you, I was deserving to return to prison. In fact, I had never really left prison. No, I was still in a custody of my own construct. Sure, no physical walls surrounded me, but incarcerated nonetheless.

Damien was at home one morning, when he went into the living room to relax and watch a movie before doing some more housework and/or studying. Sitting in Dr. Reily's favorite recliner, Bob was comfortably sipping his coffee while mostly ignoring the local news being broadcast: the top story was still about the major earthquake that struck the San Francisco Bay area and disrupted a scheduled World Series game the previous night between the Giants and the Oakland A's. A graphic on the large TV screen showed the "Death Total" at sixty-three, although a majority of live coverage focused primarily on a collapsed section of a bridge which nobody was driving on.

"Sixty-three people died in that earthquake," Bob calmly reported in between sips.

Wait, who earthquake? Damien mindlessly asked.

"Up in San Francisco. They said that it was centered somewhere around Santa Cruz, but look what it did to the Bay Bridge hundreds of miles away."

Wow, where have I been? Damien mumbled to himself, completely unaware of this catastrophic event in the northern half of the state. He watched the news footage for a few more moments before asking, *Can I ask you something, Bob? Do you ever think about death? Worry about it, I mean.*

"Well, yeah. Prob'ly no more than anybody else does."

Uh huh. So, do you believe in God?

"I guess that I do believe, Damien. I think God created the world, but prob'ly not the way it says in the Bible."

Oh, this sparked Damien's interest, *what do you believe?*

"Not sure yet," Bob said then took another sip. "What do you believe?"

Damien sat down on the davenport closest to the recliner, *Well, Bob, I really don't know either, but I don't think that I can trust the Bible to solve that. I guess that I believe that God used a process already in place: Evolution.*

"What do you mean?"

Well, I don't believe that the sixty-six books that make up the Bible are a reliable source of history, regardless of which translation you read. I don't approve that the early church limited the Bible to only those specific sixty-six books, and excluded so much other material or did not canonize others. I also do not think that what was included was written perfectly. I believe that it does communicate to us what the people of Israel experienced with God, and that it's the best source for how to live and worship. But, it's not enough.

"Not enough?" Bob sat up straighter in his chair. "What's not enough?"

The Bible. I still don't know a lot, but I do want to know more. Until I do know, I don't think I can worship in any church.

"Isn't that why people go to church? To learn more about the Bible? Not the other way around."

Not me, Damien admitted, *"I prefer to read the instructions before I start to build. Another thing is I don't want to just go to any church. I've been misled all of my life about so many other things, the last thing I want is to listen to the wrong interpretation of God's expectations for my life.*

"Damien, since you've told me more about what you <u>don't</u> believe that what you really <u>do</u> believe, why don't you start over."

Hmm, well, I do believe that the Bible is a collection of sacred man-created stories about the Israelites, their history and wars, their experiences with God, and what they believe that God was doing and telling them about their lives.

"'Man-created'? So, the Bible isn't exact truth? I shouldn't really believe all that it says? Is that watcha saying?"

Well, that's not quite true. I meant to say that it isn't an exact history, but it does express aspects of their lives with each other, in relation to their lives. Much of the Bible, the most important lessons, aren't taught but symbolically expressed.

"But isn't that the whole point of the Bible? To teach you God's word?

You'd think so, but the most important lessons have to be discovered on your own, by your own interpretation or someone else's. The Bible is supposed to be Holy, without blemish or errors; yet these sacred stories have a bunch of inconsistencies and unconformity, some contradictions...

"So tell me the difference between 'sacred' and 'holy'?"

Well, Bob, it's a matter of degrees. The Bible is sacred because it talks of God, about God, and it's inspired by God. Mostly the Bible is historical; it talks about the Israelites, their relations to their neighbors, and all of their struggles. However, I also believe that the term 'holy' needs to be saved for things that are made or created directly by God. Something for a sacred purpose. Follow?

Yeah, I do follow. I guess that if God <u>had</u> written the Bible, you would call it 'holy'? Right?"

Yep, you're right. That's the only way the word should be used. I just don't see that it can be called 'holy' for the reasons that I told you. There's just too much left wide open for interpretation, as well as all of its errors. The Bible is supposed to be God's Word, and yet there's too many typos for it to represent Him. God is perfect, and so should be the book about Him. As should our relationship with God be...perfect.

"You think we should have a perfect relationship with God?"

God wants us to have a <u>personal</u> relationship with Him, but we are full of sin and blemishes which would never allow any relationship to be perfect. But, still, we can try our very best to include him in our lives.

After this conversation, Damien went into the kitchen and removed some frozen pork chops from the freezer in order to thaw. Later, he would prepare them for cooking, along with all the fixings. While Damien was a strong believer in God, trusted in most of the Bible, he was still uncertain if the laws in Deuteronomy chapter 14—especially verse 8—were still enforced or not. In Acts, chapter eleven, Peter had that experience with a large sheet loaded up with ritually unclean animals being lowered out of heaven, then being given permission to eat any of them...but many believe that this symbolic event had only to do with his preaching to the Gentiles, and nothing with any changes to the laws about eating pigs and badgers, Even Jesus, himself, said that He hadn't come to change the Law, "It is easier for heaven and earth to disappear than for the least stroke of the pen to drop out of the Law." [Luke 16:16 NIV]

Regardless, Damien wasn't about to give up his love for pork chops and/ or bacon. No, for these two reasons, Damien hoped for God's forgiveness in their relationship.

CHAPTER THIRTY-TWO

Higher Education

As previously mentioned, Damien really was planning to get good grades in his college courses, so that he could get a decent job and pay his own way through life like a normal guy. His largest problem was a combination of hang-ups which hindered him from doing his best, or the best which he thought that he could do without anyone else's help. He started off the most recent school year with a blown-up estimation of himself and quickly bit off more than he could chew, let alone digest.

My skills were "boo boo" to say the least. Not only did my Asperger's syndrome impair my social interaction, but my attention span. I had so much schoolwork to study every night, yet none of it held my interest for long. I would end up either back in the living room or at the mall to watch a movie. Sam woke me up on a few occasions on the sofa—I never did see the end of the movie "Equus" after numerous attempts—while, of course, I still had homework that should have been done. This happened a lot with me and I still don't know why.

One morning after an evening of movies and wine, I awoke to realize I had completely forgotten to write a paper for my psychology class due that very day. I rushed to throw some basic concepts together in a literarily flamboyant way, and behold I got an "A" for it. It's not that I didn't have the brains or "smarts" for college; it's that I had a problem that I needed to tend with alone, and I was able to hide this from Sam ... and even, far too often, from myself.

December 1989 arrived, and Damien spent much of it—including his own birthday dinner—preparing for his first exam of the semester finals, which included a paper on "the first five years of human development." Damien's own first five years were neither humane nor provided much development, so he found this topic rather ironic.

After I did my paper, Bob invited me to his bedroom where we continued our earlier conversation about the Bible and God. I considered it a pleasure to talk about God, about the Bible, and about their relationship with each other. And with people, I found it particularly satisfying to talk about God and the systems of faith.

As Damien joined him in his room, Bob started with, "The last time we talked, I kinda got the understanding that, well, that you do believe in God, but differently than most people. Am I right?"

Yep, Damien answered. *You're right on the mark. Is that where we should start today?*

"Sure, why not."

Okay. So, why don't you finally tell me what you believe in.

Damien considered it a privilege to talk with Bob about something as very serious and personal as religion, because they rarely talked about hardly anything important. Although it had originally been Damien's suggestion that Bob move in with Sam and him all of those years ago, Damien still knew very little about this young man, other than his addiction to porn and fast women.

Answering Damien's request, Bob replied, "I don't know <u>what</u> to believe in about God or the Bible. I think that God is very real, but I don't know. See what I mean?

Yeah, I understand. Let's see. As I said, for me, God is 'very real,' and clearly He created the world, or—at least—put things in motion so that the world turned out the way that it did. Earth isn't some freak accident, and neither, too, are us humans. We are intelligently designed after several prototypes which we call apes.

"Alright, I can agree with that. So, you think that humans are just final versions of a science experiment?"

Experiment, yes. Final versions, no. I think that we're not quite as perfect as God was hoping that we'd turn out. Much like our first versions, the apes and gorillas, there'll be an even better species called human beings later on in the future.

"Wait," Bob interjected. "You think that God screwed up?"

What? No, I don't think that He screwed up when He made mankind. But, for all that we know, we aren't precisely 'in our image,' like it says in the very first chapter. A human skeleton from two-thousand years ago looks quite different from someone who died yesterday. The skull has a more round shape, the spine straighter. It's no mystery that humans are taller than they were during the times of Moses. So, either God's own image is changing, or we are evolving, generation after generation, into something better than our original ancestors.

"So, you think God created monkeys first, different kinds of them, until what? He finally made something that looked like Him?"

It's possible. We know that things existed on this planet before humans. I don't just mean dinosaurs, but there were fossils of smaller mammals from the Cretaceous period. Maybe that whole time frame, the geological Mesozoic era, over seventy-million years ago, was God's original test lab. Where and when He did some of His biggest experimentation. Finally, he wiped the pallet clean of clay and started all over with the epoch we're in now.

"Epoch?" Bob asked, then, after receiving Damien's definition, went on questioning, "But doesn't the Bible say God created everything in a week, and that the world is only a few thousand years old?"

There is no way that the Earth is less than three million years old, if not billions. Yeah, we ask things of God and some of those things are outside God's explanation. Like why does Earth have life on it? Why would he create Venus, Mars, or Saturn, when none of them seem to serve any purpose? We view things from our human eyes, along a time line which only contains human history. We expect God is all-powerful and all-knowing, mainly because we do not understand God's nature… and this is confirmed only by those who teach us their 'nature' or god. <u>Their</u> interpretation.

We then end up believing that we may ask all matter of questions and requests of actions from God, and that no matter the response, we're to believe that it was the pleasure of the Almighty. Good or bad, life or death, richer or poorer, whatever happens to you is because of His will for your life. His master plan. Follow?

"Yeah, God gets blamed for a lot of things that He couldn't have done or have known would've happened. Is that what you're saying? How do we know what things God can or cannot know... or do?"

Wait, I never said He couldn't 'do' all things. As far as 'know,' I believe God can see into the future and knows where our destinies are headed today. He will give you a little nudge in the right direction if you've walked too far off the path He wants you on, like when He sent me to prison and—.

"Hold on!" Bob interrupted. "You think it's because of God that you went to prison?"

No, no. I went to prison because I was paranoid on coke, and thought I needed my rifle to defend myself from something that wasn't even there. But, whose to say that God didn't influence my delusion that somebody was climbing over the fence? Damien took that opportunity to point out a rear window of the house, pointing directly at the same fence he'd shot at three years ago. *Or, for that matter, that God took over control of my randomly-aimed bullet and directed it towards the man's neck it hit? Yes, I pulled the trigger, but I believe that God was involved somehow. He knew I was in trouble, or He wanted me to meet with the people I did in prison. It changed my life forever.*

"Well," Bob admitted, "that's a point outside my understanding about God. I always thought that God had a plan for us written down before we were even born. That He knows what we'll be doing every hour, of every day, of our lives, before we even do them."

That's simply not possible. God couldn't possibly know that I would become homeless. I can't accept that he would want me to be a male prostitute. In the Bible, He hates homosexuals and hates prostitutes... and I became both of these. Why would God want me to become something that He hates? No, I don't believe that He controls our daily decisions, only the major ones. The ones which don't involve sin. God doesn't want us to sin against Him and His Law. I can't see Him wanting us to deliberately commit sins, even if it's to prove some point of God's.

Please remember that what I have to say about God is only part of what

I have come to understand. It may or may not agree with what the colleges and clergy and synagogues are teaching these days. But that's okay, because it's what works best for myself. I believe that what God is seeking in each of our creation is for us to reach out and engage God in a meaningful and everlasting relationship with Him. There is nothing else in the world that we can offer to God than this.

Bob looked confused at this point. "You think we should, what? Make a friendship with someone we can't even see or hear?"

I know how that sounds. I used to be unable to even believe that God existed, because I couldn't see or hear Him. But the fact is, He talks to us every minute of every day. We are just too busy listening to our minds rather than our souls. From what I have come to understand from other people and from Scripture, our God is very intimate. And that intimacy requires trust on both sides of the relationship. I realize that this relationship is difficult in it nature, but is vital. We must become willing to engage God, get to know God, and meet Him halfway. Only through our getting to know Him, does the possibility of heartfelt trust arrive.

We should give it a real try, for we are in a relationship with God whether we want it or not. I truly believe that God wants a father-and-child relationship with us; hence, it's our reason on why to pray to God. I do not know for certain what character that relationship takes when we're talking about God as our Heavenly Father, when other devotions and denominations consider it as a kingship-and-servant one. Could it be both at the same time? I guess so.

"Um," Bob took a moment to absorb all of this. "So, it's our responsibility to have a relationship with God, our King and Holy Father?"

I wouldn't say 'responsibility," I would say our moral obligation. Our entire purpose for existing in the first place! It should be an honor, a courtesy, that we have daily conversations with our Creator. Think about it. There is simply nothing we have to offer, no gratitude which we can offer Him, no object we can build, no invention, no artwork, nothing that He couldn't simply snap His fingers and instantly have created for Himself. No, the only way that we can thank God for our lives for being a human instead of a guppy, is through our worship and prayers.

"Seriously? A guppy?" Bob snickered.

Or a sloth. Maybe some sort of mollusk. But you get my point, don't you? We have a lot to be thankful for, and God is deserving of our thanks. Of our daily relationship with Him. With that being said, Damien let the conversation fade away, then excused himself to go resume his piles of schoolwork for the upcoming exams.

One morning while at Golden West College, Damien went to the campus lounge to get himself a cup of really bad coffee and a raspberry strudel for a midday snack, when he ran into a couple of classmates of his Abnormal Psychology course. Both students were regular attendees of Calvary Chapel of Huntington Beach, a local Christian church which Damien had once thought of checking out.

One of these two young men introduced himself, "Hey, you're Collins, right? From class? My name is Brian."

Yeah, hey, Brian. He then noticed the gold-chain necklace and two-toned cruciform pendant Brian's wearing. *I'm Damien. That's a nice cross. Are you Catholic? Christian?*

"We're both born-again Protestants. Hey, you interested in joining us? We're on our way to Bible study."

Yeah, that's exactly what I want. Damien said in earnest. *But, uh, I didn't bring my Bible.*

"No problem." We'll just share ours."

Cool! I had no idea there were any Bible studies held here on campus.

"Yeah, well it's not exactly advertised. It's just a few of us. We meet here, then go to the Snack Shop on Mondays through Fridays at 11 a.m. Usually run until around one. Is that okay with your schedule?"

Oh, yeah, that's perfect.

The other boy with Brian spoke out, "Tell us Damien; what does studying the Scriptures get you?"

You're... I'm sorry, I didn't catch your name.

Say, I'm sorry. I am Dennis.

Thanks, Dennis. Nice to meet you. Anyway, I study the Bible because I might get to know the mindset of those who wrote them.

"Anything else, Damien?"

Sure, I don't know about both of you, but I study the sacred Scriptures completely, to be able to know how life was for the Bible writers, and their society, and the world outside of their home of Israel. Yes, the Bible is to see how their relationship with God peaked and plummeted throughout the Old Testament, that only through Christ could we be saved from sin. But, more importantly, is the story behind the stories.

Both Brian and Dennis looked at each other with raised eyebrows. They weren't only impressed with Damien's answer, but had been apparently looking for someone like him—an 'open-minded thinker' of the Bible—for quite some time. They excused themselves from the third member of their party, whom Damien hadn't shared a word with, then invited Damien to sit down with them at a nearby Snack Shop table.

"Okay, Damien," Dennis started while opening his Bible to the Book of Isaiah, chapter eleven, which Dennis had bookmarked, "Why do you think Isaiah wrote his books?"

Isaiah wrote what he did, so that he could share his various experiences with God, with his people, and to the world. Isaiah saw that his nation of Judah wasn't only being threatened by the might of their powerful Assyrian neighbors but by his people's own disobedience towards God. He foretold that a lot of them would be captured and taken off to Babylon mainly as prophetic messages of encouragement, so that their hopes of freedom wouldn't be later crushed.

"So, tell us about the prophetic messages within them."

Again, guys, you can read all of that, Damien pointed to Dennis' occupied hands. *The question is what did Isaiah experience with God in his life? What those experiences tell about the mindset of the Creator and what the Creator wanted to get across to His people.*

Dennis then read aloud verses one through three of that chapter: the coming of a new king from among the descendants of David. Then asked, "Please explain the prophetic verses here. Is Isaiah talking about Jesus or—"

Let me ask you this, Damien countered. *Did Isaiah have an experience that he wanted to share with his people?*

"An 'experience'?" Brian asked, "I don't see—"

"No, that's a good question, Brian," Dennis interrupted. "It is clear that this is a set of statements, um, prediction of things to come that express some experience that Isaiah had with the Lord. He didn't just come up with this message on his own; he didn't make it all up."

"I see them as being about the near future," Brian clarified. "I'm not willing to drag them across time to the days of Christ, yet."

Ah! Damien spoke out, *"But that's just it. It wasn't 'the near future' at all, Isaiah lived in the latter half of the eight century, before Jesus was born. King Uzziah, of Judah, died in 742 B.C., which is mentioned in Isaiah chapter six. That was the year when Isaiah was blessed with God's presence. Isaiah actually saw God, not just one of His angels.*

"Hmm, so... you're saying that almost seven-hundred fifty years before Jesus was even born, God wanted Isaiah to what? Give them false hope?

No, not false—

"But, why would God want to have a prophet spread around a message about a future king which none of them, not their children, not their great-grandchildren's children would see within their lifetimes?"

Because of the other events going on at that time. Damien went into detail about how Assyria was an invincible superpower which not even Zion—another nickname for Jerusalem—couldn't possibly defend itself against. In fact, because of Israel's disobedience, God even helped the armies of Assyria punish the Israelite nations, just as Isaiah warned them. *God's children were about to be scattered all over the known world. God not only knew this was going to happen, but allowed it to. However, before His people were taken into exile or running for their lives, God wanted the message about the future to be taken into exile along with them. The timing was very important. Isaiah's prophecy about a Messianic King would be spread as far and as wide as those who heard it would eventually be spread.*

"Okay. What about verses five and six of chapter eleven?"

Damien took a sip of his horrible coffee before answering. *Brian, that's a good question, to which I don't have a concise, short, and simple answer. The Messianic King is not only promised to be a better king than any of the ones that came before Him, but is supposed to pass judgment fairly on the day of the Lord.*

"Wait," Dennis jumped in before Brian could reply. "So, now you're saying that Isaiah, in the same chapter, saw some prophesy about a king coming in seven-hundred years, as well as the End of Days which still hasn't happened yet, over two-thousand years later than that. How do we know the difference between the prophesy of a near-future and one of a distant future... one that is so incredibly distant to someone like Isaiah, that he would know about it?"

Isaiah wouldn't have known that the day of the Lord wouldn't happen during his own lifetime, nor after another two- or three-thousand years. In fact, I believe off of the top of my head, that in chapter thirteen somewhere, Isaiah even thought that the day of the Lord was near.

"Uh," Dennis muttered as he started flipping pages. "My study Bible has a footnote about that. It's verse six you're thinking about, and it says that 'the day of the Lord' used there refers to the overthrow of Babylon, its destruction, not the Apocalypse mentioned in the book of Revelation."

"I don't get it. How could Jesus 'judge the poor with justice and decide aright for the land's afflicted,' if He hadn't even been born yet?" Brian asked, quoting Isaiah 10:4 from his <u>New American Catholic Study Bible</u>.

Clearly, Isaiah was a prophet, and did wonders for his people by delivering the Word of God—both messages of hope and warning—to them, as accurately as he could. He taught the people what the Lord commanded and clearly the prophets of the Bible delivered prophecy that was not limited to telling the future; they also included the desires of the Lord. So, only to talk about these prophecies as fortunetelling or predictions, limits the true works of the Lord's prophets.

"Hey, Damien," Dennis pointed out, "I noticed some resentment in your voice when you said the word 'fortunetelling.' You don't think that Isaiah was telling the future?"

I believe that there, um, that telling the future is impossible, because the future doesn't exist. That is, God expressed His concerns and plans for the future to Isaiah, but even God has to wait and see how the future unfolds before us. Our free will' often ruins God's expectations, and then He has to make adjustments.

"I don't get it," Brian admitted. "For the most part, you agree with us regarding the future, except that God isn't telling someone, about something, that doesn't exist yet. But, we just read chapter eleven of Isaiah together, and clearly Isaiah is talking about something that God will make happen in seven-hundred years... the birth of Christ. I'm just wondering why you don't 'call a duck, a duck' as it were."

My point still remains, that God doesn't know the future. At least, not for certain. God may see where each of our destinies are headed, can predict them just like a forecaster of the weather. But nothing that we've done or will be doing in the future is carved in stone. We haven't done them yet, and—especially with me—there's little chance that what we'll do will turn out anything like what God expected.

"Alright, Damien. So, the future doesn't really exist? No one, not even God can know what tomorrow actually brings. Correct? That's what you're saying? Then, tell us how God predicts the future in the Scriptures? The destruction of the Temple? The fall of Nineveh and Babylon? Micah's own predictions of Jesus and national catastrophe... oh! And also Amos, and Zechariah..."

Again, Damien defended himself, *you are asking about something that doesn't exist. Or, well, didn't exist until God made them happen. I believe that God has the past and the now—the present—all under control, and is smart enough to predict what <u>might</u> happen in the future without His own, personal involvement. Those prophets you mentioned weren't predicting the future; they were spreading the message of what God intended to do. What He told them that He was going to do Himself or to otherwise allow to happen.*

"Well, Damien," Dennis nodded, "that helps explain why you don't believe in prophesy. You don't think God... excuse me, don't believe God lives in the past, present, and future."

Throwing away his empty paper cup, Damien responded, *"You're right, Dennis. I don't believe that God can exist in nonexistence. He is limited to the same laws and movement of time as we are. Don't get me wrong, I do believe that God exists and is powerful, that He can see where our futures are headed, just not their overall outcomes because of our 'free will' to change events, make bad decisions, or totally screw things up. This concept, the concept of making mistakes and committing sins, cannot happen in a meaningful way if God already knows the future.*

"Damien, that's absolutely crazy!" Dennis argued, raising his voice in a manner which Damien didn't like. "Help me understand this. Every priest and preacher will disagree with you about that. God has a plan for all of us! A master plan that –"

No, Damien uncommonly interrupted. *"We must remember that we have, in fact, evolved such that we truly have the ability to change our minds in our responses to a particular set of circumstances. Hence, making the task of predicting the future or living by some 'master plan' impossible. The fact is, as I understand things, nature <u>itself</u> has a certain amount of this free-will ability. Weather, earthquakes, forest fires, these—too—can be spontaneous, or acts of God. But, in either case, they make telling the future even more difficult, at best.*

"So, God doesn't have a plan for our lives?"

That's <u>not</u> what I said at all! He might have expectations for how your life is supposed to turn out, maybe several critical events here and there, who you choose to marry or how many children you'll someday have—if any—but, He gave us the human right to screw all of that up! If we do a sufficient job of screwing it all up, then God gets involved and causes something to happen that'll put us back on the correct path…that is, until we 'screw the pooch' again.

Damien, Dennis, and Brian talked for only a few more minutes, mostly small talk about the college, when Dennis brought an end to the conversation by noticing that it was "ever so close" to his next class. Damien, privately, was getting extremely bored with the two of them. Although he liked to discuss the Bible with just about anyone, these two students made Damien feel constantly on the defensive.

Arriving that evening at home, Damien took a shower and dreaded the idea of fixing dinner. He felt dog-tired and was grateful for Bob's willingness to tend to both the oven and the dishes afterwards. Damien still had some studying to do for his next final the following morning.

CHAPTER THIRTY-THREE

Screwing the Pooch

I really thought that I had better "smarts" than the barely-passing grades which I earned in school, but I settled for a "C" average, so I thought. But even this goal was out of reach. I was filling my life with overwhelming distractions which I truly didn't need at that moment. My obsession with becoming romantically involved, my becoming addicted to freebase all over again, even this unexplained desire to watch every movie available to me when I really needed to be studying.

Again, thanks to the grams of cocaine being fronted to me by my down-the-street neighbor, I was in debt to my eyeballs, and no way to pay for it! Although, with Mark's generosity—mixed with greed—I was allowed to keep digging the pit of debt incredibly deep. After all, my drug dealer knew where I lived, and would get paid one way or another, eventually. So, I abused my friendship with Sam again by selling things that weren't mine, in order to pay off this debt.

The anger inside me changed to rage. I hated myself, and before the end of January 1990, I would end up taking it out on others. Yet, before I get to that, let me set the scene for you. My friendship with Cameron and Kristy was becoming as regular as Dr. Reily's drive to his office. I was spending more and more time at their shared apartment, almost to the point of being considered as a third roommate, yet not quite that much. Another thing *that changed was my fascination with Kristy…particularly after finding out that she was still just a minor, but also for another reason—or should I say, a different person.*

Walking into the apartment, Damien greeted the group there, *Hey, everyone. How's it going tonight?*

"I'm well, thank you, and you?" asked an extremely stoned Cameron.

I'm fine…thanks. Did you guys already have dinner? As if I have to ask. You never have dinner this early.

"You're right about that," Kristy answered. "We haven't ate yet. You?"

I thought that I would get pizza before starting up with the weed."

"You're always such a Boy Scout," Cameron chuckled out, then attempted to do some math in his head. "My wallets over there, get three larges. Two supremes, one veggie. Kim is here, she's in the shower…and Joseph should be over soon with his girlfriend Sandy.

Damien had already met Cameron's girlfriend, Kim, on several occasions—they had been an item for two weeks—but hadn't yet been introduced to Joseph's. In fact, this wasn't the first time he had heard this name. No, this 'infamous' yet unseen Sandy had dated Cameron a couple of times before sleeping behind his back with Cameron's own brother, before moving on. Now, she'd sunk her insatiable claws into Joseph's heart, albeit only temporarily until she would move onward yet again.

I thought you said Sandy was nothin' but trouble? Damien asked.

"She is! She's nothing but fast and loose."

B-but then, why is Joseph getting' himself involved with her. Doesn't he know?

"Oh, he knows. The thing is, well, Damien…you haven't seen her."

At that moment, just as Damien was fishing two twenties out of Cameron's wallet for the three pizzas, came a knocking at the door. It was, as expected, Joseph and Sandy…what wasn't expected was how exceptionally pretty this young, blonde-headed girl would be. Sandy was a petite and spunky fireball, who reminded Damien a lot like actress Sally Fields in the original "Smoky and the Bandit" movie, with the exception of hair color. Damien was instantly smitten, as well all of Sandy's previous victims of lust.

Joseph was my friend, so I wouldn't make any "move" on his girlfriend. But, I am telling you the truth that having sex with Sandy was constantly on my mind. It was a fixation I just couldn't shake days after meeting her. Then, a week had come and gone when on a certain afternoon I was called by Kristy. She called me to ask for the favor of taking Sandy to the airport. Her and Joseph had split up and she needed to catch a flight back home to Georgia.

Part of me wanted to slam the phone down on the desktop as my response—which I probably should have—however, I chose to accept the favor. But, the plans to get her directly to the airport changed rather suddenly. Once I had Sandy in my car, it was my sex drive which did all of the actual driving. I'd decided to take her to my house instead, then told her that I just needed to get a couple of things before we'd be on our way again. Sandy could see right through me, and this scared her something fierce.

I freely admit now that what I did was wrong, dead wrong. All that I could think about that day was wanting for this young blonde lady and I to have some quick sex… which, according to her reputation, was something she had done a lot. So, why not with me? My ego was riding on her decision and nonetheless, I had frightened her enough to make her feel she had no choice. Her consent to engage in sex was bogus, a lie… what lawyers would later call a consent given under duress.

Here's another thing. Why did I take this to places that made me utterly sick to my stomach? To the date of this writing, I still don't know, but it is sadly and horribly true. I found no enjoyment in having sex with this innocent girl. Her being afraid of me made the sex that we had miserable and wretched to my core. It wasn't until the release of my pent-up sexual frustration did I finally realize that she wasn't having any enjoyment either.

The only right thing to happen after this sick crime was that I was arrested and properly convicted of rape. There was no need for a jury trial; I took the very first plea bargain offered to me, because I knew I was guilty and really an abuser. I also didn't want to put that innocent woman through the emotional distress of testifying and reliving that crime moment-by-moment in front of twelve people; it would be like raping her a second time. I didn't want to put her through that.

Damien was arrested within an hour of dropping Sandy off at the airport. The same instant he left her standing curbside, she had turned and entered the terminal with the full intention of reporting the crime to the very first police officer she saw. Days later, at the arraignment hearing, the public defender assigned to him advised Damien to simply enter a plea of "not guilty" until he had enough time to look over all of the evidence, but Damien flat-out refused.

No, I did it, he told his lawyer within earshot of the judge and bailiff, *there's nothing to argue.*

Damien was sentenced to three years back within the walls of prison.

Chuckawalla Valley State Prison in the desert town of Blythe, was just seventeen miles west of the California-Arizona Border. This was a relatively brand-new prison to the state system, only two years old. Another new prison to be named "Ironwood" was still under construction right next door. In fact, between the years 1984 and 1994, the Department of Corrections had built fourteen new prisons, most of which were located along the fringes of the Mojave Desert or just north of Bakersfield. Fourteen additional prisons in just ten years?!

About a week after I was transferred to Chuckawalla from the reception center in Chino, I met a tall slender man in his early thirties named Shaun. He was very inviting whenever he talked, and I almost instantly looked forward to having a conversation with him, even though he always ended up talking about God and salvation. He would urge me to make up my mind "for or against God." Finally, we started having regular discussions.

Damien accepted Shaun's invitation to join him at church that Sunday. For no known reason at all, Damien chose to tell him that he wasn't at all a Christian. However, he told Shaun that he would go, mainly because he had nothing better to do. He did this because Shaun had an institutionalized version of understanding in what it was to be a so-called Christian. This, plus Damien didn't want to come out too strong... that it would be better to pretend to be a beginner than it would to say you're an expert.

Parting ways, Shaun asked, "Sure, okay. What building are you in?"

I'm in C3.

"Alright then, I'll be waiting for you in front of your building. See ya on Sunday."

With that said, Damien went to his assigned bunk deep within the dormitory designed for two-hundred inmates. Resting there, he thought about the differences between Chuckawalla and the liberties he'd left behind at San Luis Obispo only a short time earlier. Not only was the security much more strict, the facility itself was designed to keep people both in or out. You couldn't come or go to your cell as you pleased, not... unless you had authorization you remained inside the dormitory or out. There was also an electrified fence that—according to the many posted signs—was charged with ten-thousand volts, which would cause severe injury if not instant death.

I saw that I was in desperate need for Jesus the Christ in my life. Maybe, that was the reason why God had sent Shaun to spend so much time with me. He barely knew me, yet challenged my faith, much as I questioned myself. I had left California Men's Colony as the leader of a Bible study, was out of prison for only three years or so, and now here I was... claiming to not be a Christian. I didn't at all feel like one. In fact, I felt very little other than disappointment in myself. I felt sorrow unlike any I'd ever felt in the past.

So, at that moment, I fell to my knees and prayed for the first time in a very long time. I asked God to forgive me my mistakes, my sins, and for ignoring both Him and Christ Jesus all of these years. I wanted Jesus in my life, to be my Lord and Savior. To my surprise, a voice came to me, but it wasn't from God or Lord Jesus, but a correctional officer. Being that it was 1630 Hours, it was mandatory standing count time... and there I was, down on my knees instead. Maybe, I should have prayed for earplugs, because that office ridiculed me for ten minutes straight.

The following day, as Damien's building was being released to the chow hall, Damien was so distracted by his thoughts for just a moment that he ended up banging his lowered head into a window. Instead of his usual cursing of foul words, his gibberish response sounded so funny that he couldn't contain himself. His fellow inmates, likewise on their way to dinner, asked if this apparent lunatic was alright—both for his bruised forehead and for not a normal response of cursing.

Damien stopped laughing only long enough to say, "Gee, who put that window there." However, what he failed to realize was that this comment was spoken entirely in French, and nobody around him understood what was said. Damien's Grandpa, if he was there, would've been so proud of that moment.

Sunday morning arrived, and it was time for Damien to check out this prison's church. Unlike the C.M.C. prison in San Luis Obispo, which featured a rather impressively sized, standalone chapel, the so-called church at Chuckawalla Valley seemed more like a janitor's closet. Perhaps this was its originally designed purpose before the prison's architects realized that they forgot to include a required room for worship. In any case, the relatively tiny room sat roughly twenty-five to thirty shoulder-rubbing inmates and a lackluster wooden podium. By the time Damien arrived, it was "standing room only", a mistake he wouldn't make again.

Damien was happily met by his new friend, Shaun—as agreed—just outside his dormitory, and they both walked to and entered "the Chapel" together. Shaun introduced Damien to the prison's hired chaplain, a tall and slender African-American man named Brown. He personally facilitated the Pentecostal services, while only simply sponsored and sat in on the other denominational services offered there. After the handshakes, a serene quiet took its place and washed over the attendees; all murmuring instantly faded away. Chaplain Brown took his place at the podium, yet said absolutely nothing while looking up at the ceiling.

Standing in quiet meditation, Damien perceived a strong sense of God's presence surrounding every single inmate. He, himself, wasn't sure what else he needed to do at that very moment, nor why Chaplain Brown wasn't saying anything, but respected this ritual of peace and quiet. Finally, the very dark-complexioned preacher lowered his eyes upon the congregation, and without any notes nor Bible, quoted from the book of Romans chapter eight.

"'Hence, now there is no condemnation for those who are in Christ Jesus. For the law of the spirit of life in Christ Jesus has freed you from the law of sin and death.' Let me say that again, through the redemptive work of Christ Jesus, you have been liberated from the terrible forces of sin and death."

Stopping there for a moment, Damien felt as if Chaplain Brown had made direct eye contact with him. In fact, if your were to ask anyone within that tiny room, they would've felt the exact same. "Do you not see, my beloved that your old self, your self-interested, self-centered self, is now changed! Yes, you live in that flesh, you travel this world in that flesh, 'but you are not of the flesh. On the contrary, you are in the spirit, if only the Spirit of God dwells in you.'" (quoting Romans 8:9 NAB)

Listening to Chaplain Brown, the effective result is was giving me, I had the feeling of being spoken to directly... which sort of scared me. I felt as if he had somehow been listening to me the night before when I knelt down and prayed to Christ. Did he listen to my prayer? I was doing time for a horrendous sin... well, all sins are—in God's eyes—horrendous... and I had asked Christ to forgive me and to be my Savior.

But now, now Chaplain Brown was bringing the concept of having the Holy Spirit of God living inside of me. I wasn't sure if I wanted a ghost living inside of me; it was already crowded enough inside my head as it was. I, of course, had already read "The Acts of the Apostles" and knew that having the Holy Spirit of God within you was an amazing and positive benefit, to guide and strengthen me... but I didn't feel worthy of such a sacred gift or presence in my life. No, not yet.

Chaplain Brown's sermon was brief, sweet, and to the point. He took an intermission to allow the "Worship Team" to sing a selection of jubilant, energetic songs, which—after a cue from the Chaplain—they brought to an end and seated themselves for "round two" as it were.

"Our Lord God hears you!" Chaplain Brown started up again. "Our Lord God blesses you! Our Lord God wants you in His life, in His Kingdom! All that you, my beloved, have to do, is let Our Lord God in. Let Him in your life, let Him into your flesh, let Him into your thoughts... let Him in!"

It was a little scary because I felt as if God told this chaplain to encourage me ... that I should redo my prayer for salvation again. This time, for community! For His spiritual goodness to replace everything that I am. I found myself walking forward, towards the podium, before I even heard

Chaplain Brown's complete invitation. I just did what I thought was the request of God's spirit, and I was actually pleased to have that moment of public speaking. We one-by-one took turns at that podium and publically asked Jesus to be our Savior.

Shaun was more than simply pleased that Damien had publically asked Jesus to be his Savior, because this was exactly what Shaun wanted in the first place upon meeting Damien. Shaun was now his "brother" as well as a friend. Damien's prayer for Christ to remake him, to make him born again, to be a Christian, blessed the both of them with a bond which went beyond mere friendship.

At the end of the service, Shaun introduced Damien to other Christian brothers, and nobody was in any rush to leave the Chapel. Damien felt complete for the first time... he belonged to a group, a community of brothers. Several inmates congratulated Damien for choosing God's spirit over a life of sin and a punishment in hell. However, even with their words of encouragement, Damien felt that he needed continued growth.

Frankly, I was glad to belong in something other than just myself. I now no longer felt alone... I had "brothers" who would help me grow spiritually in my faith. It felt good having a family of any sort, and so much better that this family was a Christ-centered community. One that would help me at my slow pace, not at another's pace. I was on target as long as I believed in what and how they did.

However it wasn't long before I saw that things were about to change again. There were notions that the brothers believed in that—simply put—I didn't and couldn't believe, not as they did. I didn't have the same belief in the aspects of God nor of Scripture as they did. Despite my having an honest belief in being "born again," asking Christ to be my Lord, Savior, and Master, and being "faith born" a new child and brother in Christ— and what it all means—I still believed differently about the Bible and the nature of God.

I wondered what on Earth that meant. I even prayed that God would <u>fix</u> my erroneous beliefs about the Scriptures. I felt confused because I had asked God to remove any and all defects in my life—Wow! What a concept! Nevertheless, I knew that the brothers would declare that I couldn't be a *brother of theirs, because I didn't conform to their comprehension towards the nature of God.*

Damien felt that he was headed for trouble with the Pentecostal brothers because of his conflict with their teachings. Just a few mere days after being publically born again, he was invited to join a few of these brothers in a Bible study group which didn't fair well at all. It was under his own certainty that "God didn't want robots for children, nor did He want children that were made into duplicates of each other." That got this group riled up.

Look, Damien argued with his Christian brothers, *God sent His only begotten son, Jesus, to free people from the consequences of sin. It's true that to enter the gates of the city of God, one must be reborn and created a new creation. But, we are still sons and daughters with distinctly different ways to individually understand all matters or issues. This is also true about the matters regarding God, Creation, and the Word of God.*

For instance, I believe that God did create this planet of ours, this home called Earth... yet God did so through the tool of evolution. Furthermore, I believe that this world is still evolving, and so is the human race. Just as new lands are appearing out of the Pacific Ocean, the skeletal structure of mankind is altering and being revamped.

"What!" A group member exclaimed. "You're actually comparing volcanoes in the ocean to people being born taller? It's all the handiwork of God, not some morphological process of development. Those islands are there because God wanted them there. Your spine is straighter because God wanted it to be straighter. It's not some random scientific 'luck of the draw' that these changes are happening throughout the universe."

So, Damien argued, *you're saying that every time a leaf on a tree turns brown and falls off, it's because God wanted that specific leaf to fall off? Don't you realize just how many trees and leaves that there are in the world, and how much of God's attention to all of those leaves would be required each and every day, especially during October? God has more important things to be doing with His time, than to individually pick which leaf falls off of which tree every second of every day.*

"Are you saying that God isn't all-powerful? That He isn't

omnipresent and involved in all things?"

Of course, he's powerful, but no. He isn't involved in every tiny, little event in our lives. God lives: He created the world to be self-sufficient an— sustaining. He did so by way of evolution, by putting everything into motion, so that it would all turn out like He expected. However, things didn't always turn out absolutely correct, as the history of the world and in particular— the people of Israel clearly proved in their repeated disobedience. Even the Bible, itself, is not a perfect library of absolute truth—

As you can anticipate, this final comment wasn't as well received as Damien could have expected. No, he was immediately placed on the defensive on this, to which he brought up the issue of inconsistencies and contradictions he'd previously brought up with Charles "Tex" Watson: whether Adam came before or after the animals (the first two chapters of Genesis); Noah's iimprobable ark and where all that floodwater went; the burial place of King Ahaz (2nd Kings 16:20 versus 2nd Chronicles 28:27; or why only the Gospel of John believed that Lazarus being brought back to life was "newsworthy."

Damien also stuck to "his guns" about his belief that the world was several billions of years old and not just six or seven thousand. He received mixed responses from everyone in the Bible study group. Nearly everyone else was solid on the notion that anything and everything either happens due to the handiwork of God directly, or that these events were allowed to occur. Their reasoning was confusing to Damien because it implicated that some very negative actions and events, including the Holocaust in Nazi Germany; Stalin's genocide of millions; all of the assassinations, slaughters, and butchery of innocent lives, were by God's permission. Either things of nature and human beings have their own power—hence, God doesn't have complete power and control—or God had all the power during these moments of decimation and atrocity… and this was something Damien simply couldn't accept about a loving God.

I chose to study all that I could on my own. I left the brotherhood and avoided both Chaplain Brown and his church, until I could finally go home and resume my spiritual growth within a church family of my choosing. I knew that I would eventually find a church that would help me through my growth as a Christian man. I will, naturally, be forever grateful for Chaplain Brown's sermons and his encouragement to publically declare myself one of God's own children. I could safely say that I could feel God's Spirit within me. However, in hindsight, I've come to realize that being inside of me was all that I was allowing the Holy Spirit to do. During my years at C.V.S.P., I failed to put God's wondrous gift to use or to work, in the lives of others.

Accordingly, God's stimulation of a more and more complex world, which has the capacity for more and more intrinsic value, means the development of creatures with more and more freedom to reject divine aims. Increased freedom in relation to the world necessarily means increased freedom in relation to God.... [E]ven if the environment in which we find ourselves is not objectively negative, we can make ourselves miserable....We can even do this deliberately—which is the essence of moral evil. Hence, increasing the freedom of the creatures was a risky business on God's part. But it was a necessary risk, if there was to be a chance for greatness. ~ John B. Cobb, Jr. & David Ray Griffin, *Process Theology: An Introductory Exposition*

CHAPTER THIRTY-FOUR

On the Road Again

Damien was paroled from Chuckawalla Valley State Prison in the Autumn of 1993. The time remaining of his three-year sentence had faded away at an unimaginable pace for him. It wasn't until he was down to forty-five days left that he indeed recognized that he would soon be released. In fact, the month before his release, he hadn't even made any plans toward being so.

As unlike as this sounds—it even astonished Damien—Dr. Samuel Reily was not only willing to pick Damien up from that prison in the desert, but he also was going to let him move back in with him <u>again</u>. Sam was once more proving himself to be deserving of the highest humanitarian award available, in Damien's personal opinion. Damien would have his own room back; yet, in exchange of rent, a lot more would be expected of him, including the impossible task of staying out of trouble.

None of that was going to be difficult this time, because I really did ask Jesus to be my master. I was a very different man from the one who went to prison. I knew I said this to Sam in the past, the last time I was released; however, the last time I wasn't a born again son of God. I was going to do well on parole because I'd quit all manner of foul habits, such as lying cursing, and even cigarette smoking... although, in all honesty, this last addiction was quit simply because I couldn't afford to do it anymore, while in prison, not because I actually wanted to.

Sam came to get me at prison, as promised, and even surprised me by letting me drive his brand-new jet-black 4x4 car. He called it a sport-utility vehicle, which was a marketing term I'd never heard of before. No, this helluva sexy Nissan Pathfinder SUV handled like a dream, even though I thought of it as just a really big station wagon, and called it as such. It was indeed a very nice drive from Blythe, past the Salton Sea (a 370-square mile lake of stagnant saline), back to the coast and to Huntington Beach.

Damien was greeted at the front door by three strangers: a pair of collies with full-bred or pedigreed features from the lineage of the Hollywood film stars of the "Lassie" movies and TV shows, as well as an Alaskan malamute with an equally gorgeous coat of gray and white, instead of brown and white. The two sheepdogs were named George and Barbara—after the married couple currently occupying the White House—although they were both actually female dogs. The Alaskan sled dog was named Prince... although Damien never knew why.

The collies were all grown up, and I was so very happy to finally meet them. Sam had adopted them the same month I'd been sentenced, and they were well taken care of... which was mainly done by Bob, before he'd moved out. In fact, Bob's old bedroom had been converted into a makeshift kennel for all three dogs, complete with their own TV to watch... gone were the pornos, here now were wildlife videos and two educational tapes designed for canines. It was a "puppy paradise" in there.

The truth be known, I actually liked Bob, despite of the fact that he had a way about himself that truly frustrated others, especially me. Maybe, it was simply the fact that I'd encouraged Sam to allow Bob to move in with us in the first place but he didn't repay our generosity in kindness, only in agitation. But, then again, perhaps this is how God must feel about me: He'd allowed me to be born, to live on His world of creation, only to rarely thank Him for His generosity.

Damien's life was starting to take shape, and he was ready to do his part in the everyday business of living; however, this included something he was ashamed of and would never be able to rid himself of: he now needed to take care of his annual registration as a sexual offender. This would become a constant, yearly reminder that he had done harm to a woman... and for no reason whatsoever than his own self-centeredness.

The following morning after his release from prison, Damien needed to borrow Sam's Pathfinder to take care of his Penal Code 290 registration. He returned from the police office in time to start taking care of the household chores. However, when he arrived back at the house, Sam was home early from work, and with a job proposal.

He told me that his sister, Barbara—the same one who had helped Sam with finding this house back when it was for sale, and had been working as the office manager of Sam's private practice ever since Damien shot that man in the neck—had gotten married while Damien was locked up and was moving out to the East Coast. This meant that Sam needed someone to take her place and assist him with his office needs, including the making and rescheduling of appointments... something I'll admit I wasn't great at in the past.

Naturally, I accepted. Sam had done far too many favors for me in both the present and the past, I knew that I couldn't pass up the chance to provide him a favor. Although his private practice was growing and providing him a substantial income, I knew that he could afford both the house and hiring just about anybody to be his receptionist. The point is, he had faith in me and a huge amount of love for me. Personally, I still do not know why he forgave me as often as he did, except that he was hopeful for a change in my heart at being his lover, but I wasn't that person anymore.

The next morning, Damien went with Sam to the office, so that Damien could get familiar with all the changes to Barbara's office. There was newer office equipment and a completely different business phone system from when he had last worked for Sam. Even the filing cabinets had changed, with billing now being performed on a desktop computer instead of pen and paper. Damien had never used a computer before, had never heard of the company called Microsoft, and it took quite some time to get used to using a mouse within something called windows 3.51 Workstation. The revolutionary leap to Windows 95 was still fourteen months away.

Between patients, Sam surprised me yet again. He sent me to get us lunch from a local deli and, on the way back, to take a look for an inexpensive, yet reliable, car at the neighborhood dealerships. After getting our sandwiches, I went to the Nissan dealer on foot. It wasn't long before I saw a car that fit my understanding of inexpensive and reliable. It was a 1993 Altima. The question was would Sam agree or not to buying me this new car rather than some old clunker. But I would've been satisfied even if Sam bought me the ten-year-old Datsun 240ZX in the furthest corner of the lot.

Three hours later, I was blessed as it was near time for Sam to end his short day. He was well pleased that I used my brains when looking for a car, and I was able to take a test drive. It both met my needs and handled great. It was exactly what I was looking for. Come that evening, we were both home, parking in the driveway with both these cars which we both liked. I was grateful for the car, but I was more anxiously looking for something else: the right woman to have as my bride.

Damien had needs that, on his own, he couldn't obtain. He had realized that he was in need of some changes, but he had no idea where to start, nor how to effect those changes. Asking Jesus to make those differences in him would put his life more in the hands of the Christ than his own. This is what he knew would make the correct changes and as fast as possible for him.

One detour I knew I needed was to start going to church. What I didn't know was which church was the right one for me. I did know that I couldn't go to any Evangelical or Pentecostal body of believers. We just did not believe the same things about God and the Bible. I'm not saying that they are wrong, only that they were the wrong fit for me. The truth of it is, I didn't know what denomination of Christianity nor which church would accept me for who I was, and I was so tired and scared of rejection! I'd been rejected enough.

I grabbed a Los Angeles County phone book, the Pacific Bell Yellow Pages, and ran my fingertips down the long listing of different religious sects. To my dismay, the listing continued onto the following page, then the page after that! I had no idea there were so many "flavors" of Christendom. Nor did I know what each represented, their creeds and ethics, or how they differ. The major ones included: the baptists, episcopalians, Jehovah's Witnesses, the Lutherans, Methodists, Orthodox Roman, Pentecostal, Presbyterians, and Roman Catholics. But, then, there were also: the Adventists, Agnostics, Apostolic Catholic, Brethren, Church Of Christ, Eastern Orthodox, Evangelical, Latter-Day Saints, Mennonites, Muslims, Reformed Catholic, Taoists, and Unitarians, to name only a few.

For someone like me, a list like this drives me crazy. We all believe in the same God, and read from the same Bible, yet there's just so many different churches and methods of practicing a religion which is at its core, the exact same religion. Why on Earth are there so many independent denominations? Did God truly want this? To be worshipped or praised in so many different ways? For there to be a controversy over how and when we can be baptized or not? I'm still today having a hard time accepting this is what God wanted.

One afternoon, Damien made what he'd believed to be a "silly mistake" while Sam wasn't home. He had opened the door to a pair of Mormon elders performing their mission and let two young men into the house to talk about Jesus the Christ. After letting these elders in, Damien allowed them to introduce him to this unique version of faith, that he could become a joint-heir with Jesus in God's Kingdom. That theirs is the true church, thanks to the completed third Testament of Scripture restored through their founder Joseph Smith in the 1820's.

I listened to them with interest, since I had never before heard their religion's name nor its teaching about their faith. I will tell you that there were things that bothered me straight from the gate. One of these was their so-called third Testament, named <u>The Book of Mormon</u>, and the fact that the original golden tablets which this revelation was translated from no longer exist. Another thing was their temple in Utah, and how for their private reasons it was sealed and the only way to ever have access inside is by obtaining a recommendation from their local bishop.

Finally, and what struck me as being quite odd to say the least, is their practice of Baptism for the Dead. No, they didn't dip dead bodies into the water, as the name might suggest... a living person could themselves be baptized in the name or place of someone who had died before being baptized, thereby earning the deceased person a place in Heaven. So, any ancestor who died before turning their lives over to Christ could somehow still be saved simply by their grandchild or great-great-grandchild being baptized on that person's behalf? This just didn't make much sense to me.

There were several things of their faith which I did believe strongly in, and two of these were strong family emphasis and marriage for eternity. Although divorce was prohibited, it was viewed as a last resort and often considered as merely a "legal divorce" not a spiritual one. Marriage didn't end in death, unlike the traditional marriage vow of "until death do us part," you're still married in Heaven. I, for one, never took the concept of marriage lightly... the woman I would marry would be the only one for me, and forever. This might seem like a bizarre idea in today's society of rotating Hollywood marriages and drive-thru wedding chapels up and down the Las Vegas strip, but I hold onto the ancient belief that you only marry for real and lasting purposes.

Gathering their books, Damien thanked the Mormon elders for stopping by and for spending the nearly forty minutes talking to him about what they believed in. Just as they were leaving, Sam walked into the house and politely bid them a good evening, then closed the door behind them.

"You were talking with the Mormons?" Sam asked. He wasn't mad at Damien in the slightest, yet a bit concerned with his choice to learn about their religion.

Yeah, they came by going door-to-door, and we talked for about an hour.

"An hour?" Sam smiled about this, then made an astonishing disclosure, "Did you know I was raised Mormon?"

You were? Damien asked, while looking down at the copy of The Book of Mormon held in his hands. *"I didn't know that."*

"My family has been members of the Reorganized Church of Jesus Christ of Latter-Day Saints for nearly a hundred years. Well, actually R.L.D.S. hasn't itself been around that long, but my great-grandfather was Mormon and an elder of the original church. I was baptized the same week as my eighth birthday in Salt Lake City. In fact, if you really are interested in learning more about their history, I might still have some books around here… as well as connections with the local congregation."

I've never know this about you. I had no idea you even went to church.

Sam shook his head, "Now there's a difference between being an active member and attending services. I haven't stepped foot inside R.L.D.S. for some time."

Why's that? Is it because you're gay?

"Actually, being gay isn't frowned upon at R.L.D.S., not as much as, say, being in prison. You might want to keep that small fact about yourself, to yourself, but not so much your homosexuality."

Or my bisexuality," Damien corrected. This statement, above all else Damien had said that day, made Samuel cringe. *You know, Sam, it's a strange coincidence that here I am looking into a church to join—the right church—and now I suddenly find this out about you. It might just be a sign.*

"Damien, I really don't want my membership in the Mormon church to persuade you into thinking that R.L.D.S. is the correct choice for you," he cautioned, but it was too late. Damien already viewed Sam as the ideal role model, and wanted to follow in his footsteps as much as possible.

Sam took time to review Latter-Day Saints history with me, covering the foundation of the religion in New York, their persecution from state-to-state until finally settling in Utah—they were literally chased out of the northeast, viewed as heretics both then and today—plus read some choice pages from both The Book of Mormon and Brigham young's discourses. I had no idea that I had this wealth of information and facts, for months, sleeping in the very next bedroom.

I really wanted to be accepted into a church as a member, as directed by Christ. The previous Sunday, I had attended service at the Calvary Church of Huntington Beach which, in case I hadn't mentioned it before, I did as a promise to Charlie Oops a few times when I got out of prison the last term. However, I can't say that I had faithfully gone to that church… in fact, I can count the total number of times I went there with just my fingers alone, no toes required. I never felt like I belonged in that large auditorium, and grew rather tired with the sermons. I was looking to be taught, not preached at.

When Sam read me parts of The Book of Mormon, I realized that—at that time of my life—I was being called to make this Reorganized Church of Jesus Christ of latter-Day Saints my highest priority towards learning precisely the Lord's purpose and use of me. That I was somehow meant to learn from these people in how to serve Christ. So, I then decided to ask Sam where the local congregation was so I could check them out.

The closest R.L.D.S. congregation was in Costa Mesa, California, roughly twelve miles south from where they lived; which Damien believed as both a blessing and another sign from God. The following Sunday, he drove himself there and was pleasantly surprised at what he found there. At first, he was expecting a group of church-goers who were old enough to be his parents and grandparents; and secondly, he was expecting a typical chapel with row-after-row of wooden pews... he was wrong on both counts.

he congregation in Costa Mesa had a nice mix of attenders ranging from preschoolers to seniors; however, most were around my age. I was pleased to meet several young women, both married and single, who were healthy and very pretty. I never thought of going to church in order to find dates but if I were to meet just the right single woman here, well... that could be good, too.

The fellowship met at a simple, nondescript conference hall which was used for other things throughout the week, including bingo on Wednesday nights. The tables and chairs were arranged in small groups of up to twelve. I was introduced by the pastor and his wife, who then delivered me into the welcoming hands of my new small-group leaders: Dale and his wife, Henrietta.

Damien realized straight away that he would feel really comfortable in a small-group ministry. Each group was limited to no more than twelve members, which created both an enormous level of confidentiality and acquaintance. Nothing in Damien's life had prepared him for the experience of becoming a part of a small-group ministry.

During the first night of meeting everyone, our group leader, Dale, invited me to his house that Thursday for a new member orientation. I gladly accepted and got his address. My involvement with this small group was a true blessing, reminiscent to the small seven-man Bible study which

Charlie and I had started in prison; only, of course, with better surroundings and fewer time restrictions.

I was impressed, to say the least, with the closeness that I experienced with these people; they were a true Christ-centered family. I could've spent another three or four hours with my group members, except that it was getting late on that work/school night, and I wanted to share my experience with Sam before his bedtime. So, I drove straight home and excitedly rushed into the living room . . .

Sam! You still up? Oh, sorry for yelling.

"You sound as if you had a good time," he greeted, sitting there on the davenport with a glass of wine in one hand, the TV's remote in the other. He'd muted the volume the exact moment Damien had entered the house. On the coffee table sat a mostly full wine bottle and an empty glass awaiting Damien.

Yes, I had a great time. Let me tell you about it, because it was all too clear to me that God's Spirit was at work in that group.

"Pull up a chair," Sam motioned to the couch cushion next to him, then to the wine, "and speaking of spirits, help yourself. It's an '82 Bordeaux to celebrate this occasion."

While pouring himself some wine, Damien went on with his details, "Dale and wife made it clear that they loved people in general, and that they love the church and its leaders in a special way. I believe that they were receptive of the workings of the Holy Spirit. We read scripture together and shared ourselves with others—

This last part concerned Sam enough to interrupt, "You didn't mention prison or being on parole, did you?"

No, I stayed within the context of the night's conversation. But, to be honest, I really don't see Dale or anybody having a problem with me being on parole. Sam, do you remember Navoo, Illinois?

"Yeah, I took you there a couple of years back."

Like that! If Joseph Smith was around today, he would be proud of them and so would the Mormon church's stake. It's just fantastic.

"Wait, what did you mean when you said, 'like that'? You had no idea that I was Mormon at the time. We were only driving through and I suggested stopping for some sightseeing."

You're right, I didn't know. But, for a simple sightseer, I remember you being, uh, enthralled with everything to do with Joseph Smith's model city and early attempts at building the ideal community. Well, that is, until he was executed. I believe Joseph Smith would be proud at the church's growth and over-all maturity. He definitely would have loved the idea of small groups and would've wanted to see more of it. The group of wards is Christ-centered, just what my soul needs for me to grow.

"The problem," Sam remarked, "for the most part, was the political nature of the surrounding communities and states of Navoo, Illinois. Did you know that Joseph even tried to run for state governor? Not only did he lose the election, but—perhaps because of it—drew a lot of attention to his unorthodox religion and what others believed as a socialist commune."

You mean, communism?

"More or less, but really, Navoo was <u>communalism</u> at its best. All of its original residents took care of each other under the church's leadership. A fully-engulfed spiritual lifestyle and community."

That's true, but that doesn't mean that the idea can't happen today. After all, the street gangs are doing a slow yet effective takeover of Los Angeles and many other cities. All of the drugs and crime, drive-by shootings, guns at elementary schools; this cannot be what we want.

"Damien, the separation of church and state exists for a reason. They have learned from history that church-run governments easily turn into dictatorships and the loss of religious freedom. We just had a bad example with that cult near Waco, Texas; the Branch Davidian compound which federal agents tried to gain access to, ended in an over 50-day standoff and around seventy-five people dead. We wouldn't want a repeat of that."

No, we definitely wouldn't. But you could build a community without it turning into a cult, per so.

"So," Sam asked after another gulp of wine, "what do we do differently to grow this movement in the church?"

What must be central to it function is growing a number of small, autonomous groups in each city or town, that is encouraged by its leadership in the depth of each group. They would care more about the purpose of these individual groups rather than subject matter. This will allow them to truly be focused on its members' concerns and not so much with the message.

"Wait, Damien, you think a church shouldn't care what its group leaders are teaching their members? That doesn't make sense."

The message will come, one way or another, regardless of having someone dictate a leader what to teach on a specific day. As long as the Bible is involved, the subject should be up to the group members. The main goal or purpose needs to be the healing of our many communities and societies. The growth of the church will happen on its own, the popularity of small groups will do all the actual promotion and growing on its own. No, the driven purpose of the church will be in sponsoring these small groups to bring what the local communities are in need of: close-knit associations and relationship.

"Well, my friend, clearly you have been thinking about this problem for a while. You didn't get all of this from just <u>one</u> small-group meeting, that's for sure." Sam put down his empty wine glass, then turned serious. "What started you on this problem?"

You're right Sam. I didn't get all of this from just one meeting. In fact, this whole thought started the first time I was in prison. C.M.C., actually. I have seen the mess of street gangs and how attractive they are to teenagers, and have looked for a solution ever since.

"Wait. 'Attractive'? How is joining a street gang attractive?"

Because the one that gang members do better than normal society is that they take care of their own. They watch out for each other. Both the closeness and support they give each other is attractive, more addictive that any drug. Kids want their lives to mean something, to be a vital part of something bigger than just themselves. That's why they join sporting teams, cheerleading, the school's band... they belong to something important. A family. But, if you can't play sports or music or aren't otherwise gifted enough, you will join whatever else is out there in order to 'belong' to something.

"It's human nature to be accepted by others and to belong to something bigger than just yourself." Sam nodded.

Yes, it is, but there's just so few options out there for kids today. Especially on the weekdays between the hours of two and five. Small groups is the answer. You helped me see the solution. I didn't realize it at the time, that's for sure, but when you took me to Navoo and I saw <u>what</u> Joseph Smith *had started to build there, and after tonight's small group meeting... you see, the church has always been the solution all along.*

Some tears had welled-up in Sam's eyes, although he wasn't an emotional man,, nor did Damien ever see him actually cry. "What you said about small-group ministry is impressive. I always knew that you were meant to be a member of a Christian fellowship; I just never thought you'd be interested in Latter-Day Saints. I guess I was wrong in keeping my Christian family from you."

I fell in love with the idea of a small-group ministry and its dynamics the moment I stepped inside Dale's apartment. I knew instantly that I was on the right road again.

"Well, that's good. Great, even. I'm just so glad that I was able to help you get involved in a church that makes sense for you."

Damien noticed a hesitation in Sam's voice, then asked, *What about you? Are you interested in returning?*

"I—well, now Damien, I've been away from the church for a while... and for what I thought were pretty good reasons."

But? Damien urged him on.

"But... hmm, I guess you couldn't be more right. I don't have an excuse towards <u>not</u> going."

Damien smiled, then hugged the older man, much as he would his Grandpa. *I'm glad.* Pulling away from their embrace, Damien then requested, *"I have a favor to ask of you, but first I need to make certain of something. Did you tell me that you <u>are</u> a priest after the order of Aaron.*

"Yes, I told you that last week. Why?"

Because I've been reading <u>The Book of Mormon</u>, in chapter eleven of Nephi, I saw where Jesus commanded the priesthood to baptize all of the people of faith—in the name of the Father, Son, and the Holy Spirit—and I want you to baptize me so that I can become a member of the church.

"You want <u>me</u>—"Sam was so overwhelmed by the weight of Damien's request, that he couldn't get his words straight. He found a great joy in the younger man's honest request. "Of course, I'll baptize you. I'm just so touched." And once again they embraced.

CHAPTER THIRTY-FIVE

Becoming More Centered

Looking for a Christ-centered church had been difficult for Damien at first, partially because of his misunderstanding with the terms 'Bible-centered' and 'Christ-centered'. He had seen these as being the same, and this is simply not true.

In Bible-centered faiths, the follower can be grounded in the Bible without also being grounded in the teachings and life of Christ Jesus. A Bible-centered person is one that trusts that everything the Bible says is true and nothing else is true.

Meanwhile, the Christ-centered student can recognize that there may well be other sources that contain the life and teachings of Jesus, the foretold Deliverer and King. A Christ-centered soul respects the incarnate Word of God, yet seeks to know as much as possible about Christ Jesus both through literature and worship.

Being one certainly doesn't mean that you're the other. Someone can be Christ-centered and doubt the authenticity of the Gospel of John; someone can accept that the story of the Maccabees is factual yet choose not to read it purely because it wasn't included in the King James Version of the Word. The truth is that Christ-centered churches and their parishoners are more open-minded in the acceptance of faith.

The Reorganized Church of Jesus Christ of Latter-day Saints is very

Christ-centered and liberal in nature. I wasn't what you'd call liberal nor open-minded. While I was willing to accept The Book of Mormon at face value as an additional Testament of the Bible, but—as you'll soon see—I found nearly as many inconsistencies with this Third Testament as I did with the original two. This troubled me, but not enough to cancel any plans to become both baptized and a member.

I had another problem to focus on: Prior to going back to prison, I had been expelled out of Golden West College. I found myself looking for another school in order to finish my degree. Although I had a job, working for Sam in his office, and didn't absolutely need an A.A. degree, Sam believed that finishing what I started was important, plus he saw more within me than spending the rest of my life as a receptionist. I needed a career, not just a job.

The following Monday morning, sitting there on the edge of my bed, I realized that in my thirty-six years of life, I had accomplished a whole lot of nothing... except bringing pain and suffering to the very people whom cared for me. As things were—in my previous life with Sam—I was living a toxic life without any future. I knew that I needed to end the way I had been living. Sam had invited me to live with him in part because he loved me, had believed in developing a meaningful love-relationship with me, and out of sheer convenience as his live-in housekeeper and receptionist working at below minimum wage (which was $4.25 per hour nationally), nearly double what is was in 1975, only eighteen years previously.

Immediately, I bounced off my bed and showered. I decided once-and-for-all that this troublemaker named Damien Collins, had made his last set of problems and that he was going to become a troubleshooter instead. I was going to get some education, I was going to earn my A.A. degree, needed or not. I was going to be "the best me" that I could be, no matter what I had to give up in order to achieve this goal. I was going to center my attention towards getting the best grades I could.

Damien went to Cypress College to register in a full load of college credits; using his unspent two-hundred dollars "gate money" he'd received when paroled from prison, on used textbooks and supplies. The rest of his expenses Damien had to borrow from Sam—who, coincidentally, thought Damien made a good choice since Cypress College was offering certificate programs designed to get graduates into the job market faster.

Finally, fully centered on his road forward, Damien was on his way towards completion of what he wanted for years. He wasn't using drugs—except for caffeine, the most addictive drug legally available—so he truly believed that he would do better than he did at Golden West College. Actually, as part of the process of registering at Cypress College, he had to request his abysmal records from Golden West... a printed history of his deterioration. He vowed that he would do much better, and he did just that.

For the first time in my thirty-six years of life, I was a very active member of a church, and I was very proud to serve Christ. Although going to school was important to me, it wasn't more important than my attending my church group, which felt like an honor. I truly loved the members of the congregation, as if they were natural brothers and sisters of the same family, of the same parents... something I'd never had before. I had obligations for the first time since the military academy—another lifetime ago—and these were important to me.

I also had a realistic goal for the first time ever; for I was learning about counseling. Watching my behavior throughout those first few months, I saw that I had learned more about how to care about others than myself. I was learning how to treat people, and not just the ones that liked me but those who didn't! To accept people just the way that they were. It was important to me that I'd learn what it meant to be called a "disciple." This love for others gave me purpose to study and cause to learn how to counsel those who needed to be loved back to health and beyond.

While learning to become a counselor, I found my heart wanting to help those who were in my shoes: leaving state prison under the pressures of becoming productive members of the society which they left. I had the all-important advantage of Sam's support, but many—like Charlie—had no such support from family nor from friends awaiting them. Realizing that, this meant they would need to quickly learn how to succeed, how to persevere, and how to love unrequited of anything from others.

Damien decided that he would create a nonprofit organization which would aid former inmates in becoming productive citizens. He first studied what the legal requirements were and went to work on the paperwork—sadly, with any knowledge of what it took to get such an association off-the-ground! He filed all the required forms to have both state and federal status as a 501(c)(3) corporation. However, he failed at obtaining a board of directors, as well as raising any money—other than Sam's—which turned out to be rather vital for starting up a business up... who would've thought?

We were the Community of Hope Ministries; only without any community, nor ministries, nor any real hope. It turns out that intentions which are good don't actually count unless the "intended" studies how to put his or her dreams to action. I didn't fail because my dream wasn't worth doing, wasn't a noble one... but because of sheer ignorance and that I didn't study what it takes to convert a business idea into reality. No, I wanted to get to work in helping people right away without figuring out how to run my organization.

It was the summer of 1995 when my dream financially failed, and I was feeling sad at its death. It hit me so hard, that I decided that I wouldn't attend small group for an entire week. I called our group facilitators wanting to skip out of that week's meetings, when who did I get but Dale's wife on the phone. Her voice and words stole the winds from my sails before I could even explain why I'd called...

"Damien," she greeted, "I am glad that it's you. I need a favor, if at all possible."

Sure, Henrietta, what do you need?

"I need a couple of pies from Marie Callender's"

Uh, Damien stammered.

What do you think Dutch Apple or Cherry? Maybe one of both?

Sure, no problem, Henrietta. I'll be there in about twenty minutes.

With that said, Damien washed up and got ready for the group meeting he previously had no intention of going to. He then told Sam that he was leaving for group and that he agreed in getting some pies for Henrietta which he would need some cash from Sam to buy two pies. Henrietta would be repaying for them, that is if Damien remembered to ask her.

Sam gave Damien a fifty-dollar bill, part of it was for Henrietta's much-needed pies, plus Sam wanted Damien to get the two of them a couple of pies as well. About twenty minutes later, Damien was walking out of the local restaurant with a Dutch apple, one cherry, one Pumpkin, and a Boston crème pie. The cashier had whimsically asked Damien when he placed his order for all four of them, "Is this for here or to go, sir?" Damien didn't laugh.

Arriving at Dale's and Henrietta's new home—they had moved from his apartment into a three-bedroom house—he had to open the pie boxes once or twice, until he located the correct ones for this address, putting the ones which Sam favored back into their bags. Walking inside, almost immediately Dale knew that something was troubling Damien.

"You look like you have the weight of the world on your shoulders, Damien."

Nah, these pies don't weigh that much.

"No," he chuckled out, "I don't mean those. What's troubling you?"

Oh, it's—well, Community of Hope is, um, we're bankrupt.

"How terrible," Henrietta said while the pies. "What happened?"

I happened, he said with a smirk. *Our fiscal issues were too many. Society, perhaps rightly so, prefers to raise funds for programs which deal with the needs of our very hungry homeless, and for children... not inmates. Clearly that set of complex problems should have priority over, well, mine. Over any and all ex-felon programs.*

"Maybe, but don't most released inmates become homeless?" she asked.

Yes, exactly. However, nobody wants to help them until they hit rock bottom. We are in need of the sort of preventative program that Community of Hope provides to keep parolees from becoming homeless. It's a simple fact that statistics show, well, that the majority of ex-felons return to our neighborhoods much the same as when they left society: criminally minded. Our prisons don't reform them into citizens, they merely collect and restrain them. These men and women—mostly men—return to our communities unprepared to be anything other than burdens to our neighborhoods and resources.

"Damien," Dale started to contend, "you really don't think that our state prisons reform their inmates?"

"*I*—" he suddenly decided to choose his words very carefully, even though he had no intention at misleading or lying to these kind and loving people. The problem was, Sam had given Damien advice which included concealing his arrests and convictions. *I had a friend named Charlie Osborne, although we called him Charlie 'Oops' because, well, he was kind of accident prone. Anyway, Charlie went to prison several times, each time for commercial or residential burglaries, mostly to support his drug habit. Through a friend of a friend, I recently found out that Charlie was once again in prison for yet another burglary.*

Since Damien was still on parole, he could not contact Charlie directly, whether he wanted to or not. No, instead, a friend of Damien's who was familiar with something called "the Internet" and using some sort of software Damine had never heard of—by a company named Netscape—was able to determine that Charlie was once again in prison for another five years. This fact had upset Damien rather substantially both because of his friend's choice to re-offend and Damien's failing organization which could have helped someone exactly like Charlie.

"Your friend, Charlie," Henrietta commented, "seems to have a history of poor judgment."

My point exactly. The prison system doesn't provide what he—or anyone else like Charlie—needs to correct this poor judgment. Instead, he goes on living the only way he knows how, which harms our neighborhoods, or communities, including our children. Once we have identified the criminals, locked them up for a while, this would be the perfect time to retrain them with the skills which they need . . . so they don't go back to their previous lifestyle of survival. If you can call it survival.

"So, you're saying that we should redirect our fundraising away from helping children and the homeless, to keep ex-convicts from becoming homeless?"

No, I will never argue that our monies should go to aiding ex-felons before our children. Our children are our only hope. Yet, that hope is commonly dashed by criminals and gang members, many of them are ex-felons. We, instead, protect our children from the criminal environment by aiding the troublemakers before they become homeless. You see, homelessness is a very deep pit that, well, I'm embarrassed to admit that I once experienced.

"You were once homeless?" Dale asked with a raise brow of concern.

Yes, I was living in a motel, barely scraping by. I lived and supported several likewise homeless teens without a place to stay. Most homeless are young, several are drug addicts, yet nearly all of them are destitute! They're stuck without means of building any kind of savings to dig themselves out with. Being an ex-felon only worsens any chances of becoming employed.

"What can be done?" Henrietta earnestly wanted to know.

My answer ... don't release inmates prior to them being trained how to be mature members of our world and not the other way around. Our court system sentences prisoners to years, not requirements, Years don't change a person, it only makes them older, not wiser. No, my solution would be the same as it is to get into the college classes I want to get into: You want to be released from prison, you need to meet the requirements.

"Wait, what prerequisites?" Dale asked.

Inmates in prison waste their sentences playing basketball and handball, instead of voluntarily taking parenting classes or anger management. But what is a judge told them that they could only be released if they graduated from these classes and job training ones, like resume writing, interviews, office services, something that included customer service. Instead of only doing time, they should be sentenced to training. Pass or don't get out.

"Wow, I'm surprised. I thought our prisons already did that."

No, trust me, they don't, Dale.

Henrietta then asked an impossible to avoid question, "You seem really adamant about this, Damien. What caused you interest in helping parolees? Is it only because of your friend, Charlie?"

No, Henrietta. I have seen first-hand what ex-felons go through when they are released. I was once released from prison. There's no easier way for me to say this, but I went to prison for doing something violent to someone. Actually it was two separate people but Damien wasn't thinking about this at the time. What I did was inexcusable, and I can only hope that my victim and God have forgiven me for what I did. But, more importantly, I had Sam's support waiting for me when I was released—which was a miracle—where most inmates have nobody.

Both Dale and Henrietta looked at each other with something which could have been concern and/or anxiety when Damien admitted to being a parolee. Dale, nodding silently at his wife, turned towards him when he finished speaking.

"Damien, maybe not tonight, but sometime soon I'd like to hear more details about why you were sent to prison. But, after everything you've said tonight and these past weeks, I believe in your honest regret and struggle for forgiveness."

Absolutely, Dale, I understand.

Other members of their small group's meeting were starting to show up, but Damien felt compelled to continue where he left off. During his two times in prison, he clearly saw the internal problems with the prison system; not that he could affect any changes from that side of the fences. He returned to his previous suggestion about sentencing prisoners to "freedom prerequisites" instead of lengths of time. Placing burglars into a structured agenda that's centered on anti-theft and victim awareness. Placing violent offenders on a plan focused on relieving their anger in positive ways and understanding their core emotions.

Treat their problems as a whole. The best medicine is a holistic approach: We should never have it in our minds that we should lock up people unless the punishment resolves the crime and precludes recidivism. We need an attitude that there are two parts of punishment, there is the punitive action and the restorative action. The state of California only cares about the first. Our best hope would be to make our parents' jobs easier so that they can protect their children. We should do whatever we can to prevent crime! That must incorporate the activity of rehabilitation of those inmates who have demonstrated the highest desire to avoid gang activity and return to society as a productive citizen.

In the year of 2006, California's Department of Corrections changed its name to include the words 'and Rehabilitations' to the end of it. However, the following years of operation under this new moniker didn't change much. In 2013 the department reinstituted programs to assist inmates with re-entry services and resume writing. In fact, to appease federal mandates, the new and improved C.D.C.R. converted a handful of prison facilities into so-called "Reentry Hubs" to provide job hunting skills for those inmates due to be released within six months... unfortunately, an additional list of requirements limited which inmates qualified for these Reentry Hubs, and a majority were deemed disqualified. In Damien's most recent opinion, nobody about to be released should ever be disqualified to receive job hunting skills.

Our meeting that night quickly fizzled to a close, as everyone made their way to the dining room for seconds—or thirds—of the treats and coffee, as well as to say their good-byes and give their hugs. We weren't just a group anymore, we were a true family. All were glad for the weekly meetings, yet only one or two of us were glad for the untimely end to each meeting. Returning home, I remained in my car meditating and reminiscing on the events of the meeting.

I was very glad of my decision to be baptized that following month, which would officially make me a member of the R.L.D.S. church family. Clearly this family loved me, respected me. True, they had concerns of the fact that I was an ex-felon, but later that week, I sat down with Dale and gave him my full details, this fact didn't bother him nor his wife at all. It was the greatest feeling I ever had: I finally had a family which would guide me along the path of spiritual maturity I'd longed for my entire life. I finally felt like I belonged to something bigger than myself, at the center of the universe!

CHAPTER THIRTY-SIX

Death and Rebirth

*I*t was Sunday morning, and in a matter of a few hours Damien was to die. It's the moment he had been looking forward to for several months: He was to be reborn a new creation, full of the Spirit of God and Christ. That wasn't at all easy to understand, the concept of being submerged and arising from those waters a completely blank slate. The same flesh, yet a totally cleaned soul. He was looking forward to killing off the old self.

Sam and I had spent the previous night listening to some Bach and reading Scriptures. He had asked me what my favorite verse was, and although there were far too many to choose from, everything from Deuteronomy 8:3, the sixteenth and twenty-third psalms, Luke 11:2-10, and all of Romans chapters six and eight. However, since we'd most recently been reading from *The Book of Mormon*, I responded with 3rd Nephi, chapter eleven: "I heard the Lord invite me to join his church, where I could best serve him." Naturally Sam grew misty-eyed by my choice.

We finished the last of the wine and just sat there, allowing silence and its healing powers wash over us, taking sleep with it, giving us cause to remain there for a long moment until eventually we made our way to our beds. In short order, we were traveling the river of sleep and would arrive at the mystical island of dreams. Now that's quite a mouth full, but this is exactly how I felt... my sleep was a voyage of the mind's eye, bringing my *soul along merely as a passenger on that ship.*

What I knew with clear certainty was that in what seemed like only a few minutes later, I was up and eating a good breakfast. At some point I must have showered, for not only was my hair still damp, but I had put on my Sunday clothes without even realizing it. After breakfast, I retired to the living room where Sam was listening to Gustav Mahler's second symphony, which was most appropriate for my coming event… my funeral.

Unquestionably, Damien was overwhelmed by a variety of emotions that morning which words couldn't possibly describe: ranging from enormous delight to deep remorse. He was particularly contrite for the things which had landed him in prison… the near-fatal shooting of that innocent man, and the young lady whom he'd caused to suffer physically and emotionally. Damien knew he could never go back and undo all the harm he had caused; so he focused on the present- and future-self. To change himself, who he was prior to that day, through his rebirth and resurrection as a part of Christ.

All that I could do to correct my past is to give back to society as a different person; one who had compassion for others and showed each person the respect and love they duly deserved. It wasn't up to me anymore to judge or even consider whom needed my attention or help, I was a servant of God and Lord… and He would direct my heart and eyes to whomever he pleased.

Damien felt surprised when he saw Sam in the living room wearing <u>his</u> Sunday best: Sam was 'to the nines', complete with a bow tie.

"I thought this would be to your liking," Sam said in reference to the music being played.

Not as much as seeing you dressed like that.

"Dressed like <u>what</u>? Exactly?"

Like someone about to go to church, Damien remarked with a smile.

"Well, you know. I woke up and just thought that I'd go watch my friend get baptized. You know, the same old thing as usual."

This snide comment made Damien laugh; sounding as if Sam saw a friend become baptized every Sunday for the year.

Yeah, friends do that, don't they? I almost forgot just how popular you were. You've got friends getting baptized all the time, huh?

"Well, not enough to have earned my own personalized parking space... speaking of which, we ought to hurry before we end up parked three blocks away."

We've got time. In fact, there's about five minutes before we have to go, and a little Tubular Bells would be relaxing, indeed calming.

"Sure, it's right there. Next to Pink Floyd's LP, Mike Oldfield." Sam's vinyl record collection—he would never convert to CD's nor would ever own an MP3 player—was meticulously kept in alphabetical order by composer's last name or a band's first few letters.

Thanks... you know, for everything! Not just the music, but for all that you've ever done for me.

There it was, the Baptismal Font. In moments, I would be laid out as if I really was dead and, in a very important way, that's exactly what was going to happen: I was going to be quite dead. In the following moment, my best friend was going to raise me up from the ashes—technically, it's water—of what had once been my life, much like a mythological phoenix. Reborn and renewed!

So, why was I so nervous? I was standing behind the font in a small dressing room, where I could look out across the stage and see who all was there in attendance. I was rather surprised—not sure why I shouldn't have expected this—just how many people were there to attend my baptism. When did I acquire <u>this</u> many friends and supporters? There were dozens!

In my own opinion, it was a beautiful service... although, maybe I was expecting lightning and/or thunder, because I felt exactly the same, physically. Only wet. Most of my changes happened later and over time, with my spiritual maturation. The first thing that I noticed was that I became much more patient with others. My drive to reach Christ was also enhanced: I was eager to find my place within the church.

After baptism, Damien still had difficulty trusting in God to help him with the finding of a bride... a wife suited for him. Damien noticed that the women in his own age group, with his Mormon stake, "weren't all that great." The attractive ones were already married and the single women were either vastly obese—not that they didn't deserve to be loved—or were old enough to be Damien's mom. For him, that simply wasn't going to work. No, he focused his attention on those who were attractive and single, and this combination seemed only available in the much-younger age group of coeds.

I was thirty-six, but mentally I was closer to twenty-two... which was the average age of the women I approached for dates. It's not that I wanted to date someone that much younger than myself, just that women in their mid-thirties were already taken. Also, I believed that marriage was forever; I didn't ever want to be divorced nor to "fall out of love" with whomever I did marry. Having an attractive wife wasn't as important as having someone who I could never regret marrying.

Of course, at this point, I'd forgotten that the R.L.D.S. church was bigger than our own local stake. There were plenty of congregations throughout California and neighboring states; all of which, there were women whom God might favor towards satisfying my desire to marry a fellow church member. Over time, my previous difficulty in trusting God and His ability to aid me faded tenfold. Until finally, all lack of faith died completely; along with all of my doubt.

Damien was still a student at Cypress College at around this time, working towards earning a Certificate of Accomplishment in drug and alcohol abuse counseling. As previously mentioned, he didn't do well at all—earning practically no college credits—while attending Golden West College. Another small issue that Damien had refined his major from general education to Human Development, which required a different curriculum. In short, he was only a 'freshman' in terms of his undergraduate status.

I had a long ways to go until earning my A.A. degree—Cypress didn't offer A.S. degrees at that time—which would lead towards me transferring to the state university system eventually, in order to get a bachelor's degree in Human Development. Along the road, I would also earn another certificate in codependency counselling—learning to treat those in a relationship with an addict or having a self-destructive behavior which impaired them, such as a wife of an alcoholic.

However, I must admit that one of the reasons that I went to Cypress College was to see if I couldn't meet the right woman. Yes, I'm going to use the Top Gun movie phrase again: It was a target-rich environment. Thousands of beautiful young ladies, most fresh out of high school and still under the legal drinking age. It simply isn't my fault that I am male and that I have testosterone playing ping-pong with my common sense.

Now, what I will warn you about is that one must be cautious at what they ask of God... He may end up giving them far more than they counted on. Also, in my opinion, God has a strange sense of humor. There I was, having trust issues still about God finding me the right woman, looking for one on my own. I was doing all of this legwork after having asked God to bring me one. So, probably out of spite, God just closed the door. I received nothing but rejection from every woman I approached!

It was currently a full year after Damien's baptism, on or about the twenty-fifth of September 1995. Although the school year had just started, he was already behind in his schoolwork due to his overambitious "full" load of tough courses. The days, weeks, and eventually months of the previous semester had sped by him; however, amazing as it seems, Damien achieved a 4.0 grade point average of nothing but all A's in all his classes.

I was achieving everything in school with the exception of finding a mate. I was starting to lower my standards... perhaps females weighing over three hundred pounds were still off of my radar, but I was having second and third thoughts about the ones missing more than three teeth, exhibiting full mustaches, or other abnormal amounts of facial hair. Yeah, I was getting desperate, maybe. Until I had realized that this was my problem all along; God wasn't providing me with a woman of my choice because I had never told Him what my heart desires in a woman. Sure, the Bible says that He knows our thoughts even before we think them... but He probably still wants to be asked. In Matthew 7:7, we are old to ask and it'll be given, even though God already knows what you've been wanting and dreaming about. We must ask! So, I took this to mean that God was waiting for me to tell Him what I really wanted in a bride.

So, that's exactly what I set out to do: I prayed to God on the night of the twenty-fifth, and told Him about what I thought would be the ideal woman for me. I even wrote it down and kept that list inside my Bible: I was hoping for someone mature, close to my own age, interested in having children, preferably shorter than myself—5'6" to 5 foot—bright and educated, an art appreciator, someone down-to-earth and authentic, but—most importantly—*I'd like her to be a Christian or member of the R.L.D.S. church. I didn't care about the frivolous details like hair color, eye color, or even her race… she could have yellow eyes and be a Martian for all I cared, just as long as she fit my other preferences.*

This is what I'd been looking for, on my own, for over a year. This is also what I'd wrote down and prayed God to send me. And, behold, not even a full month passed from this prayer when a woman I'd described would come into my life.

In the middle of October, a friend of Damien's named Linda had invited members of his congregation—or the "Orange" group—to join her in a celebration of the growth of her "Monrovia" group. Their service to God was one of the success stories in their local Mormon stake. Damien knew that going was very unlikely to be enjoyable for him; such celebrations for the growth of a small group usually only further humbled him or made Damien believe that he wasn't doing enough for his own small group.

Things were beginning to happen for our local stake, and I loved every minute I was a member. As things turned out, I had a couple of reasons for going to their celebration. The first was because I really enjoyed Linda: she was a married other of two, born a year or two before I was, so we shared a common generational bond. Second, I just couldn't get enough of small group ministry, and wanted to see how the other groups differ. They truly worked wonders wherever they were developed. So, even though it wasn't my own group being rewarded, I went to the celebration.

I still thank God for the way He had put things together. It's rather fascinating how God made all of the following events work out. As I've said, I went to celebrate with Linda and her husband, Dave, over the growth of their "Monrovia" group. That God had worked wonders far more than what could be seen before our eyes with their group. Arriving at 7:30 p.m. that night, I was warmly greeted by my friends who invited me to join them at their table.

Linda and I were deep in conversation and listening to David Heinz—a locally-published crooner—sing six wonderful worship songs of his own creation. I was becoming so very pleased with the fact that I buried my pride in participating with this celebration. It was refreshing to say the least. Although, looking back on that night and the way in which God works His plans, life was about to get very interesting for Linda, the group, and for me.

It was about 7:45 p.m., when God's personal gift to Damien walked into the meeting hall. It is of no exaggeration when we speak about heavenly persons, descended angels, walking amongst us; however, when Damien spoke to me about this beautiful woman who just walked into his life, attempted to describe her using insufficient works, I understood completely his admiration.

Her name means "victorious one" according to most baby names books, and it fit perfectly with her demeanor... although, at first, Damien simply referred to her as Miss Vicki.

> Shall I compare there to a summer's day?
> Thou are more lovely and more temperate.
>
> ~ William Shakespeare, Romeo & Juliet

CHAPTER THIRTY-SEVEN

Miss Vicki

Coleman, a small town in the middle of the state of Michigan, is where she was born, lived, and was educated. Miss Vicki was born a farmer's daughter, however, she wasn't born to be a farmer herself. She earned a bachelor's degree in Education from Central Michigan University. Miss Vicki was a well-loved young lady in her community, the church, and the world in general.

Following her graduation, she still had the task of obtaining a teacher's position within a state which no longer suffered a shortage of elementary school teachers, as she'd planned to become. Her inspiration, her father, had also taught middle school part-time, as well as farmed wheat and soybeans. Yet, now the schooling market in central Michigan was practically shutdown with a surplus of young instructors. What was she to do?

There was one bright light in her mind regarding both education and a job: her church. Since she was eight-years-old, shortly after being baptized, she had longed for a job within the Mormon church in which she was raised. An elder of the R.L.D.S. church doesn't make much—if anything—but, as the church was working towards expanding its size, the number and need of the congregation elders increased. Even more important, was the demand for stake bishops, which was a paid post.

Miss Vicki wanted to serve the church and be hired to do this, instead of simply volunteering as an elder.

Since she wanted to secure a paid position with the R.L.D.S. church, Vicki went back to school again... this time she would earn a master's degree in Divinity: a minister's education. Miss Vicki applied at four of the best schools and was accepted at The School of Theology at Claremont, located in Los Angeles County.

To help you visualize, Miss Vicki stands just a shade over five-feet tall. Her eyes are a very deep brown, as was her hair. On the night when Damien first met her, she had recently turned twenty-five. Thanks to her young age, her skin was clear of blemishes... and, according to Damien, was quite soft to the touch. In fact, one touch and all of your pains and others hurts seemed to flee you... never to return. In a word, she was <u>magical</u>.

Damien about had a massive heart attack the moment Miss Vicki came into both view and his life, for her presence was that incredibly alluring. Linda had actually seen her first and called Vicki over to join them at their table. Miss Vicki—as Damien routinely called her, based on her own preference—had only recently moved to the Los Angeles area. She became a member of a group within the "Orange" congregation, although neither Damien's nor Linda's. It was called the "upland" group, located just a few blocks from her college.

Sitting down, Vicki reached over and gave Linda an awkward hug across the table, then offered a hand to the timid and suddenly shy Damien. "Hi, I'm Miss Vicki."

<u>*Miss Vicki?*</u> Damien questioned, not sure if they term 'Miss' was in fact a title or nickname.

"Oh. Sorry. I's a force of habit. I teach kindergarten, well, not actually <u>the</u> teacher, more of an aide. I'm sorry, I'm rambling. And who are you?"

Uh, yeah... D-D-Damien, he stammered, *Damien Collins.*

"Pleased to meet you, 'uh-yeah Damien'," she playfully mocked. Her eyes, according to Damien, twinkled in such a way to cause the stars of the heavens grew dim.

The three of them—Damien, Linda, and Vicki—talked for a while about church-related news, about being "saints of the latter days," and our aspects to draw others nearer to God. What Vicki did next caused Damien to know that he was loved by God... she changed seats in order to sit next to him. There were plenty of other seats she could've gone to, yet chose to sit near him.

Putting out his hand, as if to receive some change, Damien responded playfully to her movement, *Sorry, it costs fifty cents to sit there.*

Slapping his hand away with pretend outrage, then sat prominently with a raised chin and look of nobility, as if a queen on a throne. Then, breaking out of her role of royalty, Vicki gave Damien a huge mischievous grin. After this, they fell deep into conversation. Damien couldn't remember what their conversation was about; his mind was too busy coping with the overloading excitement which flowed through him at meeting this ideal female.

Here I was, sitting next to a woman who was naturally smart and beautiful, that is, she never wore makeup and virtually no jewelry, nor needed any such adornments. No, to enhance her distinction and grace, she simply had to smile, which likewise came naturally to her. This was one of the first things I'd noted about her: the fact that her spirit was so powerful and in constantly serving God. She was the very definition of "angel."

After that night, Vicki and I regularly visited Henrietta's group and occasionally at the "Upland" congregation. I wish I had the vocabulary to clearly describe the happiness I felt when we spent time together. Neither of us had lots of spending cash for elaborate dates, nor did we have much free time—since we were both in college—but I'm not saying that we didn't spend quality time while dating, because we most definitely did. We simply had to be creative about it: we commonly would eat at home, go places or do things which didn't require an admission fee, such as television at her home for the most part.

On one occasion, we went to my home, where Sam was gracious to meet her. This allowed me to cook dinner for the three of us, showing off my skills as much as possible. Sam even treated us to a show or play from time to time, which neither of us could afford on our own. We had the "for richer or poorer" part of typical marriage vows well-rehearsed and in practice long before either of us even brought up the idea of a wedding; yet, there was nothing that I didn't enjoy while with Miss Vicki.

I know you're probably thinking to yourself that I'm just exaggerating about her and our relationship, but I'll tell you that I couldn't, not even a little bit. I was far from unfortunate with her... Vicki was the girl of my dreams and the answer to my prayers. Down to every detail which I'd asked of God. I have not experienced a single day nor occasion that I can say otherwise about her.

It was during their regular participation with Henrietta's small groups in the "Orange" congregation, when Damien was able to see that they shared much of the same theological understandings, and that neither were ashamed to say that their belief differed from what is commonly taught outside of the R.L.D.S. church. In fact, they spent hours talking about the different churches throughout the Christian world, comparing them to one another; as well as to both their "Reorganized" Mormon church and its original Latter-Day Saints church.

Our very first Thursday together as a bona fide couple; we drove separately to Henrietta's house. Being that I lived closer to Henrietta's, I arrived there much earlier than Vicki did; however, I waited for her in a parking space behind my own car, keeping anyone from parking there. Thankfully, since it had started to rain, I didn't have long to wait before Vicki arrived.

The more time that we spent as "a team," the more we felt like one, which suited Vicki just fine. Vicki was bright as all get out, and I saw her as more than just a qualified church elder. No, Vicki was most deserving to be given a bishop position, only none yet was available. Even if we weren't dating, I would be more than pleased to be a member of a group or congregation which she was leading. Her skills as a teacher made our sessions much more rewarding and hearty.

That specific evening, we talked about the nature of God, and openly voiced our thoughts on the matter. I shared with the group several of the opinions I have already shared with you earlier in this book. A member named Dave and I got into a discussion over God's choice to grant humans free will. Another regular group member, Jason, was much older than the two of us.

Damien began by telling them, Well, Dave, I see God as—well, um. I see God as having all the power that God can have, and that God doesn't coerce creatures to do anything that they don't want to do. Free will cannot mean a thing if God would coerce any particular action, that's also true for nature.

"Wait, that's not necessarily true," Dave contended politely. "After all, in Exodus eight, God directly caused the Pharaoh of Egypt to deny Moses' repeated requests after each of the plagues."

Does the Old Testament say God 'caused' the Egyptian king to deny his requests? Damien inquired, *Or did God 'influence' the king?*

Dave took out his Bible and flipped to Exodus 4:21, quoting it our loud: "'Again the Lord said to Moses, "Now that you are going back to Egypt, be sure to perform before the king all the miracles which I have given you the power to do. But I will make the king stubborn, and he will not let the people go"' (Good News Bible, Today's English Version [New York: American Bible Society, 1978])."

God only caused the Pharaoh to be stubborn, Damien pointed out. *God didn't direct the man's every action. No, his choice to deny Moses was still all his own.*

Jason then asked, "How do you mean, earlier, that God doesn't coerce nature?"

Well, Jason, I mean that if God had all of the power, then nothing on Earth would have anything to fulfill its desires. Neither animal, nor man, not even plants. If God coerced, then we still don't have free will to do as we actually pleased, and we couldn't sin for it was all dependent on what God wanted us to do.

"Plants?" Jason half-chuckled. "Plants commit sins?"

Sure they do, ask any experienced botanist. They commit murder, competitively strangle each other's root systems, some devour insects or spread toxins. There's also a lot of vanity, and blotting out each other's sunlight on purpose. My point is, every specie of every living thing on Earth has some leniency in what they'd like to do.

"So," Dave spoke out, "God isn't all powerful? He doesn't control everyone and everything?"

Yes, Dave, that's what I believe. Under the description I just gave, God has all the power that God can have, and none of the power—your power—to obey or disobey what God wants you to do.

"I dunno, Damien. I think you're confusing the words 'power' and 'will.'

God gave us the gift of life, and along with that life is our will to survive, our will to thrive, and our will to be significant. None of this is true power. No, I believe that God still has all of the power, if not the control. He has a plan for our lives, but it's more of a goal; not a day-to-day, minute-by-minute schedule which we are destined to follow."

I agree with you, on many of those. But control and power are basically the same things. God is also not a 'He' nor a 'Him.' God is god. And—

"Wait, seriously?" Jason interrupted. "You honestly want to argue the nature and gender of God in the same breath? Yes, God is the Creator, and we associate females with creating new life. But you can't overlook the fact that not only did God create Adam first 'in our own image,' and that Eve was more of an afterthought after all the animals proved to be an unsuitable companion to help Adam." He said, paraphrasing Genesis 2:20.

Sure, but that's all dependent on the accuracy of a story written a thousand years after its events. Not even Adam and Eve's great-grandchildren had a written language, ink hadn't been discovered yet. They might have had cave drawings or other artwork—un, what's the word? Pictographs? But my point is, by the time the Book of Genesis was written, society had already become a male-dominated one. Whose to say that Eve wasn't created before Adam? We cannot base our belief of God's gender—that is if God even has one—on the oldest Scripture there is.

"Alright, then how about the Gospels then?" Jason suggested. "God is repetitively referred to as the Heavenly Father by Jesus."

Really? By Jesus? Damien teased, then seriously asked, *Where? Doesn't Jesus refer to God as the <u>one</u> who sent him?*

"Well, sure he does. But, in Luke eleven, the Lord's Prayer, Jesus is quoted with 'Our Father in heaven,' and they wouldn't misquote him. Again, while on the cross, Jesus shouted out, 'Abba' which meant 'father', as he died. Are you, Damien, saying that they all got it wrong?"

Probably not, Damien admitted, *but I'll never say they all got it right either.*

After spending a little time getting used to the people of the "Orange" group, Vicki spent a little time sharing herself with its members. She did this out of her respect and growing love for Damien. She described her being raised in Michigan, the township of Coleman—an outlying of Warren—how she earned her bachelor's and was working on a master's. And how she was dating s smart man, someone she could be proud of.

This, naturally, made Damien blush. It was no secret to anyone in the group that Vicki meant him. He was likewise happy to admit that he was dating "a solid woman," only that he just didn't know how solid she was. He couldn't have been prouder of her… or more fortunate to be the one dating her!

It felt a little strange to me that we felt so similar about our theology. She also didn't believe that God coerced anyone to act in a particular way. That God wouldn't intentionally cause someone to sin, only to tweak or tune their feelings and dreams. Our reactions were still all of our own doing. We also were in agreement regarding the nature of Scripture, which pleased me on the account that I was no longer the only person that held many of the same notions about one subject which was so dear to my heart.

I was gratified in my being able to share in the same spiritual experience with Vicki and nothing could have ruined my mood that or any night. Nothing in life ever prepared me for the joy I would feel in attending small group meetings with her; as the one person I truly cared for was there beside me. This felt much more like doing church together and finding joy in the doing. It was no longer just a Bible study at all. It was no longer an intellectual exercise in who understood Scripture best, but I felt a nurturing and community building going on in that house. I honestly felt fulfilled by her presence and participation.

Since having Vicki in my life, I continuously felt blessed by the hand of God.

At a following group meeting together, Vicki showed further interest in personal growth for the both of them. The house was filled with Dale and Henrietta, Fred, his wife Martha, and their daughter Breanna, Alan, Dave, Jason, Vicki, and Damien. On that night, Alan started their group in prayer and asked God to heal his mother who was dying from cancer. Everyone was moved in hearing of his mother's struggle with cancer, but probably no one more than Vicki—whom had never even met the woman.

The group spent time talking with each other about what they believed in drawing forth the power of God to bring around healing. It was a very in-depth conversation, mainly because of the diversity of thoughts they shared on the subject. They were all concerned for the health of Alan's mother and voiced their loving regards. The group joined Alan in their prayers, both collectively and privately.

If I was asked, I would have to say that we can ask God for our needs, and God may well work in that direction ... however, it's of my opinion that God never compels time nor nature to act in any direction outside its own limitations. Indeed, I believe then as I do now, that God cannot force the hand of nature, despite what God may want for any of God's children.

I believe that we can and should pray regularly for—and hope for—the well-being of those in need of spiritual and physical health. What we cannot do is to coerce nature to do our own bidding, with or without the loving will of God. It's not that God has any limits, it's more that nobody can stop "the wheels in motion" once they've been started. A routine prayer for wellness will always work better than an eleventh-hour wish for a miracle.

The night ended smoothly, and Damien was not asked his deepest thoughts on the subject of prayer, for which he was glad. However, later that night, Vicki did want to know his thoughts. They were on their way to their cars, when she suddenly took his hand and offered to buy him a cup of coffee... and maybe a chunk of apple pie a la mode, but only if he behaved himself.

At a local diner, they were immediately ushered to a table and ordered their late-night snack of pie and caffeine. Vicki resumed the conversation regarding healing and God, by asking Damien, "What do you believe about God's ability to heal the sick?"

Well, that's a loaded question. Nonetheless, I absolutely believe in prayer, for prayer is our attempt to communicate with God.

"'Attempt'?" she double-checked.

Yeah, most of us try to pray, and I'll admit that I've rarely asked for the right things. I also believe that God does respond to our communication.

Many of us are too busy with our worries and stresses, with making a living, to stop and listen to God's response. God speaks to us through our spirit, yet we are too busy listening to our brains.

"And through our dreams," Vicki added.

"I could spend hours on dreams. Yes, God is constantly trying to get through to us, and usually the only time our minds are quiet enough to receive God's message is while we are sleeping. Not all dreams are visions, but I'd like to believe that it's about fifty-fifty."

"I believe that we need each other, and though we might not be able to directly participate in each other's world in a meaningful way, we can and do make a difference collectively. I'm not yet certain how that works, but I do feel that I'm not far from right."

You're not far from right, Damien nodded, *at least, I don't think so. Clearly you have put lots of thought to this. Can God physically make a difference to our world?*

"I'm not certain yet, but I don't think so... at least, if you mean to pick up this spoon and throw it, I think not."

At the arrival of their apple pies, they let the conversation drift away. Damien was captive to eh beauty of Miss Vicki, her shoulder-length cinnamon hair and golden-brown eyes, and equally astounding ability to communicate her clear thinking on any subject. Especially when the topic concerned God and theology. Yet, there was another side to Vicki which he hadn't yet discovered... and this involved philosophy.

CHAPTER THIRTY-EIGHT

Fundamental Analysis

Damien drove home that night, alone yet in prayer. He spent most of the drive giving thanks to God for such a delightful date. He looked forward to finding Sam up and eager to see how Damien's involvement with the church was going to be discussed. Damien was cautious not to bring up his privately-shared time with Vicki, or her name at all. Sam—as you know—was gay and in love with Damien, although he no longer felt the same for Sam, if he ever did.

I had no intent of hurting his emotions, at least not deliberately. Sam had provided me with so much; he rescued me from myself, from homelessness, from untold disasters I surely would've made without his support. Yet, no matter how much he wanted me to, and the number of times I'd tried to, I could not love him back in anything but a brotherly way.

Getting home, Damien walked in and made himself yet another cup of coffee—he had two refills at the diner along with his apple pie—then joined Sam in the living room.

Sam looked up from his book, "There he is. The Invincible Mister Collins."

Hey Sam, have a good night?

"A quiet one, which neither this book," he stated while inserting his bookmarker and placing the book stacked on top of two others, "nor these held my attention for long. But, tell me about yours. Anything interesting happen at you group?"

Sam and Damien had a lengthy discussion about what Damien's small group talked about regarding God's healing powers and Alan's mother's cancer. Damien, in his own way made it obvious to Sam that Damien was uncomfortable with sharing his thoughts. Sam leaned back on his couch, eyeing him carefully.

"So… it sounds as if you avoided the subject altogether. How come?"

To tell the truth Sam. I just wasn't sure how the group would accept it if they believed that my theology was so vastly different, and these guys aren't stupid… they would see that I view things quite differently than they do.

"I don't see why; they all share a common history of having a different theology than many other Christian churches. Your theology can't be that much different from what the R.L.D.S. church believes."

Well, do you believe in healing? That is, what do you believe about praying that God will heal a person, of say, final-stage cancer?

Sam could see that Damien was becoming 'worked up' about something untold: his fear of acceptance. "Stop worrying about it. You are a member of our church family, and they can't just disregard you without a real issue. So, what <u>do</u> you believe about praying for a miracle healing?"

I, um, believe that whatever our needs and wants are, we really must pray about them—to communicate these needs and wants—and realize that God cannot force events to occur exactly when we want them. God has a timetable, lives by a different schedule, and we cannot expect God to beat a deadline. A person prays, and God hears… indeed, God experiences the need personally. God might want the very same thing that was prayed for, but people—the whole environment—we all must play their part and do what God wants, for it to happen, as requested. Follow?

"Sort of," Sam admitted. "Everything and everyone here has their own part to play… and I'm still learning how you believe this works. I know that I need to learn more about your personal belief."

Well, I believe that God doesn't control all things, that God doesn't have all of the power. All real things have their own power to exist. The will to survive and thrive, is what Dave called them. But everything with will has some amount of control and power over themselves and their future.

"Well, it sounds as if you need to clean up your theology, Damien, then you can make your theology known to those who you wish, because you'll be able to express it more clearly."

Yeah, Sam, you're right. I need to have more information and time, to sort it all out. I think I'm beginning to understand, that is, have a clear picture of how God deals with prayers of all sorts. This is a very important part of my theology, and I am thinking that somehow it is something which God wants me to learn and share with others.

With that said, this discussion abruptly came to an end, with Sam needing to get himself to bed early. Fridays always tended to be Sam's craziest of workdays. His office was constantly packed wall-to-wall with patients, most of whom were showing up to get refills on their antidepressants or other medications. This caused a much larger crowd in the waiting room than the usual few patients for full-hour therapy sessions.

Friday morning, Damien hurried himself and made breakfast for both of them. Damien took his into the living room and put on some music to stimulate his mind and spirit, It was going to be a hectic day with him taking a college exam before heading to Sam's office. Damien found just the right classical music to recharge his batteries while he ate.

Once I cleaned up my mess, I grabbed my school stuff and headed out. I was grateful for Sam's allowing me to work around my school schedule, even on Fridays. This helped a lot with the number of classes I could complete in a single semester. I also accomplished my goal of earning a <u>perfect</u> 4.0 GPA (grade point average), much better than expected; and that was for a full load of classes.

One of my courses was an elective class in Ethics. This seemed like the course which every counselor should have taken as a required class in order to be hired, but it wasn't—at least, not when I went to Cypress. Yeah, Ethics was a very interesting class for me, partly because it's a very old subject; something I'd been looking for since my youth. Another thing that made it interesting to me was the fact that every model reflects a particular philosopher, and his or her scholarly work.

I found myself loving philosophy… and from it, theology.

As Damien put it, philosophy reflects upon the ultimate aspects of life and, as such, ethics concerns itself with one vital characteristic of life: The way to behave as a member of a society. This subject has been discussed throughout time, at least as far back as Plato, who developed his own model of how citizens should behave.

Ethics was important to Damien because—as you have read—he had been wishing to and was finally able to learn not only how to properly behave in society, but also the history of how that set of rules came to be. This was something vital to someone with Asperger's syndrome and what Damien had been missing throughout his childhood: Not only to be told what not to do, but why it's not culturally acceptable. How over the centuries of human development we've shaped our responses to society and to each other.

For the first decade of my life, I had been continuously told not to do certain things without ever a clear explanation from my parents or teachers as to why I shouldn't do them. When I was about to touch something that might've burned me, I wasn't told that it was hot or could hurt me, I was merely told "No!" or don't touch that. I believe it's vital for parents to not dissuade or discipline their children without clearly giving them a clear explanation why something isn't socially acceptable. To give them a history lesson, not just why their action(s) isn't correct.

Our world view, our philosophies, shape our lives and those of our children. As we know it, in such a way, our beliefs transform who we are and what we perceive as reality. Ethics is just one of many philosophical discussions we have regularly which shapes our existence and affects our very environment.

During my research and schoolwork, I studied several philosophers like Saint Thomas Aquinas and the controversial Soren Kierkegaard. Aquinas drew a lot of his assembled arguments and authorities from the 4th-century Greek philosopher Aristotle; whereas Kierkegaard concerned himself with individual existence… producing more than 20 books, most of which are in an opposite perspective from German philosopher Georg W. F. Hegel and others. Both Aquinas and Kierkegaard believe that individuals create their own natures through their choices and commitment to the will of God. "In *doing so one finds authentic freedom" (Kierkegaard, <u>Stages on Life's Way</u>,).*

Because of my newfound love of college, along with Vicki's own studies in theology, I found myself wanting to take more classes in philosophy... which I did at California State University in Fullerton. I wanted to learn as much as I could about both philosophy and theology, and about Vicki. I also still needed to finish my classes in Human Development and earn my final certificate from Cypress College.

So, regardless of the fact that Damien already was taking a 12-unit class load at Cypress, he still enrolled and added two philosophy courses offered at C.S.U.F. to his plate. Whenever he wasn't in a classroom, Damien was on the road, driving from one college to the other. Difficult or not, he was gaining a quick and deep respect for what his girlfriend was studying. Not only did this broaden his mind, but also their relationship... that is, when he wasn't busy studying.

The question that I still had trouble with was the nature of God. I couldn't clearly enough discuss this topic, no matter how much I prayed for easier reasoning. Explaining my views about God led people to question my faith and belief in God. There are so many things we see in the world which cannot be explained by natural causes, all of which support the existence of God. Yet, as I've mentioned before, I cannot accept that there's an intelligent Supreme Being who loves us—indeed, is the source of all love and life—but directs all things to their goal by some elaborate plan. That God controls everything and every outcome, good or bad, that occurs in our lives!

But then I read the following quote of Saint Augustine, which I found in a book about St. Thomas: "Since God is the supremely highest good, God would not allow evil to exist in His creation unless He were so all powerful and good that He could even make good out of evil."

This quote questioned my lasting belief that God would never want me to commit sins; perhaps, if the outcome of that sin would generate some measure of goodness, God would allow it. Would the infinite good of God permit evil to so freely occur that God could bring positive outcomes from that evil?

The answer is proven in Genesis chapter twenty-two: God commanded a man named Abraham—previously call Abram until chapter seventeen— to take his only son to the top of a mountain and sacrifice him. Imagine!

Being told to escort you loving child to a place three days journey away and to kill him or her! This thought gave me nightmares for several weeks.

Along the way, Abraham continued to deceive his son on <u>why</u> they were going all of that way out there, miles from home. Possibly lying or avoiding to answer the boy's questions—I would've been doing the latter—until they got to the mountain top, where he tied up his son! Yes, tied him up.

I found it hard to think about what evil thoughts Abraham must've been dealing with while he was wrapping those ropes around his only son, his child…or when he placed the poor, innocent boy onto that altar. He really was about to go through with it all! He was about to murder his son! It doesn't matter to me why, it only matters that he was thinking and planning to carry out this most evil act! If the angel of the Lord hadn't arrived or stopped him in time, Abraham probably would've gone through with it…even though he couldn't quite understand why God wanted him to do all of this.

From all of those evil thoughts, the cruelty of lying and deceiving his true intentions to his son, the heinous act of tying the boy up, putting that possibly-forever traumatized child onto a would-be funeral pyre of wood…from all of these atrocities, a huge amount of good happened! Abraham proved both his loyalty and faith in God that day by almost committing an act that completely violated his ethical convictions, what he clearly understood as evil.

At that time in my own life, I viewed this Bible story as a sign. I knew right then that some measure of goodness would come from all of the evil things I'd done in my past and had done to me! Of course, little did I realize that I wasn't done yet in committing atrocities.

I was being moved by the Holy Spirit to continue along my own road, to continue my education and interests in theology. My becoming able to convey the nature of God in an understandable way became my all-important focus. I studied whatever I could get my hands on, along with Vicki's assistance and her textbooks…yes, even with a full load of classes, I was finding time to read my girlfriend's school books for subjects I wasn't taking—yet.

Damien went to work just as soon as his classes that morning were over. Parking his Nissan Altima, he spotted Sam cutting through the lot, possibly pretending to get something from his car, when—in fact—he was just enjoying the fresh air. He often needed a personal break in between psychiatric patients to mentally clear his head.

Joining him, Damien asked, *How are you, Sam?*

"Good, Damien," he obviously lied. "And you?"

You look a little stressed. Are you sure you're okay?

"It's Friday, you know how the office gets. How was school?"

Well, Damien didn't wish to bring it up that exact moment, but went ahead and stated, *I have been thinking of taking some additional philosophy classes at CSUF. What do you think about my doing that?*

"Really? I know that you'll do well there; you're clearly able to handle your current schoolwork. You got straight A's last semester."

So, you think I should go for it?

"You do seem to love philosophy, Damien."

Thanks, Sam. Well, I better get inside and check on the messages. Get your office ready for your next patient. He looked at his wrist watch—a cheap digital model by Casio—which read ten minutes to eleven o'clock. *Before I go, could you tell me why you think I love philosophy?*

"Long story short... you're a philosopher by nature. A critical thinker."

Thanks, Sam. I'll see you in the office.

"Might as well get us some lunch. My eleven o'clock already called and cancelled her appointment. I've checked all of the messages."

Okay, I'll go get us lunch. What are you in the mood for?

And with that, Damien went to a local Denny's restaurant down the street and ordered two hot lunches to go: a bacon cheeseburger topped with crumbles of blue cheese, and a sandwich called 'Moons Over My Hammie.' They ate together in Sam's wood-paneled office. Damien sat on the psychiatrist's couch, using the expensive end table as his makeshift dinette.

While there, Sam spoke out, "You know, I misspoke earlier."

How's that? Damien asked between bites.

"When I told you why I think that you love philosophy. You'll love it, because it leads straight towards theology, at least it will in your case. Theology is your lady friend's chosen interest, and you really are an innate philosopher. Both of you love theology. Then there's always the fact that she's a member of the church and has been all of her life."

Yes, Vicki has, and being a part of the church—hopefully a bishop—is very important to her.

"And, she is very important to you."

Um, until that moment, Damien never felt comfortable discussing his love life with Sam... especially since Sam still held onto the hope of having a sexual relationship with Damien. *Yeah, she's very important. I know there's no getting around it, Sam, but things have been becoming quite serious between us. I know you were hoping that I was just having a passing moment. A heterosexual fling, but I'm happy with Vicki... I'm not going back to being gay.*

"I guess I've suspected as much."

You know, you are a handsome gentleman, and you really should get yourself out there. Start dating someone—

"No, I—" Sam interrupted with an unprepared comment, "I'm not that interested right now. There's a lot of concern with the H.I.V. stuff on the news, and I'm not what you'd call physically fit." Sam was suddenly 'saved by the bell' as the office's front door emitted its chime. "There's a patient in the lobby," Sam needlessly declared, which ended their conversation and lunch. Psychiatrists usually hate to be analyzed by their patients... or their housemates.

The rest of my day went smoothly enough. We did have one patient who came in who was in the arrears with her bills. What I'd tried to do was to secure a cash payment schedule with her, yet she disputed her promise to pay anything anytime soon. Sam refused to see her, as he felt it wouldn't solve the problem... and truthfully, he was likely right. The patient merely wanted something for nothing, and life doesn't work that way very often.

Right before his last patient of the day, I delivered him all of his messages—three or four of them from regular patients—and left him a note informing him that I was going home to start making dinner. On the way, I'd stopped off at a Lucky's grocery store just to get some much needed vegetables to make salad. Next door to the store, I saw a Chinese restaurant which had just opened for business the previous week. The smells coming out of it were heavenly, and I instantly lost all interest in doing my own cooking that night.

I got myself home with several Chinese dinner dishes sitting on my passenger's seat in Styrofoam containers. After dumping out those containers into glass dishes and bowls, I preheated the oven to keep everything warm, then went to listen to Pink Floyd's Delicate Sounds of Thunder. *About an hour later, I called Sam's cell phone, which went straight to voice-mail without a single ring, which meant that Sam was likely to be another hour before coming home, so I made a caramel flan.*

That done, I returned to the living room where I started reading for my Ethics course. I never found a college class as stimulating as I did with that Ethics one. It was composed of a sampling of philosophers, such as: John Stuart Mill, an 1800's English philosopher and economist; another English philosopher from the 1600's named John Locke; and—born between them—a German by the name of Immanuel Kant, who was a particularly fantastic thinker.

Kant was famous for his ethical, categorical imperative which states that we should always treat others as "ends" and not as "means" in themselves—or as a mean to our own ends. That each of us have individual value and no one should be subjected nor used merely as an instrument to satisfy another's ambitions. Of course, slavery could have been on his mind at the time he wrote these words, but the fit for any type of servitude, including my former occupation and status: whether it was as prostitute, or homeless orphan, or even prison inmate; I still retained a value when others perceived none, as far as Kant's concerned.

About ten minutes later came a knock on the front door, which turned out to be the most unexpected of possible guests:

Bob! This is a surprise, Damien greeted, then gave the old house guest a partial hug. Bob looked terrible, as if he's spent that last two nights living at the city's landfill, and hadn't showered since. *You look like you've been hit by a bus, then decided to take a nap under it.*

"Thanks. Nice to see you, too." Bob smirked, then asked "Is Sam home?"

He should be getting home any minute. C'mon in.

"I can't really stay. I just wanted to repay Sam the loan he lent me."

Damien was astounded to see the three one-hundred dollar bills being handed towards him by someone dressed and appearing to not even possess any money at all, nor a place to stay. Both of these seemed to be false impressions. Instead, Bob had embraced the latest trendy fad called "the grunge look." His faded and threadbare jeans actually cost extra in stores because of the holes intentionally made in the knees and butt cheeks. Believe it or not, this was a "step up" form his punk rock days during his second year of staying with them; Bob had dyed his hair a color called "pussy pink" and wore a lot of cashmere.

Seriously, c'mon in. I made something you'll like.

"Hell yeah, I can smell it from here. You made another caramel flan, Damien? Sure, maybe I'll come in for a bite or two."

Shortly after this, Sam did return home only to find one of his <u>least</u> favorite persons standing in his kitchen with Damien. "Bob? Huh, what brings you here?"

Always the smart aleck, the much younger man answered with, "They have these new inventions, called automobiles."

Damien, not understanding the joke, replied, *They've had those for a while now, cars are not 'new' inventions.*

"No," Sam corrected himself, "I mean <u>why</u> are you here? I see that you've already eaten some dinner and the flan. So, the rest is for Damien and I?"

"Damien invited me in. I only stopped by to repay you the loan you lent me on the day I moved out." Bob fished through his pockets until finding the cash he'd showed Damien earlier. "There's enough flan left for all of us to have three portions."

"Sure Bob, are you that greedy?" Obviously Sam still held onto some resentments towards the young man he knew as an inconsiderate houseguest.

"Look, I was pointing out that there's plenty left. I know that Damien's flan tastes good, but it's oh so sweet. Anyway, here," he said while practically shoving the money into Sam's chest, "I should be going."

Wait, Damien pleaded, *You don't have to leave right now, do you?*

"Actually," Sam insisted, "I'd prefer it if he did. I've had a long day and just wish to eat in peace. If you don't mind."

Damien escorted Bob to the front door and shared a somber

good-bye. Then the two of them ate dinner until Sam was full and headed to his bed where sleep quickly found him. Damien, on the other hand, stayed up and entertained himself by reading another act of Shakespeare's <u>Richard the Fifth</u>.

Clearly I was quite spent, for I fell asleep while still reading. Come the middle of the night, I woke on the sofa with Shakespeare resting quietly on the floor next to me. Not wanting to disturb "him", I stepped over the fallen king, grabbing my school backpack along the way to my bedroom, and laid myself down for sleep.

That night, my only rememberable dream was interesting to say the least. I woke up to a scene of Shakespeare's <u>A Midsummer's Night Dream</u>. Indeed, it was the very finale when we witness the character Puck wishing the audience a good night. I guess my mind was telling me I wasn't ready for sleep, even though I slept well enough. In any case, I truly liked Puck and associated myself fairly well with his unconventional personality.

No human being can think, feel, will, dream, without all these activities being determined, continued, modified and directed, toward an everpresent objective. This result, of itself, from the necessity of the organism to adapt itself and respond to the environment. ~ Dr. Alfred Adler. Understanding Human Nature

CHAPTER THIRTY-NINE

Two Loves Develop

Damien discovered a new facet in his being. He had fallen in love—not merely lust—with a woman for the first time in his life. Not since his short relationship with Charlie "Oops" Osborne had Damien truly cared more for another person besides himself. He honestly worried about Vicki's health and wellness more than his own. All of this personal fears and concerns had been replaced with the focusing on her needs and his undeniable love for her.

Just as striking was the fact that Damien loved going to school. Back at his early ages of six and seven, he viewed school as a place worse than any imaginable hell or pit of poisonous snakes. Instead, now with the increased maturity of his classmates, there isn't any ridicule or criticism for his slowness to pick up on certain things, nor for his offbeat questions to the instructor. Granted, he often times felt like "the oldest student in the class"—and was statistically correct.

I also give credit to my choice of taking Introduction to Ethics to the persuasion of God. In fact, I was starting to take back everything I ever said about God coercing people, for I recognized that I never would have signed up for this elective class—what turned out to be the greatest, most positive mistake I'd ever made—without some outside persuasion. My interest in obeying the guidance of God had developed into a crescendo, and this made me very happy, indeed. I was dating the woman God wanted me to date, and taking the college courses which felt like the correct ones, because they were also what God wanted for me.

Damien had discovered in himself a general subject which he could make a lot of sense of: various thoughts about the nature of the world, and—for that matter—the fundamental character of God. He began studying Aristotle's metaphysics, the study of the nature of being and likely existence of God. He delved into Rene Descartes philosophy of dualism; however, only from a religious standpoint, not from the astrophysical view of how many substances the universe is made up of.

At around this time, there were personal problems to resolve. The largest of these was how to balance Damien's relationship with Vicki and his desire to complete his A.A. degree and be transferred to state university. This wasn't going to be easy for Damien, even though it was important to his development as both as adult and a mature Christian.

Settling the problem, I realized that I would focus on my education during the week and date Vicki only on the weekend. This simply was good sense, not like following my still adolescent sex drive. Vicki understood completely with me, for which I am eternally glad. After all, she had school work of her own to help distract her from intervening hormones.

That weekend was no exception to our rule. I had chores to tend to, which included going to Sam's office to put away charts and photocopying business files so that I could take care of Sam's billing needs. Once that was done, I went shopping, cooked some things for Sam's dinner, then washed up and got ready to be with the love of my life.

There wasn't a thing that I wouldn't do for Vicki. She never actually asked me for anything, but she was always there for me. As it happens, that Saturday she saw an ad for a movie that she wanted me to see. To that end, she'd prepared a surprise dinner for us and suggested going to the movie after. We closed out the night with some snuggling on her futon. Vicki lived on campus in a studio apartment the size of a shoebox with "paper thin" walls to match. She wasn't permitted to have overnight guests, and I wasn't about to violate any rule which would result in her getting into trouble.

So, then came the curfew time for me to go home. I was saddened, of course, although the return home was an eye-opener of sorts. At a red light,

I envisioned my life unfold before me. What I saw was exactly what I'd prayed for: I had fallen in love with a young woman who I was hoping for; someone to reveal my world to, reveal my spiritual self, and to enjoy being with. I pulled over, parked along the shoulder, and immediately prayed that God would bless my relationship with Vicki. That "going home" would soon mean to be going home to her.

Damien was pleased with his life and his home with Sam. They were friends and really cared for each other. However, Damien knew that a major change would be required to his living arrangement if he continued to pursue a life with Miss Vicki. Sam's continued generosity hinged on this fact.

On the following Sunday morning, Damien got out of the shower and went right for the kitchen and a Crock-Pot stored on a shelf. Even though it wasn't yet seven o'clock in the morning, Damien was already thinking hours ahead to Sam's dinner and other important chores. He wanted to spend all afternoon and evening with Vicki.

"Good morning," an uncommonly bedraggled Dr. Reily greeted while rubbing sleepiness from his eyes, "Any coffee yet?"

Sorry, no, I just got up myself.

"Yeah, I bet. I never even heard you come home last night, must've been a good, long night? You and Vicki?"

Yes, sir. Very good. I'm not trying to offend you, Sam, but Vicki and I aren't sleeping together. We've agreed to save ourselves for marriage.

"Really? A vow of celibacy? But neither of you are, well, virgins. Right? Haven't you've told me that? So, why the sudden abstinence?"

She and I decided that our wedding night should be extra special. As close to Levitical law as possible, seeing as God already blessed our union, it's the least we can do to repay God. You know, to not sin against the Law.

"So, you're not having sex with Vicki in order to thank God for His putting the two of you together? You do realize how strange that sounds... noble, but strange. Remember, I was your doctor at Metro. I was the one who assigned you to Nurse Robertson's sexualized victims group as an insatiable addict."

Yeah, I guess I've gone from one end of the spectrum to the other: From sex addict to sexually abstinent. But I really like her, and I want God to bless our relationship... even if it means going Old Testament on life. Even Jesus said in Matthew 5:17 that he didn't come to Earth to abolish any of Levitical law, not the least pen stroke or letter from it. Even the new covenant we have through Jesus doesn't overrule the Law. And I don't want our marriage to be out of sin or tainted in any way in God's eyes.

"So, you are thinking of marrying her, Damien?

Yeah, Damien answered, then upon seeing the hurt in Sam's eyes added. *You have been and remain my best friend. I am also blessed by my relationship with Jesus, and honored to know Him as Savior and friend. But when it comes to Vicki, she is the half of me which I have always been missing. I would be absolutely nuts not to realize this, or to let someone like her not become a permanent part of my life.*

"Well, you sound pretty convinced to me." Then in a drastic change of subject, Sam point at the aforementioned Crock-Pot. "You making' pot roast?"

What? Oh, yeah. It'll be simmering all afternoon, which should make the entire house smell heavenly. I'm also planning on putting together a peach cobbler before I leave. Let me know how it all turns out.

"Sure thing, my friend."

Damien was glad to hear that even with his expressed desire to marry Vicki, Sam still wanted to keep their friendship going. Later that morning, minutes before leaving the house, Damien knelt in his bedroom and prayed to God. He wanted to express his thanks to God for the wonderful things God had allowed to happen in his life... especially by bringing Vicki into it. He also wanted God to watch over her and strengthen her desire to marry him. He left the rest to be in God's hands, because Damien earnestly trusted God to do what He saw fit and that—at most times—it meant what they both wanted.

Sam and I liked having a clean house, and even though I really wanted to have as much time to see Vicki as possible during the weekends, I still felt obligated to my commitments: so after starting Sam's pot roast, I had to clean the whole house ... which I did in record time. Then, after cleaning, showering again, and praying to God that Vicki would marry me, I left the house with my entire life savings in my wallet.

I figured that I would have enough time to visit a friend's jewelry store inside Westminster Mall, on my way to Vicki's place. The friend was a member of the R.L.D.S. church, although not involved in our small group. I really didn't know him that well, only in passing and through fellowship; but amazingly enough he recognized me on the spot. He offered, as a church-pals discount, to waive his commission on the price of a modest diamond ring as long as I promised to later buy our wedding bands through him.

Time was against me. I had only found out the previous night that Vicki had been invited to fly back to Michigan to visit with her family. Her father would be providing her with the plane ticket. I took this to mean that if I had the slightest desire to marry her, I should ask right away. I wanted Vicki to board the flight and meet her family as an engaged woman. How exciting would that be for her folks? "Mom and Dad, I'm getting married!"

I bought the ring and arriving at her apartment, I pocketed it. Without delay, she opened the door without me even having to knock—she always seemed to know when I was nearby—and welcomed me inside. I had never felt so welcomed to a person's home, with the exception being by Sam.

We chose to spend the remaining afternoon and evening in her tiny apartment since neither of us could afford to do much—least of all me, due to the item in my pocket. I was glad, too; I really wanted to have privacy with her. We worked together as a team of chefs in the kitchen she was nearly as culinarily skilled as I was. We had a romantic dinner complete with scented bathroom candles and chipped ceramic plates that didn't match each other, yet neither of us cared. We were a pair of designer shoes living on a shoestring budget; but more importantly, we were a pair.

When done with the dishes, I decided that the right moment had come. I didn't need any fanfare, no bouquet of roses, no violinist, not even her name on a ballgame's scoreboard—as incredibly classy as that sounds—although, to be honest, she deserved all of that, plus a fireworks display I saw in my head every time she kissed me. No, I would risk it all then and there without any backup nor champagne.

We were sitting together in her large chair, her legs crossed over mine, when I pretended a need to use her bathroom. I got up, but then down on one knee at her feet. I pulled out the ring box and did my best to propose to her. To be honest, I have no idea what I actually said—it might've not even have been in English!—I even flubbed up the word 'marry' with "Will you weary me?" If I was her, I would be rather wearied; but I got across to her somehow that I wanted to marry her, and she only took a second or two to overcome the shock and accept the ring.

"Yes! Oh, yes, Damien, I will marry you."

Damien stumbled and put his other knee down to stabilize his balance, then looked straight in her eyes. "God has given me to you, all that I did was ask. Pray with me, please. Together they quickly thanked God, followed by about five minutes of heavy kissing and fondling. They took themselves to Vicki's futon, which easily lied flat into a bed, then ignored Levitical law, as well as their promise of celibacy.

Yeah, we made love like you wouldn't believe. We even got her next door neighbor to pound on the wall in protest to our lovemaking noises and climactic yelps. I know we "jumped the gun" there and should've waited until we were officially married, but we were already married in our hearts. If you believe in traditional thought of God having a plan for our lives, then Vicki and I had been destined to be husband and wife before we were even born, and our honeymoon was long overdue.

Regrettably, I still had to go home. Although we were willing to break God's Law about sex before marriage, we weren't about to break the college's rule about curfew. So, I headed home, to a place that I could no longer feel as being mine. To a roommate, who I no long wanted to live with. From that moment onward, I viewed Sam's house in a way which he always thought I saw it, as my job. Where I worked as housekeeper, and nothing more.

The levity of what Damien had just done sunk in the moment he parked his car in Sam's driveway. It <u>was</u> Sam's driveway, Sam's house. With Damien marrying Vicki, he couldn't possibly continue to live here, which would likely include his working for Sam; both as a housekeeper and office assistant. Perhaps he could keep working in the office for a few weeks, yet Sam was paying Damien less than minimum wage because of their living arrangement. Sam would feel compelled to change that which he cannot afford to. And with Vicki unemployed as merely a volunteer at their church, they would need Damien's paychecks to be as large as possible in order to survive.

All of this, plus it would just be downright awkward for Sam. No, with this engagement, Damien would need to find both a new place to liv and place to work, all at the same time as going to school. This would be quite the conundrum.

At school the following day, Vicki sat down at her usual desk next to another coed named Lisa who had recently gotten married. Although the stone on Vicki's engagement ring seemed small in comparison to Lisa's own ring, the fact that it hadn't existed before caused plenty of attention.

"I was wondering why you were all aglow this morning, Vicki, and now I know. So, when did Damien pop the question?"

Vicki was still wanting to show off her new ring to the other classmates, "Damien asked me last night. I must admit that I was hoping he would. I'm flying back to Michigan in a few days, and this—" she motioned towards the ring—"is going to make Ma so happy."

"Wow! Does Damien normally grant prayers and miracles?"

"He's never done a miracle like this. God did this, and I am the happiest woman alive. This will be the best Thanksgiving ever."

"Well, from those pictures you showed me, you truly look like you belong with each other, that's for sure. Congratulations to both of you. Mrs. Vicki Collins, May you have a long and happy marriage together."

"Mrs. Vicki Collins?" she repeated tdo herself. This was the first time she had thought about the name change, and suddenly something didn't feel right to her. No, she wasn't having any doubts about her love and marriage to Damien; something else he had told her about his past made her feel instantly uncomfortable.

Everyone truly was pleased about our upcoming wedding. We told all of our church friends and small group members—Henrietta, although married, asked to be a bridesmaid but settled for the role of wedding coordinator. The last one to find out was my dear old friend. I recognized that this change in my life would likely cause Sam much paid on account of his emotions for me. Simply put, I didn't want to hurt him at all…I wanted to delay any such pain, although every minute I didn't tell him myself, was another minute he could find out from someone else—a friend of a friend— and that would be the worst possible way of his finding out.

After group, I drove Vicki to her place and we talked for a few minutes, mostly about our current living situation. We both agreed that we could not wait until we could finally wake up every morning in each other's arms. Vicki brought up the Sam issue, to which I responded that I would tend to him soon, but not right away. She was also concerned about this man who had taken care of me for over two decades now that he might be rather protective of me. I assured her that I'd been easing the facts to him about my intentions to marry her... had even dropped that bomb about him dating someone new. Our engagement wouldn't be a total shock nor overly painful for him.

With that, Vicki went inside her place and I drove home. Never was I as happier than I was that night. Okay, that wasn't exactly true, the previous night when Vicki and I had sex was the happiest night ever, at least, up until that moment... there were plenty more happy nights to come. What made that night especially good was when Vicki suggested that I should put together a list of family members and friends I wanted to invite to the wedding. I could only come up with a single name.

Damien didn't know where his Grandpa lived, the man had moved a few years previously to northern Las Vegas, but Damien didn't have his address nor could locate him on the Internet. His mother and half-brother Martin lived together in Arizona, although apparently his half-sister no longer was a Collins, since no Michelle Collins existed in all of Tucson or Phoenix. Damien was surprised with how easy it was to get his mother's address, something he hadn't known for over a decade and a half. In fact, the last time he had spoken to her or any of his siblings was while he was living with his Grandpa, back when he was only seventeen. He was about to turn thirty-nine in another month.

So, I wrote my mother a letter, inviting the three of them to the wedding. Vicki had decided that she wanted us to wait until after the school year and her graduation, so we picked the first day of summer to be the first day of our new life together: Saturday, June 21, 1997 would be our wedding. I really had no idea on how to plan for a wedding nor what would be involved. Naturally, Vicki would need a dress and I would need to rent a tux, and we needed a minister preferably within a church... but I had no concept of music, or flowers, or wedding cake, or a reception lounge, or catering or candles, or centerpieces, or thank-you gifts, or registries, or photographers, or practice dinners, or ushers, or having something old and/or blue!

I decided to help Vicki and Henrietta with the planning by doing as little of it as possible. They both had many friends and family who had been married recently or gone through a wedding, and benefitted from their friends' help in preparing for one. I knew that the only way I could be helpful was to calm her down whenever it felt overwhelming. Her having friends who recently got married left her more nervous—not less—as all get out, so I checked out public library books which really helped. The other thing that really helped Vicki was her cool-headed mother, whom was only a phone call away... make that <u>dozens</u> of phone calls away.

CHAPTER FORTY

Increased Development

The following Wednesday, Damien had a test to take in Human Development. He was skittish "as all get out" about that exam. He also had a paper due for another class, and a stack of schoolwork for his six others which he hadn't even looked at. Thankfully, he had Sam's computer to help him. Although the Internet was still in its infancy in the winter of 1996, its original intent of sharing scientific and education information had reached adolescence; and there was tons of both. He easily found textbook Cliff Notes and other quick reference and/or cheat sheets. Although he wouldn't go so far as to completely plagiarize another student's term paper, he did get some topic ideas from the ones he browsed.

So, I had to stay at home for a couple of weekends, which upset me. Those were the only times I had to myself, to spend with my fiancée. However, I did accomplish a lot of studying which made me feel better and more confident, enough to earn an "A" on both the exam and the paper. My topic was on the development of the human spirit in connection of the being. Originally, my professor told me "This paper is undoable," and that I was taking a huge risk with its subject matter. Apparently I must've impressed him.

The Saturday night after this exam, Damien went to visit his love and they talked about their wedding and the gossip circumventing their church. While they were both glad that their small group members all knew about the engagement, this information became headline news in the rumor pool. Faster than free donuts, the entire church knew all about their upcoming nuptials. What worried Damien was: He still hadn't told Sam.

At that point, Sam might have already of known or not, but I didn't want him to be surprised about it… nor to find out through some spreading rumor. I decided that we—Vicki and I—should be the first to tell him, so that's what we did, we invited him to dinner. We had reservations at an Italian restaurant down the street for the three of us. Sam knew ahead of time that something big was up, why else would we be inviting him to a meal which neither of us college students could freely afford.

To be honest, I cannot recall exactly what was said. Sam wasn't angry—he rarely expressed any type of emotion, least of all anger—but you could tell that he was disappointed. He loved me, both emotionally and sexually; although, and I don't know why, I didn't feel the same way about him. It felt wrong for me to desire him, to even be attached to him, since I would always see Sam as my doctor. No, he was more like an older brother or father. I couldn't ever be his love, his better half, regardless of how much I cared about him.

While in prison, I fell quickly in lust with Charlie Oops without the same level of actually caring about him. And although I believed that I was falling in love with Charlie, I seriously believed those feelings were due to the situation we were in and the enjoyment we felt when we were together. It was a knowingly temporary and conditional kind of love.

Then came Vicki. I was entering a new life and that new life entered me in the form of Vicki's life. I did make certain that she knew—when we'd first started dating—that I was an ex-convict and that I had to register each year as a sexual offender. Knowing all of my past, she nonetheless chose to marry me for the person that I was, not for who I had been. So, from the moment onward, I'd set aside my past altogether.

Unfortunately, settling aside my past would need to eventually include Dr. Sam Reily, as well as his house. If Vicki and I were to begin sharing our lives, we would need to share living spaces. If I was becoming a new person—like what happened when I asked Jesus to be my Savior—I would need to change my outwardly identity and be someone able to call Vicki as my family. What a difference that made in whom I could call my real family. What I forgot was that I was becoming her family, too.

The month of December went smoothly for Damien. He was a little frustrated around the holidays because he wanted to spend most of his evenings with Vicki, but Vicki really needed family time and traveled—once again—to Coleman, Michigan. Damien couldn't afford to go with her, both financially and due to his college schedule. He likewise needed to stay available to Sam's office: the holidays are a psychiatric nightmare full of suicidal thoughts and/or attempts.

Factually, I needed quiet time of my own, because I really had to study and earn every "A" possible. I believe I've developed better brains than I had when I'd first met Vicki. At the same time, I was still building my church relationships, and they were important to me. I really loved our small group meetings; even if Vicki hadn't been a member of the church—even if I'd never even met her—I would still love it.

At this time of my life, I didn't know pastors like Dr. Rick Warren of the nearby Saddleback Valley Community Church in Lake Forest, California, who emphasizes that church leaders need to focus on the health of their church, not its growth. In Warren's groundbreaking and bestselling <u>The Purpose-Driven Church</u> *(Zondervan, 1995), Rick stresses the importance of quality versus quantity; That having a clear purpose builds morale and growth on it own. That instead of trying to grow a church with leadership and programs, we must focus on growing people with a stick-with-it process.*

Although it would be over fifteen years until I got around to reading Dr. Warren's book, I was already in 1996 living under some of its core principles.

During our lengthy courtship—and equally lengthy six-month engagement—Vici and I had many conversations on some very deep subjects. We didn't always see eye-to-eye, yet rarely got into heated arguments. Vicki understood my Asperger's syndrome perhaps better than I did—myself—and knew I couldn't always help the disorganization of my thoughts, or the distant look in my eyes, regardless of how important the topic was.

One of these being our study of the nature of God and religious truth: We debated at length sometimes about man's relationship to God. I appreciated the fact that she not only had a strong faith in the church, but that we shared a very similar belief about God and Christ.

Vicki liked fellowshipping with both Henrietta's group and the one she had originally attended when she first moved out to California from Michigan. This was the "Upland" group, and it was held just east of her college apartment by a few city blocks on Sunday nights. I also enjoyed attending the "Upland" congregation; although, at times, I felt like an intruder or spy—digging for clues on how to run my regular "Orange" group better; and even was once or twice playfully accused of such. We made a great team, and "double teamed" our small groups with our mutual beliefs and differences.

We were also driving together, which was much more convenient for her to ride along in my car than her's. When Thursday evenings came, I always looked so enthusiastically forward to that time to share with others what we believed in, both as individuals and as a couple. Going to Dale's and Henrietta's house was always a real treat, as far as we were concerned except when we had exams or papers due the following Friday morning.

During one meeting in January, I was greeted by Alan, who started the meeting off with a question regarding our belief on a woman's legal and religious right to do what she wanted to her body. This, of course, included the getting of an abortion. This was something which Vicki and I had never discussed in private, so I didn't already know what her personal opinions were about abortions.

Damien answered Alan with, *"Well, that's loaded question."*

"Loaded? I think not," Alan contended. "It's one of the most important questions of our time."

Alan, I personally, and my faith agrees with it... I believe that it is, for the most part, against what God has taught us, regarding our responsibilities towards life, in general. However, I believe there are and must be exceptions to the rule.

"Wow! Spoken like a true politician, Governor Collins," Alan teased.

Vicki, who was sitting next to Damien, leaned forward and asked, "What are some of those 'exceptions,' Damien?"

o be truthful, Vicki, I believe abortion may prove to be medically necessary at times. Whenever the life of the mother is in jeopardy, I think

God would want doctors to save <u>the born</u> over the unborn. Especially if the woman hadn't yet achieved repentance. There also has to be an exception allowed for cases of rape... the baby would be a constant reminder of that horrible crime to its mother, and probably unloved.

A married woman, slightly older than Damien, named Jan, had been listening intently to Damien. "That's a pretty good list, Damien. I feel the same."

Her husband, a regular group member named Frank, then asked, "What are your thoughts about pregnant teenagers? Should there be an exception for them?"

I, uh, unless the pregnancy poses some other threat to the well-being of the young woman, then no... the baby should be born. If she cannot afford to raise a child, or isn't mature enough to do so, the baby should be adopted by someone who can. But having an abortion should never be a first choice, a first option in cases of unwanted pregnancies.

"So, which is it, Governor Collins?" Alan asked again, "Are you pro-Choice or pro-Life?"

I cannot be one way or the other. Every pregnancy is different, and every woman is different. God wants the fetus to grow and be born, otherwise it would never even exist in the womb. But, we can't ask a mother to give up her own life so that this baby can be born healthy; and I don't think a child born as the product of rape will receive all the unconditional love which every child deserves. But I'm not about to say that abortion should be illegal, since every female atheist or a woman of non-Christian faith deserves the freedom and liberty of having a choice.

The basic response of the group was that a woman should be allowed to make up her own mind about having an abortion or not. Jan did disagree with Alan's later sentiment that God commanded us to love one another, but that God didn't give any exceptions to this command for the unborn.

"I believe that the Jews of the day did not practice abortion," Alan further explained. "If I'm wrong, then it <u>is</u> wrong now. I think that the unborn is a living person, and anything with a heartbeat deserves a chance at life. And only God has a right to take such a life."

"Well," Jan spoke out, "You're right about only God having that right. But even scientists cannot tell us when a fetus is technically alive."

"But, Jan," Alan retorted in frustration, "Didn't you and Frank tell us last week that you voted in favor of the death penalty? Is that life not also human life? Doesn't God have the only right to take that life also?"

"The courts have already decided the matter when they ruled that murderers selected their own fate. In Exodus 21:14, God ordered us to put to death an intentional murderer, 'even if he has run to my altar for safety'." [TEV]

"Jan's right," Vicki supported her friend. "God gave us permission to take a criminal's life in certain situations. The only reason why abortion wasn't clearly covered as an acceptable situation to protect a woman's life, is because medical science hadn't determined a safe way to perform them at the time of the Old Testament."

"That's an interesting statement, Vicki," Alan commented, then asked, "but how do you feel about abortion?"

"I haven't formulated my opinion on the matter," she defiantly answered.

"So... do you agree with your fiancée?" Alan asked while giving Damien the 'evil eye.'

"Basically, yes," Vicki responded, "but I reserve the right to change my mind."

Jan practically jumped out of her seat, "Yeah! Go girl! You know you do."

"Thank you, Jan," Vicki smiled, then turned serious, "but I really mean it. I have not formulated an opinion on the subject. I do think that Damien is right in that young ladies should always have the unquestionable right to terminate a pregnancy in the case of rape, or child molestation, or a variety of medical reasons."

"Well, of course you would," Alan blurted out.

"What's that supposed to mean?" Vicki protested. "Just because I'm going to marry Damien, doesn't automatically mean I have to agree with him. In fact, Honey? Wouldn't you say we disagree sometimes?"

Maybe not 'sometimes'... but a few times.

"Well, then," Alan stood up and saluted the two of them. "Let's give three cheers to the ideal couple, Mr. & Mrs. Collins."

Damien looked at his soon-to-be bride, then glared up at Alan, *It's a little too soon for that, and… and we're not going to be Mr. & Mrs. Collins.*

"You're not?" Jan sat up straighter, then turned to Vicki, "Are you keeping your maiden name?"

"In a way," Vicki half-answered, then whispered at Damien to tell them.

Actually, we're doing something a little different.

"Really?" Henrietta looked on with interest.

I wasn't born a Collins, Damien explained. *When I was only a year old, my mother had her marriage annulled, then started dating around until she met and married Arthur Collins. No, I was born Damien Shelden and was never supposed to be a Collins… and after our wedding, I won't be anymore.*

"Wait, I don't understand," Dale asked from the furthest chair away from where Damien sat. "So, you'll be Mr. & Mrs. Shelden?"

"No, we decided that we'll reverse tradition. I'm taking on her surname when we get married.

Their conversation switched back to the subject of abortion and continued there for a while longer, as the group found themselves discussing murder and a woman's right to choose from a Christian point of view. <u>The Book of Mormon</u> was referenced; however, this edition of Scripture had nothing more to add above Damien's good reasons for a woman to terminate a pregnancy. Everyone seemed to agree that abortion should never be allowed as a form of birth control.

Come the end of our meeting, we felt pretty much the same way as we did when the meeting started: exhausted. Being that we both had school and were tired, there wasn't much discussion all the drive to her apartment. I walked her to the door and kissed her passionately good-night.

"See ya tomorrow night, my love," Vicki finally said while closing the door.

With that Damien made his way back to the car and headed home. It never felt right for him to be driving away from hi soon-to-be wife, but he knew that five months were going to be a short time, then they'd be living together. The only remaining question was: Where would that be?

"Our thinking shapes our experiences of life. The way we think about something and, most important, the way we relate to our thinking, will determine its effect on us. The outside circumstance itself is neutral. Only thought brings meaning to a circumstance." -Richard Carlson, *You Can Be Happy No Matter What*

CHAPTER FORTY-ONE

A Day in the Life

Damien's typical weekday was a maddening dash from one location to the next. Every Monday and Wednesday, Damien needed to wake earlier than usual, just in time for a quick shower and a bowl of cereal, then to drive himself to Cypress College in time to be in his morning Ethics class or Human Development class. On a few occasions, Damien had walked into a classroom only to realize the day of the week wasn't what he thought it was, and that he needed to be in a classroom on the other side of the campus.

After morning classes at Cypress, which usually ended at around ten-thirty, he headed to his car and—along the way to Sam's office—would stop at either Denny's, Bob's Big Boy, Chili's, or Panda Express restaurant for a couple of lunches to go, since he knew that Sam was going to be hungry. Then, as soon as he arrived at the office, which was normally around eleven o'clock, Sam would be in his office with his final patient of the morning.

While waiting for Sam to finish up with this last patient before lunch, Damien would put away the completed charts, pull out the rest of Sam's needed charts for the day, and also finish up any billing. Frankly, Damien was glad for the desktop computers Sam had installed in the office the previous year; they were a lot faster than the one and only machine that was there when he'd first started working for Sam.

During lunch, Damien and Sam spoke very little to each other. Usually their conversations were either small talk or work-related. Damien sometimes shared a bizarre occurrence which happened at school that day or a traffic jam he got stuck in. But every once in a while, Sam would mention the upcoming wedding:

"You're now a very active member of our church, Damien."

Thank you. I appreciate your words.

"I want you to know that I am worried about how your marriage will effect your missionary work."

As you know, Vicki is studying towards becoming a bishop. If anything our marriage will help my evangelism.

Sam looked sorrowful for a moment, then replied, "Are you sure that this would be best for you?"

Sam, I thought about this for several months before I got on bended knee. I love her, Sam. She's a good woman. I know that this hurts, but I have never been in a position to live on my own. Still, I am not ready, unless it is with another person of my own choosing... and I've chosen Vicki. If this were to fail or if she had said 'no', then I will be able to say that I tried my best.

"Well, Damien, it does sound as if you have thought about this, and I wish you the best. May this be the right choice for both of you. Anything I can do I will."

Thank you, Sam.

One Thursday, Damien came into the office only to find Sam not there. After getting situated, placing Sam's lunch in his vacant office, Damien called the doctor on his cell phone. Sam explained that both his eleven and one o'clock appointments had cancelled, so he went to Metropolitan State Hospital to chat with his old acquaintances there. He asked Damien to dispose of the lunch, maybe give it away to the neighborhood aluminum-cans collector... which is exactly what Damien did.

After finishing up the billing for that day, Damien left a note for Sam on his desk which read, "I really do love you and care about you, Sam. I care about the life you have given me. In two months, it'll be time for me to try out these wings, and all I can ask is that you would allow me to land at your nest if I were to fail at solo flights. Love you." Then Damien gathered his stuff for the trip to California State University in Fullerton.

My life was totally different than it was when I first moved in with Sam from my Grandpa's place. I really needed to test life for myself, and I still needed to know that Sam would be there for me should I fail. I believed that he would. So, I spread my winds for the first time alone and I took off. By the end of that weekend, I would be fully moved out of Sam's house... what had been our house for as long as I can remember.

Damien left for his other school and was prepared for what lay before him. C.S.U.F. was a very different school, much larger, too. It opened the same year Damien was born, 1957, and had roughly thirty-six thousand students, Damien really felt as if he found what God wanted for him, and that included going to school for a higher education. He felt good inside, and finally mature enough to be where adults went.

I was taking Nineteenth-century Philosophy. I sensed that it was going to be a difficult course, but lo-and-behold, I breezed right through it. To be rather truthful, there couldn't be anything simpler, I was quite surprised. I studied and did my papers, which earned me straight A's, mostly since I was studying people I'd already familiarized myself with, like Immanuel Kant and Kierkegaard. Anyway, thanks to all of my extracurricular reading of Vicki's textbooks the previous school year, I was more prepared than I thought.

Come the weekend, I was ready to visit with Vicki, and to proudly share with her that I received an "A" for my first term paper. Vicki was pleased for me, it was my first "A" in a state university. Vicki made us a delicious dinner and we went to the movies, then we spent time together with us feeling intensely closer to each other... which was pleasing to no end.

The truth is that I was scared half to death that something—anything—would change our minds, and Vicki would cancel our marriage. I never was in the position—although I had seen men who were—of when an engagement had come to an abrupt end without warning. I sometimes think that Sam felt for certain that my relationship with Vicki would come to a sudden end. How do I secure a relationship? There are no safe ones, except for the one we have with God, and even that relationship gets to being a rough ride.

I was proud of myself though. I had become a good student and a participating member of my church community, as Vicki was in her own right. I had done lots of growing up and was getting myself ready to take this flight with a girlfriend of God's own making, one that was meant for cornerstoning a new life together.

Finally, night bore Damien home to his friend Sam, and he was pleased to be where he could rest his head. *I would have preferred that my pillow was on the same bed as Vick was. Nevertheless, it was what it was. Until, suddenly, it wasn't.*

Weekly, Damien joined Vicki at either Henrietta's house for "Orange" group on Thursday, or they would meet at the "Upland" group on Sundays, or at another congregation which Henrietta or Dave wanted them to meet at. They loved their church, regardless of any particular group; and each week it seemed to be something and/or someplace different... which kept things interesting.

Sometimes, the topic was about God and church; while on other weeks, it had to do with subjects that had nothing to do with either. Well, at least, not directly. We talked about our hurts, out habits, and other problems. One week, we talked about what part the church played in the development of communities and how small group ministry participated in the process. We were considering the role of "community" in the healing of a given population—such as Los Angeles—or a given county such as Orange County.

However, we also faced another, more personal dilemma: our small groups should be in the process of growing instead of shrinking, as they were. I was saddened that even our "Orange" group was fading away! We talked at length about this problem and our concerns about the tendency for the groups to dwindle in size, in numbers. Members were moving out of the area, some were switching to a different denomination, and we just weren't attracting enough new replacements.

At a Thursday night group, a regular member named Dave brought up this subject and asked if anyone else had any concerns towards how their group was shrinking. Damien raised his hand in response: *I do, Dave.*

"What's your concern, Damien?"

As you know, Vicki and I attend both this group and her 'Upland' group meetings. Rarely does one group know what the other is doing. I believe that the church could use the small group ministry model on a much larger scale to replace the attractiveness to those joining street gangs.

"'The attractiveness?' To gangs?"

Society, especially teenagers, needs to know that a replacement to gangs and gang membership with loving church members exists. We've been doing a poor job of publicity, and it's more than any one group can manage on their own.

"Well, I believe that you're right, Damien. But even if our group were to collaborate with 'Upland,' there still just aren't enough people to work on the many problems plaguing society."

Well, you're right about the numbers of members to these small groups. Yet groups don't have to be perfect in size nor any other dimension, do they?

"Huh?" Dave looked about the faces turned his way, then asked, "Then what do you see as a way to fix our problems?"

Well, Dave, what we need are more groups that might be tiny to start with... as we are right now. Just one family, but are willing to develop growth from the community inward. This will require that the small-group leader practice their art of evangelism within their immediate neighborhoods, and then invite nonbelievers to the small group that they are starting or involved in.

"That sounds like one of those pyramid schemes for selling water purifiers or Amway products. Don't get me wrong, my sister-in-law makes a lot of money selling Amway and Mary Kay cosmetics to the door-to-door salespeople under her supervision. But that's what you're talking about, right? A tier system?"

Sure, Henrietta, you could say that it's like a pyramid scheme... only it's not a scheme and the only thing that we've got for sale is the news of God's salvation. Looking around this room, several of us have been coming to this same group week-after-week. Are we merely stuck in the habit of coming here together, the familiarity of it, or are we stuck in a rut? Each of us are at a level of leadership, and might not realize that we are holding ourselves back.

"You know," Jan admitted, "I've been a member of this group for almost a year now. And, I have been wondering why I haven't moved up to leading my own small group. I guess I've only been waiting for someone to tell me that it's the right time."

It's past the right time, Jan. Damien encourage her, *"In fact, you are long overdue.*

"<u>Wait!</u>" Henrietta—their official group facilitator—practically jumped out of her seat. "Are you <u>actually</u> insisting her to leave our group? Look at us, we are already down to <u>only</u> eight members!"

I'm sorry, Henrietta, but you actually have the wrong attitude. You should not be worried about holding onto existing members, especially one as mature in her faith as Jan, but on bringing in new ones. Jan needs to spread her wings and leave this nest, so she can build a much-needed further nest. To stay here in your wonderful group is as helpful to Jan as giving a crutch to a man whose leg is already fully-healed. You know what I mean?

"B-But, I like having Jan with us," Henrietta admitted.

So do I, and just because she'll be leading her own small group—he looked over towards Jan—*that doesn't mean she won't visit us, right?*

"Of course I will," she promised.

Don't you see? Damien asked the entire group. *We all need to be beginning our own new groups which would be known for its focus on one specific problem in society. Not everyone cares about the homeless, not everyone cares about drugs, or gangs, or gun control; so each group's members would have to consider the concern that they wish to address. They would tailor themselves into addressing that issue in a Christian way; perhaps without its members really knowing that it's in a Christian way until after they're having success at it.*

"This sounds a lot like deception to me," Dave warned. "I'm concerned that, well, that you're saying the small group won't be centered on religion. Right? It's the whole reason of why we come together as a group."

No, that's incorrect. The whole purpose of why we come together should be to focus on the problems in society, the problems that people bring us. The human needs. To take their concerns and turn them into action. The fact that we are performing that action in a Christian way will be revealed in and of itself. Yet the fact that our group's main goal is to encourage others to live a more Christian life will become more obvious to them as they are living that life.

"Damien, you just can't do that to people. You can't encourage them to behave like Christians, live like Christians, without telling them about Jesus Christ."

Why not, Dave? Why can't you encourage someone who doesn't even believe in God, let alone Christ, to live a life of empathy or generosity? If you have them 'love thy neighbor' and live a Christian life, those new seekers will eventually realize that perhaps being a true Christian isn't as bad as they had thought.

"This sounds as if you've thought this through, Damien," Jan said.

Oh yes, I have. I'm borrowing a little from my own mental notes for the nonprofit corporation I'd failed to develop. I just learned a valuable lesson with how Community of Hope fizzled.

Mark, a recently-started attendee of their 'Orange' group, then asked for clarification about Damien's attempted preventative program to assist ex-felons and inmates being released from prison in re-establishing themselves. Damien explained how, by himself, he had failed at raising any funds to keep his organization going, and admitted that he had no prior business knowledge, only a very noble dream.

"That's a shame. My wife is an expert at organizing fundraisers," Mark replied. "Wish we'd known each other while you were still in business. I would have helped with that goal."

Well, the dream hasn't died, Mark. Only my organization has. And now that I'm more involved than ever in small group ministry, I don't see why the dream cannot become reality through a group's action.

Although Damien didn't know it at the time, nor until several years later, this short discussion with Mark got the wheels rolling in bringing a much-needed organization almost exactly as Damien had originally planned into reality.

Getting back to what I was talking about, Damien started up again. *No offense to you, Dale and Henrietta, this is such a lovely home… but all of us sitting here have been so stuck in the routine of driving here every Thursday night. That's why you Henrietta, feel as the leadership is already taxed; because nobody is being promoted fast enough. There's eight of us here, that's eight new groups that can be started by the end of the month.*

Henrietta suddenly felt a moment of 'empty nest syndrome' wash over her, then said, "Well, we shall keep you all in our prayers and hope for the best."

"Well," Alan disagreed, "I—for one—am not ready to leave you, Henrietta. I like how you've been running this group, just fine."

And that's okay, too, Damien reassured. *But, Alan... don't hold yourself back for too long. You'll someday make a good group leader. In fact, it's your calling to do so. I honestly don't believe that you want to be stuck at evangelizing for the rest of your life.*

"No," Alan leaned back in his seat, "you <u>are</u> right about that. Thank you, Damien... you, too, Vicki."

Their evening ended shortly after this 'high note,' and the group left on the agreement that nobody was to do anything <u>too</u> drastic until their next meeting. Damien, however, had gotten himself all fired up about starting and leading his own small group ministry that this was all he could think about. That is, until Vicki brought him back-down-to-earth with the reminder that they both were overly involved already with both school, finding a future place to live, and planning for their wedding—less than two months away.

CHAPTER FORTY-TWO

Learning a New Process

  Our lives were being shaped by a number of factors, some of which we were not aware of until we were in the midst of them. One of these ever-changing developments was my theology. Admittedly, I commonly saw that Vicki and I believed in Christ Jesus in the same way: as being the living "Word" of God and that He sacrificed His life for the salvation of those who both believed and asked Jesus to be their personal Lord and Savior.
  Yet, I sought to learn whatever else I could, both from the church as well as from books by a variety of theologians, including a couple from Vicki's collection. As I've mentioned, I was blessed to not only have her in my life, but that she was a student of theology and was actively earning a master's degree in Divinity. She was the very resource of love and knowledge which I so desperately needed for decades... a gift from God in every possible way!
  Vicki was in her final year and was studying Process-Relational Philosophy—also known as Process Theology—which was a field pioneered by Alfred North Whitehead (1861–1947). His vision underlies much of contemporary process philosophy, educational theory, and a holistic vision of interrelated nature. Whitehead's <u>Process and Reality: An Essay in Cosmology</u> is generally considered the most important, systematic expression of how basic reality is constantly in a process of flux and change.

Process philosophy is a speculative world view that a fixed and permanent reality does not underlie the changing or fluctuating world of ordinary experience. Whereas traditional "substance philosophy" emphasizes static existence, process relational philosophy accentuates the dynamic becoming of being.

One sunny afternoon in March, Damien had a question of a scriptural nature he presented to Vicki. She suggested that he ask one of her favorite professors, Dr. John B. Cobb, Jr., who was a divinity professor at Claremont School of Theology. Dr. Cobb was also a published author of several theological books, including a re-issued classic, <u>A Christian Natural Theology</u>, and <u>The Structure of Christian Existence</u>. Damien had never before heard of him nor of Alfred North Whitehead until that fateful day.

Not wanting to disturb Professor Cobb, I asked Vicki about her taking my question to him for me. She insisted that Dr. Cobb had an open-office policy—active student or not—and that he'd welcome my questions. So, without delay, I went to the conference hall where Professor Cobb was still discussing some matter of importance to a small group of students. Again, not wanting to interrupt him, I quickly a wrote down a brief note, then asked one of the participants if he would pass it along to the professor.

It wasn't so much that I was shy or frightened of him, but that throughout my life, I held authors in a high regard of respect. Although I hadn't yet read anything that this particular man standing before me that day had written, the esteem that he wrote something left me in awe. During of my time within prison, particularly the latest time—which was at Chcukawalla Valley—I read countless books on Plato and Rene Descartes. Whatever was available at the inmate library, which regrettably wasn't much and/or missing pages.

Lo and behold, while sitting quietly towards the back of the hall and listening to the rest of their conference, I received a verbal response from Dr. Cobb saying that he would gladly spend a couple of minutes once he'd finished. Professor Cobb was gracious with me, in that not only did he answer my tough question, he invited me to join him at his home for some tea. Me?! This very important man wanted to have tea with me?!

"Absolutely," Dr. Cobb reassured, "I would love to hear more of your opinions. Bring your fiancée along, she has a very inquisitive point of view."

So, this is exactly what we did. We would spend "tea time" or an occasional lunch with this exemplary instructor. It didn't take long before I "saw the light." I was quite right in my decision to change my focus in college from Human Development to Theology. I just wasn't certain how to make a living at it!

Regardless, I knew that this was the direction of my life was supposed to now follow: I would take everything I've learning about counseling those stuck in habitual living of drugs and alcohol and other hang-ups, towards a greater purpose.

However, back then, I understood that my understanding about the nature of the world and its relationship with God was indeed different from much of what was currently being taught in many churches and schools. I was surprised that Professor Cobb had no real problems with what my unfinished "body of opinions concerning God" were comprised of.

Although throughout this book I've blamed my unorganized theology on my Asperger's syndrome—perhaps a little too much—Dr. Cobb admitted that I simply lacked sufficient terminology and the technique to outline them. That it was nothing for me to be embarrassed about, yet it was also something I shouldn't procrastinate at resolving.

"Your opinions," Dr. Cobb praised, "towards mankind's relationship with God have considerable merit, Damien. However, they lack a coherent form or structure."

Yes, Professor. I've always had a problem with structure and organizing my thoughts.

"Oh, but it's more than that. Your theology needs to be composed in a pattern of harmonious action. Your listener wants to read an assembled and orderly whole. Do you believe you can develop your opinions about the nature of God into a systematic structure? An organic structure? This is what you seem to be lacking most."

I'm not sure, Damien admitted. *I've been trying for years to interpret my opinions and thoughts about God, our relationship with God and Christ, in an understandable way that is important to me. I want to get my points across in the most expressive way that I can.*

"But that's just it, Damien. You are trying to 'force feed' your listeners to what is important to you, not to what they are ready to hear. For example, which is better: For me to interpret God as an unchanging absolute Supreme Being, or for me to stress God's sensitive and caring relationship with the world? The answer is simple, the choice isn't mine."

Isn't... it isn't yours?

"Absolutely not. Unless I'm giving a lecture about God's love for us, well then, the listener knows ahead of time what I'll be discussing. They'll already know what to expect... well, not that I won't be throwing new concepts at them. No, you'll lose your listeners if you're trying to feed them a topic or subject matter which they aren't prepared for."

So, um, I should let the listener decide the topic of every discussion?

"Damien," Dr. Cobb cleared his throat. "With every discussion, there needs to be an evaluation of how in-depth you should go into a topic. Not all of your listeners are ready to explore your theology at the level you might be wishing to share with them. By letting them open their own doors, to pick the topic they'd like to hear, you can better judge where their level of comprehension is at... and how deep you can go with them. Whichever topic any discussion starts off with will eventually be finessed towards where it needs to go."

What did you mean earlier about an 'organic structure'?

"It's an important, metaphysical perspective that everything surrounding us is organic. Sure, this house is man-made, it did not grow here of its own accord; yet its basic elements are organic."

Well, sure. That seems pretty simple.

"Everything in nature fits a certain structure which doesn't contrast what is pleasing. When I said that you should just be natural... allow your vocabulary to flow with words and terms that are clear and fundamental."

I'm not sure I understand, Damien admitted. *I always try to be as, well, as possibly clear as, um, as fundamental.*

Professor Cobb tried to suppress a laugh at that moment. "Exactly. Too often, Damien, you seem to be struggling to find words and phrases that impress or assimilate your listener, instead of simply conveying your direct thoughts. Your goal is not to sound impressive, but instructive.

Always use your own words, Damien."

Dr. Cobb then shared with Damien a manuscript he'd been working on, which was to be an introductory guide to some of Alfred North Whitehead's most important yet intricate lectures. Whitehead passionately talked with a specific target audience in mind, which was the highly-educated professionals in his own field of study.

John Cobb believed that Whitehead's work was much too significant for such a limited audience, and wrote guides to help broaden Whitehead's readership, including even a "Word Book" to clarify some of the unique and inventive terminology Whitehead confounded readers with.

It was from my lengthy discussions with Professor Cobb that I learned about what he named "Process Theology," which he felt would answer my multitude—and neverending—questions. He helped me articulate what it was that I did believe in, without impressing his own beliefs. Instead, with his counsel I began to study everything I could on Whitehead's work, including a book which Cobb co-wrote with another professor named David Ray Griffin: <u>Process Theology: An Introductory Exposition</u>.

Vicki had a few books already available written by Whitehead himself, including the aforementioned and extremely formidable <u>Process and Reality</u>, the one which Dr. Cobb felt needed supplementary guides... and boy was John ever right! Reading it was, for me, a bit like taking a biology course—and understanding it seemed to require a Ph.D. For years I've tackled, off and on, to read this book, have read it cover-to-cover three times, and I'm not sure I've completely absorbed everything Whitehead was trying to say!

Although, one cool thing I got from his books was that "process thought" seemed natural to me. Some of the questions which have plagued me much of my life were finally answered! Mind you, I didn't understand "process thought" right away, but as I did come to understand it, it made the world so much clearer! That not only was I experiencing a level of growth and development, but every relationship I was involved in—especially the one with God—was affected by this enormous change.

I still have to think differently than I was taught to think particularly about the nature of things, when I study Whitehead's books. I now understand why Whitehead called his philosophy, "the Philosophy of Organism."

It is a much deeper understanding about the nature of the world in itself, which stresses creativity, compassion, and the necessity of interconnectedness of all of nature.

Process thought is a worldly view, a way of thinking and understanding the universe, which includes its Creator, for that matter. The theology by the same name—Process Theology—picks up where this philosophy sets down, in deeper regards to God, by name, and makes God and our relationship its main focus.

This was a phenomenal period of Damien's life. Finding out that God could be understood on a much more personal level was—as I've mentioned many chapters ago—extremely important to Damien and for his continued journey towards helping others… his ultimate goal.

One of the most common statements made about God's nature is the notion that God is "all-powerful," and this is a notion which Damien has time-and-time again contested throughout his past. This notion implies that God can do and/or have done anything God's Will desires, regardless of the laws of nature or physics, even when those deeds would violate those same laws.

Arguably, since God created the universe and everything in it, He also created <u>how</u> the universe functions, which would include all of the laws of nature and of physics.

However, at this time in Damien's life, he still didn't believe that God can or would violate His own laws, or they "would cease to be laws with any meaning for all that they affect."

I struggled for a long time with this concept that: If God could willfully bend time to travel to any time period, as some theologians believed, then the laws regarding time could also be bent by others. Same would be true for gravity: If God could change a planet's gravity to cause something to float skyward, wouldn't everything else on that planet likewise float?

I do now believe that God can and does lure actual beings and other entities to bring about events according to the Divine Aim, but that doesn't mean that God always gets God's way of things. Does it?

I also believe that the actualities involved have their own aim for the next moment in time. That they may choose not to fulfil the Divine Aim. We call this "free will," but really it's just basic interaction with our environment. My point is that all of Creation participates in the bringing about of a new day, a new series of events, which often isn't exactly what God wanted to happen in that moment of time.

I also read books which discussed the notion of God as being able to know all things, including things that don't yet exist, and thoughts which haven't yet been thought. What I believe is that there are things, or "future events," which God may perceive as probably to occur, but that even God cannot know for certain. The problem lies in the fact that there cannot be a real thing as "the future." God can anticipate what we'll likely do next, and even anticipate what our destinies might be without interruption or diversion; yet that doesn't mean that these future events are guaranteed to happen.

It was my goal in sharing my life with you, dear reader, to not only know me and my personal history, but where I stand with my theological beliefs... and to help you see the beauty and—for that matter—the necessity of viewing of our relationship with God for what it's worth: a two-way path. That we need each other, us and God, for we are interconnected through God's Spirit to not only God, not only to each other, but to all of Creation!

I truly believe that God needs us to develop a sense of wholeness with the world. In the midst of this shared life, we have our maturation, our fulfillment of who we are with each other.

I am also telling you all of this to show that I have no resentment nor guilt in God, for the following bad turn of events which occurred in my married life! But, before I get to those, I should get back to the timeline leading up to my nuptials...

PART THREE

Poor Navigation

To many people, the term 'process' suggests something external and objective, but for Whitehead the units of process are always as much internal as external, as much subjective as objective. They are, 'occasions of experience'.

John B. Cobb, Jr. & David Ray Griffin,
Process Theology: An Introductory Exposition

CHAPTER FORTY-THREE

A Good Ol' Boy and a Country Girl

It didn't take long for Vicki and Damien to toss their original planning for their wedding day out the window. Damien wanted for Vicki's family to have a big part in her wedding—their wedding—yet without having to spend much money getting there. It only made perfect sense to get married at her home. Besides, it is where she'd lived throughout every stage of development: from infant to child, to teen, to coed, and now the stage where she becomes a wife... to an extremely lucky man. Vicki was ecstatic with the idea of having their ceremony on her family's farm, and so was Damien—well, at first.

During our first ever visit to her Michigan home, as a couple, I was taken away by the most spectacular and seemingly endless supply of evergreen forests and farmland. Vicki had the advantage of growing up on a 187-acre—and beautiful—farmstead. Imagine, if you will, the house and its setting: Michigan is, for the most part, flat in all directions with the exception of trees. Perhaps a hill here or there, but merely by accident. The rest is all farmland and the structures that went along with farming.

When I arrived in Michigan, I was picked up at the airport by Vicki and her mother, Vera. Vicki had flown home a few days ahead of me, while I was forced to remain behind and finish two term papers, plus take an exam. I felt such a level of welcoming which one never finds in any city.

Some forty-five minutes later, we arrived at their house. There was a long driveway to the detached garage.

The entire house was an impressive sight to see. It was absolutely beautiful... and was entirely built by Vicki's dad, Victor. While he built their house, the family lived in what had become the two-car garage. This farmhouse had been built mostly with love, rather than just wood and nails. Rooms had been custom-made with nooks for heirlooms and other functionality in mind. All I could say was "Wow!" So much family love was apparent.

Since it was till March, there was snow on the ground, except where it mattered. Vicki's brother, Vincent—yes, this family really liked "V" names—was standing outside the house finishing up his chores, which included daily snow removal of the lengthy driveway and areas around the house. Her father, the master house builder, farmer, and part-time school teacher, was found inside the home. The living room was so small, I could hardly believe that it really was part of the house, every other room seemed so specious... but then Vicki explained to me that it was intentionally designed to be cozy.

Her house reminded me of the same story that my step-grandfather told us when we lived on our farm so long ago. The house Vicki grew up in—for the most part—was the garage. Her brother slept in one half of its attic, and she slept in the other half. In fact, this is where my tour of their home initially started. Vicki showed off to me her scholastic awards and trophies, which were on permanent and prominent display. She had been an active member of 4H Club, plus she'd been very active in school sports, especially track and field. She was truly amazing.

Vicki had been born on October 5th, 1970, and graduated in the class of 1988. Damien was thirteen years older than her, not quite old enough to be her father, but clearly a gap existed. Both Vera and Victor noticed the age difference right away, since Damien was closer to their own age than the one of their daughter. Although nothing was said about this right away, it was one of their biggest concerns about their marriage, however, not <u>the</u> biggest.

After their first dinner together had finished, the plate cleared off of the table, and cups of coffee poured... an important conversation was started by Vicki's father.

"Bet you haven't had a meal that good in a while, eh? Damien?"

No, sir, that was very good. Actually, he personally thought the meat was bland, but thought it rude to point this out.

"While Vera and I are happy to have you in our home we—" Victor looked to his wife for emotional support, then continued, "we just have something we wanted to say to both of you. So, let's start."

Okay, Damien nervously squeezed his fiancee's hand under the table, out of sight of her parents. He was pretty sure what was coming.

"I must admit that Vera and I were, well, are a little concerned with having you marry Vicki."

Victor's long hesitation caused his wife to place a hand on his back and rub him up-and-down. "C'mon, Honey."

"Well," Victor found his strength, "because you are a twice-removed ex-felon, we would never have let you step foot in here if it wasn't for your friendship with our daughter. So, we wanted to extend our welcome, as—according to Vicki—you have demonstrated that you are no longer the same man that went to prison. That you're now a very active member of our church, well, not of the Mormon church, but it's a church nonetheless."

Thank you. I appreciate your words.

"The problem we have, is—well—as a registered sexual offender, what kind of life can you possibly provide for our daughter? Your criminal history will forever plague your chances at well-paid employment. Mind you, we aren't afraid of you, as much as we are afraid for you... both of you."

Victor, on the flight over here I knew to expect a question like this. No reasonable parent would feel comfortable with their daughter marrying a man once convicted for rape, without getting some definite answers. That's just good parenting. I want you to know that I am eternally grateful for what God has done for me. I never thought that there was a chance like having a woman like your daughter come into my life and to be my wife. This—alone—was impossible for me to bend my head around. Thanking God for such a blessing, not that I deserved any favors, bot for granting my prayer.

God is called our Heavenly Father, although I'm still not comfortable with referring to God as being male. But, my point is, a good father will discipline a child that doesn't pay attention and misbehaves. I was sent to prison the first time because I was living a godless life of drug abuse; the second time because I allowed my hormones and lustful thoughts take over all sound judgment. Both of those times, God had me sit in a corner, just as a parent should. If God hadn't, I would still be living a monstrous existence without any chance of ever meeting this beautiful woman.

"Aww," Vicki leaned over and gave Damien a peck on his cheek.

Perhaps this mild display of affection provided a breaking point in her parents' concern about Damien, maybe it really was his lengthy response; regardless of which, they immediately seemed much more comfortable.

"You sound like someone full of regret, Damien. Do you believe you are forgiven of your sins?" Victor asked him.

Oh, most certainly. I haven't been able to contact any of my victims, yet, and nothing would be better than for me to ask them for their forgiveness. But I know in my heart that God and our Savior have accepted me. I was baptized two years ago, in full belief of Jesus as my Christ. I have been washed clean of all sin, including Adam's sin.

"You mean, the original sin," Vera corrected.

Uh, not quite. I, um, I'll take a chance here and hope not to offend anyone at the table with my answer. I don't believe that Adam or Eve introduced the first sin and the sinful nature of our race—"

"You're saying that the Bible is wrong?" Victor asked.

I believe that for the 'original sin' to occur it would have to start with Eve, but even Scripture says Eve was not the original source of sin. No! Lucifer was the one who sinned first. Sin came into this world before the Creation of Adam and Eve, by Lucifer and a third of the host of angels who followed Satan's rebellion. It is unfair to place blame on Adam and Eve for the origin of sin.

"They were the first humans to commit a sin against God."

Eve, perhaps, was knowingly committing a sin, since she knew for a fact from which tree the forbidden fruit had been picked. She followed Lucifer's deception and broke God's most important rule to her—assuming that there weren't other rules which weren't mentioned to the story's author. But Adam, in all of the translations I've read, was never described as knowing from which tree the fruit was from. Sure, maybe by its color or shape, he might've recognized it as the kind that only grows on a certain tree... the one they were told not to touch. But, there's none of that written down. I believe Adam to be a witless victim, taking a bite without knowing what he was getting himself into. He just did what any husband should have done, he trusted his wife.*

"So, you're saying that Adam didn't intentionally sin, that Eve did but it wasn't the original sin? I guess, Damien, that we ought to talk about what original sin actually was, because the argument isn't whether Lucifer disobeyed God or not. Both Adam and Eve disobeyed God's direct instruction, just as it says in Scripture."

Sin is far more than just disobedience to God, Victor. Rather it is anything that damages our relationship with our loving and pure God. Lucifer became Satan by his defiance against God, his ill-attempted rebellion against the leadership of Heaven. For his sin, Lucifer and his followers were cast out of Heaven.

"True, but that sin was committed while he was in Heaven. The original sin to be committed here in Creation was made after he advised Eve that eating of the forbidden fruit would not kill her. Being deceptive, as Lucifer was, caused Eve to sin; however, it was still her choice to make."

"Wait," Vicki cut into the conversation, "I see what Damien is trying to say. That when Lucifer had tempted Eve to eat the fruit, he was committing a sin. But, Damien, I have to agree with my father that Lucifer had already destroyed his relationship with God back when he was in Heaven. Anything he would have done <u>since</u> his eviction, it wouldn't technically be a sin... for no relationship existed to be ruined."

No, his relationship with God wasn't 'destroyed.' In fact, nobody's ever is. Sure, it would never be the same as it was when Lucifer was the first created. Same is true about Adam and Eve after eating the tabooed fruit. Nothing, not even death, shatters a relationship with God; sin only damages that bond we have. When Adam and Even failed to obey God, I believe they—much as Lucifer—had to leave God's presence, they couldn't remain with God for they were no longer pure.

I know that the 'Adam and Eve' story isn't just about sin and the eating of forbidden fruit, it's more about mankind's inability and our lack of desire to maintain a meaningful, personal relationship with our Creator. Now, Victor, I've tried for years to imagine having a one-to-one relationship with God; being able to walk—as Adam and Eve did—with God on such an interactive level. Wow! Could you imagine a close-knit friendship like that?

Victor looked again at his wife before answering, "I believe I'm having a few of those kinds of relationships, right now. Both with God, with my wife, and daughter, and—now—with <u>two</u> sons. I see that you haven't only been reading Scripture, Damien, but you've been going beyond the stories and studying their meanings. Assuming that you've gone past Genesis chapter two, I presume."

Oh, most definitely. I don't mean to be sitting here all night and to discuss every book of all three Testaments—even my thoughts on the Apocrypha and discourses—but my general opinion is a picture of God as a loving and strategic emperor who wanted to fulfill our desire to have a physical presence of leadership, although due to our own impurity just couldn't persist among us. God gave us temporary kings and leaders to see with our eyes and listen to, while God ruled the best as possible—albeit, from a distance.

Victor, Vicki's father, cleared his throat to gain everyone's attention, then—loudly and clearly—told all of them: "To tell you the truth, Damien, I started to interrupt you a couple of times, but I didn't because I remembered that Vicki said you do need extra time to get your thoughts in sync with you lips… that Asperger's thing. However, I've found your logic tonight with fairly good reasoning. You're all over the place with the topic at hand, but this doesn't mean that you're wrong nor avoiding the original question. And I respect this about you. I liked what you had to say."

Well, sir, that's quite a complement coming from you. Damien turned to Vicki with a huge smile, still squeezing her hand underneath the table.

"Any thoughts, after you officially become my son, of changing your first name to, say, Vamien? With a 'V'? It's kind of our thing."

Uhh, Damien stammered, then chuckled slightly, *"That would be rather interesting, now wouldn't it? Unfortunately, I'd be spending the rest of my life having to spell my name to people, But, Vicki and I have a separate surprise for you.*

"Oh, really?" Neither Victor nor his wife, Vera, had been made aware of this beforehand.

Your daughter isn't going to be becoming a Collins. And, well, I've decided to no longer remain being one either. As you've been told by Vicki, I never had much of a family connection, even while I was living with them. I don't even consider myself as being a member of a family, well, except for a church family. That is, of course, until sitting here at this table. I am changing my last name tdo yours, Victor. I want to—

Damien couldn't get the final words of his sentence finished before the much stronger man—and only slightly older—came out of his distant chair, around the table, and embraced Damien in the tightest of enduring hugs. In fact, for about three seconds, Damien couldn't actually breathe. The man, his soon-to-be father-in-law pulled only slightly away from him with a river of tears running down his hardened face from each eye.

Vera, an equally-strong farmer's wife, also rushed to Damien side of the table, only to embrace her daughter, whom still was seated. The amount of indescribable love and other emotions in that smallish house was immense! So much so, that even one of their dogs in the side yard appeared in a nearby window and began to howl as if she were missing out on something great. That ol' country dog couldn't have been more correct.

During our plans to get married—this is back when we thought it would be in California—we were shown a great place to get Vicki's "almost perfect" wedding gown. Both Vicki and her mother were quite the seamstresses, and would take what we'd bought on our limited budget and turn it into something both more Michigan-climate comfortable and astonishingly elegant… much like the person wearing it! Over the next month, there were still questions to be answered and alterations to be made, but this is true of everything in life, not just dresses.

I know that I have repeated myself a few times in this book, and that my thoughts and topics haven't been the easiest for you—dear reader—to read. But, I cannot express enough times how fortunate I am in having a woman like Vicki to come into my life and to be my wife. God listened to my prayers, the specific details and preferences I prayed for, and God rewarded my faith. I was unworthy of any favors from God; I had spent almost my entire adolescence doing exactly the opposite of what God wanted of me: I ignored God's Word, I disrespected my parents, I relished in homosexuality, passionately sought for sexual release from anyone willing, sold my body for pleasure, abused my mind and soul with alcohol and drugs, bought a weapon out of foolish need and fired it into someone I'd never met, raped an innocent woman based upon her reputation and my own frustration. Shall I go on?

God, as merciful as Scriptures say, somehow forgave me for these decades of debauchery and decadence. I lived no better than Adam and Eve, combined. From the very beginning, God wanted these two to act according to the simple will and rules of obedience. But, thanks to God's love for Lucifer in allowing that fallen angel to live, God lost control of mankind. Sin became a part of our nature, and this must've troubled God to no end. Even flooding the entire world didn't solve this problem, sin was here to stay. But, in my moment of need, despite all of my past transgressions, God still answered by prayer for a wife.

It seems so unfair doesn't it? We live our lives, sometimes getting the thing we desire most, sometimes not. We pray to God for health, strength—sometimes selfishly for wealth—and oftentimes receive prosperity through those prayers from God, which we truthfully don't deserve. Yet, God rarely gets the things God wants done or expects from us. Most of us never count our blessings, or even thank God for the goodness in their lives. Often—much too often—God does all of the work, and something called "luck" earns all of the credit. I feel so sorry for God; out of everything God does for us, where is the happiness and gratitude God so much deserves every second of each day?

Towards the end of another Thursday night small group meeting, the group had nearly polished off all the coffee, chips, an earthware pipkin full of melted cheese for dipping, finger sandwiches, and topics available. Damien and Vicki walked with their arms wrapped around each other's back, all the way back to his car. Normally, this would be the most depressing time of the night—the woeful drive back to her place, while Damien returned to Sam's—however, that night there would be a change in normal routine.

Do you mind if I swing by my place before I drop you off? Damien asked from the driver's seat.

"Sure, hon," Vicki replied then, after a few puzzling moments and right turns, she asked, "Hey, hon? Don't you live <u>that</u> way? You know, south?"

Perhaps you do, Damien said with a smile.

"And so do you, unless God moved Huntington Beach recently."

Nope. Huntington Beach is right where it's at. And so is Sam's place. But mine is this way, he announced with a smirk. *But I gotta warn you. It's even smaller than yours.*

"You—you?! What?! W-w-when were you going to tell me?!" she excitably asked. The sudden thoughts and possibilities of them spending the night—all of it, plus the morning—together quickly flooded her ecstatic mind.

Whaddaya mean?! He laughed out, *I just did tell ya.*

> *It is vital to emphasize again and again that God's power is not omnipotent unilateral or coercive power. Quite the opposite. God cannot coerce any creature. Every creature has its own freedom...*
>
> *So God knows what we may choose and are likely to choose, but not what we will choose. God is omniscient (all knowing) in the sense that God knows everything there is to know, but since the future does not exist it is not there to be known.* ~ C. Robert Mesle, *Process-Relational Philosophy*

CHAPTER FORTY-FOUR

Please Stand Up

Damien's and Vicki's first trip of that year to Michigan ended at the end of the weekend, both of them needed to return to both California and their respective schools. As mentioned earlier, this would be Vicki's final semester until earning her degree; Damien would be earning a final certificate from Cypress College and—at the end of this school year—be transferred completely over to the C.S.U. system.

Likewise at the end of school in June, there was going to be a series of celebrations—either involving caps-and-gowns or flowers-and-rings—one after the other in quick succession. It was going to be a busy three weeks in June, to say the least! However, presently, Damien was still living in the final days of winter.

Damien made his way to the first of two college campuses that day: parking his car, he headed straight to the central quad's coffee stand—the college was rumored to have made more residual money from the sale of cups of truly horrible coffee, than from collected tuition fees—where Damien had his first of many daily dosages (or 'hits') of caffeine.

As he enjoyed his creamy and sweetened cup of "mud," Damien took in the morning on the campus: The air was cool as it rushed by the concrete buildings, where his classmates either rushed or dragged their heels. From his table, Damien could see the freshly cut grass performing a delicate dance in a mild breeze, which brought back memories of his quiet moments while still at C.M.C. prison, with or without Charlie "Oops" by his side.

How long ago was that? Another lifetime ago. I'd forgotten all about those days and about him. My three dismal years at Chuckawalla Valley had almost completely overshadowed how prison time could be both comfortable and positive.

Damien prepared himself for his Human Development class, which was followed closely by his Pharmacology course. He chose the latter one because he originally wanted to have a broad range of knowledge, and that it would suit his future clients who would be in need of counseling. Well, that, plus he believe it was a rather interesting class.

Pharmacology had to deal with the scientific study of both legal and illegal substances, their physical absorptions, as well as the physiological effects of drugs. If I were to pursue my career to counsel addicts of drugs, I was unfamiliar with the latest family of amphetamines and barbiturates—sure, I knew plenty about smoking weed and freebasing cocaine, but hadn't any personal experience with those others. I needed to know how they affected the body, as well as the mind, if I was to relate with my clients.

As the days of April and May arrived then melted away like the snow on the Sierras, Damien kept himself extremely busy with his studies, especially his latest additions at CSU-Fullerton in philosophy. He became increasingly excited at the things he was learning at that <u>second</u> college campus. Surprisingly, Damien was finding that he had already much of the same notions regarding God and Christ as the authors of the many books he was gladly reading.

I was doing two very important things at the same time: Firstly, I was shaping my theology so that it truly made sense not only to myself but to others—particularly nonbelievers or those weak in their faith—I would eventually speak. Second, I was also learning how to present my principles so that I would be crystal clear right from the beginning. I wanted to be concise and direct.

What I'd discovered was that there was a "language" for the things I was already feeling. I just didn't have its vocabulary nor the method to clearly think about my favorite subject: that being Christ. The one and only

Christ of the universe.

Then, during that final semester, I had a philosophy professor at my first campus, Cypress College, who introduced our class to a writer named Pierre Teilhard de Chardin...

Père Teilhard was born and raised in Auvergne, France, and was a life-long member of the Society of Jesus. He moved around a bit, living many years in China, then in New York City during World War Two. Père Teilhard was barred by his Jesuit religious superiors from publishing any of his philosophical works. So, he entrusted his several manuscripts to a friend, to be published after his death (posthumously). These engrossing and inspirational works included <u>The Divine Milieu</u> and <u>The Phenomenon of Man</u> (Harper Collins), which both Damien and I would recommend to anyone.

Sitting at my desk one evening class, our instructor Professor Lau read from Pierre Teilhard's <u>The Heart of the Matter.</u> I was held captive by every word, for I saw that I was not along in my feeling that Christ was far from easy to discuss. Professor Lau treated us with the following selection.

"Alright, students. Those of you with a copy, please turn to page 61. Number one, Christ in Matter. 'My friend is dead, the man who drank from all Life as from a hallowed Spring. His heart consumed him with fire within. His body vanished in the Earth, before Verdun'." Verdun is a city of northeastern France and was a site of a prolonged battle in 1916.

Professor Lau continued reading, "'Now I can repeat to myself some of the words by which he initiated me into the intense vision which brought light and peace in his life. "You wish to know." He would say to me, "how the mighty and multiple Universe came to assume for me the form of Christ? That was something that happened gradually; and intuitions that so [remold] our spirit are the experiences that allowed the light of day to pour into my soul, from below—as though a curtain were being raised in successive jerks'." Who would like to stand up and tell me what Pierre Teilhard meant before I go on?"

Damien didn't dare stand, although he believed he understood perfectly. Instead, he privately hoped another student would provide their own opinions towards Lau's chosen passage. No one did.

Professor Lau continued onto page 62, "And, continuing my line of thought, I could not see how it could be possible for an artist to represent the sacred Humanity of Jesus without giving him this over-exact physical definition, which seemed to cut him off from all other men: without giving him a face whose expression was too individual—a beautiful face, no doubt, but beautiful in a particular way which excluded all other types of beauty'."

Intently, I listened to Professor Lau read from <u>The Heart of the Matter</u>. It is from Père Teilhard that I came to see the impossibility to "know" Christ. He who was and is the living incarnated Word of God. For it was made clear to me that if this Jesuit priest and professor in geology—among many other notable academic distinctions—has difficulty in describing the true nature of our Savior, how was I?!? How was someone as far from able as Pierre Teilhard going to ever describe to others what Christ wanted from himself, let along the church?

It was with this and more knowledge of not just Christ Jesus—let along what he looked like—that I'd returned to voluntarily reading from my fiancee's collection of textbooks. Vicki—as I've mentioned before—was working on her master's degree in Divinity at Claremont School of Theology. Those books of hers were rather advanced for a simpleton such as myself, and provided me no direct answers. After all, I had no plans at becoming a bishop, as Vicki was.

I continued to prepare for our Thursday night group meetings, using both Professor Lau's advice at reading Pierre Teilhard de Chardin, and also Vicki's textbooks, to better put my thoughts together; not just from a theological standpoint, but a Christian one.

Damien recalled for me one Thursday night in particular, when he was asked to tell the group what it was that he actually believed in regarding Jesus the Christ. This was a rather long-winded conversation which, for the most part, repeated everything you have already read in these previous chapters. However, what was of interest, was even though Damien had spent months researching and debating with others, he still found if difficult to formulate a concise statement of faith in general.

The events leading up to that particular group meeting might have caused him some amount of distraction. When Damien had arrived at

Vicki's college apartment to pick up his soon-to-be-wife, he was greeted at her door by her "scantily –clad and radiant beauty," along with a deep and wet kiss. She seductively invited him inside, which was a break from their norm. Naturally, he was well pleased, yet a little confused, and stated as much:

Were we going to group—which we never missed—or were we going to make a child? My first impulse, thanks to my Asperger's syndrome, would've been to turn away or refuse to enter her place; because I didn't like being late to important events. But, I allowed her to dictate the rest of the evening.

As it turned out, they cuddled for a spell on her futon, then—once fully dressed (or redressed)—went to group at Henrietta's… and somehow managed to arrive there on time. How they did this, Damien still doesn't know, since their foreplay seemed "to've lasted for hours." Time always seemed limitless when they were together, and moved at a tediously slow pace when they were apart and in wanting of each other.

On the following day, arriving at Sam's office, Damien quickly prayed that Sam would help him work out a "solid defense" of his position about the nature of God and Christ. He felt certain that his employer and friend held the same contention that Damien did about the many roles of Jesus. Damien knew—most of all—he needed to sharpen his debating skills.

Walking into Sam's office, Damien was pleased to find the man alone and not that busy—yet. Damien began to share with him the events of his latest group meeting, as well as what he was doing at Cypress College. Not that Dr. Reily minded the interruption and distraction, he listened and agreed that Damien needed to learn more about the skill of defending his opinions, especially in what it was he believes in.

Sam got out of his chair and found a self-help book on his rarely touched bookshelf, then handed it off to Damien.

What's this? The Missing Link by Sydney Banks? Damien asked, reading the cover out loud. *I tell you that I need help with defending my opinions about God, and you give me a book about man evolving from monkeys?*

"No, Damien. It's not <u>that</u> missing link. No, Sydney Banks writes about the power and source of thought. The origins of our thoughts, and how to better organize them. I believe you'll find it extremely helpful."

The rest of the workday went particularly smooth—even for a Friday—and Damien felt a certain calmness within himself. In between helping patients and answering the phones, he read the first two chapters of Syd Bank's book. Although, on the words regarding positive thought, only one subject kept coming to Damien's mind: Vicki.

I thought about Vicki a lot, and I can honestly say that I felt her presence beside me the rest of that day. What's more important, was that when I called her at our usual phone times—in between her classes—she told me that she felt my presence with her the whole day long. That was very moving. I believed that we were spiritually connected for a long time, not just because we were "soul mates" or lovers, but because we were humans.

My body and your body are just containers. They are physical. Your body is not who you really are. According to Sydney Banks, other writers, and even in Scripture, mankind's ability to think, our self-awareness, and life energy are all who we are spiritually. The physical body is just a tool... a machine. Sure it's a highly functional one with good mobility and an initially strong immune system, but it's still just a vehicle, like a car, used to transport the real you around and to interact with this world.

The more I read of Sydney Banks' book, the more I wanted to visit our local library... which I did as soon as I got off work. While I partly understood the differences between the physical and spiritual worlds in which we live, and the mythological "soul" we each are supposed to have, I never thought on the level that our bodies are merely a shell—a biological, organic host.

According to another author named Ami Chen Mills-Naim, we could not even be alive without the lifeforce, that "spark" inside each of us, because that spiritual energy isn't just a part of who we really are: it is us. I quickly became convinced that the source of that energy in singular; we do not have individual sources of lifeforce, nor some sort of separate—and invisible—battery packs. No, I now believe that our spiritual energy flows from the exact same place and person: whether you want to call this source "God" or "Our Father" or whichever, we are all receiving a lifeforce from this one source.

And, finally, if this is all true: that our energies are coming from and flowing from that same source; then we are all connected to that source of life… all of us… all at the same time. It is through this link that I am convinced that we humans are all connected to one another's spiritual side. This is why when I was thinking of Vicki, so intently, she could feel my presence. Souls are not independent of each other, only our misconstrued identity is.

So, when you ask me <u>who</u> the real Jesus is—whether he is Jesus the Christ, the Savior, the humble servant, or our Lord? The answer is simple: Jesus is us. Christ, like the Holy Spirit, lives through us and shares our lifeforce. The spiritual provides you with the same energy that gives me life, gives my friends life, and gives Christ life. We are all connected through the energy which provides existence.

n much of modern philosophy the physical and the mental have been drastically separated. Descartes taught us to think of them as metaphysically different. For [Alfred North] Whitehead, it would be misleading to ignore the difference, but this difference should be recognized as two aspects of every occasion, every nexus, every society, and every event. ~ John B. Cobb, Jr., *Whitehead Word Book*

CHAPTER FORTY-FIVE

A New Family Is Born

Vicki and Damien were spending a lot more time together now that they had Damien's ramshackle—and tiny—studio apartment, which was the best he could afford while working at Sam's office and going to school. However, in all honesty, Vicki did not feel very safe there, and they only spent a few overnight stays at his place. She would stay at her college apartment on the weeknights, both because it was hers and because she needed to get up early for classes.

Our life as a couple blossomed and things made it clear to both Vicki and I that we were being drawn together as life partners. We spent weekends together and planned for the beginning of our joined lives, a marriage to last for all time!

Our spiritual and emotional growth was aided by our relationship with the church. There were so many ways that we participated in our Mormon church, and so many church members who had heard about engagement even before seeing that diamond ring on Vicki's finger. We'd received more congratulations than you could poke a stick at! It was both very heart-warming and spine-chilling at the same time! If we had wanted to keep it a secret, just between a few friends, it would've been quite impossible. If wishes were horses... right?

Not only did they have to make plans for their wedding, but also for what was sure to follow. They needed to sort out how they would live with each other, when they returned from their wedding and honeymoon in Michigan—that is, if they returned. Although Damien couldn't recall for me who said this first, but neither of them thought that Los Angeles County should play a part in the their future.

Vicki found out that we could make arrangements with the state housing people, that we would be a newly-wed couple, and what financial assistance we could come up with. That is, until the two of us found full-time employment. I, never in my life, thought about so many things surrounding one event. Yet, without them all, we would've gone crazy in being hurried through the steps. The parts that we have little-to-no control over, we were grateful for the assistance from my future in-laws. I felt so much love from them, more than I could ever give back…although, I did try.

We also loved Vicki's extended families, such as the small group ministry she used to attend when living in Michigan. What a wonderful group that she attended, their service included communion and strong imagery, especially of Christian symbolism. I remember clearly the first time that we were at their group, they met in a house which was fairly small, located just a few miles off the expressway. It was a snowy, winter night when I first met them, and—for a guy who lived most of his life in southern California, a winter night in Michigan was formidable dread.

Yet, as I started to say, that night was one of the most spectacular events in my Christian life. I was going to have communion and have a role in the service to boot. A significant part of the service was the imagery that they guided us through the exercise: That the bread was really the body of Christ, the fruit juice His blood.

Now, I was familiar with the notion from my very, very early years of attending Sundays at a Catholic church; in fact, just the word brought back memories I thought I'd long repressed. But, our Catholic church never gave communion the same depth of feeling and purpose that we received that night in this group's meeting.

Close your eyes, and imagine that you are about to eat something to symbolize the body of Christ. What if—through space and time—that bread would miraculously become the very flesh of Jesus…how would you feel? What would be going through your mind? At the Last Supper, or the

Lord's Supper, which is best described at Luke 22:14—explained in First Corinthians 11:23-32—the taking in of Christ's body brings judgement on those who do not recognize its meaning.

Since this was my first ever communion, I could not wrap my mind around that image at all. I figured that God could have this switcheroo happen—our bread turned into the actual flesh within our mouths—and it would be within the realm of possibilities, though I couldn't morbidly imagine such. Vicki had similar feelings; however, she looked forward to it occurring. I was so moved that I almost broke down my usual barriers and cried.

It was worse when they presented the imagery regarding the very blood of Christ. That really was something, for the blood is what gave the body life; and I already took in Christ's body. Now I had both the body and blood within me... was the living Christ going to make <u>me</u> of all people His new home? The mere thought that I was allowing Christ into my flesh meant to me that I was likewise a part of His life, an official member of His family.

Anyway, I just wanted to share with you some of my experience. Their service, following communion, which they held in that tiny home was huge. The images that they created were fantastic. They were so real for me that I could no longer hold back my tears. I cried steadily for two minutes, if not longer; I wasn't keeping track. You should have seen this little one-bedroom house in the middle of Michigan. It was far too small to contain the heart and outpouring of profound emotion from those people... that genuine church family. I honestly never wanted to leave.

Damien was so grateful for meeting the people who were a part of Vicki's life, her life's blood, if you will. His life was good, and he was just beginning to see and understand just how it was missed by his beloved Michigan bride. There was a problem with going home, as far as Damien was concerned, and that was the fact that he really didn't think that California was anywhere close to home for him.

I was country –born, or—technically—mountain-born, as you know from the very beginning of this story. For my first ten years, I lived alongside the Olympic range and believe to have absorbed the solitude and density of my childhood landscape. That is, well, before my family ruined that for me. I believe this to be true of anyone born in the country, that they incorporate with their surrounding countryside, making their souls "countrified" and rustic. I think that a real part of my problem was the fact that although I was raised and lived longer in California than in Washington, I never could fit in there comfortably—surrounded by concrete rivers and manmade lakes—due to my established foundation as a mountain boy. I just couldn't ever be citified.

Vicki was in complete agreement with me. She came out to California for only one purpose, and that was to earn her degree, which would happen that very month of our wedding. This area was not her home, and from the two decades of farm living, she would never find full comfort within the city limits of the madness call Los Angeles—no matter how long she remained. What else can I say about the life of a country girl?

In the part of the world which Vicki grew up in, I was beginning to believe that she was related to mostly everyone. All of the residents of Coleman knew Vicki, immediately recognized her—even after years of not seeing her at all. I really mean that, too. I ran into all matters of people who were related to Vicki in one way or another, or were family friends of a friend, or the business associate of a cousin. Oh well, that's small-town living for you.

Well, we both admitted to each other that we loved being there in Michigan, and desired to live either within its borders or nearby; so we could get away from the daily rat race of southern California. So, on top of everything else that was going to be happening in June, we began researching what else was available throughout the North. Vicki wanted a job with the church, and I had to finish my degree. And, of course, there was just one more factor for us to consider: my criminal history and requirements.

The answer to their combined questions came in the form of the state of Ohio. The facts that they wanted to live in a small-town environment, be near to a Mormon church or R.L.D.S. congregation, have a college Damien could go to, plus—at that time—didn't enforce sexual offenders to register to any publically-accessible database, which, as Damien researched, would vastly improve his chances at finding and maintaining employment. The cost of living in Ohio was so reasonable, that they could support themselves just fine on a single paycheck; or live comfortably if Damien only found a part-time position while continuing school.

Their unanimous decision to eventually move to Kirtland, Ohio—after getting married—was an easy one. Kirtland was the oldest remaining of Mormon settlements east of the Mississippi. This would be where they would hopefully start their new family... provided that they got married first.

During the Memorial Day weekend, the last one of May, Damien and Vicki flew to Michigan to both visit with her family and make final arrangements for the backyard ceremony. They had reserved chairs, tables, and two large party tents to cover those in attendance; while, standing in direct sunlight, Damien, Vicki, and their minister would be on a makeshift and raised platform with an arched trellis adorned with flowers and vines as the stage's centerpiece.

Everything was coming together, and we couldn't wait to get married. Unfortunately, that Sunday night, we knew that it was necessary for both of us to return to California so that we could finish what we'd started there: We both would graduate from our respective colleges. So, although we were flying back to L.A.X., we weren't returning home. No, we were leaving one home only to say good-bye to another.

At any rate, we both had things that only we could take care of. All of the preparation could never have prepared me for the miracles which were about to happen, and in quick succession:

First, I did graduate from Cypress College with my associate's degree; and—with a lot less doubt—Vicki did earn her master's degree at the Claremont School of Theology. I won't bore you with the details, since most readers can visualize a graduation ceremony without it tediously being described to them; however, I will remind you that this was the very first time that I wore a cap-and-gown, and found the experience quite emotional. My G.E.D. certificate from Huntington Beach Adult School in 1976 had merely been mailed to me without any fanfare.

Second, Sam presented me with what he called a "retirement package" bonus check—he refused to allow it be counted as a wedding gift—on my final day of working at his office. Along with the unexpected financial generosity, he handed me a wrapped present the size and dimensions of a wall calendar... which, of course, it wasn't. No, it was my favorite vinyl record of his collection: Gustav Mahler's Second Symphony. Although I gladly accepted his gift, I didn't own—nor ever did own—a turntable in order to play it. There was a lot of hidden sentiment behind that gift, the largest being that now Sam's near-perfect collection would be missing an important one.

And, third, came the final evenings which we would share with both our "Orange" and "Upland" small groups. The amount of generosity from the members of our groups, which were in the form both the physical and the emotional, were overwhelming. Henrietta's departing love and presents for us were practically smothering. However, as usual, Alan ruined the loving atmosphere of that night:

Damien was sitting next to Vicki at the "Orange" small group, listening to Dave's clarification of his beliefs to a particular topic regarding relationships with God. Alan, possibly believing that Damien wasn't paying attention, addressed the entire group, "You know, we should get some input from our relationship expert. Damien?"

Yeah?

"Dave believes that God and Jesus have a relationship, but I want to know what that means to you.?"

I believe that God is, as Charles Hartshorne once said: 'The soul of the word, and that God embraces the world in its entirety.' However, it is more than the world. God shapes all things by influencing every moment of experience, and that God is influenced by all things as the One to whom all of our hearts are open and desired to be known.

Alan shook his head, not in disagreement but frustration, "You didn't really answer my question."

"Excuse me, Alan," Vicki spoke out, "As you remember from last week, my future husband has already talked a lot about what we believe in, so I will try to fill in the gaps for you. We believe that Jesus and God are inseparable. That Jesus is the real incarnation of God on earth, and Jesus is God. We also believe that the source of anything new in life is from the Logos, the self-revealing Word and Will of God, whose incarnation is Christ Jesus, As explained in the Gospel of John, Jesus and God aren't independent, but two parts of the Trinity."

Actually, Vicki, Damien jumped in, *I believe the Trinity is larger than three. The complete relationship is the Father, the Son, the Spirit, and the Assembly. God is within us, the Christ and Holy Spirit is within us, and we are within each of them. That is the family connection. What is called the Trinity is really a 'Quad-nity' of Father, Son, Spirit, Fellowship.*

After a quiet second, Alan replied, "Now, that is deep. So deep, that I think we all are drowning! What is that statement even supposed to mean?"

Which part? Damien asked, then didn't wait for an answer. *I'm assuming that you know what 'ecological' means? The relationship between organisms and their environments? We, of course, are organisms—or in Alan's case, the parasite—and the world of Creation is our surroundings.*

"Wait!" Alan protested over some brief chuckling by the other group members, "Why do I have to be the parasite?"

Because of your ignorance towards reality. Without the knowledge of our vital relationship with one another, our spiritual link, you are an organism that exploits the environment without contributing to its survival. What is the second most important Commandment which God gave Moses.

Almost instantly, three group members answered in unison, "To love thy neighbor…"

But where in the Bible does God limit a neighbor to only human beings? I'll tell you that I've flipped all through Old Testament, the New, and The Book of Mormon, and there isn't any such limit. However, in Genesis 2:20, for a moment of consideration, the animals were considered by God as Adam's possible companions, just not for man's purposes of mating. Everything that has life is our neighbor. God is in all things, human and animal alike! We are to love all organisms as if they were family, for—regardless of their size or species—they are a part of God. Everything that has breath is our neighbor and family member.

Vicki then chimed in with, "Process Philosophy also describes our world as being ongoing, creative, and transformational, in every moment of experience of the evolving world. This isn't limited to human experience, but to all of nature. There simply is no distinction between the two."

"Well," announced Dale, "that is a lot for us to ponder about. However, it is time to bring this meeting to a close. Who wants to pray us out?"

Immediately Vicki volunteered, and led the group in a rather lengthy prayer since it was going to be her final time doing so. She included a personal thanks for the month of this group's membership and for its ongoing commitment and health. She also prayed for each member's strength and longevity, especially for those who were soon to follow Damien's earlier advice to begin their own groups. She hoped for prosperity for everyone in spreading God's Word and love. Then a final prayer that God would bless their marriage and move to Ohio.

We prayed out and retired to the kitchen, where Henrietta had several snacks awaiting us, which were tasty. She really made some wonderful pastries for the group, and loaded us full of them and coffee before sending us home. We were always so spoiled by her treats, her love, and her maternity.

The night was indeed a little tense, as I was talking Vicki's language where appropriate to the group, instead of waiting for her to initiate it. After all, she was now the "official" and professional theologian of the family, or so I thought. I didn't mean to steal the wind from her sails about the Trinity, either; although I found out along our way home that she really didn't mind. After all, we were both kleptomaniacs: she stole my heart, and I stole hers.

CHAPTER FORTY-SIX

Arrivals

Damien and Vicki flew to Michigan just a few short days after both of their graduations and only a week before their wedding. In the short time since Damien and Vicki last visited her family's farm, the bare backyard was just an area of dirt, a tractor, and dilapidated barn. Since then, the tractor had been moved out of sight, the ground tilled and replanted with seasonal flowers and flagstone walking paths, plus the eyesore barn had received a fresh coat—or three—of whitewash.

On moment, all there was, was the bare backyard including their old barn... and the next, there were a pair of party tents; underneath them were rows of empty chairs and at the front was our altar, lined with potted flowers. It was both beautiful and a miracle; God was very present on that farm. Of course, Vicki's mom, Vera, claimed it wasn't so much a miracle as it was a long overdue reason to do some landscaping.

Within minutes of our arrival at the family farm, we were at home. And this time, it was for a new birth to occur: Although we were ready for <u>our</u> day, we weren't yet for the days after. I remember waking up that 21st of June, the most wonderful day of my life, the day we wed. Without looking out the rear windows of the house, you'd think it was just another Saturday on the farm, with Victor and Vincent taking care of morning chores... that is, then came the people!

At nine a.m., inside the farmhouse were only Vicki's family—herself, parents, and brother—and Damien, who technically wasn't her family for another two hours. He had just returned to the family room to enjoy a second cup of coffee, when they came: Aunts, cousins, family friends; hairdressers, a harpist (the kind that plucks a harp, not a loathsome half-shrew, half-bird), the caterers, photographers, and bakery delivery man. Somewhere between sixty and seventy-five guests, none of whom Damien recognized at all... yet, of course, knew who he was.

I didn't know who most of these people were. They were all Vicki's relatives, or family's friends, or former classmates, or friends of former classmates, or friends of relatives; nearly all of which lived within a fifteen-mile radius of the township of Coleman. Regretfully, nobody from the states of California, Arizona, or Washington could attend. Likewise, the few relatives I did try to invite—my mother, siblings, and Grandpa—never replied to their invitations. The most interesting things was, this fact didn't even bother me; my thought were focused on the present moments, and my past didn't exist at all.

Then came our time. It was eleven o'clock, and Vicki was dressed like the Queen of Michigan, in the dress she'd expertly sewn together herself, along with help from her mom. Absolutely stunning... and the dress was nice, too. My rented suit wasn't anything worth mentioning; although, at least the suit looked better than its wearer: Much more stable and ironed out. Thankfully, I was only a complete wreck on the inside, where nobody could see, but God.

Vicki and Damien decided they would walk up the aisle together, instead of having the father of the bride escort her to the awaiting groom. Indeed, the walk was somewhat strange since neither could concentrate on doing so. His eyes couldn't be taken off of his beautiful bride without huge amounts of effort, and never remained off of her for long.

Vicki took my hand at the bottom of the basement stairs, and we walked up them, around the tents, and finally to the altar. It felt like a mile. The lady plucking away at the harp kept going and going with Johann Pachelbel's <u>Canon in D Major</u>. Without warning, Vicki and I seemed to be the only persons there—even the harpist disappeared from all existence—as we'd reached the raised-platform altar.

Yes, I know that they were all still sitting there, but they weren't in the same dimensional plane as us. Beside me, as my Best Man, was Vicki's brother, Vincent... who honestly I didn't know all that well. Next to him, was Vicki's father, Victor, as my first groomsman. I couldn't tell you the names of Vicki's bridesmaids to save my life!

I remember much of the service, but not all that was said. We repeated out vows as they were told to us by our minister; I have no idea if I pronounced any of it correctly. I only barely remember when he asked us to put the rings on each other's finger, and how I felt wearing mine for the very first time—all fifty pounds of it—and how she looked with the wedding ring on. I never saw anything as beautiful... and the ring was nice, too.

Then, it was as if I could hear the very voice of God saying, "I now pronounce you man and wife... you may kiss you bride." We looked at each other for a silent moment, unable to move, then Vicki's own father spoke out, "Go on, son!" and we kissed passionately.

Then came the most beautiful words on earth, "Ladies and gentlemen, it my honor to present to you... Mr. and Mrs. Damien Lartigue." That was the moment when I truly realized what we had done. We had finally broken the Collins family curse, and gave birth to something completely new for the both of us. And so ended out personal/private worlds!

Vicki and Damien had to forgo any expense towards a honeymoon in lieu of returning one final time to California. They would be moving that very weekend, driving practically cross-country—approximately 80% of its width—with all of their belongings loaded into a U-Haul trailer attached to Damien's car. Mrs. Vicki—as she was now nicknamed—would sell her older vehicle for some much needed travelling money.

Indeed, we would be <u>leaving</u> California—the opposite of most Midwesterner's dreams—to being a new life in Ohio. The fact was, we were to start a marriage with a completely blank slate, no familiarity at all with the area nor its locals; yet, we had an undying zest for a Christ-filled and centered life. Thanks be to God for new beginnings.

Tell me, Love, Damien asked on their flight back to L.A.X., "Are you glad that we're about to move to Ohio? Kirtland, that is?"

"You know it, Mr. Lartigue." Vicki found unique pleasure in saying his new surname. "I know I need to free myself of this huge mess of a city. It's no place to raise children around all of this wildlife. Not even any natural rivers to play in, only concrete ones. You know how much I hate leaving home."

This is why we're moving. Ohio isn't but six hours from that place you fondly know and love: Lartigue Wood Acres. We'll be nearby without being right on your mom's and dad's doorstep.

"Yeah, I'm so glad that you wanted to live near Kirtland before you met me."

Actually, I was going to start in Navoo, Illinois, then work my way backwards from there. You know, follow the path of the early settlers, but in reverse.

"Yup, honey," Vicki chuckled out, "you always were a little backwards."

Unfortunately, the flight attendant interrupted Damien—with an announcement about 'on final approach'—before he could come up with any witty comebacks. They had arrived in Los Angeles for the final time.

Both of the newlyweds had some final details and packing to tend to before their weekend move. These included: some groceries for their road trip to buy, lots of laundry to clean and pack, bulky furniture and mattresses to sell or donate to the shelter; plus Damien needed to go and visit Sam one last time—both for a final good-bye and to collect the rest of his personal belongings left there when he moved into his studio apartment.

I also still had a copy of Sam's house key. Having to return that to Sam and the symbolism of this one act was a moving one to be sure. I had so much to thank this man for. Just as Christ Jesus is the Savior of my soul, Dr. Sam Reily is the savior of my very existence! Not only did Sam lead me to the church which worked best for me—and therefore to Christ—he saw a hidden value within me when others didn't or wouldn't. He generously opened his home, his work, and his life to me when I had nothing, and no means of ever reimbursing with anything but some housework.

Saying good-bye was never easy for either Sam or Damien, but it was so very important to end things. Sam had known Damien since he was just an odd teenaged-patient at his work, the mental hospital. Now the little boy had finally grew up and matured... although it took quite a bit longer than most to do so. No, this almost forty-year-old married man on his doorstep had earned the right to live a full and complete life with this new mate of his, which Sam acknowledged as really of God's choosing.

Finally, the day had come that these newlyweds would "hit the road" and drive to Ohio—approximately twenty-four hundred miles of highways, freeways, and interstates. Both of them felt the overwhelming desire to get on their way home. Leaving California was the only subject on Damien's mind; while Vicki still had quite a few good-byes of her own, mostly with classmates a year or two behind her in graduating, as well as instructors.

I joined her in a final visit to Claremont School of Theology, both at the campus apartments and the Administration building. She'd been a student there for so long, that most of the staff knew her by sight and by name. Since the school semester was over—it was June 26th—nearly everyone had left on summer vacation; only a skeleton crew of instructors and students remained. One such workaholic was none other than the one person at this college I was personally hoping to see: Dr. John Cobb, Jr. He was likewise happy to see the two of us.

"Mr. Collins, Miss Lartigue! It's such a pleasure to see you," the professor greeted.

"Actually," Vicki politely corrected. "It's mister and <u>mistress</u> now, Dr. Cobb." She lifted her left hand to prominently display her two rings.

And, Damien added, *I decided to take <u>her</u> last name, rather than the other way around. You know, breaking with tradition.*

"Yes," Dr. Cobb replied. "The two of you are quite the rebels, aren't you? He rhetorically remarked with a wide smile. "So, what brings you to my shanty?" *In defense of the university, I should point out that John had a rather nice office, albeit, just not enough bookshelves nor flat surfaces for all of his literature and stacks of correspondences and forms.*

We're leaving California and moving to Ohio. We wanted to say good-bye and to thank you for all of the time and help that—

"There's no need to thank me," Dr. Cobb interrupted, "Especially not you, Damien. I've immensely enjoyed our talks together. You have a fine grasp of Whitehead's concepts... I appreciate the insight you've provided from a young student's perspective. Believe or not, Damien, you've inspired me towards my mext project... It'll be a commentary to help beginners discover process theology, and tackle Whitehead's book."

I—I've inspired you? Damien was flabbergasted. Dr. Cobb, you're the one whose done all of the inspiring. Learning about process philosophy and theology have changed my life forever. I finally have a crystal clear opinion of God and Christ which works best for me. Thank you so incredibly much for everything you've written and done for me!

"Like I said, there's no need. Instead, thank God. It is by God's will that we found each other. Oh! And here," he handed Vicki a hardcover book with the professor's name as author. "It's not much of a wedding present, I'm afraid, but it is my latest."

"I'll only accept it," she said with a smile, "if you autograph it."

Without hesitation, Dr. Cobb pulled open a desk drawer, "Where's my pen?"

We were heading towards "the ten" highway, going east. Although our original route would take us north of Phoenix, on a direct line with Albuquerque; however we were going to head southeast towards Tucson for a rather important detour. And no... it wasn't to visit who you're probably thinking of, whom also just so happens to live there.

Hon, Damien asked after passing the Palm Springs area. *Did you still want to see your friend, Martha?*

"Yes. I was just about to ask you to head us to Tucson. I called her before we left, and we'll be making her place our first night stop. How's that sound?"

That's just fine with me. Whatever we can save on motel money. Plus, I want this trip to be as rewarding as possible. That's what they say, anyway, isn't it?

"Huh? That's what who says?" Vicki looked puzzled.

That life is a journey... and getting there is half the fun.

"Alright, you're getting philosophical on me. And we still haven't even left California yet. Vicki kissed her husband on the cheek. "Thank you."

'There's no need,' he replied, saying this in his best imitation of Dr. Cobb's voice, *'to thank me,' I'm just the guy behind the steering wheel.*

"And you're doing a mighty good job at it... getting us on this long journey of life, where we'll be having <u>half</u> as much fun."

Hey! Damien protested, *Now you're misquoting me. We won't be having 'half as much fun'... we are on this long road home, where getting home is the real experience. I've been on this long road since birth. Hitting detour after detour, a flat tire here, an accident there. I made several wrong turns at the wrong intersections, until I finally decided to let Christ Jesus take the wheel and steer me where I needed to go. Through prayer, I was taken to you, my love. And now, both of our hearts are telling us that this road, right here before us, is the correct one to follow.*

Vicki quite possibly never loved this man any more than she did at that very moment. His short sermon was full of obvious symbology which she caught onto immediately. Damien didn't see this two-thousand mile trip as just a long drive, but as a representation of his greatest lifelong desire: to finally be at the end of his search—finally be at <u>his</u> home: Heaven.

A calming sense of pure peace washed over Damien and Vicki for the next couple of hours until they approached their last pit stop within California, the town of Blythe. It was hard for Damien to ignore the irony of this moment, as he pulled their vehicle off the highway towards a gas station. There in the distance stood the watch towers and other buildings of Chuckawalla Valley State Prison, the last such prison he'd resided in and paroled from.

There I was, about to finally leave the state of California, and what is the very last structure I see, but the prison I'd spent my final years of incarceration at. I didn't know what to make of this: Was I being reminded of the fact that I used to be a prisoner, or that my criminal history would haunt me regardless of the hundreds of miles I drove away? Maybe God wanted me to see that place one last time as encouragement that I'd never be a prisoner ever again, not to the state of California nor to sin. I believe God meant the latter of these, even though I wasn't likely to return to this state anytime soon.

It was indeed an interesting time driving with the woman of my life.

Partly because we were each other's captive audience and never ran out of subjects to discuss, which worked out nicely for a four-day trip. I couldn't have a better navigator both in that car and in my life. Vicki never ceased to fascinate me, I never found our conversations boring, even when the general topic would bore any educated scholar straight to a whisky bottle. No, Vicki mesmerized my mind and soul whenever we spoke about anything at all.

"So," Vicki started as they got back onto the highway, "while we are in Tucson, you want to look up your mother and brother? You know, visit them?"

Goodness, no. Damien sternly replied, then softened his tone of voice. *I mean, my mother hasn't been my mother in so long, she doesn't really deserve such a title. However, according to Scripture we are to honor our parents for being who they are... but nowhere does it say we have to 'like' them.*

Damien, I know how you've felt abandoned by her, and because of that I can understand your displeasure towards her. But she still is your mother, and—well, I—if I were your mother, I'd want to know whatever became of my son."

If you were my mother, you wouldn't have ever abandoned me. You're too decent and kindhearted of a person to have done something like that. In fact, you'll someday become the ideal of all mothers everywhere.

This compliment, naturally, made Vicki blush several shades of red. A quiet moment later, after Damien veered left to catch Highway 8 south to Tucson, she asked, "Tell me something, 'Dee.' Have you spent some time on the question of children? Because I have. A lot."

As have I, Damien admitted. *Vicki, I absolutely want one... maybe a pair of kids, so they'll have a lifelong companion, like you and your brother, Vincent, have. It's something I always wished I had.*

"So tell me... boy or girl?"

Girl, Damien replied without hesitation. *I want the advantage that girls tend to grow up more mature than boys, and faster, and I will need to become used to raising children in a Christian way, before a second one, especially if it's a boy.*

"You are learning some good things already." Vicki wrapped her left arm around his shoulders, "I agree; I want a pair. But, I think we'll do just fine if the first is a boy, because you'll be a great dad."

So, tell me something, Mrs. Vicki. Why did you bring this up now? Are we pregnant?

"We?" I like that you men think the pregnancy involves you." She laughed out loud. "Besides bringing two pillows and a blanket to Lamaze classes, maybe buying ice cream at three-in-the-morning... you men get off easy. But, no really. I'm not. I'm just thinking that it should happen around our second or third year as a new couple. That we shouldn't rush into it."

Well, that's rather cool. I want to get to know you as my wife, long before we bring any children into the mix. Let's get used to being married, at least for two years, before we start buying any diapers. He smiled at her, then back to safe driving. Did I tell you that I love you, yet, today?

"I, um... I don't remember. Could you remind me?"

Sure! I love you, Vicki Lartigue!

"I never get tired of hearing that."

Several miles after this, they arrived in Tucson, Arizona; the first leg of their journey to Ohio... their journey towards their lives together.

CHAPTER FORTY-SEVEN

Finding Ohio

Martha was a middle-aged friend of Vicki's mother, Vera, who worked together at a convenience store in Coleman. Vera wasn't there long, only for a few months while earning some extra holiday spending cash. However, during those short weeks, Vera grew an unbreakable bond with the much-younger Martha. Despite their distance apart, the two friends remained in near-constant contact.

Boy was that stop at Martha's place the right choice. Both of us were road tired and once we arrived at Martha's house—a place Vicki had only seen before in pictures—we were warmly greeted by this wonderful, delightful woman. A night at her house was just what the doctor ordered.

Vicki had called Martha before we left California, then again when we stopped in Blythe. Thanks to those calls, Martha not only had a bedroom all prepared for us, but also a home-cooked meal and dessert waiting for us. And by waiting for us, I mean that she'd timed it perfectly and placed it all arranged on the table. It was such a pleasant surprise for two people she—herself—had never met in-person before. This banquet and bed were our wedding gift from this sweet Christian woman and recent widow.

Damien and Vicki, although without any real deadline, decided to only spend the one night at Martha's and not to be any further burden. In the morning, Damien surprised the two women by being the first one up and in the kitchen. He was halfway through whipping up a hollandaise sauce for eggs Benedict, when the home owner appeared.

"Good heavens. What's going on in here?"

You surprised Vicki and I with dinner last night. I thought the best I could do would be to handle breakfast. Do you have any Canadian bacon?

"No, I don't believe so. But there's some smoked ham in the meat drawer." She joined Damien at this side, eagerly wanting not just to help, but to take over his entire operation.

Just then, Vicki came out of the guest bathroom. "Good heavens. We've been married for less than a week," she tried hard not to laugh, "and you're already poaching another woman's eggs."

*I—*Damien actually dropped his spatula onto the floor. *I'm, uh, I don't have a comeback for that one.*

"Sweetie," Vicki stepped forward and removed the mixing bowl Damien had cradled in his left elbow. "Why don't you relax and let Martha—"

Hon, seriously, I got this. Nothing would please me more, than to cook the two of you these eggs, Damien stated to both women. And, sure enough, they stepped away and allowed the chef to regain his domain.

Coincidentally, the hollandaise sauce came out absolutely elegant.

The next leg of their trip would take then through Albuquerque, into the panhandle of Texas—where they had lunch—and into Wichita, Kansas. Although Vicki believed that they should stop in Kansas City for the night, Damien pushed onward to St. Louis, Missouri. Vicki understood Damien's determination, they both wanted to get to Ohio in a hurry; although, she preferred to "get there in one piece."

This second stop was much needed, as our bodies were aching terribly from the countless hours of driving with only brief stops for fuel and our empty stomachs. We spent the night at a nice-enough motel just outside the main city. And in the morning, neither of us wanted to get out of bed...so, we didn't. At least not right away, and rather exhausted ourselves all over again.

We had an early lunch underneath the famous Gateway Arch, but I was too anxious to sit still...I really wanted to get back on the road. We only had five-hundred-sixty miles—give or take a few—left to drive. Vicki was less impulsive to get back into that passenger's seat again. The previous two-thousand-plus miles made her entire body throb in misery. Every time I mentioned getting back in the car, she winced and tried to change the subject...

"But look... it's so lovely here. And we'd already expected the trip to take four days. Let's do some tourist stuff."

No, Vicki, Damien contended. *Yes, it's nice here, but it's not home. We'll come back and visit. I promise. But for now, let's get established in Kirtland, first and foremost.*

"Sweetie, I know you're right. But we're here now and there really isn't any rush to get to Ohio."

No, Honey. The sooner we get this done, the happier we'll be. Besides, everything I own is in that car and trailer. I'll never be comfortable with it all just sitting there, where thieves can get at it.

"Oh, al-l-lright," she finally gave in. "But I'm driving."

They followed map directions all the way to Cleveland, and then simply followed the highway signs to Kirtland. As things would have it, they arrived in the state of Ohio during the apex of their strawberry festivals. Mrs. Vicki and 'Dee' didn't do much talking on the road that day. Both we so sick and tired of sitting in those car seats, listening to the same country music songs over the radio, and the chafing to their shoulders from those darn seat-belts really started to burn.

Finally, there it was... the sign welcoming them to the town of Kirtland, Ohio, and the tall steeple of the Mormon church. It was in Kirtland that the Latter-Day Saints—the original group of settlers led by Joseph Smith—built their second or third temple. The Mormons, in case I didn't mentioned it before, had already been chased out of New York, Pennsylvania, and Missouri as heretics and outlaws. They were persecuted everywhere they tried to establish themselves, and in constant exile and exodus, until reaching Utah.

Across the street of the temple was the Kirtland Congregation Building and the preserved house of Sidney Rigden, one of the founding fathers. It was in that house that the Mormon church would put Damien and Vicki up, in a rent-free room until they were able to stabilize their feet on solid ground. For that, they were so very grateful to the congregation.

It wasn't long before we arrived in Kirtland before Vicki was hired by the church's Visiting Center. It was a good start, but we both knew it was embarrassing for someone with her background and degree in Divinity to be a tour guide and information booth attendant. However, she knew more about our new hometown within a week than I <u>ever</u> did about any of California.

In August, I started going to school again, at the University of Ohio, Cleveland. I was filled with confidence by the fact that all that I needed to do was register for my classes and maintain a 3.8 G.P.A. or better. It felt real good being accepted to several universities, then to have the choice of a top-drawer school like C.S.U. to attend and someday earn my degree from. Vicki was so proud of her husband's freedom—slightly jealous at times—to choose between schools and attend the Cleveland campus. It was near to our home.

I knew, prior to leaving California, that the two things that I really needed regarding my furthered education, these were: patience and common sense. I knew we couldn't live comfortably on just Vicki's paychecks, that I would need to hold down a job. Although school had been a priority, since I didn't have any friends in Ohio that would hire me part-time in their doctor's office, I would actually have to find one on my own.

Damien was blessed by God in that his wife understood how school came first, then he'd look for a job the best one could around a busy schedule. He was offered a job at a restaurant which he turned down because of his class schedule conflicted with the hours they needed him. This frustrated him to no end, until Vicki finally made a decision... Damien would not get a job.

Our life was smoothing out fairly well and without trauma. Vicki was hired to teach fifth and sixth graders at the local elementary school, while I focused completely on my degree. A few months passed us by like a soothing mid-summer breeze—only that it was now October. Vicki and I were doing well to the point that we were able to rent a two-bedroom apartment in Bedford Heights, a small town just south of Cleveland, northwest of Kent.

This move to Bedford Heights proved to be to our advantage. I picked that I would change campuses and would finish my schooling at Kent State

U., which had more classes. I also found an ideal job at a C.V.S. Pharmacy, bringing in enough for us to pay the rent twice, if we chose to. Vicki was loving her job as a school teacher, even though her dreams of becoming a bishop someday still lingered in her mind—after all, this was her entire reason for moving out to California and going to Claremont School of Theology. But she was so very happy and satisfied.

A couple of years of living in Bedford Heights passed rather quickly... and before Damien knew it, he graduated from Kent State with his bachelor's degree, at the age of forty-two. Although he was certainly the oldest of his graduating class, this did not discourage him from walking across the stage at this ceremony.

That same year, Vicki and Damien were nominated as delegates to the R.L.D.S. World Church Conference at the temple in Independence, Missouri. For Damien, his life was taking on new dimensions as both a church member and a husband. Soon, he was going to be a father.

In January 2000, we once again talked about having a child, and Vicki thought of setting this dream into motion that spring or summer, since she did want to have a visible "baby bump" while wearing a bikini. She would stop taking birth control pills starting on April 1st. Life for the Lartigue family would have a completely new meaning once we introduced a new mouth to feed, a new life to nourish... not only with food, but also with the loving Spirit of God. We both prayed that God would someday bless us with a child.

Also during that January of 2000, Damien and Vicki had moved from their two-bedroom apartment into a three-bedroom condo which featured a mortgage, not a lease—something neither of them ever had before. Thanks to his college degree, Damien applied for several job positions with the count of Cuyahoga—a population of just under 1.4 million—either as a drug-and-alcohol abuse counselor, a co-dependency counselor, or—as strange as this sounds—a relationship counselor. For a guy who spent half of his life having trouble building friendships or maintaining them, Damien was looking to soon be considered an expert at them, as well as to be paid rather nicely for doing what he enjoyed: bettering lives.

I started to incorporate everything I'd learned during my development.

The books I'd read in my leisure time from authors like Dr. Cobb, Alfred North Whitehead, C. Robert Mesle, Pierre Teilhard de Chardin, Rick Warren, Sydney Banks, and just so many others, truly helped me with my goals of becoming a counselor.

Through the combination of Whitehead's process theology and Banks's psychology of mind, I came to realize that absolute self-awareness comes from how God exists in all things, how God provides all things with life energy, and that we are not of the flesh we walk around in… but we are the thoughts which flow from the higher realm where God exists. Everything else in life is inconsequential and frivolous, based on either our pasts or our own worst enemy: the ego.

I believe that we all want satisfaction in our lives, for our lives to actually mean something. Many of us want to be remembered for the people we were after we pass on… while some of us couldn't care less if we're remembered, we only want what we do today to be talked about tomorrow. My vote is for the latter of these, because the more often this happens, the former will actually become a reality! A truly satisfied life comes when we focus on the needs of others.

That March, the night before St. Patrick's Day, there came an expected knock at our door. Vicki was in our kitchen, brewing large amounts of coffee and slicing up some finger-style sandwiches. So, I got up from the couch and turned the TV off, then opened the front door. The two people standing there were absolute strangers to Vicki and I, yet we expected them and welcomed them inside all the same.

Hello, I'm Damien, he greeted his guests.

"Hi, Are—are we <u>too</u> early?" the woman asked nervously.

"No, no," Vicki came around the kitchen island and offered a hand to shake, "you're right on time."

Please, Damien urged his two guests, have a seat. With that said, the doorbell rang again.

Looks like you came at just the right time, Damien suggested to the guests already seated. If you came any later you'd have to sit on the piano bench, and it's rather uncomfortable. Trust me.

"So," the man asked, "what's tonight all about?"

Before Damien could answer, he became busy shaking more hands of people he either just barely knew from the area or didn't know at all. A total of three men and four women had arrived. None of them happened to be members of their church; which was exactly what Damien was hoping for.

Welcome, welcome everybody. Please have a seat. My gosh, is that another car pulling up? We're going to need some more chairs. Anyway, hi. I'm Damien and this is my wife, Vicki. Welcome to our home, and to the first meeting of the 'Bedford Heights' group. Shall we begin?

> One respect in which God's creative love is adventurous has already been discussed: since God's creative activity is persuasive, not controlling, it is a love that takes risks. Hence, each divine creative impulse into the world is adventurous, in that God does not know what the result will be....
>
> The point is that God's own life is an adventure, for the novel enjoyments that are promoted among the creatures are then the experiences providing the material for God's own enjoyment.
> ~ John B. Cobb, Jr. & David Ray Griffin, *Process Theology: An Introductory Expostion*

CHAPTER FORTY-EIGHT

Unexpected U-Turns

Regrettably, even with all of these positive events occurring in his life—the nice home in Ohio, the small group he'd started, even the likely prospect at a county job as a counselor—Damien's twisting road of turmoil was far from straightened out. In fact, a rather sharp, hairpin turn was directly ahead! Whether it was the application for a mortgage or a job with the county, unforeseen trouble from Damien's past had located him.

On the second Friday of April 2000, Damien showed up for work at CVS Pharmacy as regular as always. He'd worked through the ranks of stock and cashier over the previous year, and was considered a "shift supervisor," one position below assistant manager. Damien always made himself available to work any overtime, and he received praises from his bosses... none of whom knew Damien would be quitting the instant he might be hired by the county.

I had already had my first of the usual two job interviews, and to the best of my knowledge, the other three candidates—based on their very young ages—probably didn't have the college degrees I had. I was merely buying time while working at CVS. I knew that at any moment I'd be called-in for that all-important final interview.

My mood was also particularly high because Vicki and I had just held our third Thursday night group meeting at our house, which now had fourteen members. We were discussing several local and neighborhood issues and how we thought things could be improved. We talked about how things used to be different, and touched a little bit on personal feelings. Baby steps. So far, none of them knew I was leading them towards living a true Christian lifestyle, nor my year-from-now goal of encouraging them to seek earnest salvation!

Halfway through his morning shift that Friday, Damien's name was called over the store's public address system's speakers, asking him to come to the Customer Service desk; which seemed normal enough since he was called there many times throughout his shift to approve a customer's merchandise return.

One of the two plainclothes detectives standing there showed Damien his badge, before asking: "Excuse me, are you Damien Collins?"

Automatically, Damien's defenses went on red alert; nobody in the state of Ohio knew him as a 'Collins' and at the sight of that police badge he became fidgety.

I—I used to be. Damien Collins, I mean. I changed m-m-my name when I got married. It's Lartigue, now.

"Well, sir, we're going to need you to come with us."

Uhh, but I'm h-here. I'm workin'.

"Sir, we have the authority to legally detain you, unless you're willing to voluntarily come with us." The detective's initially polite attitude was hardening.

Um, okay, let m-me jus' let my manager know and, to grab m-my coat.

"Actually, I'll grab your coat, if you show us where it is."

Am...am I in trouble for something? Damien asked.

"That remains to be seen, Mr. Collins."

Damien was escorted to and seated in the back of their unmarked Ford sedan. He hadn't been handcuffed, yet, which seemed to be a positive sign that they simply needed some questions answered...or that this was a possible case of mistaken identity. Although, once the short and swift ride to their police station was over, out came those dreaded manacles.

"Please turn around and face the car—"

Wait! I thought I wasn't under arrest, Damien complained.

"This," the detective referred to his shiny handcuffs, "is only for your protection." Which was, technically, a half-truth: Damien was cuffed primarily for the officers' protection, not just his.

Damien was quickly brought down hallways and into an interrogation room small enough to double as a public voting booth for someone in a wheelchair. There were only two chairs—his bolted to the floor—and a single wooden shelf mounted to the wall for note-taking or a cup of coffee to sit on. Instead of either of these, the detective placed a micro-cassette audio tape recorder, clicking the bright red button.

"Today is Friday, April 14th. Detective Nichols and Morehead. We're with suspect Damien Collins-Lartigue. Warrant number—" and he spouted out a series of seemingly random numbers and letters typed on a form he held. Finally, this same detective took his seat and stated slowly, "We really only have one question for you Mr. Lartigue. Are you the same Damien Collins formerly of Huntington Beach and Claremont, California?"

Well, yeah, I did live in Huntington Beach with—

"That's all we needed," he interrupted purposely. "Anything else you have to say, Mr. Collins, should come after we tell you what's going on and your rights."

O-o-oka… he nervously responded.

"For the record," the man spoke towards the tape recorder, "the suspect Damien Collins-Lartigue has offered a confession of identity, towards the outstanding arrest warrant faxed to our Cleveland office from California."

The other detective spoke while paraphrasing from a piece of paper he now held up, "Mr. Collins, you are being sought in Claremont, California, for violation of penal code section 290, failure to register as a sexual offender, for leaving the state of your felony parole conditions without notification, and for evading arrest. You are—"

Wait! What? I've done none of that! I mailed the Claremont police a letter telling them that I was leaving California. I-I even have the, you know, that small green postcard they mail back to you. I—.

"Sir, sir. That's an argument between you and the state of California. Today our job is to—"

But this is a mistake! Just some clerical error or something. We, Vicki and I... we gave them the address of our church in Kirtland. I—

"Again, sir. Please calm down. Your legal fight is with California, not us. We are only making arrangements for you to get there—"

To California?! Oh, no... no, no... I got work, got group...

"Sir," the other, possibly more experienced detective spoke. "Let me explain how extradition works. Our job is to hold you because there's been an arrest warrant signed and filed. We are not sending you to California; they have asked us to detain you until they come to pick you up. That is the extent of our job. If, however, the—" he paused to read the unfamiliar city's name again, "—the Claremont police fail to pick you up within fifteen business days you will be released by us."

So, if they don't come, I'll get to go home? Damien asked and the detective nodded. *How about bail? Can I get bailed out? He needlessly asked, even though he privately knew they likely couldn't afford any amount.*

"No, Mr. Collins." Then he proceeded to recite a slightly-modified version of the standard Miranda rights, substituting instances of the word 'arrest' with 'detained.'

Sitting there on my assigned rack at Cuyahoga County Jail, I was constantly waiting to hear my name being called to be released. Whether it was released back to my home with Vicki, or released to the Claremont police officers who would be escorting me back to the place—the state—I was dead certain that I would never be seeing again as long as I breathed. I can't express in words the depth of my sadness and oftentimes frustration. I was back in jail, maybe going back to California, for a crime which I was certain that I did not commit!

Memories of our final week as California residents played backwards and forwards within my mind. Our last gas stop in Blythe and that ominous view of Chuckawalla Valley State Prison on the way out of the state... now I knew it was a warning of events to come, yet I'd ignored it then.

What I knew I hadn't ignored nor forgotten to do was what I now seemed doomed to be convicted of. As a registered sex offender, I had to update my registration information—my living address—each year or whenever that addressed changed, for as long as I stayed within California. I was last registered residing at my shabby studio apartment in Seal Beach, just north of Huntington Beach, and legally obligated to notify the Claremont police before I moved anywhere, including leaving the state... which I had done.

Although I kept the nature of my violation private or fictionalized it from my fellow inmates—nearly every day in county jail I'd hear the question, "So what are you in for?"—none of them thought that the police way out in California would spend the amount of money needed to fly two cops to Cleveland, perhaps stay a night someplace, then fly three people back out there... all just for a simple parole violation. I, of course, hid the facts that I was no longer on parole when I'd left California.

At the first chance possible to use the phones, which turned out to be a full twenty-four hours later, Damien called Vicki. Her voice was understandably in a panic! It had taken her three hours and twice as many phone calls to finally find out why Damien had not come home from work the previous night—she'd even called the local hospital to see if he was a patient there. Damien could not recall for me exactly how Vicki figured out he was in jail, only the following snippet of that highly-emotional collect call:

They're saying I didn't tell the Claremont police that I was moving to Ohio.

"B-But," Vicki stuttered a bit, "you d-did. I remember you writing the letter. You even asked me for the address of the church in Kirtland. I had to look it up."

Yeah, I remember that, too. We looked up their address online.

"Did... didn't, um, you send that letter certified, right?"

Yes, I went to the post office near Sam's office and paid extra. I told these cops here that I got the green receipt card back when the Claremont police received my certified letter.

"You know, I remember seeing that same postcard in a box when we moved into the condo. I swear I'll look everywhere for it, Honey."

Oh, that would be great! You have to find that card. It'll prove that

I followed their rules. That I told them I was to move out of California.

"Well, it won't really prove all that... only that you sent them something. I'm going to start looking right away. Oh, Dee, this needs to be just a stupid mistake. I need you home, with me."

That's all this is, just a mistake. Some clerical error. We didn't do anything wrong, Vicki. If anything, I'll get a free trip to California out of this, may say hi to Henrietta and Dr. Cobb again.

"I don't want you to. Not without me. What are we going to do?! They could drag this on for weeks."

It won't take that long, my love. They'll realize it's just a simple mistake. You'll see.

During the following two weeks in Cuyahoga County Jail, Vicki visited her husband every chance she had—each non-contact visit lasting only one hour—even taking time off from her work at the elementary school. Damien also called her several times each day, until they realized that each fifteen-minute collect call cost nearly ten dollars! They agreed to cut visits and calls down to only twice per week.

A few of their calls dealt with "best case" scenarios involving Damien not getting picked up by the Claremont police before the deadline; while one or two involved Vicki possible flying out to California, or—heaven forbid!—need to move out there and await a lengthy prison sentence. Their most painful conversation happened ten days into his incarceration; this call centered on her impossibility of finding that green postcard proving that Damien factually sent the certified letter.

On the morning of what Damien perceived as his sixteenth—and therefore "illegal" or "one too many"—day in custody, he voiced his outrage that the arresting detectives lied to him. That he was told he'd be released if nobody from California arrived. On several occasions, Damien demanded to see the warden of the county jail, which fell upon deaf ears.

Finally, that evening, one correctional officer from another part of the facility overheard Damien's rants for freedom: "Hey! Settle down!"

But I'm not supposed to be here! It's been sixteen days!

"Hey! Calm down and start over. You're an extradition case, right?"

Yeah... and those lying detectives said I'd be released if nobody came to get me by yesterday! Fifteen days! That's what they said!

"First off, it's fifteen <u>business</u> days," the experienced guard strongly emphasized the word 'business,' "So the weekends don't count. Secondly, you're leaving for California tomorrow. A transport team called this morning and they will be in town tonight, pick you up tomorrow. So, have all of your shit ready to go by breakfast."

Oh... umm, thanks.

It was the morning of Damien's last day in Cuyahoga County Jail—and, perhaps ever, within the state of Ohio—and he had one of the worst of sleepless nights in his life. Much like a death-row inmate the night before his scheduled execution, Damien's thoughts filled with both fear of the unknown and hope for an eleventh-hour reprieve from this pending punishment. Being extradited back to California seemed to him even worse than the blessed mercy of euthanasia!

Lying there with my eyes open, I could remember that long last week we had as Californians just like it was yesterday: my hugging Vicki and getting into our car with the U-Haul trailer attached and driving away from Huntington Beach and the area we'd know for so very long. On that previous evening, the final time of checking my mailbox, and the fact that I'd received the proof of delivery by the U.S. Postal Service.

It was a small, green postcard indicating that someone at the police station had received my letter giving both notice of my leaving California and giving them the address we looked up on online of what would become our new regular church, since they would be the ones providing us with temporary housing.

That final morning, I found myself eager to be picked up by the Claremont police, because—as the arresting officers explained—my legal fight was with California not Ohio, and I wanted this simple clerical error put behind myself. I was already more concerned with how I was going to be traveling back <u>to</u> Ohio [from California], than to worry about what might go wrong in court.

Then, several tremendously long hours of waiting later, at around noon, the announcement was made for Damien to report to the floor officers' podium. He was directed to grab his already bagged-up personal belongings—what few commissary items accumulated over the past two weeks, plus his work clothes worn at CVS Pharmacy, including his name tag and vest (which technically didn't belong to him any longer).

Two plainclothes detectives he'd never met before—and who never offered any names to him—had Damien switch out of his jail clothes into his own, as well as replaced his shackles for regular police-issue handcuffs. After some half-hearted pleasantries and salutations with their Ohio counterparts, these men from California escorted Damien to their parked rental car, followed by a short drive to Cleveland airport.

The officers and I had three seats at the far back end of the plane. It was not the most uncomfortable of flights to Ontario which I've been on—I remember Vicki and I flew back and forth from LAX and Ontario airports to her parents' farm prior to our wedding there—it's just this was one flight that I'd remember every detail of because it was the saddest of moments.

There I was leaving my home city... the city that I'd grown to call home, the city where my wife and I lived at, and now it was just my wife whom lived there! As our plane rose in the air and the view of Cleveland and it suburbs—Bedford Falls, included—an image of Vick crying on our sofa developed in my mind. It suddenly occurred to me that images of her within my memory and imagination were the only photographs of Vicki I now possessed.

Damien was allowed to eat the same snack foods served to all the passengers, and even once allowed to use the seasoned 737's lavatory. A movie was played on the four-hour flight, yet Damien wasn't offered the chance to receive headphones to listen to it... not that he really was in the mood for entertainment, only for this situation to be over with.

Finally, we landed and since all we had was carry-on baggage, it took no time at all until I was getting into the back of their unmarked police car. Almost immediately, outside of the airport, the scent of the salty California air refilled my lungs like the breath of a former mistress, and practically made me gag. It was both familiar yet unwelcomed all at the same time. I was truly back where I absolutely didn't belong!

For all at least returns to the sea.
~ Rachel Carson

CHAPTER FORTY-NINE

Ever Increasing Excrement

Ontario airport, located just within San Bernardino county, pales greatly in comparison to nearby LAX International in both grandeur and number of travelers; however, it's widely considered a much more convenient and efficient airport for these same two reasons. Secondly, the airport wasn't far from the Claremont police station, where Damien and the two detectives would first be going, prior to his eventual booking within the county jail.

Damien could not recall for me in any detail the events which transpired at this police station, only that they interviewed him in an identical fashion as the Cleveland detectives had weeks previously, including both verifying his identity and the more formal reading of his Miranda rights. He was dog-tired from both his sleepless nights at that other jail and from jet lag.

Once again, although needlessly, he brought up the fact that he'd sent a certified letter to that <u>very</u> building, informing them of his plans to move out to Ohio. Unfortunately, the interviewer neither had any recorded confirmation of this nor Damien's letter—or a photocopy of it—within his case file, which was "normal police procedure." Another interviewer asked Damien the same quintessential question which I, myself, had wondered about while editing this story: "With something this important, why did he rely on sending a letter? Why didn't he come to the police station in person?"

Damien explained that their police station nearly always has hour-long waiting lines for those needing to register as a sex- or narcotics-offender, and with all of his preparations with their move, sending a letter was the most convenient. In hindsight, he now realizes that he should've not only gone to the police station in person, but also brought along a video camera to record everything, especially the date and time.

Finally, after an unknown amount of time in that interrogation room—what probably felt like an entire week—Damien was led back to their car and driven to his new deluxe accommodations… the single-most expensive apartment building in all of Los Angeles.

As you know, I've been to that same country jail before and there was nothing about the booking process and my stay there that surprised me; not even the taste of the awful, flavorless meals served there. I would spend some thirty-six hours before I would go to arraignment court, and my prior hands-on knowledge of the legal system brought me some measure of comfort which many other inmates around me didn't have.

It was always so absurdly early when we were woken up—nearly an hour or two before sunrise—and served our so-called breakfast, which was some sort of substance which supposedly resembled scrambled eggs, cold brown water called "coffee," and a type of sausage suspectedly-made from imported, Alabama roadkill… possibly armadillo or mongoose. At least the milk tasted like milk, even if it was only the non-fat variety.

After the rush job of eating breakfast, inmates going to court are all herded not unlike cattle, then loaded up onto a county sheriff's barely-functional school bus older than I am, and taken to one of the court buildings throughout Los Angeles County… whether your case was state or federal or otherwise. That morning, along the way towards the central court district, the inmate sitting next to me asked the usual question of: "So, what are you in for?" and I replied with my common response that I'd violated parole…

"A violation?" the young man asked, "But then, why are you on this bus? I mean, don't all violators go to court in the afternoons?"

This was Damien's first sign that, perhaps, his case was a bit more serious than just a simple paperwork mishap. Still, driven by hope and positive thoughts, he believed that his "private" attorney could get this matter resolved quickly... it seemed so straight forward, just a clerical error. His letter had been probably placed in the wrong sex offender's file, and someone would eventually—and hopefully—find it.

I thought my paid lawyer—hired over the phone by my wife—would be explaining the entire situation in court that day, and I'd be going home... or, at the worst, required to perform some community service.

At his arraignment hearing, Damien met his attorney for the first time; a pleasant-enough looking white businessman with dark-brown hair and in his forties. However, due to all of the rapid activity and time constraints within that courtroom, they only had two or three minutes to talk—technically, it was all whispering.

"The good news, Mr. Lartigue, is that the district attorney has dropped counts two and three of your indictment, the fleeing and violation of parole conditions, since you clearly weren't any longer on parole when you'd moved out of state. They are now only pushing forward with Count One, your failure to register under Penal Code 290."

Yes, I understand that, Damien replied, *"but as Vicki already told you, we sent the police a certified letter telling them we were leaving California.*

"Your wife did explain that, and if this case goes to trial we'll be calling her as a witness." The middle-aged man then frowned because he disliked being the bearer of bad news: "Unfortunately, no trace of this letter can be found. The Claremont police have no record of ever receiving it in the logbooks."

It's probably in somebody else's file, Damien complained.

"No, Mr. Lartigue, you don't understand. Their mailroom clerk's log doesn't have you sending anything since the one you'd sent a month earlier about going to Michigan for your wedding."

Well, that's their fault, not mine, Damien rightfully grumbled. *So, what am I looking at? A year in jail? Do I have to pay some fine?*

"No, it's much more serious than that, Mr. Lartigue. This is a third-strike case... unless we can afford some leniency from the judge at your <u>Romero</u> hearing, you could be sentenced to twenty-five years."

During Damien's prior times within any jail or prison, California hadn't yet enacted its current Three Strikes law... an outrageously written felony sentencing enhancement section of their Penal Code. This was something entirely new to Damien; although, months after being paroled from Chuckawalla Valley State Prison, he'd heard of guys receiving indeterminate sentences for the most minor of offenses:

From the years 1993 to 2012, criminals were being given 'twenty-five years to life' for stealing their neighbor's lawn mower, as long as they had "once upon a time" been convicted of a violent or serious felony within any state. It didn't matter if your latest crime was violent or not, you were instantly deemed a rehabilitation failure and threat to society, locked away for over two decades, if you survived that long.

Thankfully, in November of 2012, the state's voters realized that—from how erroneously Three Strikes had been written into law—the inmate population was swelling to nearly two-hundred thousand! Shoplifters and drug abusers were serving life sentences, and that this needed to stop. Almost as much as taxpayer money was being spent on state prisons as was being spend on public elementary schools. They voted for some minor changes to the Three Strikes law which helped bring the prison population down slightly; regrettably, not nearly enough.

For ex-convicts of any sexually-based crime—as Damien's 1990 rape—these 2012 changes to sentencing enhancements do not affect them: Once a person has been found guilty of rape or any other type of sex crime, any minor offense committed years later can still cause them to spend the rest of their lives in prison.

In reality, that was the first moment I realized I was facing twenty-five-to-life! No wonder they flew out to Ohio—the expense of it all—to bring me back here, I was suddenly public enemy number one! The shock of it all was only further submerging because neither Vicki nor my attorney seemed to be able to prove that I really hadn't attempted to escape my responsibilities of having to register as a sex offender. Simply put, I was neck-deep in manure and other fecal matter!

Under the advisement of council, Damien entered a plea of "not guilty"... an answer with which he not only he honestly agreed, but which would also give his paid attorney time to maneuver towards a more-reasonable bail and the best plea-bargain possible. All of which, in Damien's opinion, meant more lawyer's fees and more time he would be spending in the county jail.

Looking back, Damien honestly couldn't find any noticeable differences between having a "private," paid-for attorney and a court-appointed public defender: *Neither are easier to get ahold of than the other. Plus, although paid lawyers are known to have fewer cases to burden them, those cases they have are usually in multiple counties throughout the state... miles away from the "most important client."*

Damien was returned to the courtroom's crowded, standing-room only holding tank to await hours for his ride back to county lockup. By far, that particular waiting room was the single-most dismal place on the planet! Filled with shackled individuals plagued with uncertainty or knowledgeable doom! Most coming back from court after being sentenced to an abhorrent amount of months or years in custody; others merely receiving a postponement or "continuance" until finding out their own fate. Commonly, due to a scheduling mishap, there will be one or two inmates still waiting to be taken into the courtroom, either later in the afternoon or, for whatever reason, had been scratched from the day's docket... a so-called "dry run." Regardless, everyone held within a holding tank is always eager to get back to their jail cells or dormitory bunk beds as quickly as possible... freedom from the jail within the jail.

Los Angeles County Jail in Lynwood, California, was very different from the previous jails Damien had been housed in. Due to this prior criminal history, Damien was placed within a much-needed protective custody unit which lacked any serious violence throughout the entire time he was there. Amongst all of the types of felony charges his fellow inmates were facing, a majority of them were for various sexual offenses, including child molestation... the undeniably most-heinous of all crimes; and yet, even these known offenders were safe from harm.

I was in a dormitory housing unit at Lynwood. There were a fair number of "dayroom hours," which meant us inmates could entertain ourselves with a variety of board games, cards, watching TV, and doing artwork. You could make use of the showers anytime during these hours, even shower three or four times if you so wanted to. However, out of all these uses to fight off the overwhelming boredom, the only event I ever looked forward to was the use of the phones to call my wife, two-thousand miles away.

Due to the differences in time zones, she was normally home from working at her school at around two p.m., my time. However, on that day, nobody was home to accept my first four collect-call attempts. Finally, at nearly seven p.m., her time, Vicki did answer the phone.

Hello, my love, Damien happily greeted his wife before she said anything.

For two seconds, there was only silence from her end, making Damien to initially believe that the phone system was having technical problems, but soon he heard her response: "Damien, I—we hafta talk…"

Immediately, Damien noticed something odd with the tone of Vicki's voice; it sounded as when someone had embarrassingly injured themselves—hurt and angry at the same time.

Hon? What's wrong?! He inquired out of concern. The first assumption to spring to mind was that she's pregnant, but then why would she be sad?

"I spoke with, with some lawyer… yours, I think." The person she'd spoke with was actually a paralegal of the District Attorney's Office, performing background research of exactly when they'd moved to Ohio. Vicki then loudly cleared her throat: "Dee… what <u>aren't</u> you telling me?"

What? What do you mean? the confused husband asked.

"They—nobody gets sent to prison, <u>for life</u>, because they violated a condition of their parole! Stop lying to me! What did you <u>really</u> do?! What are you hiding from me?!"

I—I'm not—

"Did you kill somebody… is that why you were so eager to leave California? Oh God. Did we move to Ohio just so you could hide from the police?!"

No! There wasn't any hiding or killing! I never did anything like that!

"But, then, why are they threatening to send you to prison for <u>life</u>?!"

They want to sentence me under this new Three Strikes law, because I have that—he suddenly lowered his voice to a whisper so nobody could eavesdrop, "—that sex crime on my record. But, I didn't hurt anybody, Vicki! I swear! You know we sent that registered letter, and I was following all of their rules.

"B-But this, just doesn't make any sense! People don't go to prison for the rest of their lives for—for what you told me! Damien, if you truly love me, you'll tell me what you really did wrong!"

Vicki, I s-swear to you, this failure to register nonsense is all that I did... all that I'm being charged with.

"Oh, why can't I believe you?! That doesn't sound right, the legal system doesn't work that way! Nobody gets twenty-five-to-life because they forgot to send paperwork! Damien, she said with a particular sadness in her voice, "if you can't be honest with me, then I can't be with you."

What?! What are you saying? He exclaimed out of frustration.

"Damien, I can't be married to a liar," she was obviously crying at this moment, and Damien couldn't do nor say anything which would comfort her from so many miles away.

B-But, I'm not lying, Vicki. I love—was all he could get out before her voice was replaced with an annoying dial tone.

For the following two days, each time Damien dialed and attempted to get through to Vicki, the collect phone call's charges weren't accepted. Most of his calls weren't even answered on the Ohio end, thanks possibly to her having Caller-ID on the phone.

On Thursday night, Damien received his first-ever letter sent to this latest California address, an upbeat and cheerful letter from his wife full of renewed hope that he'd soon be released and able to return home to her. The letter, because of the delay with incoming inmate mail, had been sent by Vicki long before she had spoken to anyone about the possible maximum prison sentence Damien could very well receive, as well as their shockingly unpleasant phone call. He would receive two more such "happy" letters from her until all mail abruptly stopped.

Meanwhile, not a single day went by when Damien didn't handwrite and send a letter—or three of them—to his wife. In fact, of the few remaining dollars within his inmate canteen account, Damien spent over thirty of it on stationary and stamps.

Damien couldn't "for the life of him" remember Vicki's parents' phone number, although if he could, he doesn't believe he would have called them: *If Vicki didn't want to answer her phone, she wouldn't answer her phone. Only time would heal any resentment she had towards me.*

The only other phone number he could remember by heart was for his life-long friend and former employer, Dr. Sam Reily... however, for presently unknown reasons, even Sam was likewise not answering his phones—home nor business numbers.

Indeed, I was so sad that I was trying to come up with ways I could just end it all by ending my life. What kept me wanting to live was the slim possibility that Vicki was still my wife, and would find out that California's new law was, in fact, the problem; that I was completely truthful with her. I was still clinging onto the hope that my lawyer would clear this all up, maybe reach a deal with me serving only a year or two... anything less than twenty-five!

I realize now, as I'm telling you all of this, that my reasons for not committing suicide were all based on things which I had zero direct control over. And, while I was frantically calling upon people who weren't answering their phones, I was completely neglecting the one person who both always "answers the phone" and influences all situations... our Heavenly Father God. I know and see <u>this</u> now, but I couldn't and didn't back then because my attention was only focused on my growing turmoil. I had six weeks to wait for my next of several court hearings to come, while spending the remainder of my incarceration dealing with the fears of becoming utterly alone. And through it all, I admittedly never once prayed nor included God in the events going on.

It was a full month later that I had my first attorney/client meeting about what this lawyer was recommending and what the deputy district attorney was willing to do in my case. The prosecutor—of all people—was actually in agreement that this matter really was too minor for sentencing under Three Strikes, yet both his and the judge's own hands <u>were tied</u> by the sentencing enhancements required under state law. The judge would simply not be able to give less than six years—one year for the offense, and five for all of the mandated "prison prior" enhancements stacked consecutively.

I still did have the choice of fighting my felony charge and taking things to a jury trial; however, as my lawyer warned me, if I lost at trial the judge would be forced by law to imbue all twenty-five years <u>plus</u> the enhancements for previously being in prison, totaling <u>forty</u> years in prison! Those seemed to be my only two choices: Either I take six years, or four decades... there simply wasn't anything less, and my chances weren't good at a jury trial; especially since our "star witness," Vicki, wasn't even speaking to me anymore.

The news brought a wave of tears to my eyes; I was so filled with confusion and a deep depression. I could not understand <u>how</u> the sex crime I was convicted of, and punishable by only three years, paled in comparison to my so-called failure to register as an offender of that crime, and would earn me <u>twice</u> this original amount of prison time!

As it turned out, this depression was just the tip of the iceberg for Damien. After dinner that every evening, mail was passed out by their correctional officer on duty, including one for Damien. Within an official looking envelope from a law office, were two items: a handwritten letter from Vera Lartigue, Vicki's mother, informing him that Vicki had moved back in with them in Michigan and Damien isn't to contact her; plus a set of divorce papers and forms.

CHAPTER FIFTY

A Reintroduction to Hell

Following Damien's conviction by plea, in August of 2000, he was transferred to North Kern Valley State Prison—technically, a reception center and transportation hub—located in the city of Delano, midway between Fresno and Bakersfield. Across the seldom-travelled street of West Cecil Avenue, the preliminary construction work of yet another new prison—to become a level 4 maximum-security prison—was just getting underway with its land clearance; that next-door neighboring facility not scheduled to open for another four years.

With respect to the residents of Delano, the area is rather desolate. Thanks to its close proximity to Death Valley (the lowest point in the Western Hemisphere and record holder of hottest surface temperature in known history), the local agriculture and wild plants struggle to survive on the ever-parched ground. There were very few trees which Damien could remember, both on his trip there and during his short stay.

I was nervous again, not because of anything about being processed into the prison system per se—remember, this was to be my third state-issued prisoner I.D. number, so I was rather experienced in what to expect and when—except, this time I had a 'R' suffix on my paperwork because of that 1990 rape charge. It didn't take as long as it did my previous two times in reception to calm my nerves down. After all, because of that 'R' suffix, I was to be kept in a protective custody yard, what we call a "soft" yard.

A fair number of men at that North Kern center were convicted for a sex crime or something which made them want to "P.C. up." Unlike my previous times in prison, there was a growing percentage of inmates who were "dropping out" of their former gangs; either because they'd gotten tired of being bossed around by someone younger than them, or because they were feeling disrespected by fellow gang members. This was something very new to me and the prison system in general: prison gangs were failing, at least to some degree.

I saw pretty shortly that all I had to do to become more comfortable with my latest situation, was what I always did in prison... and that was to do my own time and stay out of the others' business and their lives, unless I was invited in—which was extremely rare for someone like me.

Damien had shed his nervousness as if it were rainwater on an umbrella, involving just a couple of vigorous shakes until mostly dry... <u>mostly</u>. Yet he kept to his lonesome while at reception; not necessarily trying to be unfriendly or to avoid making any friends, just simply not putting any amount of effort into doing so. Again, in hindsight, he now knows this "wasn't very Christian of him," but he also knew he'd likely never see any of these fellow inmates again since, from a reception center, guys are sent by buses all over the state and/or to neighboring Arizona.

My first cellmate at "Delano" was a man who made the claim that he was in prison for life, yet it wasn't for the crime which landed him back in prison. No, his initial crime was car theft and the possession of cocaine for sale. When we talked, he shot right by these charges and he focused on his fantasy... that is, the crime he'd created in his mind. His "more-impressive crime"—apparently hoping for a level of notability with the inmate population—was for killing one of his most recent cellmates! In his own words, he was easily convicted because he was caught with his victim's decapitated head resting in the sink.

Wow! Really?! Although I didn't believe a word of this cockamamie decapitation, I still needed to worry if I was safe from someone capable of visualizing such an event. I'd been around, and even lived with my share of the mentally deranged, while in my youth at the Metropolitan State

Hospital—*where I'd first met Sam—as well as a few crazies during my previous stretches of prison time. We call them "J-cats," short for 'J' category, used as a designation decades ago. The key thing is, I didn't know if this man named Mark was going to be potentially violent towards me, or if he simply wanted me to believe he was a lunatic, out of his own fear of an unknown future.*

Tell me, Mark, Damien responded to his cellie's story, *Am I safe?*

"Sure, Damien. For now. I mean that I'm not currently hungry, and besides... I don't very much like to eat white meat." This element of cannibalism was something entirely new to their conversation, which only further told Damien that this man was trying to scare Damien... perhaps to the same level of fear that Mark was at.

Well then, that's over with... I guess. So, what do you do for entertainment around here? Damien politely asked.

"I read. Do you need a book?" Mark questioned without any real tender.

Actually, yes! I love reading, practically anything. You have one you aren't reading?

"Maybe, maybe not. Most of them are missing some pages, though. I've been using them as napkins after eating whatever crawls into my cell."

That's fine. I don't mind missing pages... kind of used to it, actually, Damien calmly replied, then pointed at their shared toilet. *"Do you mind me sitting there while I'm reading?*

"Hold on now!" Mark was becoming infuriated with Damien's apparent lack of personal concern. "You haven't become afraid of me? Why's that?"

Well, Damien paused to collect his thoughts, *because if you were going to kill me, there isn't a whole heck of a lot that this thin body—*referring to his own scragginess—*can do to stop you... so, I just prefer getting along with you. We're not going to be cellies for long... this is just reception. An' this isn't my first rodeo.*

"You've been to prison before?" Mark asked with uncertainty in his tone.

Yeah... twice. In fact, they almost nailed me with Three Strikes this time, but gave me only six years at my Romero hearing.

The look on Damien's new cellie's face just then was one of bewilderment; the phrases 'Three strikes' and 'Romero hearing' were as foreign to Mark as they had been to Damien several months ago...yet, now, these flowed from Damien's mouth like household words. The unknowing look in Mark's eyes told Damien that this person was relatively new to the system—possibly a 'first termer.'

"Good. You're not afraid of me because you used your head," Mark complimented, then foolishly added, "which prob'ly tastes delicious."

Back to offer of a book, Damien insisted, *do you have one I can read until the library cart comes by? Which, I believe, is only on Wednesdays.*

"Thursdays," Mark corrected, then sat up straighter on his lower bunk bed and lifted one end of his mattress, revealing three hidden books plus some large manila envelopes stuffed full of old letters and paperwork. "Here, I have these two you can borrow."

Ahh! Charles Dickens' <u>A Tale of Two Cities</u>. I really like that one, I don't mind reading it again.

"You've read it already?" Again he asked in obvious doubt. "What other authors do you like?"

Wow! Now there's a question that'll take <u>all day</u> to answer! I like to read, well, everything. Philosophers like Plato and Immanuel Kant. Classical writers like Shakespeare and Mark Twain. Religious books by—

Damien was interrupted as, during his summary of authors, his new cellie located yet another book underneath his mattress and presented this to him.

Mark handed me another surprise that day, in the form of <u>The Adventures of Tom Sawyer</u>, in paperback. Since I'd already read <u>Adventures of Huckleberry Finn</u> during a previous prison term, but not this one, this was indeed a real treat. Who'd ever guess that a decapitating cannibal would have such an excellent work of literary delight hidden under his bedding, if only to provide some much-needed additional cushioning.

With that said, things returned to where they were before out brief—yet informative—conversation. I climbed up on my assigned upper bunk, or 'rack' as we called them, and our tiny cell returned to dead silence until dinner/chow and the usual "mandatory standing count" time. It was a routine which I'd lived for so very long, and yet for nearly a decade had completely forgotten. I truly believed that day we drove out of California—Vicki and I—that this prison lifestyle was never again to be a part of my own life... yet there I was, all over again.

Only a handful of days later, I was blessed by my cellie Mark's transfer to Soledad prison, or what was now being called a Level Two correctional training facility: "They must mean that the <u>officers</u> receive training there, because it's got almost <u>nothing</u> to offer the inmates!

Okay, perhaps 'blessed' is the wrong word in that statement. After my cellmate's claim to fame of not just killing his former cellmate but that he also chopped him up and ate most of the victim's internal organs whole... Mark and I were getting along rather famously. Two peas in a pod built for an infant. We tolerated each other and our tight quarters quite well, in fact.

Speaking of facts, obviously since Mark was being sent to a Level Two medium-security prison, all credibility of him killing someone—as if there was ever any credit—went right out the sealed-shut window. I'd learned over the years that most of everything that's heard around a prison should be treated with considerable care, leaning more towards insincerity and falsehood than truth... even when from the staff! Roughly ten percent of <u>truth</u> <u>be</u> <u>told</u>.

I believe I've mentioned before about gossip in prison, and how male inmates are worse than old women at a hair salon. On a daily basis, there's always rumors of better TV channels, better food, longer recreation times, and—biggest of them all—shorter prison sentences coming right around the corner. <u>Any</u> minute now<u>!</u> But, as I learned the hard way, it's best to not hold one's breath whenever the news is regarding something which will benefit us inmates.

On the morning when Mark would leave out cell for the last time, on his way to Receiving and Release (R&R), he rewarded my efforts of staying both quiet and at arm's length away at all times with a handshake. His final words to me were out of gratitude that I wasn't "a mindless asshole." All things considered, he wasn't a "bad" cellmate; although, even if he had been or his fiction was true, I believe I still would've wished him some measure of good luck, as I did that day.

Following Mark, Damien was housed together with another

prisoner who spoke very little English, and whose name he couldn't recall for me. This Mexican or "further south" immigrant chose not to interact with Damien as much as possible, perhaps due to their <u>impenetrable</u> language barrier (unlike the U.S. border). Instead, or in favor of not being able to converse, Damien buried himself in both his readings and also his journal writings.

Even back then, in the year 2000, I knew that at some point in my life I was going to want to write something autobiographical. This is one of the many coincidental benefits of being in custody, whether it's within jail or prison: you have plenty of spare time to pause and reflect on your past. I was remembering details I had long forgotten, and I wanted to capture as much of these as possible on paper. The conversations, the people, and the places weren't as vivid in my memory as they once were, and it would've been a true tragedy if I'd lost even half of it.

Another five weeks went by for Damien "like a winter's chill in the desert," until he was to be transferred to his 'parent' or more-permanent facility. Damien had been endorsed to be transferred to his "alma mater" prison in San Luis Obispo, called California Men's Colony, where he'd spend time together with Charlie "Oops" Osborne in 1983; unfortunately, crushing those dreams of reunion and reminiscence, he was transferred to Pleasant Valley State Prison, located along Interstate 5 in Coalinga.

Sitting there, on the yard, on one of my first of many Saturdays, I'd wondered how this place got its name...for there wasn't anything "pleasant" about it, nor the surrounding valley. Perhaps this prison was named by the same idiot who'd called a town in Kansas: Oceanside. No, there wasn't anything at all remotely pleasant there; not the weather, not the air quality, and especially not the correctional officers.

Again, and I apologize for repeating myself so often, even when I'm repeating myself about repeating myself: I'd been in prison a good portion of my life up till these moments I'm retelling you about; so, I've had quite the experience with prison staff—meeting several of the "good" ones and the "bad" alike. I'd grown used to expecting encounters with bone-headed individuals, or inexplicably uptight persons, or downright hateful instigators, and—most prominent of all—the exceptionally lazy; mind you, I'm talking about the officers themselves, not just the inmates and other prison staff.

So, when I state that Pleasant Valley had more than its fair share of the "bad" ones—the angry, hateful, lazy, and/or pettish about every little thing which we did or which brought us added comfort—I hope that you'll consider my observation more as an expert's opinion rather than a plaintive whine. The level of contempt which most of the officers held towards us inmates—especially the ones who dropped out of a gang in efforts to better their own lives (and, in turn, better society)—was thicker that San Francisco fog; and just as visible.

It is not my intention to bore you with absolutely every event, the names of every cellie I had, nor all of the nonchalant things which occurred over those pair of years spend at Pleasant Valley prison. Nearly all of, well, most of it, was spent pretty-much alone... I acted in a way which expressed how I felt.

There were several moments sitting on the bleachers on the yard when I either wanted to and did cry out over the loss of my wife. The loneliness formed out of our divorce was a direct hit in my nose. I really couldn't begin to know how I was supposed to live without her. "I'm not alive now. I am without the spark and spirit that is life!" And yet, God—in some personally perceived methodical or purely sadistic way—was keeping me alive for unknown reasons. I wanted it all to end, to stop being God's punchline or punching bag, or both.

My reasons for being in prison, for becoming divorced, were all so backwards... much how the character Job must have felt in that story of the Bible. Vicki couldn't believe me about why I was being sent to prison, and I didn't feel as I was in prison due to any fault of my own, and by the look of things to come, I had nothing less than a bleak future to look forward to: just more loneliness and despair. If my past had anything to prove to me, it was I should only expect more abandonment from family or friends, and separation from any good situations, such as those I had at military school and state hospital.

After several months in prison trying to make life work again for me, to locate my lost will and desire to live, I was found by my cellmate tying a noose around my neck in order to hang myself. I really wanted to physically end that which I had no spirit to continue... I wanted death! It no longer mattered to me that I religiously had no right to end my life; that had I succeeded—which I obviously didn't, or this book would be over—I would've committed one of the most heinous and unforgivable of sins against God. Yet, a biblical hell seemed so much more "pleasant" than the physical hell I'd been living in since birth.

My cellie at the time—let's call him John, since it doesn't really matter—had unexpectedly returned from his inmate job too early, and immediately yelled "Man down!" upon seeing what I was up to. The rope I'd made out of torn sheets was already around my neck, just wasn't yet tight enough nor ready to support my full weight. My cellie, of course, had another reason to be calling for medical assistance: If I'd gone through with it, my cellie would've been placed in administration segregation pending a full investigation into my death; and those take forever to complete.

Damien was quickly stopped by custody staff with his suicide attempt, handcuffed, escorted to the medical department, and placed in a suicide watch cell...wearing nothing but a paper gown, sleeping on nothing but bare metal and an unpliant quilt, for seventy-two hours. As a blessing, this experience opened the doors for Damien to receive closer, more intensive psychological care. He was immediately placed on antidepressants and received required counseling; although, thanks to his years of helping Dr. Reily at his office, Damien believed he both knew and was more experienced with mental health than the so-called prison specialists he met with.

There was nothing that I could do to lessen the pain within my soul. I had previously asked God for a chance to become a "healthy" husband, someone who could be a good husband, maybe even a father which someone would be proud of knowing as "Dad." I asked and God delivered: God brought Vicki and I together as husband and wife. I had promised at our wedding that I would take good care of my relationship with this woman of God's choosing. A marriage which seemed so completely compatible, so lovingly strong, yet lasted only three years.

It was there, in that closely watched cell, shivering in that paper gown, that I realized I'd lost my wife because I failed to keep my promise to the Lord, my God. I felt myself as being beyond the grace of God to ever be forgiven. I'd become too focused on my relationship with Vicki, on the small group we'd started, on making a living for myself, that I'd forgotten to take good care of the relationship which God had with me. I failed, and to this day I pay for it in my loss of Vicki.

During that time, I felt a sample of what Hell actually is, because I could imagine what it is like to wake up and live each day totally unloved, especially not by God. In the days that followed the seventy-two hours of suicide watch, I made another new promise to God never to hurt myself. I knew at my core that I wouldn't still be living <u>unless</u> it was because God wanted me to be here or to achieve something unknown to me... if God didn't, I wouldn't be breathing. A snap of God's fingers, and I'd be no more. So, I promised God that no matter what my feelings were, that I wouldn't force God's hand... or fingers.

I did this promise by declaring that "my" body doesn't belong to me. I only travel with it. "My" soul doesn't really belong to me, either. I belong to God and I won't hurt that which belongs to God! I want to die or to be used by God in such a way that I know that I'm serving my heavenly Father, my spiritual "Dad." I may not love <u>me</u> that much, but I love God.

God help us to change. To change ourselves and to change our world. To know the need for it. To deal with the pain of it. To feel the joy of it. To undertake the journey without understanding the destination. Amen. ~ Michael Leunig, *The Prayer Tree*

CHAPTER FIFTY-ONE

Man in a Bottle

*A*s time pushed itself through and dragged me along a path of its own creation, I have learned how to be a modified version of myself... a <u>me</u> who doesn't have deeply felt emotions. I still have trouble, today, not expressing my intellect, but otherwise doing okay in conversation—especially when I don't have to share what it is that I feel.

Prison is not a place for <u>real</u> people that are used to expressing what really is on their minds and in their hearts. I'm a person that has always had a fair amount of trouble knowing my feelings and mind for that matter—it's an Asperger's thing. For me, prison was really "bad business" as I so desperately wanted friends, well, at least one friend that allow me to be <u>me</u>; allow me to talk about what I was feeling, especially about Vicki and our divorce.

Pleasant Valley wasn't an absolutely horrible place to do time—at least when you stayed "off the radar" of the hard-bitten—except for the ways which one might feel trapped inside a bottle, which I commonly felt. One does not have any sort of sense of privacy, or safety of who one is or what one feels. Instead, many guys like me become students of personal deception, putting on masks of fake personalities.

Although Damien was regularly being seen by a psychologist, as well as taking multiple medications, these counseling sessions weren't a replacement for having a good friend to vent his frustrations and concerns to. There wasn't a real chance of developing that kind of friendship with his psychologist nor any other staff member. He decided to slowly build on seeking a friendship with his coworkers and cellmate, for starters.

At Pleasant Valley, I had gotten a job fairly quickly which I liked. I was a building porter—basically a janitor for the housing unit I lived in. I even earned a whole seven cents per hour; unfortunately, that's before taxes (in prison terms, the percentage they take out of your pay to satisfy restitution). My particular job was the scrubbing of the shower on the ground floor of "C" section of the building, as well as helping with the distribution of toilet-paper rolls, bed sheets, and other supplies.

It was a rather boring job, because within fifteen minutes of cleaning, mopping, and—at times—some minutes of either sweeping or tending to the trash cans, I would be done for the day. On the plus side, after taking care of things, I was technically still on the time clock, even when all I was doing included reading or playing Pinochle. It was through the latter of these—the four-player card game—which I became less insecure around people, and even developed a handful of acquaintances which eventually could turn into friendships over time.

There was also my cellmate, this one called "Bear." He was considered an "Other" race—neither Caucasian, Afro-American, nor Hispanic, which were the three majorities. No, Bear was a Native American, or what Christopher Columbus mistakenly first called an Indian. The nickname fit, for Bear was built like a freight train. He was really massive, without an ounce of unwanted body fat. As a former U.S. Marine, Bear kept himself on a daily regimen of personal discipline, while remaining kind-hearted to others... a Herculean teddy-bear.

Perhaps and because of my Asperger's, or just my rather unique upbringing, I had lost all trust in my ability to judge a man's truthful character. I was very slow, but I would, on occasion, make an exception on my willingness to test the waters of untried relationships. Upon entering my cell for the very first time, standing there before this Goliath, I chose to risk making a fool of myself of offering a hand of friendship to Bear. As it turned out, my often faulty perception of someone's friendly nature was uncommonly accurate that time, and we became fast friends.

Damien described for me his first few days at Pleasant Valley State Prison, both before his suicide attempt and after; unfortunately, the timeline differing these two periods had become blurred, both due to the heavy medications he'd been prescribed and he occasional loss of a page or two of his handwritten notes. The cellmate named Bear wasn't the one who found Damien tying that noose around his neck; no, he'd become the cellmate who would remove the lasso around his potential.

When we were first unloaded from the bus and escorted to our prospective yards, the correctional officer (or "C.O.") warned us that "C" yard was called a "fifty-fifty" yard, meaning that there was very little violence, due in part to the fact that about half—fifty percent of it—were "soft" or gay inmates. The other half were regular "mainliners," including the rigid members of various prison gangs: the blacks, southern Mexican, northern Mexican, the Aryan brotherhood, other white and Hispanic groups.

The point of the C.O.'s foredoom was that "hard heads" and those who enjoyed getting into fights, would be transferred to another prison lickety-split. I was determined to be someone who gets along far more than not... so, I was glad for the 50-50 yard, regardless of which "fifty" I best fit the description of in the minds of others. In fact, all of us arriving on that yard for the first time were glad to be housed there because of its system-wide reputation.

Protective custody, or P.C., is for the most part a rather bad term to those of the general inmate population, because anyone housed on a P.C. yard—or what was also being labelled as a Sensitive Needs yard—was viewed as a weakling, a snitch, or a child molester... regardless of what their paperwork said. Nobody either doing time or had done a prison term before wanted to associate themselves with protective-custody inmates—or, even worse, to be one! To do so makes you abnormal, and convicts despise nonconformists.

I had learned during my two previous trips through Corrections, as well as my short visit to Juvenile Hall—almost forgot about that one—that inmates prefer a structured lifestyle of predictable routine. They get irate whenever a regularly scheduled recreation time gets cut short or all-out cancelled, disappointed whenever there's a change to the posted weekly menu, really pissed when their personal property gets searched or when abruptly told to move to a cell or building. But, most troubling of all, whenever someone peculiar and/or eccentric lives within their midst: Nonconformity is by far the worst form of disrespect to these hardened chameleons.

Thankfully, my cellmate Bear was a rare exception. Although he had done time before, for an undisclosed crime, which he'd spent on the "mainline," due to his intimidating girth and height Bear was subjected to a lot of provoking by newer inmates whom merely wanted to create a name for themselves. Fighting someone stronger than you—whether you win or lose—traditionally earned a guy some "street cred" with his buddies... especially when blood split, usually regardless of whose. This is primarily why Bear "P.C.'ed up," because he did not want persistent prison-yard or chow-hall fights, and the loss of good behavior-time credits due to fighting, to remain part of his future... Bear wanted to someday be prison-free! To go home!

His example, by the way, is why I have such a difficult time understanding why other "mainline" inmates and most correctional officers treat guys on protective-custody or sensitive needs yards differently and/or more harshly. I never intended to become labelled as a career criminal, and Bear never intended after his military service to be the biggest man on a prison yard. Yet both of us were aiming for the same thing—to avoid any situations which would cause us to remain in prison an extra thirty-days, sixty-days, or anything longer than absolutely necessary! And yet, we were looked down on because of this, because we didn't wish to make remaining in prison a lifetime goal, like so many others.

So, if you want to know why Bear and I wanted to be nonconformists—to be housed in a "soft" yard with other inmates who'd rather sleep all afternoon, than to be part of a twelve-man brawl because a man of a different race had touched my "shot caller's" shower bag hanging on the wall—our answer is simple: Because we don't belong in a bottle! We want to be ourselves, our true personalities, and—most of all—to have our freedom. And if this is so horribly wrong of us, so completely backwards in the thinking of gang members and other career convicts, then we are glad our bottles are broken.

On the first Sunday morning since becoming Bear's cellie, after my suicide attempt, I discovered that he wasn't only a Native American but *an active Christian. This surprised me because Pleasant Valley had about twenty participants of their "sweat lodge," and yet Bear chose to practice Christianity. This pleased me to no end. Until that moment, nearly all of my previous cellmates this prison term were atheists, Catholics, or of some other undisclosed faith—either because we never talked about it or I chose not to know this about them.*

"Yes, I am, Damien. I am very happy to say that I am a Christian. If you'd like to come, make haste. On Sunday mornings, because yard release is right after breakfast, there's no time to ready ourselves for morning service. It starts right at nine," his cellmate offered.

Thank you, Bear. I'll be quick. Just have to get cleaned up and comb my hair.

"You'll really have to hurry because I need to wash-up too, and they just released the diabetics for their shots. About your hair, here. Try some of this." The larger man reached around Damien and grabbed a plastic jar of Palmer's Olive Oil Hairdress. After unscrewing the lid, Bear angled the jar's opening towards Damien... who viewed the greasy contains with abhorrence.

'Olive oil'? he truncated from the label. *Maybe if my hair was a salad, I would.*

"Try some," Bear offered with a little more insistence. "Trust me, you'll never go back to using those gels or sprays."

Damien gave in and tried some. To this very day, he still only ever uses this hairdressing, for whatever few grey hairs which remain on his head.

After thanking Bear for the use of the pomade, they both barely had time enough to lace-up their state-issued shoes, until the cell's door "popped" ajar along with the other eighteen cells along their section of the tier. They now had two minutes to leave and lock the door behind them before the floor officers would become upset and/or threaten to "tear the cell apart" for taking too long.

We ate our large Sunday breakfast—which consisted of a pair of fried eggs, hash-browned potatoes, slice of turkey ham, really good oatmeal, frozen orange juice, milk, and really bad coffee. Gone were the days of what us inmates from the 1970's and 80's called a "grand slam," yet the food was filling enough. Well, usually. Another one of the issues with being on a protective custody yard is that it's everyone for themselves, which translates to "everyone looking out for themselves," and there's a lot of stealing in the kitchen area: handfuls of ground beef snagged from the vat of spaghetti sauce, slices of pepperoni plunked off of the pizzas, and chickenless chicken stew.

I actually was happy because God was looking after me; even despite my failure at the loving relationship which God had given me in the form of Vicki. In this time of need, God allowed me to become cellmates with this kind-hearted and every bit of a Christian man. Bear showered me with the generosity of a supply of coffee, creamer, sugar, and a spare mug to drink from, along with a small supply of some much-needed hygiene products. But, of all of these simple luxuries, the most important one was a new leather-bound <u>Scofield Study Bible</u> which his family had accidentally ordered two copies of.

Regularly after Sunday morning service, Bear's desire to hear God's Word—"God's Voice," Bear called the Bible—was unfulfilled and he craved more. Bear invited me that morning, and every Sunday afterwards, to join his group of gathered students of the Good News. He introduced me to the like-minded men waiting for us on a small parcel of lawn outside the chapel, running parallel to the asphalt jogging track. We sat down on the grass with our Bibles opened in our laps. It wasn't the most comfortable way to study the Bible, yet the company we kept sure was. I instantly felt like I could share just about anything personal with these complete strangers... these servants of God.

In that moment, I chose to do a lot more than get to know Bear; I wanted to imitate this true believer and man of God. These men who lived according to the way Jesus taught God's people to live, and to embrace the Lord's parables. Even though I was "not of the same cloth," as it were, at least not the same theological cloth.

Damien's cellie, Bear, opened their study time in prayer, asking for the Heavenly Father to guide their study, so that they could learn whatever prudent topic God wanted them to learn that moment. Bear asked that God would help them be of one mind in their discussion, and to remain that way after the end of their study, if not for the rest of their lives. Damien had never before heard someone pray quite like that, asking God to not only pick their topic as needed, but to bring their thoughts to a form of unity!

A middle-aged white man introduced himself to Damien as George, offering him a hand to shake. "Nice to meet you. If you're in need of supplies, just let me know and I'll get you taken care of. We have a benevolence fund... it ain't fancy, but some basic needs can be taken care of.

Thank you. I'm alright, because God had me celled-up with a fantastic human being. Damien smiled and nodded towards Bear.

The rest of the group introduced themselves quickly, yet it was done warmly. Damien enjoyed both the study group and their choices of study; that morning's topic was Jesus' parable of the Pharisee and the tax collector, starting at Luke 18:9. The group identified with the boastful Pharisee and how God would reckon the tax collector to be righteous because he showed true grief and contrition over being sinful.

One of the members of their group broke out in tears—his name was Isaac—confessing publically to them all that he's had this same difficulty affecting his prayers; that he had asked God the previous night to show him what he was doing wrong in his attempts to be free of stress and worries. The reading of this parable was just what Isaac needed to hear this morning.

Damien impressed the group by pointing out something he'd remembered reading in another study Bible, which was that fasting—under Mosaic law—was only for the annual Day of Atonement, and that the Pharisee unnecessarily abstained from eating from eating twice a week only because that's what their priests told them to do. Bear and a few others were inspired that this newcomer to their group knew this tidbit of information... and whatever else Damien might have to offer.

I was feeling pretty darn good about going to church, even if it was only a worship time. But <u>boy</u>! Could that worship team sing a hymn! Let me just say that they sounded so crisp and clear. The church singing made a real joy to partake within me; I could feel their earnest worship. I knew that God was warmly moved by all of their contributing voices. One could just feel God's presence every time that worship team let our any song they *would sing.*

I was blessed double because our inmate preacher was clearly trained by God to deliver each morning's message. Truly, I was blessed by God's hand in my life and upon my being...my spirit! On a few occasions, I couldn't help crying; I was just so deeply moved by the fact that God was clearly in charge of my life—my future—despite the way I'd refused to heed the directions of God's spirit.

It was at my first study group meeting that I'd also met a young white man named Ryan. No, he was only barely a man, on that borderline of immaturity and age of consent—which will hopefully someday be raised to twenty-one. Yet, as spiritual strength and development went, Ryan was twice mine! There simply wasn't a moment when one could catch Ryan unprepared for a Scripture pop-quiz. He was a walking encyclopedia of biblical facts and quotes. Let me just say that I was ever so happy to have this student—a professor, really—of Christ and God's Word, although the cost to meet him was time within prison.

It is such a shame to think that someone like Ryan would be spending the remainder of his existence on the planet locked up, stuck inside that horrible, cramped space. This is one of the biggest problems with our judicial system: The judges and prisons only look at the crime committed, and rarely at the person whom committed that intentional or spontaneous error...the parole board rarely considers the respectable nature and goodness, which now resides inside that forgiven sinner's heart. The person released from prison after ten or more long years in custody is never the same as the one who was arrested; yet, unfortunately, inmates are punished for their potential to reoffend, not rewarded for their potential for greatness.

CHAPTER FIFTY-TWO

Illogical Inconsistencies

Bear and Damien had many good times with each other while housed within that cell at Pleasant Valley State Prison. For the most part, they had little to say, while at others they were like passing ships in the night: Damien arriving home from work at around the same moment Bear was leaving for his inmate assignment. However, as prison life goes, during time of facility lockdowns—which according to Damien were awfully frequent at Pleasant Valley, and without any just cause other than staff laziness—Bear and Damien had good, lengthy conversations or quiet chess games.

My days at Pleasant Valley were pretty much the same, while off of lockdown, doing much the same from breakfast till after final count, at nine p.m. I didn't do any plan-making ahead of time, for there was no guarantee that we would be getting "yard" or "dayroom" program. Nonetheless, I made it a solid part of my routine to study the Bible so that I could have interesting discussions regarding God and Christ Jesus, as they affected my life.

The one thing that bothered me, back then, was not having anything significant that I could learn while locked up. At least, nothing which would benefit me in the long run. I enjoyed reading... I just didn't know anyone "on the outside" who could send me books that would motivate my brain, or to learn new things which I could apply to my future.

As I've mentioned, I had lost my only true resource in life, my wife Vicki. I was barred from contacting her. Meanwhile, and still for then-unknown reasons, I was unable to reach Dr. Sam Reily over the phone. And although the inmate library on our yard offered a decent variety of donated paperbacks—mostly of the mass-market suspense-fiction genre—it held forth very few books in the fields of philosophy and theology, my favorite subjects.

I often found myself unhappily settling for whichever on Earth I could find at our yard's library, and borrowed quite a lot of them... even fantasies I'd already read before, such as J.R.R. Tolkien's The Lord of the Rings trilogy, or the lesser-known books penned by J.R.R.'s son. Although these were rather entertaining, I'd have preferred something more academic... or biblical. So, I once again returned to becoming more involved in a Bible study.

Like most other inmates I wanted to go home and resume taking on college classes at any campus elsewhere. The circumstances involving and surmounting my peaceful life needed to change, and I associated going to college as a dependable means towards that change. This is perhaps why I was constantly changing my majors and enrolling in college classes, because I found a level of certainty in attending them. In hindsight, I guess you could say I was stuck in a routine of always preparing, educating myself for a future yet to come, instead of playing a role in the here-and-now around me. Well, a role better than that of society's punching bag or spittoon.

Then it happened... Bear got me more actively involved in the leadership of our Sunday morning Bible study. Sure, it was presently only a group of a dozen very-conservative Evangelicals, but these men "ate" the Word of God like it was chocolate mousse! As I've said, we met on the small lawn after our more-official Sunday service inside the chapel, all of us craving ever-deeper digestion of the Bible. Yet, naturally, I "ate" with slightly different table manners, as well as a more cultivated palate than most.

The biggest separation I had with those who came to the Bible studies was that I earnestly did not believe that the Scriptures were the "spoken words" of God. I believed back then—and still do today—that God teaches "His" children what God wants us to learn, and much of this is by way of "His" Scriptures. Not that they are spoken truths but, rather, a collection of various stories; some of which taught by the only begotten living Word of

God... the Messiah, whom I'd accepted as being Jesus of Nazareth.

Unfortunately, as I explained this to other people, that the Bible is a series of stories—some quite possibly as fictional as J.R.R. Tolkien's... especially Noah and his Ark, or Jonah and his whale—which were written primarily to teach and nothing more. Of course, some of it—such as the sayings of Jesus—really might've been exactly what Jesus actually said, or a close enough paraphrasing. As I told this to other people, I'd unintentionally created distance from some of them, and cross-examination by others.

I had offered an answer to someone's question regarding Adam and Eve's son, Cain—who killed his brother, Abel, out of pure jealousy. As the story goes, Cain is kicked out of the land, that his dad had prepared for farming, as punishment for his murderous crime. Then, Cain sojourns, in the "land of Nod" and he is protected from being killed by the people there because of God's mark. My concern was the fact that Cain got "the boot"— is forced by God to leave the land east of Eden and forced to seek a living among people who he's afraid would want to kill him... so, where exactly did these people come from unless they, too, got kicked out of Adam's land?!

I went backwards and forwards with my fellow Bible study participants on the unanswerable question: How could there be people in the land of Nod, unless those people—direct descendants of the first man and woman, living in the land just east of Eden—had likewise been kicked out of their homeland. My answer to this was, and today it still remains: that God must have created more than one genetic pool by way of more than one set of "creation parents"... more than just one Adam and one Eve, in order to expand the initial world population. How else could mankind have prevented the biological troubles associated with inbreeding?

Likewise, the thought that mankind had spawned from massive amounts of sibling fornication and parental incest is absolutely revolting, even if there wasn't any established laws against it back then. In Genesis 4:17, it says that Cain slept with his wife... who either had different parents than Cain had, or was biologically Cain's sister, since no other family trees yet existed in recorded history. So, either all of mankind stemming from Cain and his wife are genetic mutants thanks to the product of inbreeding, or God had made more people from dust of the ground and/or from rib bones than what's currently recorded in the Bible.

This topic, as you can imagine, didn't go over too well with these conservative Evangelicals I was speaking with—especially the subject of incest and having sex with one's sister—inside a men's prison. The fact that I was housed on a yard known for having a percentage of child molesters and rapists made a few of these study group members concerned about my point of view towards this subject. The following Sunday, I was respectfully asked not to attend the Bible study group, since my thoughts and opinions were a bit too fanatical or, dare I say, too liberal... although I'm not entirely sure just when in human history "liberal" became a bad word.

Although Damien agreed to "taking a break" from their Sunday morning group, he continued to attend the religious worship services held within the chapel. He even built up the courage to ask a few of those churchgoers his unanswerable question of: Was not the bride of Cain also Cain's sister, born of Adam and Eve? To which Damien either received some peculiar stares or honest consideration and/or feedback.

It was through these moments of positive deliberation when Damien pondered the ideas of starting his very own Bible study, as he'd done before at C.M.C. prison over two decades ago. Damien was hoping that he could finally apply his head and "heart knowledge" of his learning.

On Sunday mornings, I was indeed happy to attend early-morning church service. Our chaplain was Bishop B. Brown of the Church of God in Christ, Holy Trinity. After one service, I really wanted to ask the bishop a question on the subject of faith and healing, as it had touched on the Holy Spirit.

I was under the belief that all the faith in the world does not mean that, even with all that support, a person would necessarily be healed of his or her physical problems, if that healing wasn't a part of the "plan" of God. Sometimes, evangelical saints seemed to believe that one's faith is all that it took and that person in question would be healed. But someone praying for their own healing doesn't seem as powerful nor as acceptable as the selfless praying of others, for others. So, I was wondering and wanting to see what this bishop would say on the matter.

Bishop Brown agreed with me that nothing could be done without God's participation in the healing. Also, Brown believed that what was really going on whenever Jesus Christ healed someone, was the fact of a real need of spiritual healing and not just physical healing...

"Well, Mr. Lartigue," Brown answered him, "it is my belief that if one were in need of healing, and if he were to believe God could heal him, then yes... God will heal that person. If one has faith that it is the Will of God, then by His Will, that person will be healed."

Okay, Damien started, *but that still leaves the question of the Will of God. How do we <u>know</u> if it <u>is</u> in the Will of God?*

"Good question! Jesus taught us that if we merely were to ask, believing that it would be done, then that healing would be in the Will of God."

B-b-but, how do we learn what actually is the Will of God?

Bishop Brown then smiled, as if the answer were obvious. "Follow Scripture. Mainly in the Gospels. There is where we find the Will of God in everything which Jesus did and spoke of."

But I have, Chaplain. I've lost count of the number of times I've read the gospel according to John or to Luke. I have most of Paul's letters memorized by heart, more so than my own personal letters to my wife... well, ex-wife.

"That's impressive. So then, when Jesus said that by faith anyone could tell a mountain to move, and it would move, you do not believe the same would be true if by faith anyone asked to be healed?"

I believe you left out that part in Matthew 17:20, where that faith could be as small as a mustard seed and that Jesus was probably referring to the problems of great difficulty hampering society, not really a mountain. But I see what you mean... it's just you still wouldn't be able to move a mountain unless it's God's Will that the mountain be moved.

"Yes, but you are forgetting what causes something to become the Will of God." Bishop Brown again smiled as if the simplicity of this topic could be recited by a kindergartener: "You have to ask your Father."

Oh, right. Um, okay. Good deal. I'll see you next week then—

"Why wait a 'week?' I run a small Bible study with about a dozen believers, at various levels of scriptural understanding. Would you be interested?"

Damien was momentarily flabbergasted, but then couldn't seem to say the word 'yes' fast enough! Yes, absolutely! Thank you!

"Alright then, come here Wednesday, after dinner, okay?"
Yeah! That sounds very cool! Again, thank you a lot, Bishop!

This was going to be rather different and new for Damien, because the groups he'd been a part of at C.M.C. and other prisons, were with men mostly at the very beginning of their faith. Bishop Brown's study group sounded to be a much more intellectual challenge, at least Damien hoped so. Likewise what would be different, was that the chaplain himself would be leading it… all of Damien's previous groups were run by the inmates themselves.

Damien was determined to make this chance be positive for him. That as long as God's nature or character wasn't the subject for the day, Damien would be able to attend and keep his unique understandings to himself. Unfortunately, being as Damien's track record towards staying out of attention is an incredibly short list, not voicing his opinion on the subject didn't last long at all.

Damien was very glad that he loved going to church, craved knowing as much as he could about God, and at all times of each day. Damien was also really glad to have Bear as his cellmate, who also was a Christ-loving man and went to this same Wednesday evening Bible study Damien had just been invited to join. Damien viewed this as an added bonus, since he now knew <u>who</u> he could ask questions to both on the way to group, and on the way back to their cell.

I could finally sense that everything was going to be better than only "fine." Bear had become my unofficial greeting party, and he introduced other Christians to me. Also, whenever there was another new inmate that just arrived to the yard, Bear made it "his business" to greet and introduce himself to them. He was the unofficial Welcoming Committee to our little world.

It was strange at first, but I truly saw the spiritual rightness of Bear's introductions to newcomers. This made me feel at ease right away; this man, my cellie, held a very natural love for others… the core of being a real Christian. Clearly, this heart-warming activity of Bear's was innate—or at least something I thought he was born with, since I completely lacked it—and I'd began to be slightly envious of him and this deep love which flowed so fundamentally throughout his existence. His inwrought charisma was as soothingly fluid as it was embittering since I'd never have it.

People like me, born with Asperger's, are not only introverted but we have a constant feeling of unintentional disregard or disengagement with other people... especially those we don't already know. This natural severance I have usually causes me to latch onto one or two really good friends, sometimes as many as six with considerable effort, while remaining reserved and aloof to others, and not because I want to. Although I've been characterized as shy by those who don't really know me that well, I constantly desire to be anything but shy or internal; after all, personally-absorbed is the opposite of being a true Christian.

After a month or so, time in prison no longer felt like a waste. No! Every day before dinner, Bear and I made healthy use of that hour of being locked up for count time, to study the Bible. Bear had started taking a correspondence theology course through the mail, which Bishop Brown had highly recommended. Bear and I benefitted from that course, which was paid for by my cellie's quite-proud grandmother. She—sorry, I forgot her name—didn't at all mind buying the books and tuition for these college-credit earning courses... she was overjoyed to hear how her previously violent grandson had turned his dark life over to Jesus Christ!

As we grew more comfortable and trusting of each other, Bear shared with me some events of his gruesome youth. I will not get into the details with you, since what he shared with me was in confidence, but Bear wasn't at all a peaceful person to be around. His childhood led him down the only path which made any sense to him: death and destruction! Although he'd been a punching bag like me—and likewise raped while really young—Bear punched back! He'd hurt quite a few people, several of whom were totally innocent of causing him any pain. And now, at that point, the man standing before me expressed the very handiwork of an Almighty God! A completely reformed Christian.

As I've said, I enjoyed having Bear as my cellmate. Yet, as all things do, change for me was inevitable! Time rapidly slid by Bear and I, and before long I had completed both a pair of years as well as enough good behavior to receive a reduction in my security level. I was about to go to my annual review—what us inmates call "going to committee"—and for once I was dreading it, because if my classification points dropped low enough, the prison could ship me off to just about anywhere!

To my unexpected and personally pleasurable surprise, I was put up for transfer, once again to California Men's Colony—the one in San Luis Obispo which I'd been at before—to their West facility. This got me rather excited, since in my personal opinion, based on my previous experience there, C.M.C. is the best place to do time at... that is, of course, second only to being released from prison and doing time out there! This was really "sweet." A homecoming of sorts for me.

However, this chapter of my life is about inconsistencies, and my latest arrival at C.M.C. would continue to be such an example. In late December 1982, as you know, these facilities were just about the pinnacle or optimal of prisons every inmate wanted to do there time at. But in early August of 2002, almost exactly two decades later, the atmosphere and general respect between inmates, staff, and within each group had drastically changed.

While each prisoner still possessed keys to their own cells, this advantageous privilege was now disrespectfully being used for all sorts of debauchery, including—but not limited to—theft, vandalism, and gang rape of unsuspecting and defenseless victims. Inmates had copies of forged keys or figured out which limited number of cell keys open which set of tumblers, in order to break into whichever cell they chose.

There was plenty of smuggled-in drugs or homemade wine—we called it "pruno"—practically everywhere, plus a very high percentage of openly gay men actively French kissing or fornicating other men where others could see them doing it, without a care in the world. The correctional officers were absolutely disgusted by this behavior, and treated all inmates with the same loathing regardless if you were anything like them. In fact, the guards seemed to be more uptight and rude to those who <u>weren't</u> publically engaged in sexual misconduct even more so than those who were! After all, inmates not misbehaving or being written up for rules violations were a threat to these officers' job security... as if the state of California would ever run out of inmates.

Because of this debauchery and loathing, those of us arriving off of the buses were treated with an unusual disdain I'd never experienced in all my years in the prison system before. The Receiving and Release (R&R) officer went through my personal belongings with a cruel vengeance: scrutinized each and every piece of paper, tearing manila envelopes along their sides instead of simply opening the reclasping flap, and—which I'll describe in detail—when it came to the number of books I possessed...

Officer Clath stood before Damien across a long counter, sifting in a not-too-gentle way through the contents dumped out of a cardboard box, namely the property which Damien had brought over with him from the previous high-security level 3 prison. Yet, for some unknown reason, C.O. Clath was declaring several items as not allowed at the current medium-security, level 2 facility, even if they <u>were</u> permitted at the more-secure institution. With each item Clath removed from the shrinking pile and tossed into a nearby trash can, Damien grew more and more infuriated... which may have been Clath's goal:

"Nope. Nope. What the hell is this?! Nope, can't have this either."

Wait, I bought those from Pleasant Valley's canteen. I even still have the receipt, Damien rightfully protested.

"Well, it's not sold in our canteen, so it's not allowed. And, holy crap! How many frickin' books do you have in here! Don't you know the fuckin' rules! Ten books and magazines! Period!

When I left Pleasant Valley they didn't have a problem with me—

"If I hear the name Pleasant Valley one more fuckin' time, you're spending tonight in Ad-Seg!" meaning administrative segregation. "Here! Pick out which books and magazines you want! Be quick about it!"

Asking Damien to pick only ten books or magazines is in close comparison to asking a Hollywood movie critic to spontaneously pick his or her ten favorite actors of all time... there's just too many difficult choices to consider. Each time Damien placed a hand on a book, even if he'd already read it twice or more, he kept eyeing that trash can this officer had been tossing confiscated—technically, pillaged—items into. He just couldn't bear the sight of <u>any</u> literary work being thrown away.

After four excruciating minutes, Damien had made his selection of ten books in one pile, and ten magazines in another. This only further exasperated the hurried office to no end.

"Don't you fuckin' listen?! I said ten! Not ten of each! Ten books or magazines! And what about those?!" Clath pointed at four bound notebooks which Damien kept handwritten notes and his daily journal in.

They're notebooks!

"Yeah, genius! 'Books' is part of their fuckin' name! You're wasting my ga'damn time! I'll pick your fuckin' books!" And with that, the officer grabbed at the top two paperbacks of the 'books' pile, the top two magazines of their pile, and only two of four notebooks within Damien's diminished belongings. The rest were then scooped up and tossed into that rather-full trash can.

You said I could have ten, Damien rightfully complained, *that's only six!*

"Be glad you're gettin' any! Now, get the fuck out of my face, Chester!"

The officer's amalgamation of 'Chester' stood for "child" and 'molester,' which Damien certainly was not. In fact, this officer had no idea for what crime the inmate standing before him—nor any of the others within the nearby holding tanks—were 'in' for. He lacked the access to such information. Regardless, the reference to Damien being an offender of children, caused him to emotionally outburst more than anything else this "worthless human being" said or did:

TO HELL WITH YOU!! I ain't no chester! And you've got no fuckin' right to call anyone fuckin' that! Damien exclaimed loudly enough to be heard through walls. *You're supposed to be an officer! An example of who we are supposed to be and behave! You are—*

Damien wasn't able to finish his sentence before being tackled to the dirty tile floor by an officer responding to his yelling from down the hall. Although, this was perfect timing, since Damien was likely to have said something highly disrespectful about Office Clath which would have resulted in Damien spending several days instead of only one night in 'the hole.'

"Get him the fuck out of here! I don't need this shit! I've got work to do!" the irate R&R officer's final words echoed in Damien's ears as he was being escorted around a corner, then locked in a wire cage featuring the same dimensions as a 1960's public-telephone booth... minus the pay phone, of course. His personal belongings, what little were left after the vicious reaping, sat in a clear-plastic trash bag just outside the wire cage; practically teasing Damien into believing that this was what his life has boiled down to, as well as his self-value.

Unfortunately, this would be only the first of such emotional turmoils and personal intrusions which Damien would face at this once-optimal prison.

CHAPTER FIFTY-THREE

Regressing Reputations

D amien spent only that night—of many, many more nights—within a solitary confinement cell, then in the morning was escorted to the West Facility, which was their Level 2 unit and featured large dormitories housing on average eighty inmates each... all snoring and farting practically all night long. During his walk there, with an officer he didn't know, Damien caught glimpses of his old home-away-from-home, the East Facility—which was Level 3 cell-living.

With his first three steps into his new dormitory, Damien instantly knew he would not like it there. Although the entire prison yard was considered "soft" or a protective-custody type of facility, the hardened faces looking back at him showed a mixture of gang-membership experience and/or homosexual desire of "the new fish."

I had seen the west dormitory being much the same as my previous level three and four facilities. Boy was I wrong! And this wrong presumption worked against me. As I was settling myself in, taking the knot out of my bag of property for the very first time, I was pretty much minding my own business, and this was somehow perceived as disrespectful by the others in close surroundings of my assigned bunk. But then, of all moments for a new guy, my past came before me.

As you know, I was openly bisexual during my first prison term, which included a trip through Tracy D.V.I. and this very prison—although the East side of it. I didn't send out any feelers, at least I didn't mean to, but I must have had some invisible "Gay Pride" bumper sticker taped on my back, because even though I hadn't said more than the words "What's up?" to a limited few onlookers, I ws instantly rumored as being gay!

Then came the moment when I was approached by a mid-forties Mexican dud whom claimed to know me...

"Yeah, I know you," this stranger stated. "Back in Tracy, somethin' like in '85. You got some weird first name, like Duncan? Denver?"

No, I—Damien paused to reconsider the ramifications of lying, especially in a room of eighty guys without a place to hide. *It—it was '82, and my name's Damien.*

"Yeah, I would've gotten it. Damien." The American-Mexican moaned something despicably in Spanish, then translated for everyone close enough to hear: "Yeah, I remember. I paid your pimp Danny for a taste of you. Sweet as sugar."

This public declaration, especially the name of Danny, instantly brought back long-lost memories for Damien: His months of being prostituted out by a man named Danny, his cellie Jim, and a disgusting homeless bum nicknamed Bob the Dog. Damien had forgotten all about those Tracy D.V.I. months, as well as the total number of men he was forced to provide sexual services for. Apparently, this man standing before him—with his exceptionally good memory of faces and events from two decades ago—remembered what services Damien had long ago provided, and <u>hopefully</u> would be providing him again!

The exact same fear I had back in those days of first meeting Danny and his other friend, Jim, was resurfacing right along with those forgotten memories! I was scared back then, and I was equally scared right then and there in C.M.C. West. I was not prepared to start whoring myself out in a dormitory-living joint, nor to let someone else force me to. But it was obvious to me that this well-equipped and buffed Mexican guy was going to let my past reputation dictate my future.

Wow! Really?! Damien teased. *You remember all of that, yet you don't remember I'm the one that gave you herpes?* Then Damien turned serious, *I'm not for sale anymore. I'm forty-six years old, and nothing down there is sweet anymore. Pro'bly give you gonorrhea this time, he lied again. At least, to that moment, Damien had been 'lucky' at never contracting any long-term diseases from a john or lover.*

"Shit, I pro'bly gave you your herpes, and I've had gono' plenty of times before. At least you mouth seems to work fine."

I'm not going to be anyone's whore! Damien defiantly stood his ground.

"Who said anything about being a whore? I'm greedy, I don't share my toys. I want you all to myself!"

It was in that instant when Damien realized he would have no choice: either he would have to accept this man as his monogamous lover or, thanks to this man's earlier public declaration about Damien's past, someone else—and perhaps worse—would be taking "possession" of the former prostitute.

I really couldn't believe my rotten luck. If this Mexican dude hadn't recognized me, nor remembered that twenty years ago I sold my body for food and protection, my first few days within that dormitory would've been a lot different. I had forgotten all about my past, yet my past hadn't forgotten all about me! However, these days were going to be short ones thanks to the unknown wheels I'd put into motion back on that afternoon I'd gotten off of the bus.

The events of that yelling match between myself and the R&R officer, plus my one night spent in "the hole," had not reached completion. In fact, just four days after arriving at C.M.C. West, I was being out up for transfer to C.M.C. East.

Damien had been called into the facility captain's office to discuss a Rules Violation Report filed against Damien for the offenses of disrespecting an officer and disobeying a direct order. The second of these charges did not make much sense to either the captain nor Damien, because the "order" he was said to have disobeyed was to select ten books or magazines from his personal property and Damien was reported as refusing to do so.

Regardless of the truth of these accusations, Damien saw this R.V.R. hearing for what it very well could be: An escape from dormitory living. Not only did he enter a plea of guilt before the captain even asked him, but Damien clearly added, *And I'd do it again, 'cause C.O. Clath is a fuckin' prick if there ever was one!*

"Inmate Lartigue! I'm not going to allow you to speak that way about one of my officers."

But he is a prick! Everyone knows that I'm telling the truth.

Then the facility captain smiled, "Well, of course it's the truth. But, I still can't have you saying it. Your plea of guilt is hereby accepted. I'm afraid this is going to increase your classification points to level three, and I'm going to have to rehouse you to Facility East.

Oh, really? Damien sarcastically replied to the news of being transferred to exactly where he wanted to go. *Darn! I hate having to leave.*

"Well, my hands are tied. Sorry," the facility captain needlessly apologized, completely oblivious to Damien's true desires to get the heck out of a dorm.

California Men's Colony East Facility, Damien's old homestead, hadn't changed much since the early 1980's. Everything was pretty much the same, with the exception only to Damien's earlier mentioning of the frequent misuse of keys to burglarize others' cells or to "butt swindle" the occupant. C.M.C. East consisted of four yards known as quads, with each quad roughly one acre in size; Not bad for six hundred men. The biggest difference was that the one-man cells themselves had been converted to two-man rooms no bigger than they were when Damien originally stayed there.

I wasn't at all expecting to have a cellie, since I hadn't had one back in 1983, and to be honest: the cells just weren't large enough for two guys. Sure, when Charlie "oops" and I were sharing the same bedroom—and bed—we rarely noticed the extreme closeness... instead, we savored it. But now, in 2003, the unwanted closeness with someone you barely know was intrusive! The second bed, or upper bunk, wasn't arranged directly above the bottom one, but connected to a metal wall which acted like a room divider down the middle of the cell, with nothing but wasted space located underneath the top bunk. It was a horrible configuration which made the already small room smaller!

What was really strange was, the cellie that I had—the man already living in the cell when I was moved in—was immediately told by the officers that he would be moving out. I found this as an unexpected blessing, but I guess I really should have seen this as a warning sign of something on the horizon. It had been so long since I had a cell—prison or jail—to myself. It was luxurious! However, it only lasted six days.

On Damien's fifth day of having a prison cell all to himself, a small piece of paper was delivered by an officer: a note of a classification hearing on the following day. He went to breakfast as usual that morning, then to the counselors' office for the committee meeting. Once again, it was decided that Damien would be moved, although <u>this</u> time to an entirely different prison, in the city of Avenal. There was no clear reason on why this transfer was being done, only Damien's confrontational nature towards staff… namely the officer who threw away a majority of his books and notebooks.

I was going to be placed on the next bus to Avenal State Prison just because I raised a fuss about my books and notes being trashed. In the quiet moments of waiting for that bus, I sat down with pen and paper to reconstruct the events which had been recorded in those lost notebooks, but most of this was an impossible task. I could vividly remember certain things and conversations, with crystal clarity; yet, I couldn't always remember the dates nor the sequence of those events of my past. It would end up taking months of memory reflection for me to rewrite those two notebooks; so I believe my fussing on that fateful afternoon was justified, if not the subsequent "adverse transfer" to that other level two prison in Kings County.

I was once again leaving one of the best prisons in all of California for one of the most mediocre and boring!

Just three months before Damien's forty-sixth birthday, which occurred on December 6th, 2003, he'd been "put up" for transfer to the one place his correctional counselors believed as adequate: Avenal State Prison, near Bakersfield, California. Damien would be spending his next two-and-a-half stale years there.

Boy, was it dull… as far as things to do. What I mean by that is, although living within any prison is a lackluster, routine experience, Avenal prison managed to surpass and excel at that level of monotony! This boredom was the child to the overwhelming lack of mind-stimulating activities and inmate-assigned jobs… as well as a staff whom didn't care one bit about the population.

Back in the late 80's when A.S.P. first opened, it housed just under three-thousand men, as it was originally designed to hold. However thanks to the implementing of California's absurd Three Strikes law, state-wide prison overcrowding caused Avenal to follow the footsteps of other cell-living facilities by declaring their single-man cells as being large enough for two inmates, as well as converting the gymnasium—once used for indoor recreation—into "temporary" dormitories... which remained being dorms for over a decade.

But presently, when I arrived there, there weren't enough services nor inmate assignments available for the some seven-thousand two-hundred inmates living on those six individual yards. In fact, at the unit I was housed, with its eleven-hundred or more men, the waiting list to receive any kind of mind-stimulating position, outside of adult education or the single vocational program being offered, was longer than the amount of time I had left to serve. Granted, if I had somehow managed to "sweet talk" my way into a yard crew job or kitchen worker assignment, I would've gained additional time credits towards being released sooner; however, I would never be one of the "popular" people in a crowd of a thousand, nor would I reduce myself to groveling for a job.

Although it is true that prison had "yard programs," which included various sports such as softball or even basketball tournaments where winning participants could win sodas or other junk food; due to the massive amount of inmates housed on a particular yard, being picked by a team captain to play was as equally improbable as the odds of your tier of cells receiving any recreational time that specific day. The local correctional officers' union was really strong in dictating to the prison administration towards how many inmates could be out of their cells at any given time; unless, of course, if the prison hired more officers... which they couldn't afford to do.

Gone was also all the funding for inmate hobby and craft programs, the highly-sought lessons in woodworking and cabinetry back in the 70's and 80's. Inmates still learned how to draw and perform beading, but through purchasing their own supplies through family members, and instruction from fellow inmates or library books; absolutely no staff support. We couldn't even get photocopies of Sudoku or crossword puzzles made by staff, even if we had funds to pay for those copies, which was never a problem in the 80's. More and more common privileges we used to have and/or count on were evaporating before my very eyes, and the primary cause was due to overcrowding and poorly-trained rookies replacing all of the retiring baby-boomers.

As Damien noticed, more and more of his own generation—those born between the late 1940's through the early 1960's—were retiring from the prison system, being substituted with a younger and "more pretentious" class of staff whose primary focus is towards their paycheck amounts and promotions than any earnest belief in rehabilitation of anyone. Also, this idea of retirement troubled Damien because he'd soon be in his fifties without a single dime saved up for a rainy day, let alone any lengthy employment. No, Damien was looking towards a dismal future of homeless shelters and working until the day he died. These thoughts led him back to prayer and Bible study.

There I was, regularly praying that God would not only help me get out and stay out, but also to watch over me as I'd struggle to restart my life. Keep in mind that I still had a difficult time back then knowing the differences between having a life and "making a living." I wholeheartedly believe that I had a brand-new life through Christ Jesus, yet I completely lacked a means of supporting that life, as my thirty-year employment history only listed three short-term, minimum-wage jobs. I would need God's proactive assistance now more than ever before!

I knew my biggest problem was that I just never really followed God's lead. I thought I knew what God wanted from me, or what I believed was best for myself; yet look at where I'd ended up time and time again! God would not have led me to this nor any other place but "home" if I had listened. How did I end up so darn blind and deaf towards God? Towards God's voice and the road signs God had placed along my journey? God had the perfect alternative towards going home... I would have been safe from myself! Yet, as inconceivable as it is for someone so well-versed in Scripture—someone whose not only started a Bible study in prison, but also a small-group ministry out of his own home, once upon a lifetime ago—here I was exactly where I would not have been, had I simply "lived what I knew."

My fears were growing, not shrinking, as my release date was approaching ever closer. One of my worries back then was I had no notion of who would hire this ex-offender. The fear of failing at getting a job—a job that would keep me off the streets once again—or making a living that would be manageable, was driving me crazy. No company would hire a former rapist and convicted gunman—the fact that I was under the influence of freebase during both of these events wouldn't necessarily help my job application neither. So, rightfully, I was starting to panic about being paroled and let loose on the streets again!

Damien's rather common doubt of being able to find employment as an ex-felon—especially when your criminal history is longer than your list of past employers—is the number one reason why parolees recidivate. They are made to fell <u>unqualified</u> because of their past behavior and record, until these men feel that their only choice <u>is</u> to return to that very behavior which they are known for and/or most experienced at. The failure to break out of one's reputation is the greatest reason why a parolee reoffends, as well as why California's prisons are so overcrowded.

Listen to yourself, and in that quietude you might hear the voice of God.

CHAPTER FIFTY-FOUR

Returning to What Works

On July 22nd, 2005, after several long years of attending Bible studies and mostly keeping to himself, Damien was released on three years parole from Avenal State Prison. All of his earlier fears and worries about getting out of prison without any real plans towards where to stay or how to live, all came to fruition within that final 24-hour period of excitement and dread.

It was a busy night, the one before my release from A.S.P., and I was a busy boy—and by "boy" I mean the quite literal definition of someone full of childlike elation. I was anxiously rushing around saying goodbye to those few inmates—mostly fellow churchgoers—whom I thought of as friends. Then, between the hours of 2100-hours count and one o'clock Friday morning, of my actual release day, I finally wore myself out enough to finally climb up to my rack to see about getting any amount of impossible sleep.

Finally, I was awakened just before sunrise by an officer calling me to the podium. In my hurried pace, I went to that podium without as much as a last quick-glance at my former space or locker. No! I just grabbed by stuff—what little of it I'd packed the day before—and left. It wasn't until I'd arrived at Receiving and Release that I noticed I'd left behind my treasured battery-operated AM/FM radio headphones... the kind joggers used to wear before the invention of iPods. I inherited them from someone else who'd gone home, and now in my absent-mindedness someone else would be inheriting them from me.

A moment later, my depression over the loss of my radio faded away, as a familiar form was handed to me for a signature. The process of releasing us prisoners was smooth and quick...far easier and faster than in the opposite direction! It wasn't long before the few of us guys being paroled that morning were hurried into an awaiting white van—"kids, do not try this at home"—and for my very first time, I was in a van without chains nor other restraints.

During Damien's last two times being released from prison, Dr. Sam Reily personally drove out to whichever prison and picked Damien up. Likewise amazing, Sam offered Damien a place to stay, place to work, and financial support during those tough transitional periods back into society. However, this <u>third</u> time, Damien had none of this! No obvious help from anyone.

A month before being released from Avenal, Damien had called Dr. Reily's home number completely on a whim, since all of his previous calls went unanswered; plus, and for similarly unknown reasons, the doctor's work and cell-phone numbers came back as being "no longer in service." To Damien's surprise that June day, his collect call was both answered and accepted; albeit, not from the good doctor himself. Instead it was Sam's younger sister, Barbara-Anne.

"Damien?" she greeted him over the phone. "I'm so glad you called."

Umm, hi—he paused to place a name to the unexpected voice, *Barb? Wow, haven't heard your voice in, well, forever. How are you, and Sam? Is he home? I've tried a bunch of times to—*

"Wait. Slow down, Damien," she urged, then cleared her throat. "One question at a time."

Sorry, it's just been so long since I got through to someone over the phone. I'm a little excited. Is Sam home?

"Well, of course he's home—"suddenly she interrupted herself, as if something suddenly came to mind. "That's right, you don't know. Do you?" she asked in a very somber tone.

Know? Know what exactly? The only thing I know is that Sam doesn't like to answer his phone.

"No, Damien. Sam is... well, he had a stroke. It happened a while ago. Sam lost all feeling on the left side of his body, Damien. His arm, his hand, his leg. He's partially paralyzed, Damien."

This news was quite a shocker to him. The infallible Dr. Reily suddenly losing control and feeling of the entire left half of his own body. Barbara-Anne went on to explain that Sam doesn't like to talk on the phone, due to his excessive slurring of words and the frustration of correcting himself after each mispronunciation. That after his stroke, Sam was forced to close his office of psychiatry, to focus on his dilemma and needs. Without the business, Sam would be soon slipping into financial ruin... he's already considering the sale of his Huntington Beach home.

I had had no idea that all of this was occurring in Sam's life. I felt so completely out the loop and distant. Sure—and I blame this feeling on my Asperger's—I was concerned with this shock that Sam wouldn't be able to help me out... not that <u>he</u> still owed <u>me</u> any favors; it was completely the other way around! However, as Barbara-Anne made it sound, and as I suspected, Barbara-Anne had the entire situation under control; she would take excellent care of her big brother.

So, back to Damien's release from prison, he wasn't previously experienced nor prepared for what it would be like to be released on his penniless own. What was it going to be like in the world without his old friends, without a job or place to live, and without his wife, Vicki.

In hindsight, I realize the irony that had I <u>not</u> failed at starting my non-profit organization: Community of Hope (which was designed to help parolees in the exact same circumstances I was now in), that this organization would've been around to assist its founder! And boy, did I need some rapid assistance right then and there with my return to society.

As I believe I've mentioned before, when someone like me gets released from a California state prison, that parolee receives two-hundred dollars, also referred to as "gate money." With this absolutely <u>exorbitant</u> amount of money—yes, I'm being rather facetious here—a released prisoner is supposed to travel to his or her parole region, afford housing, purchase new work clothes, and completely start their life all over! Yeah, with two-hundred bucks.

We were in that van for about a half-hour, before the officers pulled *into a Stop 'n Go station, to get some refreshments. They opened the back doors to that prisoner-transport van and invited us parolees to stretch our legs—since we had another twenty-five minutes to drive—or to buy a few things. This, again, was very different for me to be coming out of a sheriff's or prison van <u>without</u> any handcuffs on, as well as this sudden humane treatment by these correctional officers; normally the comfort of their passengers in the back of the van is the <u>least</u> of their concerns!*

Merely walking around that gas station's parking lot as a "free" man was an enjoyment like none other! There I was after five years, back amongst the living members of civilization: the air smelt different, the direct sunlight felt different, and everything surrounding me was new and exciting. I splurged some of my invaluable cash on a pack of cigarettes and a Pepsi. It has been such a long time since I'd last smoked—all of the prisons were smoke-free, although tobacco was still smuggled in somehow—and I knew it was an expensive luxury which I couldn't afford on my limited budget, but I so desperately needed something to calm my nerves right then. I wasn't at all willing to restart my earlier addictions, yet as most people do, I could see myself easily returning to what best worked for me… and I was terrified.

Damien and his fellow "releasees" were dismally loaded back onto the van, albeit still without any shackles plus knowing that they'd never be inside a van like this one ever again—or, at least, for a very long time. On the road for another half an hour, they finally reached their next stop: a Greyhound bus depot in Fresno. Under regulations, the officers still maintained custody of each parolee until that person purchased a bus or train ticket. Damien's chain of custody was broken the moment he bought a one-way bus pass to West Los Angeles, thereby proving that he was returning to his region of parole.

The question haunted me: How was I supposed to live? What was I supposed to do? I was, for the first time, quite literally on my own without a place to live nor any support from my friend Sam, my grandpa, or my step-father. I knew I was capable of taking care of myself, and had during my early twenties as a prostitute, supplemented by Sam's generosity in paying for a motel on Santa Monica Boulevard, for the first couple of months. Yet, naturally, I was edging towards my fifties, plus the potential clientele of a fifty-year-old male prostitute wearing a sex offender GPS anklet was nonexistent outside of, perhaps, Las Vegas. Not that I was honestly considering "hooking" again.

However, what I did do since I knew the area rather well—or thought I still did—was to return to the Hollywood/Santa Monica area. After some five hours on a Greyhound bus, I disembarked and entered that depot in order to figure out where I was supposed to go until Monday morning, when I would need to report to my parole officer's office in Pomona. I studied for an hour a roadmap of the city's buses, learning what routes would get me from points <u>A</u> to <u>B</u>, without winding up in <u>Z</u>.

The weekend alone was intimidating me! Here I was, doing what every inmate in prison dreams about nearly every night: being free! And I hadn't a clue on how to make my remaining one-hundred and forty dollars last me the rest of Friday, the following two whole days, and into Monday. Granted, while I was in prison and working as a building porter, I made less than thirty cents per day, and survived on even less than that; yet, I had a taxpayer-funded roof over my head, and hot meals provided.

I knew that I needed to get me a room for the night—my first priority—and took a city bus to, of all intersections: the corner of Hollywood and Vine. The area had, of course, changed in the last three decades; although, most of the businesses were still recognizable, despite the fancier landscaping. The Golden Cup coffee shop was still there, under the same management I believe; however, thanks to local tourism, the cheapest hamburger on the menu was now six bucks. Everything had been revamped or repainted to appeal to the thousands of out-of-state visitors.

From 1979–1980, I had called this neighborhood mine; yet in 2005, while most things seemed familiar, nothing felt the same. The motel I had paid-by-the-week to stay in was long gone, bulldozed and replaced by something more ritzy. Even my old haunt, the adult theatre called "The Cave" had a modernized touch of class it really didn't need, other than to justify its increase in ticket prices. Yet, above all these, the most noticeable change to me was the decrease in number of prostitutes and complete absentness of the homeless. I didn't see any of either kind, even for a Friday afternoon.

As I approached one motel known for its cheap hourly rates, I realized the conundrum that I didn't even own a driver's license nor any other official type of identification. Don't most hotels expect you to prove your identity or *provide a credit card to cover any damages made to your room?* As I walked into that place's lobby, I was hoping that the clerk would make an exception for this recent parolee. No such luck! In fact, the details of my recent release from prison only further encouraged the clerk <u>not</u> to help me! That I'd better off finding someplace even more seedier than his.

During my last few days in prison, I spent hours considering all possibilities of being released: In none of them was I expecting that I'd have to be homeless for my first weekend. I often thought that the prison system would put me up in a halfway-house type of place until I got myself a job or an apartment—which California used to do prior to the 1970s, and some states continue to do today. Like most parolees, I just didn't know where I was supposed to be, only that I needed a place to crash until seeing my P.O. on Monday morning.

After my disappointment at possibly the worst motel in L.A., and as it was close to dinner time, I spent another seven dollars I couldn't afford to be spending at a fast-food restaurant. Beside the door to the restrooms was a public pay-phone—remember those?—and decided to call the only phone number I'd memorized: Sam's home.

Before I get into the details about that call, let me reiterate that I was deeply troubled about my impossible situation. Life on parole, for me, used to be easy… after all, both of those times I lived with my dear friend, Sam. Sam was, at minimum, a true friend… one which I didn't deserve. So, this experience of "restarting life" on my own was not only new, indeed, it was scary! I was most uncertain of what to do and when to do them; I only knew that I'd better be more frugal with what little cash I had left, as well as a friend or just some helpful advice.

There was also the fact that I was forty-seven years old in July 2005, and yet I still was dependent on others. This unfledged lifestyle alone made me feel so shameful. I mean that, even while married, I was still dependent on Vicki's financial support—the one soul I wanted to grow old with and to make a healthy family with, and I was dependent on Vicki for quite a while; at least, until obtaining the CVS Pharmacy job which—in all actuality— did not contribute all that much towards the household.

Standing there in that fast-food restaurant and dialing Sam's number, I felt bad for "dumping" him and his obvious love for me, in exchange for *a female partner in life. This was something that he couldn't compete with: my desire to be with a woman, to become a husband, and to someday be a father. He had hoped during our years of living together, that my bisexuality would eventually be swayed towards a monogamy with him; yet I had an obligation to myself to be true and this includes being a wholly me, who I honestly was, and this meant someone attracted to both genders... which brought Sam nothing but disgust.*

As with my previous call—albeit a collect one from inside prison—the home-owner himself wasn't the one whom answered it... instead, I got Barbara-Anne again. She told me that Sam wasn't doing well, that twice he'd been admitted to the hospital for this or that. She also told me, that most likely due to pain medication, Sam was becoming more and more of a recluse. A zombie, really. Then our conversation turned towards myself and my own needs. Within minutes of describing my plight, Barbara-Anne pledged to Western Union me some much-needed money; yet, when I told her about my lack of a driver's license and credit card in order to rent a motel room, Barbara-Anne changed her plans and stated that she'd meet me in the restaurant's parking lot in an hour.

Thanks to Sam's sister's generosity and proof of identity, Damien was checked into a hotel which his remaining gate money couldn't lease by its own. The few extra dollars she gave him really did help break Damien's insecurities, a small boost of confidence in his immediate future, if not his attitude towards life beyond bars. Although Damien promised not to waste the money or "go on any wild shopping sprees," one particular peer pressure was building up within him on Saturday.

The world changed while I was in prison: Everyone, even preschoolers, seemed to have cell phones now. True, cell phones existed in the late 1990s, but those early pieces of technology only made phone calls... but now they did practically anything! Music, movies, games, GPS, movie tickets, sports scores, texting—whatever the <u>heck</u> that is?!—and access to everything on the Internet... you could even turn your coffeemaker on with a phone! It just seemed like you couldn't officially be a member of society without ownership of a phone. So, I bought one of those "throw away" models with a pre-paid amount of minutes, you know, just in case somebody wanted to call me.

Barbara-Anne rented me the hotel room for only that weekend, which was fine by me. After all, my housing problems were to be overcome that Monday. Or, so I'd thought. But in the meantime, thanks to Sam's sister, I was living with a lot less stress and a bit more assurance. It's simply amazing what a few spending dollars can do to a person's morale; yet at the same time it's surprising how society works against those who have so very little. When I'd gotten off of that Greyhound bus I felt like a foreigner in a strange land; yet when I wasn't allowed to check into that motel, I felt like I wasn't even recognized as a human being!

The one thing I'm sure of in this world, and of this world, is that God never intended mankind to live this way, paycheck-to-paycheck. That someone with only a few dollars in his or her pocket should have a lower morale than anyone else living comfortably. We humans attach too much of our personal well-being and emotions to our financial status; the amount of money in your wallet or bank account should never dictate the amount of happiness in your life... yet we do this all of the time! Things shouldn't work that way.

It was on Monday morning when Damien made a call—on the hotel's phone, not his cell—to his parole agent's office. The receptionist there gave Damien driving directions to the Pomona parole office, roughly thirty miles away. When Damien stated that he'd be travelling by bus and needed to know which ones to take, the female voice grumbled that her other phone lines were ringing and hung up on Damien. Thankfully, he still had his copy of their map, as well as the mapping software on his smartphone.

It took me quite some time to finally reach my parole agent's office, just a little bit after ten. However, the man assigned to handle my case wasn't there. I was told to have a seat, that it shouldn't be long... followed by "he shouldn't be much longer." At around one o'clock, as the other parole agents of that office returned from lunch, I again questioned where mine was at. "Oh, he should be here any moment." I wasn't about to take up residency in their waiting room, so I told the receptionist I'd "come back tomorrow," and left.

Once again I was faced with the dilemma that I'd need a place to sleep that night. I was waiting for my first of three different bus lines, in order to return to the Hollywood area, when it occurred to me that there really was no need to travel all the way back there. Maybe I could find a motel closer to this office building, preferably within walking distance. But then the realizations regarding proof of identity, lack of credit cards, and the few belongings which I'd left behind in the hotel room. So, I called the hotel's lobby using my cell phone, and informed the desk clerk I'd be staying for one more night. It was going to cost me every last dollar I had left almost, minus tomorrow's bus fare and tonight's cheeseburger. I'd be in serious trouble if my parole officer stood me up again.

CHAPTER FIFTY-FIVE

Only Halfway There

On the following day, Damien did meet with his parole agent, Jorge Simmons, who seemed to be a nice-enough guy in his forties. Their first interview together lasted only ten minutes, covering Damien's agreed parole conditions, expectations, and current financial status. One positive surprise was that Damien wouldn't be required to wear a GPS anklet, as originally feared, because the initial sex offense happened in early 1990, and his failure to register this latest time didn't trigger that particular embarrassment and hassle.

Towards the end of the interview, Officer Simmons handed Damien a prearranged stack of blank forms to fill out, which included applications for food stamps, unemployment insurance, state identification card through the D.M.V., and Medicaid. The agent suggested applying for food stamps and ID card immediately, and to remain healthy as possible until the government health insurance kicked in, Finally, Officer Simmons handed Damien one last item, a sealed envelope addressed to a place he'd never been at nor recognized.

"And this is for your landlord," Jorge said about the envelope.

Wait... my what? Damien asked, while shuffling the handful of loose papers and blank forms around.

"That's for your halfway residence. It's an excerpt of your case file, notice of your parole conditions, and authority to stay there." The officer then noticed the puzzlement in Damien's eyes and asked, "Haven't you been on parole before?! You've got two strikes, right? So, I know this isn't your first rodeo."

Actually, I'm as new as they come. I stayed with a friend the last two times I was released. Never dealt with food stamps or halfway houses before.

"Ahh, okay. Well, that address there," he points to the sealed envelope, "is where you've been assigned. Staying there is up to you, unless you don't have a permanent address. As a registered sex offender, you'll need a residence, not homeless shelter. And to re-register every time you move, whenever you stay at a friend's house for longer than a few days. You already know what happens if you don't."

Yeah, you could say that, Damien added sarcastically.

The halfway residence is state-funded and rent free until you get a job… and it is your responsibility to get a job. You don't qualify for any S.S.I. disability, an don't be relying on unemployment checks. That'll be a violation of your parole. Get yourself a job."

Umm, what about going back to school? I thought I either needed to get a job or be a full-time student?

"Aren't you, um, forty-seven? Forty-eight?"

Yeah, but… but I've never felt fully completed in my education. I was working towards my degree while I was living in Ohio. Damien had actually earned his Bachelor's degree, yet this was in a field which he no longer felt interested in pursuing. Besides, as you may have noticed, Damien preferred the life of an academic above any other career choice, rewarding or otherwise.

"Well, yes, being a full-time student covers the requirements of your parole… but you just told me you have no family and no money. Who's going to be paying for you going back to school?!"

Oh, there's grants I can get towards tuition, and loans that'll meet me halfway on the cost of books. I've been thinking all of this out before my release from prison.

"True, but community colleges don't provide housing or food. You'll have to come up with those on your own." He then cleared his throat, and offered Damien a handshake. "I'll be in touch. Don't fuck this up."

Oh, I won't, Damien promised, then left the office.

As feared, Damien didn't receive any financial support from his parole officer. No, not a single dime! Thankfully, the halfway house Damien was assigned to was practically right around the corner, less than two blocks from the parole office. If not for Barbara-Anne's help, Damien would be completely penniless right now, as he's already spent much more than his original gate money amount. Whatever little he's got left would have to go towards the price which the D.M.V. charges for an I.D. card, and the bus fare to get around town.

After a quick calculation, Damien realized he wouldn't be able to buy himself dinner that night! Nor any other night! The halfway house didn't provide any meals at all, only a place to sleep. In Damien's own opinion, nothing could have been worse than staying at the halfway house... most homeless shelters would be a vast improvement! However, through scuttlebutt and suggestions from the other parolees staying there, Damien picked up some tips and locations of where to find the best free meals.

I wasn't completely destitute, mind you. Until my food stamps kicked in, I did manage to sell a few of my prison belongings, as well as cook some of my leftover food from the prison's canteen I'd brought with me. This was the only benefit to staying at the halfway house as opposed to a motel, they allowed us to do our own cooking there. They had only a few pots and utensils to cook with, none of which would be accepted at a Salvation Army donations center due to rust and dents. But I rarely felt starved.

The residents of the halfway house were required to attend house meetings regarding career planning or educational goals. You had to show that you were either making progress towards getting a job, getting into school, or they would throw you out of the halfway program. Nobody really helped each other out; if anything the dozen or so of us cared only about ourselves and our few belongings the most. While those who could afford doing so were constantly doing drugs and getting high, without any regard to violating their parole, if they got caught.

I would like to say that there were a lot more guys than just me who were taking this chance to restart their lives seriously. I often felt like a diamond in the rough, or a rose amongst the weeds, but nobody else staying there seemed to fear being sent back to prison... and this terrified me. I couldn't count on any of my housemates for any amount of honest nor respectful conversation, let along friendship. I really needed a friend right then.

Being jobless and utterly unemployable as both an ex-felon and registered sex offender complicated things, and—for that matter—so did not having anyone to discuss things with. I tried to talk to people I didn't know, which was incredibly difficult for me, but most of my initial conversation was rather self-involved or otherwise revealed a little too much of myself, which turned aside interest and attention faster than you'd ever believe possible.

My job hunting and interviewing skills were, well, <u>crappy</u>! Almost as bad as my making friends at a coffee shop. The fact that I had practically no employment experience other than my working for Sam—who was no longer in business nor available for comment—and that I was in my late forties, plus the eye-catching criminal history section of my job application, well... let's just say the interviewer rarely offered a departing handshake nor the common lie of "We'll keep your application on file if anything comes up."

So many things seemed to be fighting against me when it came towards obtaining <u>sustainable</u> income. I wasn't looking for a minimum-wage job, simply because I needed a paycheck which someone can <u>live</u> by. The halfway house would be expecting a percentage of each paycheck I earned—to be honest, I forgot what the percentage would be, but it was a big chunk. I also still owed the state of California some court-ordered restitution fines, which would likewise be taken out of any paychecks once I started getting them. It seemed like staying unemployed was, in fact, more profitable for me than having a job, since I'd only be keeping a small slice of it.

This belief of Damien's is a rather common one amongst parolees. Why should someone work eight-hours-per-day yet only get paid for one or two hours of that hard work? As Damien once suggested to his parole agent, there really should be a "grace period" between when someone is released from prison and when he or she is first required to start reimbursing the state any leftover amounts of restitution. How else was someone like Damien ever supposed to rebuild his life, save up for first month's rent (and security deposit) of his own place, when most of his money disappears before he can even smell it.

As Damien witnessed within that halfway residence, most parolees "work over" the system instead of work at a job. Several halfway residents Damien was forced to live with were collecting government grant money or disability checks which weren't theirs—in the names of inmates still housed in prison—or other manipulations of either the welfare system or unemployment insurance benefits, which they were likewise not entitled to. The temptation for Damien to follow their criminal footsteps was indeed high, yet he wanted to do everything to avoid going back to prison—getting his <u>third</u> strike—and staying clean... which included finding that ever-elusive job.

There was also another job-hunting problem with me having nothing for transportation, except for that which I was born with: one left and one right! On the serious side, with all of the walking I was doing, to and from interviews, I would soon require a newer pair of shoes. What I knew of the city of Pomona was limited to everything within walking distance, featured on maps, or mentioned in advertisements and TV commercials. It sucked not having a car, and I couldn't rightfully afford to spend anything on bus fare to get me further away from the halfway house.

After my first two weeks there, I finally received in the mail my new state identification card from the D.M.V., complete with my horrible picture. Back then there was very little difference to shape and design of a driver's license and an ID card; in fact, college students used to rent cars from the airport quite often using a state ID card rather than an actual license to drive. On several hot August afternoons, I would've been half-tempted to do the same, if I only had enough cash to rent a car. I was that sick of my surrounding area, and even feared I'd never again see beyond the city limits of Pomona.

On top of the fact that I was soon turning forty-eight and searching for any job paying more than ten-dollars per hour, I was an ex-felon and—to add grief to this mess—I was a registered sex offender who only wanted to do things right this time around. I just didn't know how! But then, a real and honest change at making it happen for me—legally, as opposed to dealing drugs like some of my housemates—came at last: I was told about a seminar being given by one of the local schools which specialized in eighteen-month vocational programs, such as medical assistant certification.

The fact that I had previous experience with working in a mental health office, plus a degree in counselling, my parole agent believed I'd be a good fit when I told him about it. My P.O. seemed disappointed that I was unable to find a job on my own, although I'd documented on the required forms all of the interviews I'd been to that and every month since my release; with the job market the way it was in the autumn of 2005, nobody seemed interested in hiring just about anyone with a criminal record, sex or otherwise. I was assured that this vocational school not only taught the necessary material, but also they aided graduates—even an ex-offender like me—in getting a job in their specialties.

Damien began aiming at becoming a medical assistant, if for no other reason than he couldn't find a job on his own and was at risk of being kicked out of that horrible residence. Although many parolees report mixed feelings towards whichever halfway residence they are assigned to—most just thankful enough to have a place to sleep for a few days until finding a friend's couch or ex-girlfriend's bed to move onto—nearly all homeless shelters are found to be vastly more preferred... or, at least, are perceived a cleaner than a halfway house.

The name "halfway house" is misleading; it's more of a motel or slum than a house, plus the adjective 'halfway'—which might've once meant halfway between prison and civilization—now stood for halfway between Hell and Gomorra. It literally was a "crack house" in every sense of the term, because everywhere you looked were addicts and their vices. The peer pressure for me to join them in getting high was almost overwhelming, but I knew what would happen if I ever did give in: complete ruin and probably prison. I'm not sure when exactly I developed the necessary self-control I needed those months, but I managed to refuse all offers to get high and get fucked.

I forgot to mention one last thing about this halfway residence, and this goes towards the difference between such places and with prison: While incarcerated, I was kept on a protective-custody or "sensitive needs" yard for my own protection since "mainlines"—those not in protective custody—dislike fellow inmates convicted of sex crimes or anything involving children. While my own case didn't involve kids, but did involve raping a woman,

I was involuntarily placed in a S.N.Y. prison. However, there's no such thing as a protective-custody or "sensitive needs" halfway house! No, all parolees without a place to stay are just lumped together under the same roof, regardless of which prison or yard-type they stayed at.

I was once again forced to lie to people about why I was in prison when they asked. I also had to fib about which prison yards I was on—mainliners seemed to have memorized which ones are S.N.Y.—and when I was there. Yet, regardless of what I said, or how "good" of a liar I could be, the truth was out there, and I knew evidence would be discovered at some point. Sure, I had already thrown away every piece of paper or envelope with either C.M.C. or Avenal state prison mentioned on it, all of my court papers, everything incriminating or revealing about my past; yet all this would prove to be wasted effort.

After about four months of living "incognito" amongst former inmates who hated rapists, rumor of Damien's apparent misgivings about being housed at a particular prison and particular yard of that prison were proven false. While Damien wasn't home—if you can call being at the halfway house as such—an unknown resident ransacked Damien's personal belongings and this person found a large manila envelope with the address label still affixed... the address to Damien's old cell number and yard letter of Avenal prison; a widely-known S.N.Y. facility nicknamed as "Tellin' All, Avenal."

Damien was confronted with said-envelope, accused by three men of being, "a baby-raping snitch!" and promptly beaten halfway to death.

Directly after the vicious beating—of which Damien wouldn't be able to recall had the event not been so well documented—Damien regained consciousness in the back of an ambulance. For an immediately unknown reason, his left wrist had been handcuffed to the safety railing of the gurney he was lying on. His memory of walking to the front door of the halfway house was still a thick fog which to date is vague. His first question to the paramedic treating his multitude of wounds was a pretty obvious one, *What happened?*

"You were involved in a fight," the attractive female reported. "Three men held you down until the police arrived."

Fight?! Did—did I win? Damien coughed out.

The paramedic smiled at this. "Oh, yeah. You won the grand prize! You are the only one being transported to the hospital."

What? Which hospital?

"Memorial. We're about halfway there."

Ohh. Did—did I men… tell ya, I—I'm in school… to be a medical assistant?

"Well, in that case, pay close attention," she stated while busily untangling some unused I.V. tubing. "This is how to start a new I.V."

CHAPTER FIFTY-SIX

The Fight of the Decades

Damien was visited by two people while being treated in the Emergency Room; neither of whom he was particularly interested in seeing... nor they of him!

First up, a Pomona City Police investigator arrived to ask Damien for "his side" of the story. He wrote down notes while the heavily-injured man mumbled semi-coherent words regarding the events which were beyond blurry and didn't make much sense to either the interviewer or the interviewee. As the officer asked questions, brand-new details were freshly becoming realized by Damien's mind. He often answered the cop's questions with questions oh his own.

I know I mentioned the envelope and that I'd lied about being at a S.N.Y. prison, but I couldn't remember if <u>this</u> was what started the fight, nor who hit whom first. I said I didn't remember getting punched or kicked, and this turned out to be the wrong thing to say in the long run.

Second to visit Damien was his parole officer, Jorge Simmons. The agent was less than pleased to be at a hospital after his normal business hours, and even less pleased to see Damien. He noticed the handcuff on Damien's wrist rather quickly; albeit, now on Damien's <u>right</u> wrist and securing him to a bed's railing and not a gurney's. Simmons stated that, although he didn't yet have a copy of the police report, the fact that Damien had been entangled in an incident involving the police, Damien had likely violated his parole. Jorge was nothing if not chockful of good news.

My parole agent warned me that I was likely facing county-jail time for the police contact, perhaps a misdemeanor for fighting with my housemates, regardless of who started the fight. Any kind of violence is grounds for a parole violation, even if I never threw a punch or otherwise defended myself. How crazy is that?! Well, stay tuned... it's about to get even crazier.

As soon as Damien was deemed to be in stable condition—medically, not emotionally—he was taken under custody of the Pomona City Police and escorted by two officers to an awaiting cop car parked beside an ambulance. This would become Damien's fourth trip to a county jail: the first two times to Orange County, and these last—or <u>hopefully</u> last—two times to Los Angeles County. Even though it had been more than five years since Damien last went through the booking process, he felt overwhelming sensations of just recently being there, sitting within the exact same holding tank, even seeing familiar faces of the staff whom worked there.

Being back in county jail was the worst kind of déjà vu, because everything I was experiencing actually did happen before! In fact, far too many times before. Being booked into county lockup was frighteningly becoming a way of life for me, and without just cause these last two times. I couldn't believe anyone could end up going to jail for being beaten up! Yet, in my case, it was more than <u>that</u>... just because I was on parole and had a criminal record which included violence in 1982 and rape in 1990. And here, two decades later—yet only months since my release from prison—I was suspected of committing another serious crime. Actually, make that <u>three</u> crimes.

Since the only witnesses to the one-sided fight at the halfway house were the same three individuals who had bombarded Damien, this would become a contention of viewpoints: Damien's word versus theirs. Naturally, the multitude had the unfair advantage of collaborating and supporting each other's elaborations or complete falsehoods, while Damien's voice stood alone. As such what had originally been an ambush by three men developed into an issue of self-defense from a raving lunatic whom thought he could vanquish three men on his own; in other words, that Damien started the fight and threw the first punch. This constituted three separate felony counts of assault.

As anyone from my past could tell you, or a judge, I've never started a fist fight in all of my life, and certainly not against unprosperous odds. In 2005, and at the age of forty-seven, I was not a formidable boxer; although, I did have the advantages of being five-foot eleven-inches in height, and on average two-hundred thirty pounds... long gone were the skin-and-bones days of my youth. I blame my then-present obesity on the fact that I'd only recently been released from the inactive lifestyle of only a few hours of recreation per day—if any at all sometimes—and thus still sported a rather common "prison belly," which a lot of parolees end up with. So, the thought that I could take on three hard-nosed ex-felons by myself... is absolutely ludicrous!

And yet, this is exactly what they were saying, according to my public defender. That I'd come "home" from an appointment at Kaplan College—so that I could be enrolled in the very next cycle of classes—and become irate when I'd discovered that somebody had rummaged through my stuff, removing a large-sized envelope with my name on it. That once I located the man who had stolen it, I became hysterical and started throwing my arms around at the closest man, and that the three of them were in fear of their safety. They end up "regrettably" striking back at Damien in order to defend themselves. To the public defender, their version of the event seemed plausible, especially when in light of both my criminal record and history of being committed to a juvenile program at a state mental institution.

Oh, by the way, with regards to my court-appointed attorney—let's call her Sylvia Allegro—she was quite young, maybe only a year or two out of law school, and was likely born right around the same time I was in the aforementioned Wuchium Program at Metropolitan State Hospital (in Norwalk). I was amazed that evidence of my being there, back in 1973, was still floating around, especially since I believed my juvenile record of contributing to the delinquency of two girls had been long-sealed shut! Yet here my own attorney was bringing this archaic information up as if the district attorney was planning to use it against me! I began to view her as more of an intern than an actual lawyer, but my lawyer she would be.

Ms. Sylvia always tried to sound positive while presenting me with bad news or her personal opinions. She had the air of the typical confidence you'd expect from a seasoned attorney, yet she lacked the pizzazz of one; there was obvious inexperience in the way she phrased certain things. It was also quite apparent that she was terrified of trying this case before a jury, as it would be her very first trial against a defendant facing a third-strike conviction. Actually, to be more accurate, a <u>fifth</u>-strike, since my so-called victims had collaborated in saying that I'd tried to throw punches at all three of them, earning myself three separate assault and battery charges.

I was scared for my life, yet there was nothing I could do in my own defense for that life. Although I, myself, after being arrested five times (once as a teenager), had never experienced a jury trial firsthand… I had come to know that despite what the United States Constitution says nor its guarantee that it's the District Attorney's or other prosecutor's burden to prove guilt, that I would be the one whom had to prove my innocence! But how? Sitting there, in a county jail, my heart was ever so worried about my situation and inability to do anything to help by criminal attorney's work on my case in the slightest!

During Damien's first week in county jail, he once again reached out to the only phone number which he had memorized: the home of Dr. Sam Reily. It took three attempts—on two separate occasions—until Damien's collect call was accepted of its charges by someone at the other end; and once again it wasn't the homeowner but his sister who answered the phone.

I was surprised to find out through Barbara-Anne that my long-past friend, Professor John B. Cobb, Jr., had called Sam's house the previous week. I had forgotten that I had listed Professor Cobb as my emergency contact on the move-in forms for the halfway house. John had received a most-unexpected phone call from the halfway-residence staff approximately the same time I'd been handcuffed to a gurney and loaded into the back of the ambulance I cannot—even today—remember riding in very clearly.

The now-retired professor had left Barbara-Anne his home phone number and address which I promptly wrote down on the back of a medical request form, then called John. He greeted me warmly over the phone—almost like we'd just talked the other day, and not half-a-dozen years ago. John informed me that everything which I'd owned at the halfway house had been mailed to him—at his own expense, including—and most important of all—the journals and my other handwritten notes regarding my life and Bible studying. Many of those precious pages—many of which I'd never be able to recreate from memory—had been ripped out of their bindings or otherwise torn in half, most likely by the same individuals who wanted me to spend my mortality in prison. Yet, at least these pages were not safely in John's possession.

We talked about my not-so-distant future and the unlikelihood of my receiving any fair justice. The inevitable jury trial would be my own word versus the word of three others, with no other evidence to support either side... or so I thought, but this would come up later. Professor Cobb, who still held the title of professor in honorary or "emeritus" status only, was surprised by Sylvia's unbalanced chances at winning over a jury, especially since she didn't have the same resources or a team of paralegals and investigators as the Deputy District Attorney had.

John couldn't financially help support me in mounting a privatized legal-defense team, but there was absolutely no delay in his charity of providing me some much-needed canteen (jail commissary) items and other funds to make life behind bars a little more comfortable for me—whether I was truly deserving of such generosity or not. John was the perfect example of Hebrews 13:3 and Matthew 25:35, in that he never forgot me during this crisis, and gave without personal thought of reward. I spent three years waiting in county for my fateful day before a jury of my peers, yet I never felt completely alone thanks to John.

Damien spent from January 2006 to January 2009 both figuratively and quite literally twiddling his thumbs, while his court-appointed (and under-appreciated) public defender continued to request one continuance after another; *perhaps* hopeful that some previously unnoticed piece of evidence or witness would mystically show itself during these delays. Nothing actually did, yet wouldn't it have been great if it had? Such as a guilty conscience of one of Damien's alleged victims or the recorded video-footage from an unconsidered security camera. However—and regrettably—none of these surfaced during the forty long months of postponements.

How does one, such as I, describe the heartache, their pain and miseries, at not only losing their freedoms and liberties, but also all mental and emotional well-being?! I was beyond angry about my situation, yet this unnatural emotion did nothing to serve me... it would do nothing to help me cope through this mess I'd been forced to create! Yes, "forced"... for not a single misstep nor misfortune this decade seemed voluntarily mine.

All that I knew about my current battle for wellness, for happiness, was that my downhill fight started the day I'd been escorted out of my job at CVS Pharmacy in Ohio, flown back to the so-called Golden State, and compelled to live step-by-step in ways I'd have no recourse to deviate from! Such as in my divorce from Vicki, my five years in prison, and my release to a halfway residence for lack of anywhere else to legally go.

I was facing three felonies for assaulting people whom I not only didn't know—nor knew me—but also who I'd never threatened to harm. Neither did my so-called victims have any injuries nor even the slightest of bruises, and yet I was about to be sentenced to the same length of time as that of any premeditated murderer! Three consecutive terms of twenty-five years!

And through it all, when you really stop and think about it, I was the real victim—left broken and bleeding—by both my assailants and the system which required me to live there! How could the state of California ever expect someone like me to fight against such odds: a protective-custody inmate paroled and housed in a place full of protective-custody haters— without ending up bloody and back behind bars for decades more to come?!

Finally, the opening days of trial (which mostly included jury selection and motion hearings) had arrived for Damien. Although his public defender, Sylvia Allegro, had never expressed much confidence in winning Damien's case—in fact, she'd only visited with him twice at the county jail during the entire three-year span—she did her legally-obligated best... with both the limited resources and spare time she had available to prepare for this fight.

Personally and statistically, criminal trials are lately becoming more "battle of wit and charisma" than a proof of facts and/or justice! To Damien, both sitting there in that courtroom and afterwards, jurors seem to watch for which attorney "put on the best show" or entertainingly presented his/her evidence in the most provocative way, not the importance of that evidence itself.

Damien's lawyer relied heavily on his medical records from the emergency room visit, showing no bruising to Damien's knuckles and crystal-clear signs of defensive wounds to his forearms and shins. This was her only real evidence to show the jury, other than Damien's own testimony; and, in hindsight, putting her client on the stnd might've been a mistake, but what else could she have done?

On cross-examination, the prosecutor—an experienced debater in his mid-forties named Peter Brown—relied heavily on "character assassination" via Damien's lengthy and "colorful" criminal history, plus the fact he'd just been released from prison. Brown also called the alleged victims of these assaults—the men whom had beaten the heck out of Damien "after he'd started it"—yet they turned into a 'mixed bag' for both litigating sides; particularly since two of the three were back in prison because of violence, and the third had died from an overdose.

The Deputy D.A. jumped right into my being arrested for getting two teenaged girls drunk, one of them pregnant, while deliberately leaving the detail that I, myself, had been a teenager at the time. No, all that the jurors saw, was a now fifty-year-old defendant sitting before them... leaving their imaginations to consider me as a molester of children when I was nothing of the sort! I was only a year older than those girls, only fourteen-years-old in the spring of 1972; and yet, that lawyer made it sound like I'd gotten the girl pregnant just the other day, when I was forty-nine!

Second, came what he labelled as my "intentional shooting" of a loving father of two, in his head. As you've already read, there was nothing "intentional" about it! I didn't even aim at that guy, but at a drug-induced demon or phantasm climbing over the backyard fence. Yes, the bullet did hit someone after passing through the wood, but I had no idea that it would eventually harm anybody. The district attorney seemed to disagree, only because my aiming at someone sounded better for him.

Next, the "recidivism of raping innocent, young girls" in my sexual assault of Sandy... who wasn't actually "a girl" nor was she all that innocent. But I did admittedly force myself onto her that day in 1990 when I'd driven her to the airport. True, the drive to L.A.X. should've been as nonstop as her flight would've been, but my lustful rage was fueled both by her beauty and reputation of being an "easy lay." I gave into my desires and knew that what I was doing was wrong at the time I was doing it.

Finally, and most recently, my "blatant disregard for authority and public safety" in not registering as an offender but fleeing to Ohio... the same old incorrect story as before, that I'd run to Ohio just to avoid jail time. I once again contended that there was no "running" involved, but that Vicki and I had spent months in our preparations to both get married and move out of the state we equally disliked. The concept that anyone could dislike living in sunny California was probably inconceivable to some of the jurors, but it was the truth, the whole truth, and nothing but the truth.

In the United States, rather than other countries which actually care about justice being served, the prosecutor's task is to make a defendant look as much as of a heinous monster as possible—nothing personal, it's just his job—using artistically crafted phrases which leave out those small-yet-essential details which make an ex-felon out to be even worse of a criminal than he or she already was. This is because human instinct about someone's trustworthiness has been somehow culturally associated to one's reputation, regardless if the person never told a lie in their life! There's never been any real proof of connection between criminal behavior and a tendency to prevaricate, yet most district attorneys believe anyone once arrested has accumulated such a tendency to lie.

If I didn't know who I was, I'd want the person Mr. Brown was describing in his closing arguments to be locked up for life, too! His exaggerations and deliberate misguidings about me and the testimony given were easy to overlook by me and my attorney, yet they changed everything about the person I was and my past intentions. He made me out to be a calculating manipulator; that I was a threat to not just society but all of mankind.

My attorney countered as best she could by explaining to the jury why I was required to live at that halfway house; that during my five years previously in custody, I had exhibited no negative behavior—violent or otherwise—to earn any administrative write-ups; and that I was actively a full-time student of medical assistance at Kaplan College when arrested... which was a slight stretch of the truth, since I hadn't even attended my first class yet.

However, in my personal opinion while sitting there in that courtroom, even if Sylvia had called the Pope himself to testify at how much of a saint I'd been in the last decade, the prosecutor's damning portrayal of a half-century long long history of "Damien the sexually violent predator and absolute menace to civilization" had already made up those twelve people's minds for them. Of the D.A.'s opinion, regardless if I actually had thrown the first punch or not, the jurors would be crazy to allow me to roam free amongst decent citizens even again!

Something else Damien previously never knew about California's legal system—it's rarely shown on TV or in movies—is that during closing arguments of a jury trial, the prosecution "gets to go twice." The deputy district attorney may give the first batch of final statements to summarize all of the evidence and testimony presented; then after the defense attorney's turn to address the jury, the prosecutor gets a <u>second</u> chance to either reiterate the facts or "rip into" how the other lawyer "failed to prove innocence." Since these statements are the last things the jurors hear before going off to deliberate and choose a unanimous verdict, they tend to be the most vocally creative and, at times, remarkably outlandish! This, too, needs to be changed.

When the jury at my so-called 'fair trial' came back with their expected verdict of "guilty of all charges," my mind revisited earlier considerations of killing myself. The suicide attempt I'd been foiled at decades ago was on the forefront of all my thinking, and I had two months from that reading of their verdict until my sentencing hearing and committal back to state prison... this time forever; at least as a physical, earthly being. Or lived to the rather-young age of one-hundred thirty.

But why should I wait for nature to run its course! Why not help it along and voluntarily end this accursed existence right then and there? I'd asked myself this, again and again; and the only answer I can provide to anyone on why I did not kill myself, was because it would've gone against what God intended of my life.

Keep in mind, however, that throughout my research of the Bible and involvement in Bible studies—whether the ones I've shared excerpts with you which took place at various prisons, or held within a small-group ministry—I have never faltered in my opinion that God doesn't have any schedule nor a master, all-controlling plan for anyone's life. God intends us to do good deeds and to follow the groundwork of the Christ towards a hopeful goal; plus God will nudge some of us—from time-to-time—with a challenge or experience to bring us back to the path which leads to that hopeful goal.

Yet, I will never say that my life went exactly how God wanted it to. Nor that God was behind all of it, pulling the marionette's strings, as it were, for my life. No, much like the creation of the universe and this planet, our futures and destinies operate by means of the evolution process which God put into motion and inspires with as events unfold, preventing losses which God perceives as likely to occur, and being blindsided—just like us—by the unimaginable or eccentric.

No, I'll never believe in a master plan, but in an intended purpose for the life of Damien Lartigue. And I wasn't yet presumptuous enough to cut short that purpose, whatever it may be or lead me towards.

Damien had originally asked me to end this story here, at this point in his life, during his return to state prison; however, I didn't believe it to be fair to those readers believing that Damien's "long road home" wouldn't lead to a much more cheerful ending than that of someone being sent to prison for the remainder of their perceivable lifespan. After all, don't most novels and memoirs end with the hero, main character, or protagonist living a much better life thanks to the encounters and experiences he or she had throughout their story?

While Damien's search for some ever-elusive happiness has been tougher than most people's—finding only small portions of it while attending military school, as a patient in a state hospital, involved in a forbidden passion with a gay inmate, a friendship—and love—with a doctor, and a wonderful-yet-short marriage to a believed soulmate—Damien's fight for wellness never ceased.

One common belief or "taboo" which Damien has hopefully proven wrong to you, is that life doesn't end just because a person has been sent to prison. Sure, each inmate has lost his or her liberties and freedoms, but life continues onward, evolving progressively. And Damien had done just that! He didn't put his life nor service to God on hold just because he was sent to state prison; but, instead, Damien fortified his life and salvation in lieu of his predicaments.

Although I was back in prison, this time "for the long haul" as it were, I knew in my heart that God wasn't through with me, nor I through of God. There would be plenty of work for me yet, along this final road home to Heaven. I was oddly at peace now that I was returning to an environment I understood yet despised... that being state prison. Also, there was a lot of fear as well, because of both my needing to be to be housed on a protective-custody yard again, and a maximum security one at that. I'd never been on a level 4 yard before, where predominately every inmate was serving an indeterminate sentence (or life without possibility of parole), had an improvised shiv in a pocket or sock, and nothing to lose... or so the rumor goes.

This, my fourth trip through the system, started at a designated reception facility at the Richard J. Donovan Correctional Facility at Rock Mountain in southern San Diego. To this very day, I haven't the foggiest idea who in the world Richard J. Donovan was nor what he was famous for... other than being a convenient name for a prison. The popular prison rumor is that he was a former warden who was killed during an uproarious riot—the melee of <u>all</u> melees—at some imaginary institution; yet, most likely, he was just some local politician whom pushed for the funding to have the place built.

Oh, and one more interesting thing about Donovan—the prison, not the man—from certain areas of the facility, the higher vantage points, you could literally see the border crossing between California and Mexico. Let me tell you that just knowing I was <u>that</u> close to a border with another country, was knowledge enough to fuel dozens of fanciful dreams about climbing the electrified fences and escaping into that foreign land, never to be seen from again! It was awfully tempting for a guy with three counts of twenty-five-to-life, if not totally unrealistic... those ten-thousand volts might hurt a little bit.

I was seen by a counselor in record time and endorsed to go to two different places, yet ended up actually going to neither of them. Instead, I was later "transpacked"—in other words, preprocessed to be transferred, with all of my belongings packaged up in cardboard boxes days beforehand—and sent to a prison us inmates called "New Corcoran," but went by a different, official name which didn't make much sense either..."

CHAPTER FIFTY-SEVEN

Celebrating My Recovery

In mid-December of 2009, Damien was transferred to the California Substance Abuse Treatment Facility in Corcoran (roughly halfway between Fresno and Bakersfield). Although this was just another state prison when Damien was brought there, the original intention of California S.A.T.F. when it opened in 1997—as the name implies—was to house only those inmates whose cases involved alcohol or drug addiction, which Damien's latest crimes were neither of the sort.

This transfer didn't make much sense to me, since I hadn't involved myself with freebasing cocaine nor any other kind of drug in decades! I hadn't even had a strong drink since my wedding reception, and even that was done in moderation, In fact, the only addiction I was under recently—other than that of being other people's punching bag—was to caffeine, which was still legal in most states, unlike marijuana, which should be legal in all of them.

So, why was I being sent to a prison which doubled as a substance abuse recovery center? Well, your guess is as good as mine; yet, the most likely cause was: because they had room. In 2009, California's prison overcrowding mess had finally achieved national news coverage. The United State Supreme Court (in Brown v. Plata, 131 S.Ct. 1910) approved an order issued by a three-judge federal court, requiring California to reduce crowding to *approximately one-hundred-forty percent of design bed capacity... in other words, they could continue to crowd, just not <u>as</u> crowded as they had been, which had been like living in a can of sardines.*

Naturally, since at the time I reached S.A.T.F. the Supreme Court's decision had just been made public weeks prior, no actual reduction or "realignment" had started yet in late December. We inmates were still being packed into dormitories, or—as I was—into cells originally designed for just one man, not two or three of them. Worst yet, it took weeks to see a doctor, and even longer to have a tooth pulled. There were just too many inmates and never enough staff.

Getting back to the name of the place, the word "treatment" should've logistically been removed. This place was a "substance abuse facility," meaning there were far more drugs available for purchase on the yard than there was counseling against its use. The governors of California—first Arnold "the Terminator" Schwarzenegger, the Jerry "the Eliminator" Brown— repetitively cut funding to rehabilitation programs and vocational classes for us inmates, despite the department's name change from C.D.C. (California Department of Corrections) to C.D.C.R. (...and Rehabilitations). No, all that money was needed elsewhere, such as for custody staff salaries and pensions.

In fact, back when I was at Pleasant Valley State Prison, I saw a lot more counseling classes, A.A. meetings, and other treatment going on than at this institution with the word "treatment" in its name! The place was literally a ridicule—a parody—to its name, especially since the custody staff and other state employees were providing most of the drugs and cellphones to be sold on the yard... only to be later confiscated by these same officers and sold all over again. Eventually these guards would get caught by other staff, after being "snitched" on by their dealing inmates; yet the punishment normally was minimalized by their local union representative down to <u>paid</u> suspension or loss of vacation time, which suited the drug supplier just fine... hardly anybody ever used their vacation time anyway, except for Christmas or other major celebrations.

Damien's life at "Sat-F" wasn't uncommon of his previous experiences in state prison, with the exception of the level of violence he'd witnessed. Most of the fighting he saw was one-on-one wrestling matches—more UFC-style talking or sucker punching than old-fashioned street boxing—and usually over a loss at a poker table or outstanding drug debt. Very few fights were because of race or former ties to a particular gang.

This was one of the huge differences between being on a protective-custody (or S.N.Y.) yard back in the 1990's and now; there was almost no intolerance towards race or religious beliefs any more. Whites and blacks were getting along, playing basketball, volleyball, and chess against each other without all of the old disrespects nor any racisms. The northern and southern Mexicans still call each other insulting names from time-to-time, but basically they got along, whether they were drop-outs of a gang or not.

No, the number one reason for the fighting was over gambling and drugs. For several days at a time on "my" yard, things would run smoothly, but then there'd be two fights on the same day and the whole facility would be placed on lockdown, for a few days or so. And, what I meant by "my" yard, is that the sat-f program was run on two prison yards, with some inmates on "D" and others on "E" yard, which is where I was.

The "D" yard regularly had more fights on it than ours. Every time we came out of our cells for recreational time, we'd wonder just how long that day's peace would last before someone would start punching another—and you'd personally hope that a weapon doesn't become involved; otherwise we'd be fed inside our cells for a week, escorted in handcuffs back and forth to the showers, the whole nine yards.

Oh, yeah, before I were to forget, although both yards were protective-custody facilities, "D" was a maximum-security or level 4 yard, and I'd been placed on "E," a high-security or level 3 yard. To be honest, the prison administration must've made a mistake! I'd been sentenced to three life terms and had been through the system too many times to count, that I should've accumulated enough classification points to spend several years on that Level 4 yard before being downgraded—trust me, I redid the math plenty of times. Yet, for reasons which couldn't be explained, I ended up being housed on the "lesser violent" yard. All I can say is, thanks guardian angel!

Within a month of Damien's arrival at S.A.T.F., he was assigned an inmate job with the Education Department, as a classroom teacher's assistant (or T.A. for short). The classrooms themselves were located separately from the regular facility, beyond a "Work Orange" gate and security checkpoint, and adjacent to the classrooms for the vocational programs. Because of this, there was both a lesser amount of custody staff presence and a persistent animosity between educational students and vocational workers.

Oh boy did they not get along! We'd be walking to class, and you'd hear derogatory remarks like "Don't forget your crayons!" and "Did you copy off the right guy's homework?!" The students really hated it because nobody truly wants to be assigned to adult education, and those vocational guys usually got paid for showing up. It's difficult to learn eighth-grade math while knowing that your buddies are back on the yard playing handball and having fun, and then to have a bunch of jerks rub your nose in the fact that they're getting career skills and earning around a dime per hour doing it... and you're not, because you still don't understand algebra.!

Although I was tutor and not actually a student, their rude comments shouldn't have affected me; yet I often felt compelled to verbally defend my pupils by yelling a witty retort across the way back at them—well, at least I believe them to be "witty." Something like, "Hey, why don't you grab a screwdriver and tighten your brain!" Unfortunately, instead of being received as implied—that the person had a screw loose—the vocational guys thought I was trying to say "go screw yourself." And I often made the tension worse.

As far as the jobs went, being a T.A. was perhaps my favorite of all previous assignments! The instant gratification when you're tutoring someone and their eyes light up with comprehension, is intoxicating! It was rewarding to see that my tutoring was making a difference in the lives of those men in my class... and I'm using the term "my" class quite literally, since the state employee hired as our teacher would write that day's assignment(s) on the whiteboard, and then basically ignore the students unless absolutely necessary. No, us three T.A.s did nearly all of the actual teaching, and it was an enlightening experience for students and tutors alike.

Along with the rewarding chance to help those other grown men out, as well as awakening skills and knowledge I'd long forgotten I'd learned, I also did several clerical and janitorial chores each day. This placed me in the awkward position of walking past the aforementioned vocational classrooms to acquire mops or brooms, or to dump out trash to the Dumpsters. This, as you can imagine, set me up for several precarious encounters which—thankfully—always remained vocal not physical; after all, none of those inmates with "pay numbers' wanted to lose their job assignments over a shoving match. Of course, not everyone thought this way about consequences—they were in prison for this same inability—and during my two years at SAT-F I did get knocked down twice, while out of eyesight of authority.

But then came the reason why I was transferred from SAT-F; and, once again this wasn't because of something I'd personally initiated (just like at the halfway house). There are certain inmates who understand how to circumvent the prison system through use of intentional bad behavior: if you dislike the prison you're at, just get into a fight with someone who's timid and, after a few weeks in "the hole" (administrative segregation), you'll get your wish of being housed elsewhere. This tactic is also used by guys who have accumulated enormous drug and/or gambling debts without any means to repay them: just punch somebody you don't even know, and you'll be moved to a prison where that enormous debt doesn't exist (and you can start a new debt!).

This is exactly what happened to me. While I was coming off of work, both of my hands full of either books or my empty coffee mug from breakfast, I barely had time enough to react to a punch aimed at my head! He missed, but I'd stumbled backwards far enough to lose my footing, and ended up on my butt. The attacker—someone I didn't recognize at all from either work nor around the yard—proceeded to kick me one time in my left hip, then did something rather strange: Before any alarm sounded or correctional officers came running up, this bruiser got down on his hands and knees, then laid down prone way ahead of time, nearly thirty seconds prior to being told to.

In other words, it was completely orchestrated in advance. I just happened to be in the wrong place and with my arms full at the wrong time. Nothing personal, he's just wanting off of the yard. However, and unfortunately, I'd likewise be receiving an adverse or disciplinary transfer to another institution after roughly a month in "the hole" for being involved in a confrontation which I had no control over.

However, during this time of sadness and anger over losing my T.A. job and being forcibly moved yet again to another place, I'd received something in the mail to celebrate: An appellate attorney assigned to me by the court after my trial had successfully gotten one of my charges dismissed on appeal! Turns out that the Court of Appeal agreed that since my third "victim" (a.k.a. assailant) had passed away prior to my trial and being cross-examined by my public defender, and that the testimony given by the two living "victims" (a.k.a. assailants) didn't fully corroborate the third guys involvement nor even his whereabouts when the fight started, this one count shouldn't count. In layman's terms, I got one of my twenty-five-to-life's dropped.

If I hadn't already been over fifty-years-old—I was fifty-four when I received that letter in the hole—I'd be even happier that my seventy-five-year sentence had been lowered to fifty. Now I just needed to stay healthy enough to live to be a hundred years old, and I might parole someday. Although, without being sarcastic, having any time knocked off of one's sentence will always bring out a positive rush of encouragement that even more time might get dismissed someday, or when sentencing laws get changed. Also, simply telling other inmates that you just have two life sentences instead of three of them, was personally comforting: absurd as that may sound to some reading this.

On January 19th, 2012, Damien once again rode on a prisoner-transportation bus, which in his own words, was one of the nice buses which once were owned by Greyhound or Trailways before being converted to carry inmates. This was the first time Damien would travel to northern California, north of the Fresno area. As Damien reminded me, the entire state of California is, in fact, northern California or "Alta" (Upper) California; whereas everything south of the border with Mexico is "Baja" (lower). Yet, as far as being within the U.S. state currently known as just California, Damien had never been this far north before, as a state prisoner.

The long bus ride's final stop (and Damien's) was named the Sierra Conservation Center in Jamestown, eleven miles west of Sonora. However, upon seeing the all-too-familiar sights of raised guard towers and electrified fences, the misleading name didn't convey that this place was just another overcrowded state prison, like all of the rest. One difference between S.C.C. and Damien's previous institution, was that the Level 3 yard he'd be staying at was topographically separated from the other yards of the prison... which were at a lower elevation.

The so-called lower yards, "Calaveras" and "Mariposa," were mainline (non-protective custody) level one and two yards; although, for the most part, we forgot they existed at all... couldn't see them, couldn't hear them, unless an alarm went off down there. Also, it should be noted, that on the minimum-security yard—I forgot which one was which—several dozen inmates were being trained daily in wildfire prevention and extinguishing, before being voluntarily shipped out to remote "fire camps" throughout the foothills.

We, of the upper yard, nicknamed "Tuolumne" or just "C" yard (for those bad at spelling the nearby river's name), were high-security Level 3 inmates with "sensitive needs" to be under protective custody from the general population. As such, we were excluded from learning how to become fire fighters or conservationists... so, we focused on just being good Christians instead. And I truly mean this, that everyone at S.C.C. Level 3 yard was involved in one denomination of religion or another, and that there were <u>plenty</u> available to choose from!

In all of my years—decades, really—of coming to prison, being sent from one place to the next, I'd never been at a facility which offered more services of religions, meetings for alcoholism and substance abuse, classes for parenting, anger management, victims impact, and creative writing, in my life! Each day of the week, there were at least three different church services of worship, or Bible study, or of personal recovery going on somewhere within that prison yard. The number of outside volunteers and sponsors who were taking the time out of their free daily lives to drive out to this remote prison was staggering! There was just so much outside love and attention being poured into our facility on a weekly-basis, it was infectious.

What I mean by the word "infectious" is the <u>good</u> kind: that the happiness and goodhearted cheer of these selfless volunteers was rubbing off on us inmates. I rarely saw a fight on the yard, and whenever there was an alarm going off on our yard, eight times out of ten it was an accidental push of a panic button against a chair or other furniture. Nearly everyone got along with each other, regardless color, age, or belief. Yet, for me, it was so *strange not having fights kicking off or smelling pepper spray at least once-a-week... no, there was almost none of that.*

The simple fact that this new place had such a significant reduction of violence made me so very grateful. But, just as quickly, I began to concern myself as to just why there was so little violence at this prison? What was S.C.C. doing so differently that others, like SAT-F, weren't? Both S.C.C. and SAT-F were level 3 S.N.Y. facilities, both had the same number of staff, roughly the same number of inmates (while including the inmates which were housed inside Tuolome yard's gymnasium at the time), plus there was the usual amount of homemade alcohol, illegal cellphones, and drugs available... but where was all of the violence I was so used to?

The only possible answer to differentiate and distinguish S.C.C. as a less hostile prison than SAT-F, was the number of recovery programs being offered, and the true role models in the volunteers who showed up to run those many groups. One such program, which was very new to me, was called Celebrate Recovery. To be honest, I didn't understand the name of it. How do you celebrate something you are recovering from? I've done a lot of recovery after celebrations—namely hangovers—so I guess my curiosity in both its name and the rumor that it was a Christian-run or "Christ-centered" program.

What I'd found on the first night of going to it, was that Celebrate Recovery had all of the elements of Alcoholics Anonymous and crisis management meetings tied together into a small-group ministry! Unlike A.A., C.R. dealt with personal hurts and habits of every kind, whether it was drugs, alcohol, gambling, kleptomania, gang history, childhood abuse, pathological dishonesty, depression, anxiety, or whatever else! Everything was scripture based, as we got together in small groups of no more than a dozen guys each week, and worked through both the questions in our workbooks and the concerns on our minds. It was truly a fantastic experience those first few meetings.

Not only did our prison yard have these Celebrate Recovery meetings each Wednesday night, but the administration even dedicated an entire housing unit (in our case, Building Five) towards the C.R. programs; calling it a 24-hour therapeutic community. All of the two-hundred inmates housed in Building Five were active in the C.R. program, attended at least one religious service each week, and were under contract with the floor officers not to engage in any negative behavior or otherwise be kicked out of the unit. It was literally like living within a commune of Christian brothers, both within a prison and supported by its staff. Again, I have to use the word: Fantastic!

There's a lot more to this program than what I'm putting here, such as daily morning devotionals and public testimonies, but it's difficult to describe such an experience unless it's first witnessed in person. The Celebrate Recovery program at Sierra Conversation Center was unlike anything I'd been involved in before—much as Henrietta's Orange congregation and small-group ministry, yet with more "punch" to it: more personal familiarity with each of the members in our group.

Let me also say that even though I could easily relate to the curriculum, some of the questions in the workbook were rather gut-wrenching for me to contemplate, especially the ones regarding making amends with myself and others—my parents who abandoned me, included. No, they were awfully difficult answers, as well as eye-opening. There was quite a lot of pain I'd been hiding back, just beneath the surface, which I'd forgotten was even there, punishing me every single day. I never would've realized it without going to Celebrate Recovery.

As part of Damien's requirements for remaining both within the C.R. program and the therapeutic community of Building Five, he needed to sign up for a weekly religious service at attend—whether it was Christian, Catholic, Native American, Buddhist, or one of the two pagan services. Since Damien disliked Pentecostal worship, he first looked into the Latter-day Saints group, although this turned out to be unfavorable as well...

The L.D.S. service was held on Thursday afternoons and sponsored by two (sometimes three) elders from a local Mormon church. Events were going on just fine until we got around to introductions, with me being the only new guy to their regular group of eight inmates. Perhaps I should've just said I knew absolutely nothing about their religion, which might've been best... but, no, not me. I went on and on for ten minutes about how I was an elder in the Reorganized Church of Jesus Christ of Latter-Day Saints, how I'd been baptized and where, plus how I'd helped run a small-group ministry in—of all places—Kirtland, Ohio, and so on.

Well, this didn't go over all that great with either the sponsors or my fellow inmates. The problem is members of the R.L.D.S. church aren't all that accepted by members of the L.D.S. church, to begin with. Then for me to drop that huge list of accomplishments into their laps all at once was taken as the exact opposite of modesty... that I was either showing off or downright lying out of my all-too-arrogant ass! In other words, I was not well-received into their group, as an abhorred R.L.D.S. member.

Sensing their animosity—actually, that's perhaps too strong of a word, let's go with distaste—in me as a distant cousin, with oppositional beliefs, I went onto something else. I tried your typical evangelical worship services, which after only four weeks I grew tired of repetitious sermons about salvation and true freedom. I wanted something challenging! A Bible study which I could really sink my teeth into.

Then the most interesting thing happened. My cellie was transferred to another prison, and a guy named Eric—who I'd met once or twice at a C.R. meeting, asked if I wanted to be his cellmate. What was interesting about this moment was that only a week prior to this, I'd discovered that Eric was a self-published author of two novels and—of all the religions I'd never tried—a life-long Messianic Jew, or Jewish Christian to be more accurate.

I had already expressed an interest to Eric about understanding more of both the Jewish religion and culture. Not that I wanted to convert to Judaism, only that I'm always fascinated by cultural history and beliefs. Yet, nothing would ever convince me that Jesus of Nazareth isn't the Christ. And this is where Eric first surprised me: that as a Messianic Jew, he also earnestly believed and accepted Jesus as the true Christ. This was the first indication that I needed to do more research which, to date, I'm still doing.

Through another member of the Jewish community at S.C.C., I was loaned unabridged English volumes of The Zohar*, as well as a Hebrew/English dictionary, which are quickly becoming as worn out as my copy of Alfred North Whitehead's* Process and Reality*, which my good friend Professor Cobb sent to me. I believe there aren't any immediate connections between the principles of Process Theology and those found with The Zohar; however, when you apply process thinking to The Zohar sections regarding Genesis, I found a much deeper interpretation of the commentary presented.*

I have a much more broad understanding of our world, thanks to both of these books and the experiences which lead me to them.

Of all the peculiar things I've typed for this book, nothing could be more incomprehensible than the gratitude I have towards coming to Sierra Conservation Center. Yes, I said "gratitude," as in happy to be here. To anyone who doesn't know my full story, a comment like this would seem more than just bizarre: Happy to be in prison? Yet, as you've read, there are various ways to serve a prison sentence, whether you want to do "hard time" or God's time. I chose that nothing could be more important in my life—one which would remain permanently behind bars—than to spend it in helping others.

We are all connected through Christ and nature; so supporting someone else in need and/or emotional pain, is in turn the support of all mankind. Nothing could be more important, nor more personally rewarding in the long run!

Although I am in prison, I truly feel at home. I've involved myself as a group leader of Celebrate Recovery, signed up for multiple classes in writing and other therapy to bring help to others. While I do not have my earthly freedoms, I have infinitival spiritual liberties... and nothing could be more substantial and homelike.

> "Home isn't as much of a location, as it is a state of wellness. Humans spend a lot of effort in making themselves miserable; whereas innate happiness surfaces when you're at home with yourself, who are you, and—most importantly—focused on the assistance of others. Only then, regardless of one's circumstances and whereabouts, can a person be truly home."

~ Eric W. Senn
Damien's cellie (2013-14)

Acknowledgements

This book would never have been possible without the assistance and/or the inspiration of:

Alfred North Whitehead, John B. Cobb, Jr., David Ray Griffin, C. Robert Mesle, Richard Carlson, Marilyn Senn, Sydney Banks, Roger Mills, Rick Warren, Pierre Teilhard de Chardin, Dr. Alfred Adler, Charles Hartshorne, Vicki R. Lartigue, John David Loren, Rick Baker, Po Bronson, Michael Leunig, Robin Casarjian, and the Lionheart Foundation; the men and women of Chalice Press, New World Library, P&F Press, Fawcett Premier Book, Templeton Press, Random House, American Bible Society, The Westminster Press, harvest Book, World Almanac Books, Google, Yahoo, the Reorganized Church of Jesus Christ of Latter-Day Saints; and—most importantly—our loving Lord and Savior.

Suggested Reading

Philosophy

Banks, Sydney. *Second Chances.* Tampa. FL: Duval-Bibb Publishing, 1984.

Bronson, Po. *What Should I Do with My Life?* New York, NY: Random House, 2003.

Carlson, Richard. *You Can Be Happy No Matter What: Five Principles for Keeping Life in Perspective.* Novato, CA: New World Library, 2007, 1992.

Casarjian, Robin. *Houses of Healing: A Prisoner's Guide to Inner Power and Freedom.* Boston, MA: Lionheart Press, 2012, 1995.

Cobb, John B., Jr. and Griffin, David Ray. *Process Theology: An Introductory Exposition.* Louisville, KY: Westminster John Knox Press, 1976.

Cobb, John B., Jr. *The Structure of Christian Existence.* Louisville, KY: Westminster John Knox Press, 1968.

Cobb, John B., Jr. *Whitehead Word Book: A Glossary with Alphabetical Index to Technical Terms in* Process and Reality. Claremont, CA: P&F Press, 2008.

Descartes, Rene. *Philosophical Works of Descartes.* Trans Elizabeth Haldane and G. R. T. Ross. New York, NY: Dover Publications, 1931.

Hartshorne, Charles. *Whitehead's Philosophy.* Lincoln, NE: University of Nebraska Press, 1972.

Mandino, Og (Augustine). *The Greatest Miracle in the World.* New York, NY: Bantam Books, 1978.

Mesle, C. Robert. *Process-Relational Philosophy: An Introduction to Alfred North Whitehead.* West Conshohocken, PA: Templeton Press, 2008.

Plato. *The Dialogues of Plato.* Trans. Benjamin Jowett. New York, NY: Random House 1937.

Prather, Hugh. *Notes on How to Live in the World and Still Be Happy.* New York, NY: Doubleday, 1986.

Whitehead, Alfred North. *Adventures of Ideas.* New York, NY: Free Press, 1961, 1933.

Recovery

Baker, John. *Celebrate Recovery Inside.* Grand Rapids, MI: Zondervan, 2005, 1998.

Baker, John. *Celebrate Recovery Bible, NIV.* Grand Rapids, MI: Zondervan, 2007, 2005.

Mills-Naim, Ami Chen. *The Spark Inside: A Special Book for Youth.* Auburn, WA: Lone Pine Publishing, 2005.

Senn, Eric W. *No Locked Doors: An Inmate-to-Inmate Introduction Guide to Personal Recovery.* Discovery Bay, CA: Frog and I Services, 2013.

Senn, Eric W. *No More Locked Doors: An Advanced Guide Against Recidivism and Relapse.* Discovery Bay, CA: Frog and I Services, 2013.

About the Authors

DAMIEN LARTIGUE inspired to be a drug- and alcohol abuse counselor and relationship therapist, is a graduate Kent State University in Ohio, and currently resides in Jamestown, California. He has written a few papers on Relational theology, is working on a novel, and facilitates a local Celebrate Recovery small-group ministry and recovery program.

ERIC W. SENN served proudly in the U.S. Navy (AE-FC), worked as an IT Networking Systems Analyst at NASA Ames Research Center, and lives in Discovery Bay, California with his golden retriever and a schipperke. He has two adult sons, Rick and Andrew, and has self-published several science fiction novels, two murder-mysteries, and some motivational books, including the "No More Locked Doors" series based on Sydney Banks' work in Health Realization.

For more information about Celebrate Recovery, please visit: www.celebraterecovery.com.

www.ingramcontent.com/pod-product-compliance
Lightning Source LLC
Chambersburg PA
CBHW051030160426
43193CB00010B/896